Autos and Progress

JOEL WOLFE

Autos and Progress

The Brazilian Search
for Modernity

OXFORD
UNIVERSITY PRESS

2010

Oxford University Press, Inc., publishes works that further
Oxford University's objective of excellence
in research, scholarship, and education.

Oxford New York
Auckland   Cape Town   Dar es Salaam   Hong Kong   Karachi
Kuala Lumpur   Madrid   Melbourne   Mexico City   Nairobi
New Delhi   Shanghai   Taipei   Toronto

With offices in
Argentina   Austria   Brazil   Chile   Czech Republic   France   Greece
Guatemala   Hungary   Italy   Japan   Poland   Portugal   Singapore
South Korea   Switzerland   Thailand   Turkey   Ukraine   Vietnam

Published by Oxford University Press, Inc.
198 Madison Avenue, New York, New York 10016

www.oup.com

Oxford is a registered trademark of Oxford University Press

Wolfe, Joel, 1960–
Autos and progress : the Brazilian search for modernity / Joel Wolfe.
   p. cm.
Includes bibliographical references and index.
ISBN 978-0-19-517457-1; ISBN 978-0-19-517456-4 (pbk.)
1. Automobiles—Social aspects—Brazil—History—20th century.
2. Transportation, Automotive—Social aspects—Brazil—History—20th
century. 3. Automobile industry and trade—Brazil—History—20th
century. 4. Social change—Brazil—History—20th century. 5. Progress—
History—20th century. 6. Nationalism—Brazil—History—20th century.
7. Political culture—Brazil—History—20th century. 8. Brazil—Social
conditions—20th century. 9. Brazil—Economic conditions—20th century.
10. Brazil—Politics and government—20th century. I. Title.
HE5653.A6W65 2010
338.4'76292220981—dc22   2009018928

Printed in the United States of America
on acid-free paper

For Traci, Teddy, and Ellie

ACKNOWLEDGMENTS

I KNOW THE EXACT MOMENT I realized I had a fascination with the ways cars, trucks, and buses shape our world. I was stuck in traffic on M Street in Washington. I sat behind the wheel of my bus thinking about traffic flows and the ways automobiles had transformed the once quaint streets of Georgetown. I wasn't as upset as curious about those changes. I was driving a bus for my work-study job, not knowing then that so many of the stray thoughts I had while behind the wheel of GUTS (Georgetown University Transportation Society) buses would later influence the ways I think about the world, particularly modern Brazil. Driving that bus for three years didn't turn me into a gearhead. I don't subscribe to auto magazines, and I don't try to work on my car. Indeed, I drive a ten-year-old, five-speed Honda Civic because it's a sensible vehicle that gets very good gas mileage. Even though I'm not a classic car guy, I am fascinated by the ways automobiles shaped much of the world in the twentieth century.

Teaching modern Latin American history brought that personal interest in automobility into my thinking about history. By the time I began research on this book, I had realized that so many of the mundane thoughts we have as drivers are part of larger questions about our world. Teaching helped me understand those connections, and my experiences in the classroom shaped many of the questions I raise in this book. I am, therefore, first and foremost grateful to my students at Williams College, Rice University, and now the University of Massachusetts, Amherst, who asked wonderful and tough questions about Brazil and how it both differed from the rest of Latin America and, at the same time, defined the region by being its largest and most populous nation.

I was also fortunate to have wonderful colleagues over the years who encouraged me to take on this broad and, in many ways, new area of study. Regina Kunzel, Jim Mahon, Michael McDonald, K. Scott Wong, and the late Tim Cook helped me get this book started right after tenure at Williams. At Rice, I was fortunate to be a member of the Modernity and Modernization Writing group that included Sarah Thal, Allison Sneider, and Peter Carl Caldwell. Carl's guidance has been and remains invaluable to me. Although a Germanist, his reading of various stages of this manuscript has helped me clarify my arguments and improve my prose. In Houston, I was also fortunate to be able to rely on David Pesikoff for his great friendship and insights on economic and other matters. Ed Harris is another good friend whose counsel and good cheer have helped me throughout the work on this book and other projects. I am also grateful for his tutoring on the intricacies of auto racing. At UMass, I have benefited greatly from the advice and encouragement of Joye Bowman, José Angel Hernández, John Higginson, Bruce Lurie, Daphne Patai, and Heather Cox Richardson. Lowell Gudmundson of Mount Holyoke College and the UMass grad program has been guiding me since my first stint in New England, and I thank him for all he's done. Marguerite Itamar Harrison and Malcolm NcNee, both of the Portuguese and Brazilian Studies Department at Smith College, have been terrific and very helpful colleagues.

My greatest intellectual debt is to my mentor and friend Thomas Skidmore. He taught me much more than the historian's craft through the example he sets for all of us in the academy. His comments on portions of this manuscript and his friendship have been invaluable to me. Quite a few colleagues, many of whom are also good friends, read portions of this book or heard presentations at conferences and at invited talks. Others graciously shared some of their research when they heard about my project. Their support helped me a great deal throughout this book's research and writing. I thank Susan Besse, Jonathan Brown, Tom Cohen, John Crocitti, John Coatsworth, Mike Conniff, Doug Cope, Jerry Davila, Todd Diacon, Marshall Eakin, Farès el-Dahdah, Betsy Esche, Paulo Fontes, Richard Graham, Michael Hall, Tom Holloway, Gil Joseph, Paul Josephson, Roger Kittleson, Jeff Lesser, Linda Lewin, Frank McCann, Antonio Luigi "Gino" Negro, Patricia Pessar, Margareth Rago, Laura Randall, Katherine Sikkink, Steve Topik, Chris Wells, Mira Wilkins, Daryle Williams, and James Woodard. Tom Cohen was a great help in and around Washington, and Gil Joseph provided encouragement, advice, and critical thought during our long drives between Washington and New England. I thank them both for their friendship and support. I am particularly indebted to Todd

Diacon, Marhall Eakin, and Steve Topik for their close readings of all or parts of the manuscript.

This book was researched in a quite a few public and private libraries and archives in Brazil and the United States. I am particularly grateful to Barbara Tenenbaum and Georgette Dorn of the Library of Congress for all their help in locating so many hard-to-find materials. The staffs of the U.S. National Archives, the New York Public Library, the Nettie Lee Benson Library at the University of Texas at Austin, the Henry Ford Museum and Library, Studebaker Archives and Library, the Oliveira Lima Library, the Land Tenure Center at the University of Wisconsin–Madison, and the Bancroft Library at the University of California at Berkeley were tireless in helping me locate often obscure holdings on automobility in Brazil. Stephanie Lucas at the Henry Ford, John Kyros at General Motors, Maria Angel Leal at the Oliveira Lima, and Andrew Beckman at the Studebaker National Museum provided expert and timely assistance with many of the images in this book. The library staffs at Williams, Rice, and UMass also did great work, and I thank them for it, particularly Lee Dalzell at Williams and Peter Stern at UMass. I owe particular thanks to Mira Wilkins of Florida International University. She graciously shared her extensive personal archive of Ford Motor Company materials, and she gave me valuable advice on the project.

In Brazil, I am grateful for the expert advice and assistance from the staffs of the Biblioteca Nacional, Arquivo Nacional, Arquivo do Estado de São Paulo, Arquivo do Estado de Minas Gerais, Biblioteca Municipal de São Paulo, Arquivo Edgard Leuenroth at the Universidade Estadual de Campinas, Biblioteca de Automóvel Clube do Brasil, CPDOC at the Fundação Getúlio Vargas, and the Biblioteca de Faculdade de Economia at the Universidade de São Paulo.

I could not have researched and written this book without the generous support of the Woodrow Wilson Center. I also received both financial support and time off from teaching to write this book at all three of my academic homes. I am particularly grateful to Mike McPherson and Gale Stokes for their support at Williams and Rice. I could not have completed this book without the wise counsel of Susan Ferber of Oxford University Press. She has provided just the right balance of encouragement and criticism, and the book is much better because of her thoughtful editing.

My greatest debt and thanks go to my family. Like a lot of historians, the gap between my first and second books can be explained, in part at least, by wonderful changes in my personal life. I began research on this book just before the birth of my first child. Theodore Jacob and Eleanor

Ruth Wolfe have grown from tiny babies who needed to be rocked to sleep to wonderful elementary school children who wanted to know when the book would finally be done. I can't imagine not having slowed my work for them, and I know they're thrilled to have fuller access to their dad's Mac now that the book is in fact done. My wife, Traci Wolfe, has been encouraging and understanding. More than her admonitions that I should finish the writing and get the book to Susan, her support and love are what I am most thankful for. And finally, I thank my late aunt, Florence Greenberg. She is the only person I've ever known to have visited every continent on Earth, and her letters from afar and stories of travel instilled a curiosity about the world that led me to become a historian of Latin America and kept me fascinated by the world around me.

CONTENTS

Autos and Progress

Introduction

NEWS OF THE CRASH SPREAD throughout Brazil almost immediately. Ayrton Senna, at age 34 a three-time winner of the Formula One world championship, was traveling at about 185 miles per hour when he lost control of his Williams-Renault Formula One car. He died four hours after the crash at the Grand Prix of San Marino in Imola, Italy, on 1 May 1994. Idolized at home in Brazil, his youth and good looks were paired with his skills in the race car. Other athletes and entertainers, from Pelé and Carmen Miranda to Xuxa, have achieved national and international acclaim, but Senna's celebrity was different. Unlike a brilliant soccer player or beautiful actress, Senna's work required mastery of a highly sophisticated technology, and he was renowned for his skill and daring. In the dangerous and seemingly chaotic environment of Formula One racing, Senna controlled his vehicle and dominated the field with style and grace. His many triumphs in Europe, Japan, and the United States demonstrated a Brazilian command of both speed and technology.

Brazilians did more than mourn Senna's death at his funeral; they also celebrated their modernity through his life. President Itamar Franco declared a three-day official mourning period for Senna. He was granted a state funeral in São Paulo that was considered to have been the largest public event in the nation's history, with more people lining the streets of the city to view Senna's body than had attended the funeral for Tancredo Neves, the civilian politician who led Brazil out of 21 years of military dictatorship. At the moment of his burial, all traffic—from cars, trucks, and buses to the cable cars on Rio's Sugar Loaf—came to a halt for one minute. Coming during a period of political turmoil as the nation struggled to establish a vibrant democracy, Senna's life quickly became symbolic of

Brazil's struggle for modernity. Roberto DaMatta, the noted anthropologist, commented that Senna "was the right kind of hero. He worked for what he won. He was the Brazilian miracle." One Brazilian newspaper columnist proclaimed Senna's death "a sacrifice on the altar of modernity."[1]

This book reinterprets twentieth-century Brazilian history through automobility—broadly, the relationships among the society, culture, economy, and automotive forms of transportation—examining the country's attempts to make itself a geographically unified, socially coherent, and economically powerful modern nation. It seeks to clarify how a country that proclaims its national slogan as Order and Progress struggled over the course of the twentieth century with complexities such as its multifaceted social structure and its enormous and sparsely populated national territory. It also provides new insight into how Brazilians of different social classes imagined and worked for the creation of a broad-based democratic political system.

This book does not reject the dominant interpretations of twentieth-century Brazil that focus on issues such as race, labor militancy, and a political system marked by either a severely limited franchise or outright dictatorship. Instead, it seeks to complement those views. Race is often considered the key to understanding Brazil. It was, after all, the nineteenth century's largest slaveholding society and did not end slavery until 1888. The country's great immigrant population and the ongoing "myth of racial democracy" shaped how both Brazilians and foreigners think about the nation. Technology and consumerism do not seem at first to complement race and ethnicity, but studying how Brazilian elites viewed the introduction of new technologies and their belief that the development of a consumer-based democratic society would ease racial and class tensions illuminates the nation's social structure.

Another way this book reinterprets Brazil's twentieth century is by focusing on the physical challenges to national unification. Brazil's relationship with its geography contrasts with the experiences of the other physically large nations of the hemisphere.[2] National integration through ever more sophisticated transportation linkages has been a fundamental component of American history.[3] From the National Road and early canals, through the railroad and later the interstate highway system, the United States became a modern nation state in large measure through such physical unification.[4] Mexico, both as the Spanish colony of New Spain and as an independent nation, has been ruled from its centrally located capital. During its colonial period, roads connected Mexico City to the Atlantic at Veracruz and the Pacific at Acapulco. Railroads later tied the central valley of Mexico to its markets in the United States.[5] Railroads had the opposite effect on Canada. With the financial support of the British government, railroad construction in the mid-nineteenth century provided the means for integration and allowed regional forces to resist being overwhelmed by the United States.[6]

Brazil followed a different path. When King João III decided that Portugal should take physical possession of Brazil in the 1530s, he created a series of land grants known as donatary captancies. Parcels of land were measured out by mathematical coordinates because the Portuguese seafarers were expert in such science, and because they had little idea of what actually existed on land. The largest grant, to Martim Affonso de Sousa, was figuratively and literally without end, "entering into the back country and mainland as far as possible."[7] This initial form of taking possession of the colony had a profound impact on the Brazilian polity and economy well beyond the colonial period. Brazilian nationalism in the nineteenth and twentieth centuries was marked by the limits of colonial settlement patterns that left the population "hugging the coast like crabs."[8] Portuguese and later Brazilians moved beyond the coastal escarpment to capitalize on extractive enterprises inland. Beyond settling Minas Gerais during the eighteenth-century gold and diamond boom and Acre in the late-nineteenth-century rubber boom, however, Brazil's population remained almost exclusively on the coast. It was not until Brazilians began to manufacture automobiles in the 1950s that they built the first major roads into the interior.[9]

Brazil's export economy exacerbated these settlement patterns. International demand for coffee and rubber pushed economic activity deeper into the nation's interior in the late nineteenth century, but it did so by creating lines of communication between agricultural areas and foreign markets through their respective ports. Coffee from Araçatuba in the far west of São Paulo and rubber from deep in the Acre territory both ended up in Europe and the United States, but few in the one region traveled to or had any contact with the people of the other. The nation's infrastructure reflected this. Foreigners not only financed the vast majority of railroad construction but also planned the routes and ran the lines. They had no interest in using advanced transportation technologies for political means, such as the unification of Brazil; they simply wanted to move coffee, sugar, and other commodities from the fields to ports and then abroad. Highway and railroad construction in the nineteenth and twentieth centuries mostly facilitated the export of coffee from São Paulo and Rio de Janeiro. Brazil's railroads were so concentrated in the coffee regions that there was no national network or system of transportation.[10] The nation's one nineteenth-century highway, the União e Indústria, which connected the southern portion of Minas Gerais to the province of Rio de Janeiro, spurred the development of Mineiro agriculture but did little to integrate the nation.[11] With little physical integration, Brazil relied on the figure of the emperor and the juxtaposition of national exceptionalism vis-à-vis Spanish America to define much of its nineteenth-century national identity.[12]

The arrival of automobiles in the first years of the twentieth century challenged the status quo. Although automobiles seemed to be a panacea for Brazil's weak national unity, the new technology brought significant challenges. To take advantage of the promise of automobility, Brazil would have to create a truly national network of roads linking not only the major metropolitan areas but also those parts of the country thought of only as the frontier. During the 1910s and 1920s, politicians, businessmen, intellectuals, and others began to address the question of the Brazilian nation in terms of tying it together physically and economically through the expansion of infrastructure. The arrival of the automobile was not the primary agent in this reconsideration of Brazil's extreme regionalism, but it raised significant social questions, as well as bringing a new tool for peaceful national unification. During the first two decades of the twentieth century, Brazil experienced political rivalries among its states, and the economy splintered along regional lines. In addition to these political and economic fissures, there were great cultural and social divisions between the coastal Europeanized cities and the distant *sertões* (backlands). Both the uprising at Canudos (1895–1897) and the Contestado rebellion (1912–1916) demonstrated the lack of control Rio had over the hinterland and differences between urban, coastal Brazilians and residents of the interior. Euclides da Cunha's famous account of the land, its people, and their millenarian uprising in his epic account of Canudos has too often been dismissed by later commentators as simple geographical determinism or shortsightedness.[13] For the vast majority of Brazilians of all social classes, though, the spaces between Rio (or even Salvador) and Canudos and between São Paulo and the Contestado region of Santa Catarina and Paraná were terra incognita.

Although the millenarian uprisings were, at least in part, popular local reactions to outside centralizing intrusions, these regions were not only physically isolated from Brazil's major metropolitan areas but also thought by the nation's leaders to be distant, dangerous, and nearly uninhabited. Throughout the nineteenth and early twentieth centuries, the central state had done little to gain control over the near hinterland, and even during the empire, census taking and mapmaking made little headway in the vast

Brazilian interior.[14] The absence of knowledge about the interior was both a symptom of the weak central state and a fundamental cause of Brazil's extreme regionalism.[15] The creation of the Instituto Histórico e Geográfico Brasileiro (IHGB) in 1838 should have played a fundamental role in exploring the country's physical makeup, but instead of maps and population censuses, it concentrated on writing a national history that would "rouse the love of country, courage, faithfulness, fidelity, and wisdom; in sum, all the civic virtues."[16]

Brazil's geography and its effect on the nation preoccupied many of its early great intellectuals. In *Old Roads and the Peopling of Brazil*, João Capistrano de Abreu chronicles what he terms the "leather culture" of the cattle trade, especially as it penetrated the São Francisco River from present-day Bahia to Minas Gerais. River travel and reliance on mules and horses defined the seventeenth and eighteenth centuries he studied, but major technological changes, from the growth of railroads to the spread of the telegraph, had already begun to affect Brazil by the time the book was published in 1889, the same year as the founding of the republic. In the 1930s and 1940s, the renowned historian Sérgio Buarque de Holanda examined the ways geography and transportation shaped the culture of São Paulo and much of Brazil. The economist Caio Prado Junior, likewise, viewed transportation throughout the country's massive interior as the key to Brazil's development as a great nation.[17] These scholars understood that Brazilian republicanism sought a delicate balance between the interests of the nation's far-flung regional elites and the creation of a central state that would provide "Order and Progress." Without a large standing army or well-developed lines of communication among its states, Brazil looked to railroads, the telegraph, and even ballooning to shorten distances and transform its distant regions into a coherent whole.[18] Brazil's railroad system was in some ways impressive in scope. It not only facilitated the steadily expanding export of coffee but also managed to lower overall transportation costs for other goods moved throughout the country. Still, railroads did more to connect coffee regions to their ports than to unify the nation.

Brazilians dreamed of exotic technologies to bring the nation together. Adventurous minds turned to flight, first in balloons and later in propeller airplanes. Air travel became a key component in thinking about the nation, from Santos Dumont's experiments with airplanes in the first decade of the twentieth century to the nation's space program that has used satellites in geosynchronous orbit above Brazil to facilitate everything from mapmaking to delineating new states in the Amazon to electronic bank transfers and basic telecommunications. The place of flight is so well established in Brazilian thinking about the nation that Brasília, the new capital city inaugurated in 1960 to spur interior development, is literally shaped like an airplane.[19] Air travel sparked visions of suburban-style homes with runways and private planes parked in their garages, but the reality has been far different, with the vast majority of air transportation being regulated, scheduled, and too expensive for mundane use.[20]

In Brazil, as in other parts of the globe, the car quickly proved a realistic alternative to utopian dreams of broad-based air travel. Cars became so popular that over the course of the first three decades of the twentieth century, automobility took on an almost mythic status as the key to Brazilian national unification, social peace, and economic development. In 1925, for example, when the Ford Motor Company put early Brazilian autoworkers on display assembling Model T's during the First Exposition of Automobility, tens of thousands of spectators marveled at the transformative power of cars, both their manufacture and use.[21] The spectators witnessed their fellow Brazilians assembling some of the most modern machines on earth—machines that could help them gain control over their vast nation. Science and technology were long-standing tropes for the transformation of the Brazil. The founders of the republic in 1889 embraced positivism, and many of the military men who dominated politics in the 1890s had engineering backgrounds. As historian Boris Fausto notes, positivism "seemed to offer an orderly, scientific solution for the political and social impasses [of the day]. . . . Its reverence for technical innovations and industry attracted the emerging elites."[22] In addition to positivism, throughout the first half of the twentieth century most Brazilian elites subscribed to the basic tenets of Lamarckian eugenics; that is, they believed that the majority of Brazil's mixed-race population could be socially and culturally elevated through education and other improvements in their environment.[23]

To these elites, the automobile was the perfect tool for bringing about progress through order. This sort of embrace of technology was not unique to Brazil; it became a fundamental component of making nations modern. As historians Leo Marx and John Kasson have detailed, the United States came to embrace technology as it made the transition from a Jeffersonian agrarian republic to an advanced industrial society.[24] The French Revolution, as Ken Alder documents, owed a great deal to engineering and technology.[25] From the great national pride engendered by the Paris sewer system to its nuclear power program in the aftermath of World War II, French national identity has been heavily influenced by its relationship to technology.[26] Whereas French and American sentiments about technology evolved as a component of broader cultural and economic changes, India's founding as a modern nation was shaped by explicit debates about science and technology. The founding ideals of the Indian nation were articulated through debates between Mahatma Gandhi and Jawaharlal Nehru, whose differences were symbolized by Gandhi's simple spinning wheel and Nehru's belief in centralized planning and even an embrace of nuclear power.[27]

Such thinking represents an embrace of the "technological fix," or the belief that modern science, engineering, and machines would resolve social problems that societies would not otherwise be able to rectify.[28] Belief in technological fixes led people to view early automobiles as the answer to the environmental degradation of animal traction in the cities and to see the airplane as a tool for world peace.[29] To Brazilians, embracing automobility as a technological fix also meant believing in the notion of the so-called spatial fix; that is, over the course of the twentieth century, a steadily increasing number of Brazilians came to believe that the social, economic, and political problems their nation faced could be ameliorated or even eliminated by moving off the coast and taking advantage of Brazil's massive, untapped interior spaces.[30] In theory, automobility would solve Brazil's economic, political, and social problems without conflict or even much effort. In practice, reliance on auto travel was complicated, and it produced unexpected results.

For Brazil, turning to automobility in the twentieth century was more than an embrace of technology; it also involved purchasing foreign-made consumer goods. In the nineteenth century, Brazilians, like most Latin Americans, had relied on imported products, which were often less expensive and of a higher quality than locally made ones, while conferring higher status on the owner.[31] Cars were a new sort of consumer product, however. They were both a technological device and an expensive luxury item. The large-scale entry of the American car companies, particularly the Ford Motor Company and General Motors, transformed Brazilians' thinking about cars. These corporations marketed autos as middle-class consumer goods that were fundamental to a modern lifestyle, influencing many more people than just those who could afford to buy cars. The importance of cars, trucks, and buses to both economic development and a new sense of Brazilianness only deepened with the creation of a domestic auto industry during the second half of the 1950s. This national auto industry played into ideas about the link between consumerism and citizenship, as owning a car became a key component of Brazilian identity.[32]

The presence of automobiles fired Brazilians' imaginations about the connections between driving and engaged citizenship and, at the same time, created hope for an eventual industrial transformation of the society.

The opening of automobile factories in Brazil held out the promise of the creation of a disciplined, nonradical working class that mirrored what Brazilians perceived to be the experiences of autoworkers in the United States. This dream stretches back to the 1920s and reached fulfillment in 2003, with the inauguration of Luiz Inácio Lula da Silva as Brazil's president. Lula's Workers' Party (Partido dos Trabalhadores, PT) grew out of industrial actions in the auto factories in and around São Paulo in the late 1970s and early 1980s. Lula rose to prominence as a labor leader who represented a new stage in Brazilian industrial relations that seemed to many in civil society, the military dictatorship, and the auto companies to be more like the practices of America's United Auto Workers or Germany's IG Metall than like the old populist or communist unions of Brazil's recent past. This interpretation was driven by an established mythology about the ways automobility would transform the nation and its poor.

There is no simple, agreed-upon formula for what constitutes modernity, but several fundamental aspects of Brazilian automobility constitute its key features.[33] Automobility promised to unify the nation by shortening distances and accelerating communications. Auto travel would "annihilate space through time."[34] Driving vehicles literally enveloped people in machines that not only provided personal mobility but also allowed them to experience the exhilaration of speed as never before. Large-scale automobility is also dependent on the intervention of a modern state capable of building great road systems and other major public works. Central to all this is the notion that modernity necessitates change and a definite break with the past. Brazilian automobility sought such a break and promised to bring progress through the organized intervention of the central state working in concert with large-scale private economic interests to unite the national territory.

Too often, modernity is understood as a European phenomenon either transplanted or aped in Latin America, assuming that Europe and the United States were the vanguard or center of the modern world.[35] Although often associated with early imperialist thinking, this viewpoint has proved itself to be highly resilient and influential throughout the twentieth century, bolstered by demonstrable European and American technological superiority.[36] In many ways, the railroad is the ideal metaphor for this Eurocentric modernity, for the predetermined and linear nature of rail travel parallels traditional thinking about progress.[37] Unlike the railroad trip, there is no predetermined journey in a car; this freedom of movement holds out a nearly infinite number of possible end points for travel. Although great highway systems resemble railroad grids, autos often travel on small roads and even dirt paths. Automobility may therefore be a much more apt metaphor for modernity, especially in a country as geographically large as Brazil.[38]

Brazilian automobility also had a wide variety of political implications. In many ways, the presence of modern technology in the country became a measure of Brazil's "civilization."[39] The increasing use of automobiles in the late 1910s and 1920s forced Brazilian elites to consider wide-ranging road building and even begin to question the limits of their country's extreme form of political federalism. Debates about road building and transportation in general also revealed the limits of Brazil's embrace of export-oriented liberalism and began to raise questions about internal development. These themes took center stage during the first era of rule by Getúlio Vargas (1930–1945). Indeed, he turned to automobility to stimulate internal tourism and national industrial development. He also chipped away at Brazil's federalism by promulgating a national traffic code that applied to all municipalities.[40] The political implications of automobility were most clearly seen during the presidency of Juscelino Kubitschek (1956–1961). The developmentalist politics of his "fifty years of progress in five" program represented the culmination of more than a half century of thinking about the ways technology could allow Brazilians to finally gain control over their geography. Kubitschek's policies represented a triumph of modernity because they brought together economic modernization and cultural and political modernism.[41]

The national automobile industry also ushered in a new politics of consumption as mass production made car ownership possible for an ever growing number of Brazilians. To Kubitschek and his advisors, such consumption was a necessary component of citizenship in a capitalist democracy. They believed fervently in Fordism, which would use factory work to transform the poor into consumers and citizens. State policy makers and industrialists imagined that Brazilian workers in the new auto factories and other industrial establishments would soon own their own cars and homes. The leaders of Brazil's military dictatorship (1964–1985) had a narrower vision of consumerism and put more emphasis on controlling autoworkers than on expanding their purchasing power. In the 1960s and 1970s, the military refashioned a democratically oriented automobility into an export-oriented program that no longer sought to raise the standard of living of autoworkers or the poor. The military's development policies relied instead on expanded automobility through the great expansion of the national highway system, particularly into the Amazon. These authoritarian developmentalist policies did, however, help foster the democratic politics of automobile workers, who, along with other key segments of civil society in the late 1970s and early 1980s, brought an end to such policies and returned automobility to its democratic orientation.

These shifting ideas about automobiles reveal the complexity of debates about the political nature of technologies.[42] In fact, a central argument of this book is that knowing the meanings Brazilians invested in automobility is necessary for understanding the nation's twentieth-century struggle to be modern. Cars, trucks, and buses became not only the tools for creating the modern Brazilian state but also symbols of hope for its ongoing growth as modern, developed, and democratic nation.

| First Cars: Curiosities of the Elite

ALBERTO SANTOS DUMONT TRAVELED TO Paris to explore the world of flying and ended up learning to drive. The son of one of the nation's richest coffee barons, he was fascinated with European luxury, and he had nearly religious faith in the ability of technology to produce order and progress. In 1891, Santos Dumont visited the Peugeot works in a makeshift garage in Valentigny. There he spent hours discussing the internal combustion engine with the assembled workmen. At the end of the day, he bought a 3.5-horsepower Peugeot, one of only two produced that year. Seven months later, Santos Dumont returned to Brazil with his automobile to drive the streets of São Paulo in South America's first car. It is fitting that Santos Dumont, the man so many throughout the world thought invented and piloted the first airplane, was Brazil's first *automobilista*.[1]

Young Santos Dumont's first great triumph in flight was the creation of a dirigible, which he flew around the Eiffel Tower on 19 October 1901. That feat earned him the prestigious Deutsch Prize and international acclaim. Heads of state honored him for his accomplishments in flight, and the great jeweler Cartier designed the first men's wristwatch, the Santos Dumont, in his honor.[2] Then, on 22 October 1906, before the press and hundreds of onlookers in Paris, Santos Dumont made what was believed to be the first ever heavier-than-air flight in his airplane, the *canard*.[3] This flight not only made Santos Dumont a worldwide hero but also intensified public interest in flight. In Brazil, Santos Dumont's flight changed the ways people thought about the nation. As Giberto Freyre commented, the Brazilian discovery of the airplane seemingly made it possible to "whisk people from Amazonas to Rio Grande do Sul or from Rio de Janeiro to Mato Grosso. Perhaps this triumph would mean a new life for Brazil, a life faster even than that of

Europe, faster than that of other Americans, including the Yankees."[4] Freyre believed that Santos Dumont was a key figure in the creation of the myth of "Brazilian progress through science," and as such, the young aviator "became a symbol of Brazil's ability to conquer time and space, elements which hitherto had been the greatest enemies in its struggle to gain prestige in the eyes of the world, in its attempt to appear modern."[5]

In the 1890s, automobiles were the exotic products of a new class of inventors and engineers. The appearance of a car on a Paris or New York City street usually caused a great commotion. The vehicles were loud, unmanageable, and generally dangerous to drivers and pedestrians alike. With the development of early sedans and roadsters, however, auto ownership moved from inventors, daredevils, and the sons of the rich and powerful to the rich and powerful themselves. These older men relied on professional chauffeurs and mechanics to drive and maintain their expensive new vehicles. During the first few years of the twentieth century, the automobile became the key status symbol for the wealthy throughout Europe and the Americas.

Ever attentive to European fashion, Brazil's elite began importing automobiles at the turn of the century. Auto ownership was another example of the nation's liberal economic model at work. Agricultural exports—particularly coffee—produced great riches for planters, bankers, and merchants, who imported luxury goods, such as autos.[6] The success of the export model encouraged Brazilians to think about transcending their nation's status as an agrarian exporter and attempt to become a modern industrialized country. Although economic historians have long noted the key role played by the coffee economy in fostering early industrial development, less recognized is the role of consumerism—particularly but not exclusively elite buying habits—in shaping the Brazilian desire for industrialism.[7]

Brazil's first few automobiles would hardly be recognized as cars by 1910. Santos Dumont's Peugeot was a fragile contraption of wire and wheels. The small engine was mounted behind and below the driver, and the machine was steered with a tiller. In 1892, when Alberto and his brother Henrique drove it in the streets of São Paulo, it was the first and only car Paulistanos would see for close to a decade.[8] Another very early auto was imported merely as a public curiosity. Alvaro Fernandes da Costa Braga drove a six-horsepower, single-cylinder Benz automobile to advertise and deliver coffee and chocolate produced by his Fábrica Moinho de Ouro in Rio de Janeiro. This vehicle reportedly was involved in Brazil's first automobile accident.[9]

Santos Dumont's association with automobiles only heightened the interest of Brazil's wealthiest citizens in owning this latest European fashion. São Paulo's coffee barons and early industrialists purchased the latest French models as soon as they were available. The city's original sixteen motorcar titles issued in 1902 read like a ranking of the state's wealth, beginning with Conde Francisco Matarazzo, Walter Seng, and Antônio Prado Junior.[10] Rio's second automobile after Costa Braga's very early vehicle was, according to some, José do Patrocínio's or, according to others, Fernando Guerra Duval's Decauville in 1900. There is no debate, however, about Rio's first licensed automobile. On 29 August 1903, Francisco Leite de Bittencourt Sampaio received the Federal District's first auto license (five other licenses were issued that day). These early auto owners reportedly did not pay any import fees on their motorcars because there was no category for them.[11]

The arrival of a city's first automobile was usually a public event. On 13 February 1900, for example, the Bahian industrialist José Henrique Lanat introduced a Voiture Bayer-Clement #475 with a Panhard and Lavasa engine to Salvador. Crowds gathered in the streets to witness this "most modern vehicle."[12] But aside from the public spectacle, owning these first cars was not so glamorous. Car owners were forced to purchase fuel for their vehicles in tins at pharmacies. There were no automobile mechanics, and none of the early owners—with the exception of Santos Dumont—had driven before importing cars to Brazil.[13] Perhaps the most revealing and embarrassing manifestation of such problems occurred in Porto Alegre. In April 1906, the city's newspaper, *Correio do Povo*, proudly announced in a front-page headline, "Porto Alegre Now Has an Automobile!" Januário Greco, an industrialist and owner of the Cine Apolo, had imported a French-made De Dion-Bouton from Argentina.[14] But when it arrived, its owner faced a serious and seemingly insurmountable problem: Neither he nor anyone else at the docks in Porto Alegre had any idea how to operate the vehicle. News of the car's arrival and its owner's inability to even start it spread throughout the city. Finally, Greco learned of an Italian, Marini Constanti, who reportedly knew how to operate motorcars. The one problem was that Constanti was at that time in jail. Greco pleaded with authorities to temporarily release the man in his custody, but they refused. Greco then decided to have his car loaded onto a cart and pulled by horses to the prison, where Constanti instructed him on the operation and maintenance of the De Dion-Bouton.[15]

There were many such barriers to early auto ownership in Brazil. There were few good roads outside the downtown areas of state capitals and no traffic regulations. The *Estado de São Paulo* newspaper editorialized in early 1903 against blindly embracing this new technology, warning of the cars' ability to "produce explosions and fire." The paper further worried about the vehicles' mechanical integrity and their ability to brake for other forms of traffic in the city's streets.[16] Regardless, demand for cars among Brazil's wealthiest citizens continued to rise. São Paulo had only 5 cars in 1901 but 16 by 1903. In 1904, the state registered 84 automobiles and its first dealership. Orey Antunes e Cia Ltda. imported Darracqs at first and eventually handled Renaults and Berliets.[17] Rio experienced similar growth. In 1903, the city had 6 autos, 12 in 1905. Two years later, there were 99 registered autos in the nation's capital.[18] The major transformations of large-scale urban renewal projects in both Rio and São Paulo at this time facilitated driving by creating more than just a handful of streets capable of sustaining motorcar traffic.[19]

Other regions of Brazil had neither the physical infrastructure nor the wealth to sustain auto ownership in the first years of the century. By the early 1910s, however, most of the state capitals had at least a few cars on their streets. There were even parades of automobiles in Belém and Manaus in the 1910s.[20] Spotting a city's first automobile left a lasting impression. In his memoirs, Jorge Americano recounted the Sunday morning at the turn of the century when he first saw a car in São Paulo. He recalled the sound and appearance of the vehicle more than its occupants, but he guessed that it was Santos Dumont's brother Luís and a young Antônio Prado Junior, the scion to one of Brazil's great coffee fortunes. Americano's excitement over spotting the motorcar was tempered by his fears of what vehicles traveling at 30 kilometers per hour would do to the peaceful city streets and how such speeds would threaten the safety of children.[21] No matter where these first cars were driven, they were hard to control, loud, and uncomfortable for their passengers. They had solid rubber tires that were more often than not driven on stone or dirt streets.[22]

Manufacturers in France, Germany, Italy, and the United States rapidly produced a wide variety of increasingly reliable and sophisticated luxury vehicles that appealed to the tastes and desires of Brazil's wealthiest citizens.[23] The Columbus Motor Vehicle Company in Ohio even sold the Santos Dumont Touring Car in the United States.[24] By the mid-1910s, Rio's wealthiest residents bragged of owning some of the most exclusive automobile models available. One foreign observer noted, "The class [of motorcars] was high grade, beautiful and extremely powerful. It is said that no city in the world can show more expensive high-power cars than Rio de Janeiro."[25] Advertisements for these luxury goods first appeared in specialized journals. The literary and cultural magazine *Fon-Fon!* carried advertisements for garages and auto dealers, as well as ads for specific models, including the Peugeot Double Phaeton and the Adler Landaulet.[26] There were reportedly 150 different makes of autos from France, Germany, the United States, and Italy. São Paulo experienced similar growth in its automobile population. By 1911, one foreigner estimated there were more than 2,000 cars clogging the downtown area and the expanding elite neighborhoods around Avenida Paulista.[27]

Automobiles filled no actual need in Rio, São Paulo, or Brazil's other major cities. They had nowhere to go and nothing to transport. British chronicler Reginald Lloyd noted in the early 1910s that Rio's drivers' main activity was cruising: to see and be seen, rather than using cars to go someplace. They went "to the Rio Branco and Beira Mar avenues daily, and a very common practice with owners is to race up and down the Beira Mar an hour or two at a stretch. In the hot weather this is a sufficiently modern method of obtaining a breeze."[28] Lloyd further noted that wealthy Paulistanos did not venture far from the Avenida Paulista in their fancy European cars.[29] The latest luxury models were used in official ceremonies and, as early as 1907, became a staple of Rio's Carnaval parades. This *corso* or parade of "riding cars bumper-to-bumper, [with passengers] singing, throwing confetti, paper serpentines, and jets of ice-cold perfume on the watching multitude posted along Avenida Central" quickly became a Rio tradition. Cariocas also adopted the French "Battle of Flowers," in which the wealthy car owners decorated their vehicles with flowers and then slowly cruised the city where they were "ogled by [the] open-mouthed population lining the streets."[30]

These activities sparked consumer interest in auto ownership just as car companies in the United States began to produce less expensive vehicles. The U.S. Department of Commerce noted with some exaggeration in a 1912 report that "the market for automobiles in Brazil is one of the best in the world." It continued by stating that manufacturers should not bother trying to sell inexpensive vehicles in Brazil because those who could afford a car wanted a luxury model.[31] This sort of hyperbole about the Brazilian market continued throughout the 1910s. One study claimed that there were between 6,000 and 8,000 people in Rio ready to purchase motorcars.[32] The 1908 debut of the Ford Motor Company's Model T brought vehicles within the reach of a wider stratum of Brazilian society, as now the affluent and not just the extremely wealthy could afford a car.

Although Brazil's auto market remained heavily circumscribed, a wave of new automobile-oriented magazines provided access to the budding car culture even to those who could not afford a Model T or another inexpensive model. Two types of journals published in the 1910s focused on the new fashion of *automobilismo*. The first covered trends in auto design and repair, reviewed new models, and reported extensively on automobile excursions. The second was made up of literary journals that blended a fascination with autos and other new technologies with new styles of expression. The most famous of these was *Fon-Fon!* whose name was supposed to evoke the sound of a car horn. Another was the aptly named *Klaxon*. The publication of car magazines such as *Auto-Propulsão*, *Auto-Sport*, and the *Revista de Autómoveis* represented the growing fascination with autos among Brazil's literate, urban population. People who might not be able to afford a car could at least read about auto culture in Europe, the United States, and Brazil in these new publications. Each issue reported on developments in automotive technology and on races and raids, and all were filled with shiny photographs of cars and advertisements for the latest vehicles imported from Europe and the United States.

The first few issues of *Auto-Sport*, which began publication in 1912, combined reporting about foreign car trends, such as the French police using autos, with a nearly messianic editorializing about the importance of *automobilismo* to Brazil's future. The use of motorcars was described as "one of the most powerful forces in our development." The magazine's first issue sold out its 5,000 copies in a few days, and so another 10,000 were printed.[33] The initial issues of *Auto-Sport* also included articles on two topics that would fascinate and worry Brazil's auto enthusiasts for years to come. First, it argued that auto-based transportation, including an eventual reliance on trucks over railroads, was a key to national unification and economic growth. Second, the magazine's editors worried that Argentina, although smaller in size and population, already had more automobiles than Brazil.[34]

Another early magazine, *Auto-Propulsão*, declared in its 1915 inaugural issue that it intended to serve the interests of people involved in driving and aviation. By 1917, the magazine had become the official journal for car clubs in Rio, São Paulo, Juiz de Fora, Curitiba, Mato Grosso, and São João del Rey. *Auto-Propulsão* reported on adventurous drivers, referred to in Portuguese as "os sportsmen," as well as on the activities of the steadily increasing number of professional drivers, such as chauffeurs.[35] Unlike *Auto-Sport* and *Auto-Propulsão*, the *Revista de Automóveis*, when it began publication in Rio in October 1911, was explicitly geared to the most elite members of Carioca (people from Rio) society. In its first issue, it proclaimed that it sought to "defend the interest of *automobilismo*...for the progress of the city, the furthering of its elegant life, and the fascination of its means of transport."[36] These magazines, along with *Auto*

Federal and *O Auto Ilustrado*, were both a product of and further stimulus to the growing fascination with automobiles in urban Brazil. Along with other new technologies—the phonograph, typewriter, and later radio—motorcars came to Brazil just as the nation's mass publishing industry was getting started. City newspapers flourished, as advertisements for new consumer goods filled their pages. Specialty magazines, such as the automotive press, advertised cars for sale and hire, as well as every sort of service and product needed for driving. In this way, the automobile and its press promoted each other.[37]

Several of Brazil's leading writers addressed the profound changes associated with the ongoing adoption of new technologies from Europe and the United States. Brazil's great *cronista* João do Rio (Lima Barreto) wrote: "And suddenly, it's the era of the automobile. The transforming monster erupted, snorting, among the city's rubble.... It needed and accented an epoch entirely its own.... Automobile, Lord of the Era, Creator of new life, Enchanted Rider of urban transformation."[38] That João do Rio was fascinated first by Santos Dumont's flights and then by the arrival of the automobile is not particularly surprising. It is interesting, however, to note the ways in which his and others' writings were influenced by the advent of new technologies that challenged established notions of space and time. As Flora Süssekind, Nicolau Sevcenko, and others have demonstrated, various Brazilian writers of the first two decades of the twentieth century began to blend new content with new forms of writing, particularly in the most modern media of the day, the newspaper.[39] Indeed, Süssekind contrasts the venerated poet Olavo Bilac with João do Rio: Bilac saw himself as a craftsman and his work as free of modern interference. He wrote by hand. João do Rio used modern instruments (e.g., the typewriter), and his columns were literary expressions of cinematic or grammophonal representations of life in Rio de Janeiro.[40]

The automobile remained, above all others, the key technological innovation that fascinated a new generation of Brazilian writers. For João do Rio, Raimundo de Meneses, Júlia Lopes de Almeida, and others, the car was the perfect instrument for accelerating and decelerating time and altering the meaning of distance and space. From its very first issue, *Fon-Fon!* was closely associated with the growing automobile culture. A drawing of a car chasing caricatures of Brazil's leading intellectuals graced the cover of the first issue. As an introduction to that first issue, *Fon-Fon*'s editors compared the magazine and its offerings to "a little race, without great use of gasoline, or an excess of speed." They continued, "For a journal as agile and light as *Fon-Fon!*, we don't need a predetermined plan (or should we say an exact distance)."[41] Throughout its first few years of publication, the magazine contained both fiction and news reports related to the growing culture of automobility. This growing literary connection spawned material ties between young Brazilian authors and the new field of advertising. One advertisement in *Fon-Fon!* for Benz automobiles used a fictitious scene from the Brazilian Academy of Letters to try to sell cars. Other issues included sayings for drivers, pictures of new cars, and chauffeurs' jokes.[42] (Figure 1.1).

João do Rio's and other *cronistas*' writings celebrating the new culture of *automobilismo*, along with the advent of *Fon-Fon!* represented a new sort of hope among segments of Brazil's urban intelligentsia. They began to

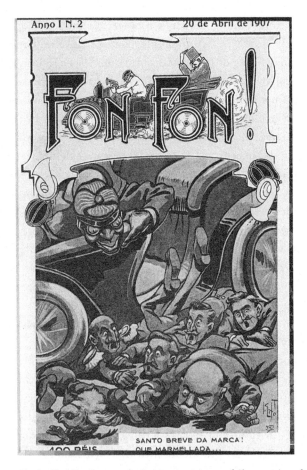

FIGURE 1.1 Early *Fon-Fon!* cover depicts a new automobile mowing down members of the traditional political and military elite with the comment "Good God! What a windfall. . . ." Photo courtesy of the Oliveira Lima Library.

imagine that technology, specifically the motorcar, would transform Brazil into a unified, modern nation. New technologies shaped not only their imaginations but also the ways in which they communicated. *Automobilismo* became much more than an interest in cars and driving; it was also a set of ideas about Brazil's future.

The press connected those who owned and operated cars to those seeking to promote and profit from expanded automobility. With fewer than 100 cars in Rio, gasoline was sold by pharmacies and auto parts by hardware stores. As the number of cars steadily increased, a few entrepreneurs opened garages that provided fuel, tires, and auto repairs. In 1908, Alfredo Elysiario da Silva opened one of the first large-scale operations in Rio, the Fiat Garage. Fiat, which was not formally associated with the Italian manufacturer, could garage and service 50 vehicles. It provided full repair services and even built custom bodies. The garage bragged of employing skilled Italian workmen and drivers, whom it would also rent, along with cars, to its customers.[43] These garages eventually evolved into two different types of businesses. Some became machine importers and fabricators. The Auto-Garage Pessos e Cia, on the R. Ipiranga in São Paulo, repaired many types of machines but specialized in automobiles.[44] Other garages transformed themselves into formal automobile dealerships. As early as 1904, Orey Antunes e Cia Ltda. operated as a dealership for a series of French cars (Darracq, Renault, and Berliet), but this was more the exception than the rule.[45] When the Ford Motor Company first came to Brazil in the early 1900s, it looked to sell its products through garages, but they were, more often than not, interested in European vehicles. In the major cities, Fords were initially sold by department and hardware stores. Outside Rio and São Paulo, they were available through an ad hoc collection of outlets, from individuals to farm supply merchants. One Ford executive recalled the trouble he had creating the initial network of dealerships in Brazil: "We had to appoint blacksmiths and even dentists and doctors and whoever we could. We actually had to make dealers."[46]

Drivers and mechanics ran these garages and rented their services to wealthy men who had little interest in driving their vehicles and even less interest in maintaining them. São Paulo's mayor in 1900, Plínio da Silva Prado, for example, bought a Delahaye in France and looked in Europe for help with the vehicle. He ended up bringing two Swiss brothers to São Paulo to serve as chauffeurs and mechanics. This arrangement was so envied by the Paulista elite that others searched for European brothers to serve as their chauffeurs.[47] Chauffeurs were prestige employees to the Carioca elite as well. The first presidential driver, Felisberto Gonçalves Caldeira, became an important figure in Rio's automobile culture. He helped to found the Centro de Chauffeures (which later became the Sindicato dos Motoristas) and was involved in crafting the city's first examinations for chauffeurs' licenses.[48] Mechanics also occupied a privileged social position at this time. Their monopoly of knowledge about the operation and maintenance of this new technology brought them not only high salaries—mechanics in the early 1900s often owned their own cars—but also a good deal of prestige.[49] Given the extraordinary wealth of this generation of car owners, this arrangement did not produce social tensions between servants who operated vehicles and the rich who owned them. The ability to employ chauffeurs and mechanics, who were more often than not Europeans, conveyed even greater social status on Brazil's first generation of car owners.[50]

The increasing number of cars slowly fostered the creation of an infrastructure for the development of a full-fledged automobile culture in the major cities.[51] Car owners quickly formed clubs and associations to organize their social activities related to driving and auto ownership, as well as to coordinate efforts to expand *automobilismo*. The Automóvel Club do Brasil (ACB) was founded in June 1907, and it inaugurated its headquarters on Rio's Praia de Botofogo on 23 July 1908. It was first and foremost an elite social organization with close ties to the old, elite Club dos Diários. In addition to throwing lavish balls and banquets for the city's wealthiest car owners, it sought to promote driving with safety regulations, street improvements, and pedestrian education.[52] Paulistanos founded their own Automóvel Club de São Paulo in 1910. To distinguish itself from its counterpart in Rio, the São Paulo club chose to concentrate on the nuts and bolts of expanding automobility. It advocated government support for road building and increased car imports. The club, which had an initial membership of more than 230, also promoted driver education.[53] Other cities' car owners followed these examples and formed their own auto clubs.[54]

Once established, Brazil's various automobile clubs set about to create an urban environment that would better support automobility. Preceding the clubs, the city of São Paulo had led the way by issuing Brazil's first traffic regulations on 26 February 1903. Antônio Prado, the city's mayor and an auto enthusiast, felt compelled to regulate automobile operation, even though there were only 25 vehicles in São Paulo at the end of 1902. These initial basic rules required that all drivers have a license issued by the city. All cars had to meet certain basic standards and had to have license plates produced by the city government. And all cars had to have lights if they were to be operated at night. A general speed limit was set for 30 kph in open areas, 20 kph in areas with populations, and 12 kph in the city center or throughout the city when conditions did not allow higher speeds. Two additional aspects of this first set of regulations reveal not only the novelty of cars but also the general suspicion such a new technology engendered. Car owners were responsible for the maintenance of their vehicles in full working order, and drivers were obliged to avoid accidents at any cost. Operators were more or less presumed responsible for most accidents involving their vehicles.[55]

Rio's ACB attempted in 1915 to have Brazil adopt an international accord on driving. The main goals were to tie Brazil's regulations to those used in Europe and the United States and, more broadly, to standardize driving throughout Brazil.[56] The first goal is understandable, particularly given the heavily European context of Brazil's nascent automobile culture. The attempt by the ACB to standardize driving throughout the country was, however, completely unrealistic. There was simply no mechanism for disseminating or policing a set of national traffic standards. Indeed, not until the late 1930s and early 1940s did Brazil unify driving regulations.[57]

The ACB proved much more effective in limiting the Rio city and national government's attempts to control traffic in the nation's capital. Car owners were particularly put off by a 1917 proposal to introduce speed limits in Rio. In 1911, the editors of *Revista de Automóveis* had argued strenuously and successfully against imposing a 20 kph speed limit on Rio's city streets. The 1917 proposal was more detailed, calling for three separate speed zones: center city (15 kph), general urban (40 kph), and rural (80 kph). Epitácio da Silva Pessoa (Brazil's president from 1919 to 1922), while serving in the Senate, supported the idea of establishing these as national standards. Unfortunately, the speed limits were applied to neither Rio nor the rest of Brazil for another 25 years. The absence of such basic regulations had profound effects on life in Rio. One local magazine commented, "One of the characteristics of Rio de Janeiro to the foreign eye is the lack of a speed limit for motor cars. This is a practice which does not honor the capital of Brazil and the numerous disasters are a proof of the assertion. Nothing is more pitiful than the death of a young man who was sitting on the sidewalk of Avenida Beira Mar last Sunday who was run over and killed."[58]

Indeed, driving was a real danger for Cariocas. From 1908 to 1918, there were 20,907 known auto accidents in the city. Of those, 1,743 involved cars colliding with cars; the others were cars hitting people, horses, carriages, buildings, trees, and other objects. There were 279 vehicular deaths in Rio during this ten-year period.[59]

Like all areas during the introduction of the automobile, Brazil's cities—particularly Rio and São Paulo—faced the complex task of integrating new, noisy, difficult-to-control vehicles onto already crowded streets. Although neither Rio nor São Paulo had the sort of street traffic found in New York, London, or Paris, the introduction of even a few automobiles in certain sections of town caused major disruptions.[60] Early reports of accidents point to the unwillingness of pedestrians to respect cars' right of way and to appreciate the power of those machines. People were not yet accustomed to automobiles' high speeds and poor braking. The police in Rio and São Paulo reacted to these problems by creating special divisions in 1910 to control urban driving.[61] During the 1910s, Rio and São Paulo began to install traffic signals, enlarged their traffic police departments, and attempted to enforce speed limits where they existed.[62] These cities were not beset by a huge number of automobiles, nor were their streets overcrowded. In fact, the poor condition of the Brazilian city streets increased auto traffic congestion because car owners tended to drive along the same handful of routes. In São Paulo, they traveled the downtown triangle and the Avenida Paulista. In Rio, the Avenida Central and the Beira Mar were favorite cruising spots. This concentration of automobile traffic made a relative handful of streets very dangerous locations for pedestrians as well as drivers.[63]

Although the problem of auto accidents was very real and dangerous, the tale of Brazil's first car crash has often been told and has even become part of the nation's mythology. The story is that in 1903, the great poet Olavo Bilac begged his dear friend, the famed abolitionist and journalist José de Patrocínio, to allow him to drive Patrocínio's new car. Some versions of this story include the erroneous claim that Patrocínio's was the first automobile in Brazil. Bilac supposedly took the wheel of the car just imported from France for a short drive of about 10 kilometers from Rio's largo de São Franscisco to Tijuca. At the corner of Rua Evaristo da Veiga and Rua das Marrecas, Bilac drove straight into a tree. Some accounts even provide the two friends' dialogue from the crash scene. Upon surviving the destruction of his new car, Patrocínio is reported to have said, "I know why this happened, it's because I was never baptized.... Without religion and with these ragged streets, progress just isn't possible!"[64] That those would be Patrocínio's first words upon extricating himself from the crash stretches the imagination. Why would Bilac even want to tempt fate in a friend's new, expensive possession? It is impossible to know who first told this story, but its significance is not so obscure. Patrocínio and Bilac were the sort of old-style intellectuals that younger writers who became closely associated with *automobilismo* rejected as out of fashion and even antimodern. The story of Bilac's accident is perhaps best interpreted as the story of a nineteenth-century Brazilian man incapable of handling twentieth-century technology.[65]

The twentieth century began in Brazil with a great sense of hope. The abolition of slavery in 1888 and the declaration of the republic in 1889 signaled Brazil's final break with its colonial past. Throughout these political and social upheavals, Brazilians increasingly turned to science and, to an even greater degree, technology to gain control over the unruly world around them. Some intellectuals and politicians held a nearly religious belief in the power of technology to provide both the order and the progress promised by the declaration of the republic. Automobility became a centerpiece in the collection of technologies that these leaders would use to transform Brazil.

It was perhaps inevitable that Brazilians would begin to measure their national progress through censuses of automobiles.[66] Auto magazines reported on the gross number of cars, trucks, and buses in the nation and the numbers per capita relative to other Latin American nations. By 1920, Brazil had one vehicle for every 1,400 inhabitants. This compared favorably to Venezuela (1:1,421) and Bolivia (1:5,454) but poorly to Argentina (1:281).[67] The steadily increasing number of vehicles was proof to some of Brazil's growing prosperity. A variety of groups—including segments of the military, private auto enthusiasts, and foreign embassies—worked to lower or eliminate tariffs on automobile imports specifically to aid national development. The wide use of cars and trucks in the war in Europe was cited as evidence of the growing importance of automobility to a modern nation.[68]

The creation of both the Ford Model T and the General Motors Corporation in 1908 provided important new tools for Brazilians interested in using automobility to foster modernity.[69] These elites and the American manufacturers had obvious shared interests, as the car companies looked to Latin America as a key developing market. Ford, for example, identified Argentina, Brazil, and Uruguay as its only potential markets for large numbers of cars in the 1910s. Although Ford at first concentrated on Argentina, Brazil quickly became its most lucrative Latin American market. By 1912, there were twice as many Ford Model Ts in Brazil as any other single car (Figure 1.2).[70] Smaller manufacturers in the United States received help in establishing sales offices from the U.S. government. American consular officials happily aided Studebaker, Pope, and others because Brazilian businessmen were actively seeking ties to American

Garage Moderna, Sao Paulo, Brazil

FIGURE 1.2 In 1913 São Paulo, the Model T was a luxury item, owned by the wealthy and driven by chauffeurs. Photo courtesy of The Henry Ford Museum and Library.

companies through contacts with diplomats.[71] The expansion of mass production in the United States, coupled with the war in Europe, led to the eventual domination of the Brazilian market by North American manufacturers, which would last until the late 1950s. This shift broadened automobility, at least slightly, as cars became affordable to more than just the richest Brazilians. It was also an important part of a cultural shift in Brazil toward U.S. goods and culture that became even more pronounced in the 1920s. Before 1915, for example, French imports controlled roughly 30% of the market, but in 1915, U.S. companies reached 79% of all auto imports; in 1917, American auto companies took hegemonic control of the market with 95.5% of imports.[72]

In the first two decades of the twentieth century, the motorcar began to open, ever so slightly, the nation's great interior spaces. The vast majority of motorcars remained in Rio and São Paulo, but Brazilians outside those metropolitan areas began to purchase vehicles at this time. From 1907 to June 1920, Brazil imported 24,475 automobiles. About 71% of those went to the Federal District and to the state of São Paulo, with the remaining 29% going throughout the country. Those figures, however, underrepresent the rate of rural and small-town car ownership. In 1918, for example, the city of São Paulo accounted for 58% of the state's cars. The state's secondary cities (e.g., Santos, Campinas, Ribeirão Preto, and Franca) had a growing vehicle population, and quite a few small municipalities had between 5 and 10 autos; 51 towns reported having 1 car only.[73] The statistics on urban concentration of automobiles also fail to take into account the emerging used car market, through which vehicles originally purchased in Rio and São Paulo were resold in smaller interior communities.[74]

Throughout the 1910s, the press reported on the expansion of automobility into Brazil's interior towns and cities. In addition to cars, bus and private car services connected interior towns. These services brought the smallest communities in contact with railroad links to state capitals and beyond. These early bus lines connected towns in Minas Gerais with those in São Paulo. The Auto-Viação Inter-Municipal Uberaba covered 356 kilometers and stretched all the way to Goiás. These services often traveled over old ox paths and across rickety and dangerous bridges. The companies promised to improve the routes on their own, but the difficulties of road building forced them to abandon most of their plans.[75] The creation of these interior transportation links not only increased local trade and facilitated contact between the smallest towns and capital cities but also began the process of changing the national imagination. Such links began to reduce the country's great size, extreme federalism, and weak lines of communication that limited the Brazilians' sense of their own nation. As late as 1916, for example, large landowners (or *fazendeiros*) in the Contestado region between the states of Santa Catarina and Paraná did not recognize the Brazilian flag or national anthem when army troops arrived in the region.[76] Car and bus travel, along with the new idea of tourism in Brazil, held out the possibility of transforming popular knowledge about the country. Travel and tourism might, many auto enthusiasts hoped, foster the creation of a broad sense of *brasilidade*.[77]

Automobility quickly took on the qualities of an ideology, promising to cure all of Brazil's problems. It would soon even transform Brazilian agriculture. The *Ford Times* reported in 1913 on the growing use of the Model T on Brazil's coffee plantations. The company magazine claimed: "So much have motor cars meant to this industry that there has been a noticeable increase in the size of acreage of single plantations since the automobile has made it possible to adequately supervise cultivation on a large scale."[78] Such hyperbole was not uncommon in the automotive press. A more sober assessment of the matter would focus on the growing use of the Model T as a piece of farm machinery. Ford placed advertisements in a wide variety of newspapers and magazines to call on planters to "Transform your Ford into a Tractor!" and promised easy-to-follow instructions for such a conversion.[79] Of even greater significance to Brazilian agriculture, auto enthusiasts bragged, would be the revival of the rubber industry. An ever increasing number of automobiles would provide the needed stimulus for a second rubber boom, in which the rubber would be made into tires within Brazil and would develop the Amazon region into a "true Eldorado."[80]

Such ideas were not mere dreams. In 1915, Goodyear Tire and Rubber Company began work on a Brazilian factory, intended as the central plant for South American production. In addition to tire production, the presence of a growing number of automobiles also encouraged state policy makers and industrialists to consider allowing foreign oil companies into Brazil to create a viable fuel supply for the nation's automobiles. More nationalist voices called for the development of alternative fuel sources, particularly alcohol.[81] Beyond these changes, Brazilian intellectuals and political and business leaders in São Paulo and Rio began to imagine that they might eventually create a national automobile industry. As early as the 1910s, there were glowing reports of Brazilian-made truck and bus chassis. The magazine *Auto-Propulsão* reported in 1915 on the fine work of skilled Brazilian craftsmen and proposed the idea that Brazil would soon have its own automobile factory.[82] Such ideas were not necessarily far-fetched, given the impressive strides Brazilian metalworking companies made during World War I. Cut off from European suppliers, Brazilian manufacturers increasingly depended on the nascent national machine tool industry to keep factories operating. If skilled Brazilians could produce looms and spinning equipment, it was not unreasonable to imagine them making automobiles.[83]

Automobility promised to transform modes of transportation, physical space, and eventually even the economy, but it could also disrupt cultural and social norms. Driving soon appealed to women, especially the daughters of Brazil's wealthy, because it was fashionable among American and European elites. And Brazilian car enthusiasts supported women's right to drive. As early as 1912, *Auto-Sport* editorialized in favor of expanding women's access to cars. The magazine claimed that women were already driving in Rio and São Paulo because *automobilismo* was not a masculine sport "like golf or hockey." By the late 1910s, the experiences of women ambulance drivers in World War I were cited as further proof that women should have full access to motorcars.[84] One reason women wanted to drive was that it became fashionable. Newspapers in Rio and São Paulo reported on the models of automobiles used by the cities' wealthiest citizens when they attended exclusive clubs and parties. Processions of cars were quickly added to Carnaval celebrations, and the Batalha de Flores included elaborately decorated motorcars.[85] As automobiles worked their way into elite culture, they began to affect fashions and manners.

These transformations—both promised and real—did not have a significant impact on Brazilian society in the 1910s. Agriculture was little changed by the arrival of a relative handful of cars in the rural sector. The growing tire industry did not usher in a second rubber boom, and a true domestic automobile industry would not begin producing cars until the late 1950s. Moreover, the few urban women who learned to drive did not, by their presence behind the wheel, have a discernible impact on gender ideologies in the 1910s. Automobility's real significance was that it pervaded the Brazilian cultural imagination at a time when ideas about new forms of agriculture, a powerful industrial base, and even new roles for women were considered and debated.[86]

Although cruising through the cities did not end, it was soon eclipsed in the popular imagination by the daring of young men who raced cars and drove them through previously inaccessible terrain. Pierre Lesdain, a French count, provided an example to Brazil's young, wealthy car owners. He arrived in Rio de Janeiro in 1908 with his four-cylinder, 16-horsepower Brasier to show the locals how a true sportsman operated his automobile. After attending a number of social functions where he bragged of his abilities and questioned the locals about driving in Rio, Lesdain grandly announced his plan to perform Brazil's first great driving stunt. He would ascend Rio's famous mountain Corcovado in his motorcar. He began his climb through the heavy Tijuca forest at 10 A.M. on 18 February 1908, riding his Brasier along the train tracks most of the way. He blocked a tram on its way to the top and was fined 200 milreis by the Light Company, which ran the tram and the city's utilities. A great crowd greeted him at the summit and his picture adorned the front pages of the city's newspapers for days following this stunt.[87]

Lesdain's daring inspired Rio's auto enthusiasts to talk about "raids" on nearby areas beyond the city's boundaries. For the first time in Brazil, car owners discussed driving from city to city to demonstrate the possibilities of auto travel. These adventures were consciously modeled on the European and later American practice, and the English word *raid* was used in Portuguese.[88] Gastão de Almeida met up with Lesdain as both cruised along the Praia de Botofogo. Almeida suggested additional raids and mentioned his plans to travel to Petrópolis, some 90 kilometers from the center of Rio. Steering his Dietrich, Almedia drove along the Leopoldina railroad and over abandoned portions of the once great União e Indústria road. Where there was no other route, he simply made his way through the jungle. His trip took three full days and led a reporter from the *Correio da Manhã* to remark that such a raid "was the sort of thing that makes brave *sportsmen*."[89]

Count Lesdain next decided to make a much more spectacular raid, to São Paulo. He left at 4:00 A.M. on 6 March. The handful of car enthusiasts who had heard of his plans considered Lesdain quite crazy. Brazilians knew that no road or combination of roads linked the two cities, for many of them traveled to São Paulo by taking a sea route to Santos and then a train to the Paulista capital. When no news of the Frenchman was heard, many in Rio assumed he had died in the interior's jungles.[90] Then, on 12 March, the *Correio da Manhã* reported that Lesdain had sent a telegram two days earlier from the town of Belém in the state of Rio de Janeiro. Lesdain reported that he, Major Luiz Barbosa da Silva, and three mechanics had encountered extraordinary obstacles as they made their way through mud and jungle.[91] More than two weeks passed before readers in Rio and São Paulo again heard of Lesdain's progress. He reported in from Bananal, still some 300 kilometers from São Paulo. The stretch from Arrozal to Barra Mansa was the most treacherous Lesdain and his crew faced. Where there were roads, they were often made impassable by fallen trees and deep pools of mud. Some roads led directly into swamps. In this stretch of territory, the car had to traverse five rickety bridges that required repair before use. There were some rewards, however. When they suffered a minor accident outside the village of Cruzeiro on 6 April, Lesdain and his compatriots were greeted by locals on bicycles who had come out to escort them into town, where they were treated as great heroes. They had coffee, cookies, and liquor with several leading citizens; were treated to the finest rooms in the Hotel Bitetti; and later attended a special reception and banquet the mayor hosted to mark the arrival of the first motorcar in his town, as well as to celebrate the bravery of the sportsmen making the historic raid.[92]

From Cruzeiro, Lesdain made his way to Embabú and then to Caçapaya. There, on 9 April, he sent a telegram to São Paulo to announce his imminent arrival. Crowds began to gather around midday on 11 April. Lesdain and his crew finally arrived in São Paulo at 5:24 in the evening. A large group of auto enthusiasts met him in Penha and drove in a parade formation to the Praça Antônio Prado. The following day, there was a great reception at the Parque Antártica to honor Lesdain and his companions, with extra trolleys run to accommodate the celebrants. Lesdain accepted congratulations from the city's leaders and then spoke at length of the tortuous experience of spending 34 days driving from Rio to São Paulo. Finally, he proclaimed that Brazil had to build a viable motor route connecting its two greatest cities.[93] When that was finally completed in 1926, the trip would take 6 to 7 hours.

Lesdain inspired other Brazilian auto enthusiasts to attempt their own raids. When word of the raid reached São Paulo, Washington Luís Pereira de Souza, then state secretary of justice and one of his era's most vocal proponent of *automobilismo*, set out on a raid to Itapecerica da Serra. Unfortunately, Washington Luís's Fiat could not handle the rough roads, so he had to join others in a Motorbloc car that made the trip. Upon arrival in Itapecerica da Serra, the party was met by the mayor and honored with a banquet.[94] Just a few days later, another leading Paulista, Antônio Prado Junior, set out in his Ford—along with Clóvis Glicério, an engineer; Mário Cardim, a journalist; and Bento Canabarro, a backwoods guide (*sertanista*)—to make the first São Paulo–Santos automobile journey. They stopped frequently to clear their path, sometimes with dynamite. In all, their raid of only 95 kilometers between the state capital and its major port required more than 25 hours of driving.[95] Raids within the state of São Paulo and between Rio and Minas Gerais were increasingly popular in the 1910s, with drivers challenging previous times with new cars and modified routes. Increasingly, American manufacturers, particularly Ford and Studebaker, sponsored these new raids to demonstrate the durability and superiority of their latest models.[96]

Lesdain's great raid was not the only major feat of *automobilismo* in 1908. That year also witnessed South America's first motorcar race, held in São Paulo on 26 July. The first major initiative of the new São Paulo Automóvel Club was an auto race from São Paulo through its rural suburbs of Embu, Itapecerica da Serra, and Santo Amaro. The course covered 75 kilometers and had a grandstand that served as the start and finish (admission was two milreis). The cars were grouped by horsepower: Silvio Penteado won his section in a Fiat, J. Laport his in a Renault, and Antônio Prado Junior took the final and least powered category in a Delage. The race was a great success. The press estimated that more than 10,000 Paulistas witnessed the 14-car, 2-motorcycle race from along the roadside. In 1908, there were probably fewer than 1,000 automobiles in all of Brazil, but watching a motorcar race allowed thousands of Brazilians to experience vicariously the speed and power of this new technology.[97] The sports sections of Rio and São Paulo's largest dailies soon included sections devoted to racing and raids.[98] This race's success led the Rio-based Automóvel Club do Brasil to sponsor its own on 19 September 1909. Gastão de Almeida drove an hour and forty minutes to win this 72-kilometer race held on the São Gonçalo Circuit in his 60-horse power Berliet. An estimated 5,000 Cariocas witnessed the race.[99]

On race day, the *Correio da Manhã* reported that the goal of this sporting event was to encourage broader acceptance of the motorcar in Brazil. The automobile, the newspaper continued, was the only instrument capable of effectively tying the nation's various state capitals to the national capital. The race showcased modern technologies, including the telephone, which was used to augment telegraphic reporting of the event. In addition to the presence of race cars, a motorized ambulance was on the scene to speed injured drivers to medical care. Indeed, the *Correio da Manhã* story concluded, "Today's race is the beginning of the powerful triumph over a major problem, because the progress of the nation has been reclaimed."[100]

The motorcars that the coffee barons and their sons imported to Brazil as yet one more European luxury item ended up playing a much more complicated role than their owners had anticipated. At the time wealthy Brazilians imported the first cars, transportation existed to serve the coffee economy above all else; there was simply no reason to consider establishing railroads or highways to connect Brazilian cities or states.[101] Indeed, before the arrival of large numbers of automobiles, the state of São Paulo had studied and rejected the idea of building more roads. The government of Manuel Ferraz de Campos Sales believed that the railroad and the small feeder roads that connected plantations to depots were more than adequate for the state's economy.[102]

The elite of coffee producers, bankers, and middlemen who profited greatly from the nation's infrastructure being tied to its export economy inadvertently popularized the very machines that would soon challenge aspects of Brazil's liberal economic model. Auto transport opened the possibility, for the first time in Brazilian history, of unifying the nation. Business and political elites began to speak of developing national markets and of establishing intimate contact between the distant and exotic interior and the modern and outward-looking coastal cities. The motorcar's arrival forced Brazilians to ask difficult questions about the ways in which the coffee export economy had reinforced the nation's extreme federalism. This new technology not only challenged how Brazilians thought about the physical makeup of their country but also raised important issues about the role of the state.

CHAPTER 2

The Coming of Tropical Modernity: Automobiles and the Question of Nation

THROUGHOUT THE 1920S, significant segments of the population challenged the status quo in Brazil. A vocal, though small, group of politicians in São Paulo disputed the ongoing dominance of that state's Republican Party. In Rio, São Paulo, Belo Horizonte, and other large cities, industrialists increasingly questioned the supremacy of agricultural commodity production and export in the economy. And perhaps most significantly, young military officers, the so-called *tenentes*, launched two separate uprisings (in Rio de Janeiro in 1922 and São Paulo in 1924) to challenge Brazil's social, economic, and political structures. This questioning of Brazil's economic liberalism and closed political system was a by-product of the landed elites' success. The booming export economy had brought growth to the nation's state capitals, particularly in the center-south region. Urban and rural growth helped fuel early industrial development and so created new economic opportunities for the nation. This agriculture-based, export-led growth, centered primarily on coffee, created the preconditions for alternative visions of Brazilian development. Over the course of the 1920s, new technologies like automobiles became both symbols and tools for that new style of development.

Raids, races, and simple driving, however, continued to be limited by the near-total absence of roads connecting Brazil's cities.[1] Primitive roads that were nearly impassable after heavy rains connected the major cities to the nearby countryside, but the majority of interior roads had been fashioned over existing paths slave hunters (*bandeirantes*) had created in the colonial era and early nineteenth century. In the entire nineteenth century, Brazil had built one modern road, the 155-kilometer União e Indústria highway that connected the growing economy of Juiz de Fora, Minas Gerais, to Petrópolis in the state of Rio de Janeiro. Begun in 1856 and completed in 1861, the well-designed and built highway quickly fell into disrepair with the advent of rail travel in the 1860s. By 1900, the path of the União e Indústria no longer functioned as a thoroughfare. Other roads connecting São Paulo and Santos and the coast with the interiors of Paraná and Santa Catarina were also constructed, but they, too, were not maintained when railroad transportation expanded.[2]

The arrival of the motorcar forced Brazilians to reconsider road building. The urban reforms in Rio and São Paulo at the turn of the century left these cities with grand boulevards capable of handling cars, and new cities such as Belo Horizonte had smooth roads that did not wreak havoc on early automobiles.[3] The arrival of the extremely durable Ford Model T allowed some interior car travel, but conditions were so rough that even it faced severe limits. One Ford executive recalled that driving in Brazil's interior at this time required unique skill: "In the interior it was necessary to put the Model into reverse on part of the trip; otherwise the cars would smoke from overheating. If the car went backward this would cool the car. Otherwise the disks would burn. Often one would have to stop and rest and leave the car to cool."[4]

Car enthusiasts, businessmen, and government officials all well understood the limits Brazil's poor lines of internal communication put on the growth of auto-based transportation. As early as 1909, the national government made subsidies available to states willing to build new roads. In 1911, the Department of Communications and Public Works studied the feasibility of constructing a highway suitable for motorcars between Petrópolis and Rio de Janeiro.[5] In addition to these modest early initiatives, some in Brazil were beginning to discuss much broader, grander plans for the automobile. The dream of *automobilistas* was that Brazil would soon have a network of roads connecting north with south and east with west. With such roads, Brazil could take advantage of the promise of modern technology. The editors of *Auto-Sport* noted, "There are no limits to velocity and with auto transportation becoming more common every day, [roads] become a national priority."[6]

When President Washington Luís (1926–1930) declared in 1926 that "to govern is to make roads," he spoke of an increasingly obvious aspiration for the nation. The automobile held out the promise of reversing Brazil's dominant development pattern. National unification would not only push forward economic development by dramatically increasing the size of domestic markets but also diminish the likelihood of future conflicts between isolated rural communities and cosmopolitan urban elites. For the first time in Brazil's history, technology was embraced as an instrument for the economic, political, and social transformation of the society. Technology would, along with science, break down the barriers to national integration in a peaceful and orderly way. Automobility would destroy the remaining obstacles to capitalist development and, at the same time, provide the basis for the creation of a truly Brazilian culture.[7] Automobile travel would allow Brazilians to physically gain control over their massive national territory, while it also created the physical and cultural interaction of coastal and urban Brazilians. This contact, intellectuals argued, would lead to the creation of a truly national culture and identity.

Automobility and modernism were closely intertwined in the 1910s and 1920s (Figure 2.1). Their association mixed the worlds of literature and art with the hard labor of road building. While intellectuals sought to create the figurative nation through artistic and literary production,

FIGURE 2.1 São Paulo quickly became the capital of automobility. In the 1920s, the Viaducto da Chá had more auto traffic than streetcars. Photo courtesy of the U.S. National Archives.

engineers and planners literally mapped and paved the nation. Businessmen and government leaders worked with both groups to build a new Brazil. Foreign car companies eagerly, but quietly, aided these activities with generous financial and technical support. In the 1920s in Brazil, cars, trucks, and buses brought economic modernization in close proximity to social and cultural modernism, together allowing Brazilian elites to imagine the transformation of their country.

In the twentieth century, Brazilians recast as pioneers the men who had chased runaway slaves. These *bandeirantes* were no longer the tough, mixed-race backwoodsmen who captured Indians and escaped slaves. The *bandeirantes* were now literally pathbreakers who opened Brazil's interior to settlement.[8] Myths about the pioneering spirit were particularly important to Brazil's auto enthusiasts. They considered themselves modern *bandeirantes* who would use cars and trucks to explore and settle the interior. It was the less heralded leaders of Rio's Automobile Club who began planning for the nation's first road-building campaign. Unlike the fiercely independent *bandeirantes*, these twentieth-century road builders chose to work closely with the Ministry of Transportation and Public Works and some of the nation's richest and most powerful men.

The founders of the Automobile Club had proclaimed in 1908 that one of their primary goals was to build roads throughout Brazil. Particularly during its first three decades as an organization, the Automobile Club counted among its members many of Rio's most prominent citizens. In fact, the Club de Diários, which itself was a continuation of the venerable Casino Fluminense—both privileged societies for social and business networking—essentially became the Automóvel Club do Brasil.[9] The powerful Cariocas who led the Automóvel Club used their business and political connections to work closely with Tavares de Lyra, the Minister of Transportation and Public Works, to promote the idea that building roads was key for Brazil's future economic growth and military defense.[10] The Automóvel Club de São Paulo had a similar history. Its 1919 yearbook details not only its extensive ties to smaller clubs throughout São Paulo but also how powerful a political force it was in city and state politics. A past and future president of the republic (Francisco de Paula Rodrigues Alves, 1902–1906 and Washington Luís Pereira de Sousa, 1926–1930), along with the archbishop and assorted present and former governors, mayors, and other dignitaries, belonged to the club.[11] Early clubs in Minas Gerais and Bahia—both local city and statewide—played similar roles in melding existing elite organizations made up of local notables and forward-looking car enthusiasts.[12]

Rio's Automobile Club held the First National Roads Congress on 12–13 October 1916 to bring together like-minded auto enthusiasts to identify where and how the new roads should be built, as well as where the financial backing would come from. This congress did not produce any great plans for the immediate construction of national highways. It did, however, help to create the institutional framework for auto enthusiasts to debate the "roads" question in the national capital. Special committees of the Automóvel Club began to study the feasibility of constructing modern highways outside the city limits.[13] At the same time, the Paulista Automóvel Club held its first roads congress in June 1917. From that gathering, the club created a special roads group (the Associação Permanente de Estradas de Rodagem) to promote local highway construction. São Paulo's Mayor Washington Luís served as the Roads Association president, with Ataliba Valle and Antônio Prado Junior acting as secretary and treasurer. These powerful men, whose families could claim to be among the largest coffee producers in São Paulo and thus Brazil, quickly set out to design a modern road system for their state.[14] By 1925, Pernambuco, Rio Grande do Sul, and Mato Grosso had formed associations to complement those of Rio de Janeiro, São Paulo, and Minas Gerais. In January 1926, governors and other officials from four northeastern states met in Recife for the Congress of Good Roads, Instruction, and Public Health. Representatives from the São Paulo roads commission, as well as delegates from the Automóvel Club in Rio and the federal government, attended this week-long conference to map out future roads for the northeast.[15]

No actual construction of major roads immediately followed these congresses. The participants did, however, build Brazil's *Boas Estradas*, or "Good Roads" movement, which sought to copy its namesake in the United States.[16] In Brazil, the Good Roads movement promoted the idea that roads, unlike railroads, could be built much less expensively and more quickly, in response to new clusters of population and economic activity. The low cost of first roads, which were often unpaved, would allow governments to use road building to spur migration and the development of entrepreneurial activities. The movement of people and money into the countryside would begin, however tentatively, to erode Brazil's urban-rural divide. The group promoted these ideas through the magazine *A Estrada de Rodagem (The Highway)* (later *Boas Estradas*), which, even more than the roads congresses, succeeded in fueling interest in national highway construction. Unlike the early car magazines, which mostly focused on elite urban culture in Rio and São Paulo, *Boas Estradas* tended to advocate rural road construction.[17]

Urban Brazilians in the nation's center-south rarely thought about the inhabitants of the country's interior. When Cariocas and Paulistas considered interior folk, whom they often derided as "hillbillies" (*caipiras* or *caboclos*), they tended to view them as threats to Brazilian civilization, particularly after the country's two violent millenarian rebellions.[18] Uniting urban and rural interests was no small task. Although prosperous coffee barons who generated their wealth in the countryside owned palatial homes in Rio de Janeiro and São Paulo city, Brazilian society was clearly divided between coastal urban areas and their interior rural spaces. In the late 1910s and 1920s, roads enthusiasts from both Rio and São Paulo began to articulate ideas about a Brazil unified by a complex system of highways. They were not necessarily competing visions, but Carioca and Paulista ideas about transportation differed in several important ways. Cariocas argued for a road system that would reflect their city's political dominance, with highways emanating from the national capital to every state in Brazil, while Paulista road enthusiasts believed that roads should boost their growing agricultural and industrial economy. Both projects sought to finally unify the nation in some meaningful way. Such ideas were part of a growing critique of the extreme nature of Brazil's liberal economy and federated polity. Businessmen and politicians interested in automobility and road building joined intellectuals in proposing new ways to create a modern nation state in Brazil.[19]

Although automobile enthusiasts congregated in clubs, they understood that only broader car ownership would effect physical, economic, and perhaps even social unification. And so, the construction of a new Ford Motor Company assembly plant on Rua Solon in São Paulo marked a fundamental turning point in Brazil's relationship with the automobile. The factory— a miniature version of the main Highland Park plant in Michigan—rose to three full stories in late 1920. With these mass-produced Fords, cars were making a rapid transition from status symbols of the elite to tools for improved transportation and the physical integration of the nation. Ford and General Motors, which opened a factory soon after Ford's, played an important role in this shift, as their automobiles began to fill the streets of Brazil's largest cities and state capitals, and trucks and buses also became more common in Brazil's vast interior spaces, despite the fact that auto ownership remained far beyond the reach of most people.[20]

During the 1920s, Brazil was the fourth or fifth (depending on the year) greatest importer of U.S. made automobiles. From 1923 through 1929, annual imports of autos averaged 83% of the value of all goods brought into Brazil.[21] Still, U.S. government and business analyses of the Brazilian market noted that the highly skewed distribution of income limited future growth, as did the weak road system. These facts left U.S. exporters cautious about the Brazilian market, but animated Brazilian car enthusiasts saw expanded roads as spurring further economic growth and incomes and so more automobile imports.[22] One sign of the growing importance of automobiles in Brazil was the frequent counting of cars and the many comparisons of the nation's per capita auto ownership with that of other Latin American countries. Censuses of automobiles became a measure of the Brazil's modernity.[23] When the counting of cars turned up far fewer vehicles than assumed, auto enthusiasts assured themselves that the problem was one of underreporting, not limited ownership.[24] This was more than simply a product of wishful thinking. Every year did bring an increasing number of imported autos into the country, and a used car market soon developed.[25]

The distribution of autos throughout Brazil mirrored popular views about differences among the nation's various regions. São Paulo state had by far the greatest concentration of cars, trucks, and buses in the country and led Brazil in all aspects of automobility. By the end of the 1910s, the city of São Paulo led the nation in automobile registrations; by the mid-1920s, the state held half of the licensed vehicles in the nation.[26] The state increasingly relied on truck transportation between its primary port, Santos, and the growing capital, São Paulo city. The number of passenger cars, trucks, and buses steadily grew in the state's secondary cities, and motor vehicles began to appear in smaller towns in the northern and western coffee frontier.[27] By 1921, Franca, with a population of about 12,000, had 200 kilometers of roads, three garages with repair shops, and 80 automobiles (40 Fords, 5 Hupmobiles, 5 Chevrolets, 2 Spas, 2 Dorts, and a smattering of other brands); Taquaratinga, with only a few thousand residents, had 66 kilometers of auto roads, two garages to service vehicles, and 10 registered automobiles (5 Fords, 2 Essexes, 2 Chevrolets, and 1 Dodge).[28] Ford and Chevrolet, but also Dodge and Studebaker, consciously marketed their cars to those in the interior as rugged vehicles capable of handling even the worst rural roads.

In many interior states, the arrival of a car in a small town, even if it was just passing through, became an occasion for a large celebration with speeches by local dignitaries.[29] There were two separate, but not mutually exclusive, reactions to seeing a car for the first time in rural Brazil: wonder and fear. One report noted that "on June 15, 1920, there entered into Santa Luzia [Goiás] the first automobile viewed by the local population with a profound astonishment, amounting almost to terror." The car's ability to climb local mountains and connect nearby towns led to "unbounded admiration of the inhabitants to whom this form of locomotion had been entirely unknown."[30] The 1922 arrival of a car in Cuiabá, Mato Grosso, was remembered 30 years later by Afraubi Corrêa as a key moment in that city's development that brought a "revolution in social customs" due to the expanded mobility that was now available. Although the presence of cars marked the beginning of the modern epoch for this interior city, Corrêa's family Chevy spent ten years parked next to the family horse, and both were relied on for work and transportation.[31] In 1927, the Ford that Doertagnar Marinho drove into Andaraí in the interior of Bahia, a town of only 3,500, was honored with a parade and speeches predicting the coming of "a new civilization" in the *sertão* and therefore a new Brazil[32] (Figure 2.2). Other arrivals were treated less ceremoniously. One car traveling from Juiz de Fora to Petrópolis in 1920 terrorized children and adults in several small towns along the route. In 1921, outside Rio's city limits, a Dodge was rescued from a swamp by men on horses who pulled the vehicle from the deep mud. Rural folk who saw this car as it resumed its trip either stared at it or ran yelling into the woods.[33]

FIGURE 2.2 In Bahia, wealthy car owners prepare for an excursion. Their chauffeurs drove the vehicles. Photo courtesy of the U.S. National Archives.

The sight of motorcars on city streets no longer caused such commotion, but the steadily increasing number of autos did begin to affect urban Brazil. Trolleys (*bondes*) and cars often vied for the right of way in the business district of São Paulo.[34] The Praça da Sé, the public square widely considered to be the center of town, was turned into a parking lot, and jammed streets led to calls for studying ways to alleviate traffic. This motor traffic diminished the use of horse- and human-pulled wagons, at least reducing the number of animal-automobile collisions.[35] In both Rio and São Paulo, the city governments attempted to outlaw the use of animal-pulled trucks and carts in the central business districts, which was justified not only in terms of traffic safety but also by efforts to reduce the manure in Brazil's city streets, as London, New York, Berlin, Paris, and Buenos Aires had done.[36] Other large cities, such as Belo Horizonte, Fortaleza, and Porto Alegre, likewise registered large numbers of motorcars in the 1920s and also started using trucks and buses in everyday commerce. Cars and small trucks were converted for use by police, ambulance services, and fire departments, making autos an increasingly visible and useful part of everyday life in urban Brazil.[37]

Already by the late 1910s, São Paulo's and Rio's streets were well known for their dangerous traffic. In addition to the steadily increasing number of cars, trucks, and buses, Paulistanos and Cariocas had to contend with horse-drawn vehicles and trolleys. A British diplomat breathlessly described the harrowing conditions on São Paulo's streets in his annual report on social, economic, and political conditions in Brazil: "Taxis...are driven with such reckless abandon that collisions and deaths are of daily occurrence....Cars rarely stop after knocking down pedestrians, and no effort seems to be made by police either to identify the drivers or to prevent the recurrence of similar accidents."[38] São Paulo's rapid growth exacerbated the dangerous conditions, as more and more vehicles filled not only the streets of established neighborhoods and the old downtown triangle but also new suburban subdivisions that grew throughout the 1920s, 1930s, and 1940s. The constant stream of migrants from the rural sector increased confusion on the streets and led to so many pedestrian deaths from collisions with cars and trolleys that they were memorialized by Antônio de Alcântara Machado, the leading chronicler of working-class life in São Paulo.[39] A 1924 article in the *Estado de São Paulo* lamented the dangers of the city's streets caused by the ever-increasing presence of unregulated traffic. Cars and trucks were making São Paulo's sidewalks and streets too dangerous for pedestrians: "Today, the city's residents need courage to leave their homes and walk the city streets because they face thousands of unbridled machines flying through the streets as if they're in a race."[40]

By the late 1920s, commentators noted that automobility was beginning to transform more than life on the street; it also affected São Paulo's architecture. Business buildings were increasingly designed with parking facilities, and single-family homes were consciously modeled on U.S.-style houses with two-car garages (Figure 2.3). These architectural revisions spoke to even more fundamental changes the car was bringing, for the two-car garage was to accommodate both the husband's and wife's cars.[41] Broad auto ownership and two-car families continued to be more an aspiration than a fact of life in São Paulo, but those ideas reveal the power of both exotic technologies and consumer goods to shape culture.

These marketing efforts did not by themselves shape ideas about gender, but they did dovetail with important changes in social ideals about women.[42] Female auto ownership was not seen as inappropriate or damaging to women's honor in urban Brazil (Figure 2.4). The cover of the second issue of the magazine *Automóvel Club* illustrated a woman happily driving alone.[43] Young beauty queens often earned new cars as part of their prizes in various pageants. When Yvonne de Freitas was named Miss São Paulo in 1929, she was given a new Reo Flying Cloud Master by the local dealership; 1929's Miss Brazil, Olga Bergamini de Sá from the Botafogo

FIGURE 2.3 The steadily increasing number of cars owned by businessmen led to a severe shortage of parking in São Paulo's downtown. Photo courtesy of the U.S. National Archives.

FIGURE 2.4 Car companies and auto enthusiasts promoted the idea of women drivers as a basic aspect of modernity. Photo courtesy of the U.S. National Archives.

neighborhood in Rio, said she had "a passion for cars" and intended to purchase a convertible coup (*baratinha*) while in Galveston, Texas, for the Miss Universe pageant.[44]

Although cars fostered changes in architecture in São Paulo, their impact in Rio was much more immediate. Foreign and local commentators alike noted the packed streets—some even called for the construction of a subway as early as 1927—as well as the extremely dangerous nature of Carioca drivers. Pedestrians quickly became aware of the inability of many drivers to control their cars, and traffic fatalities increased each year at a rate much greater than the growth of car ownership. The high speed, stop-and-go style of driving was so pronounced in Rio that U.S. government officials encouraged manufacturers of brake linings to increase their presence in Brazil.[45]

Another important difference between automobility in Rio and São Paulo was that the vast majority of motorcars in the nation's capital until the late 1920s were taxis. This reflected the development of professional drivers as a new group of high-skill workers. The city's taxis quickly earned a reputation for terrifying both passengers and pedestrians.[46] A 1924 editorial entitled "Automobile Assassination" summed up the situation on Rio's streets: "Among the world's speed maniacs and traffic 'scofflaws,' they [the Carioca chauffeurs] are star performers.... Chauffeurs are apparently growing more reckless as the number of cars is increasing. The other night, near the Tunel Novo, two cars ran over the same person.... Both drivers ran away from the corpse at top speed."[47] Such behavior led the Rio city government to establish special posts explicitly for traffic police. New fines were created for stopping in the middle of traffic to drop off or pick up passengers.

Just as foreigners had long measured Brazil and other societies by their level of technological achievement, leading Brazilians looked at the steadily increasing number of motorcars, trucks, and buses arriving in Brazil as empirical proof that their country was making an important and irrevocable transition from an agrarian society that had only recently ended slavery to a modern, capitalist nation-state. They were incredulous that the 1924 figures showed that Argentina, despite its much smaller population, had more than three times as many vehicles as Brazil (88,550 for Argentina, 29,084 for Brazil). Worse yet, countries in Europe described as "tiny" and "exotic," such as Serbia and Bulgaria, had more motorcars than Brazil.[48] The ratio of cars to people was even more alarming to Brazil's auto backers. *Boas Estradas* reported in 1926 that a U.S. Department of Commerce study had found that there existed one motorcar for every 71 people on earth. The United States led the world in car ownership with one per every six people; China had the lowest level of ownership with one per every 31,876 people. Brazil had only one car per every 530 people (compared to 1:279 in Argentina and 1:311 in Mexico).[49] Magazines and newspapers that covered Brazil's automobile culture paid close attention to comparisons with Argentina and the poorer, southern American states that had the fewest vehicles per capita in the United States.[50]

Despite the fervent hopes of auto enthusiasts, Brazilian cities did not experience the sorts of traffic jams that U.S. cities had, despite the growth of Rio and São Paulo during the first three decades of the twentieth century. The absence of New York–style auto traffic worried Brazilian enthusiasts because they viewed bustling streets packed with motorcars, trucks, and buses as a sign that Brazil was on the path to modernity.[51] Brazil's car enthusiasts did brag that they had a much greater number of trucks than any other Latin American nation. Whenever possible, Brazilian merchants, factory owners, and even farmers purchased trucks. Indeed, truck transport quickly became the dominant form of portage both within Brazilian cities and among them.[52] In well-developed regions in the center-south, trucks expanded the reach and efficiency of existing rail lines by bringing greater quantities of produce more quickly to railheads. In São Paulo, increasing supplies of coffee traveled by trucks (Figure 2.5), and nearly the entire maté crop moved by truck. These vehicles then returned to the countryside loaded with goods for sale to farmers and other rural folk.[53] Trucks had an even greater impact in the impoverished *sertão* of the northeast. They moved cotton from Rio Grande do Norte's interior to Natal and from the *cariri-sertão* and eastern Piranhas Valley to Campina Grande in Paraíba. Bahia's sugar crop increasingly came to market by truck.[54] The developing reliance on truck transport was not as glamorous as the sight of the latest imported sedans and roadsters packing downtown business districts or chic neighborhoods, but it did reveal the importance of automobility to Brazil's economy.

Brazil's automobile owners were evangelical in their belief that the broad use of cars, trucks, and buses was the key to making the nation modern, but they did not have any coherent ideas about how to popularize auto ownership. Despite some hyperbolic claims about the growing presence of cars, they faced the reality of Brazil's narrow market for elite consumer goods.[55] Car evangelists sought to promote automobility to the

FIGURE 2.5 Over the course of the 1920s and 1930s, sugar and coffee producers increasingly used trucks to transport crops from plantations to rail lines. Photo courtesy of the U.S. National Archives.

broader public through support for the nation's growing automobile clubs. Leaders of the Rio-based Automóvel Club do Brasil moved to disband the organization in early 1921 in order to remove its association with the city's elite social clubs. Then, on 16 May 1921, they inaugurated the new Club Brasileiro para Automóvel. The new association would focus on "promoting the development of automobility" by building roads and publishing and distributing maps, driving guides, and other materials. On 12 July 1922, it changed its name back to the Automóvel Club do Brasil to align itself with the growing movement of such groups internationally, especially those tied to the American Automobile Association.[56]

The new Brazilian auto club publicly articulated its central mission: doing whatever was necessary to make using cars more common in Brazil. The ACB lowered the cost of membership and subscription to its magazine specifically to make automobility more affordable to all. It sponsored special expositions to promote the latest vehicles and additional roads conventions to plan a national highway system. It formally resolved to privately fund road construction.[57] The ACB also built formal ties with existing clubs, such as those in Minas and São Paulo, which were undertaking similar transitions, and helped establish new associations in Alagoas, Paraná, and elsewhere in the mid-1920s.[58] Foreign governments eager to export cars to Brazil aided this effort with funding and international contacts. In addition to increased ties to the American Automobile Association, the ACB established links to two international groups based in France (the Association International des Automobiles Clubs Reconnus and the Association International Permanente des Congrès de la Route).[59]

Although these efforts brought car owners together, they did not necessarily bring new people into the world of the automobile. The best way to truly popularize cars was to show them to as broad an audience as possible. Just as merchants had learned to exploit glass and lighting in department store windows to market goods to passersby in Rio and São Paulo, auto enthusiasts decided to market automobility as if the idea were a product.[60] The ACB and the São Paulo club, with considerable financial and logistical support from foreign auto companies, began to stage elaborate automobile expositions.[61] The first systematic marketing event took place at the Brazilian Centennial Exposition in Rio in 1922. The U.S. government, along with several American corporations, sponsored exhibits on modern road construction and showed movies with titles such as *The Story of the Automobile* and *An Oil Field Dodge—Automobile Picture*. The Ford Motor Company exhibit was the largest and most elaborate, with Model Ts, Lincolns, tractors, and other products on display. General

Motors, Dodge Brothers, Indian Motorcycles, HCS Motor Car, and others also brought their products to the exposition to attract consumer interest.[62] The success of the car-oriented displays at the centennial encouraged the São Paulo Good Roads Association to hold Brazil's first true auto show at the Palace of Industries during October 1923. Headlines in São Paulo's newspapers heralded the opening of the show and announced that 26 car manufacturers, along with tire makers, oil companies, and others from the United States and Europe, had displays. Thousands of people from São Paulo and Rio attended the show, with great lingering crowds around the new car displays. Demonstrations of trucks and other vehicles were also quite popular. The largest crowds watched modern highway construction machinery pave 840 meters (or a bit more than a half of a mile) of the Santo Amaro road in only 90 minutes.[63]

The success of the first show led to a more ambitious Second Auto Exposition in September 1924. This time, the Good Roads Association worked closely with the São Paulo Automobile Club. The city's newspapers covered preparations for the show and commented extensively on the use of Ford tractors in pulling cars up to the second floor of the exhibit hall. In addition to demonstrations of tractors, trucks, and even buses, the second auto show included a 700-kilometer raid of 44 cars from São Paulo to Ribeirão Preto and back. (A Marmon won in 10 hours, 7 minutes, and 48 seconds.) The show was so popular that it was held over for three additional days.[64] This second auto show, along with the third held in São Paulo in November 1925, differed from the first in one important way: Automobility was discussed and demonstrated in terms of national development. At the third, which drew more than 10,000 visitors on most days, Ford emphasized the need to travel into "a characteristic Brazilian jungle" and advertised the Model T as the vehicle best suited to open the nation's interior. Ford also marketed the Model T as the best defense against Brazil's notoriously unreliable hydroelectric supply. Factory equipment was operated using Fords as their central power supply. The magazine *Brazilian American* editorialized, with some exaggeration, to be sure: "The far-reaching results of the show of this kind in the progress of Brazil cannot be over estimated. In the future they will be high spots in the history of the economic advancement and prosperity of Brazil."[65]

The members of the ACB who had attended several of the São Paulo shows moved to hold the first national auto exposition in Rio. Everything about the show in the national capital would be bigger and bolder than the São Paulo events. General Electric provided special lighting to make the exhibits and nearby Avenida Rio Branco "like Broadway in New York

City." The First Exposition of Automobility was held 1–16 August 1925 at the Pavilhão Portuguesa. It was planned by the ACB in close consultation with the U.S. embassy and particularly the Ford Motor Company. The Rio auto show opened with an elaborate ball attended by many of the city's wealthiest citizens and continued with a series of formal lunches sponsored by car companies such as Ford and General Motors, but it quickly turned to more popular events.[66] In addition to elaborate displays of cars, auto parts, oil and gasoline, and even the latest in automobile insurance policies, the real draw of the show was the outdoor area filled with demonstrations. A special two-kilometer racetrack and temporary facilities were erected. There were daily races of cars, trucks, tractors, motorcycles, and even bicycles, as well as time trials. Truck and tractor hauling displays were, likewise, crowd favorites. One tractor pulled a flatbed truck with a 5,000-kilo horse and buggy on it. Another pulled a flatbed with two steers and a cart. A sign on the tractors read "Solve Your Farming and Transportation Problems with a Fordson Tractor."[67]

No exhibit, however, held the public's fascination as much as the special Ford pavilion, in which a group of Brazilian workers made Model Ts on an assembly line that had been shipped from the company's São Paulo facility and reassembled in Rio for the show.[68] It was one thing to imagine a new, imported technology such as the automobile being used to unify a massive country like Brazil; it was quite another for Brazilians to imagine themselves as capable of building such machines. Even though they were assembling Model Ts that had been shipped from the United States as "CKDs" or completely knocked down units, these Brazilian workers were building one of the most advanced machines available in the 1920s.[69] Even more than the steadily growing number of factories in São Paulo, Rio, and other cities producing consumer goods, the spectacle of Brazilian workers assembling automobiles revealed a nascent industrialism in this predominantly agrarian nation. Soon after the Rio show, Antônio Prado Jr. traveled to the United States to tour its automobile plants and drive on its new roads. The workings of the Packard plant convinced this scion of a great coffee family of the desirability of a domestic auto industry.[70] Increasingly, Brazilian writers began editorializing on the establishment of a Brazilian automobile industry as both a tool and a symbol of national development.[71]

Throughout the 1920s, the ACB and the São Paulo club continued to hold auto shows that focused less on new models of cars and more on demonstrating automobility (Figure 2.6). Races and raids were increasingly common components of the shows. Moreover, other cities, often with the help of both the ACB and the Ford Motor Company, held their

FIGURE 2.6 Parading in cars on a Sunday on the Avenida Paulista. Photo courtesy of the U.S. National Archives.

own automobile expositions, such as that of the Associação de Estradas de Rodagem em Pernambuco held in Recife on 19–26 January 1926. When leaders of the Associação de Estradas de Rodagem em Rio Grande do Sul announced their first auto show, they proudly proclaimed that Rio and São Paulo were not the only centers of automobility in Brazil. The gaúcho show opened with a parade of 97 cars on the Estrada de Canoas in Porto Alegre and included a race won by Brazil's best known driver of the 1920s, Irineu Corrêa. More than 10,000 people attended the show, and Porto Alegre continued to host shows that were particularly well known for their advocacy of truck and bus travel for the development of southern Brazil (Figure 2.7).[72]

No single Brazilian did more to promote road building than politician Washington Luís. As a young man, he had been an avid "sportsman" who frequently participated in raids and was often frustrated by the absence of good roads in São Paulo. As the governor of the state (1920–1924), he created a comprehensive road network that unified São Paulo and tied it to Rio and Minas Gerais. He even drove to the national capital on the new São Paulo to Rio highway to take the oath of office as president of the republic in 1926. In a message to Congress in his first year in office, Washington Luís spoke out on Brazil's need to embrace automobility because cars were more flexible than trains and less expensive than air travel. He added, with an allusion to the role of immigration in the making of a nation, "To govern is to populate, but one cannot populate [a nation] without opening

FIGURE 2.7 Bus travel grew in importance in the 1920s and 1930s, including in the Amazonian state of Pará. Photo courtesy of the U.S. National Archives.

roads. ... To govern, then, is to make roads." Elsewhere, Washington Luís noted that "good roads [presented] a prerequisite for lowering the cost of living through transportation cost reduction and the shortening of distances between manufacturers and consumer markets." He even requested that all Ford Motor Company advertisements include the slogan "good roads shorten distances, unite people, and bring progress."[73]

Washington Luís was certainly not alone in stressing the economic, social, and political reasons that Brazil needed an extensive highway system. Oswaldo Aranha, the close political ally of Getúlio Vargas and future foreign minister in the 1930s and 1940s, formulated an early plan for Rio Grande do Sul's highway system. He emphasized the economic viability of roads over rails by stressing the flexibility of auto transport over trains. Aranha also noted the complex strategic needs of Brazil's southernmost state and argued that a road network was militarily a sounder choice than the railroad because it would allow the army to send troops to various parts of the border. In the mid-1920s, Aranha also prepared a report calling for the federal government to sponsor a comprehensive highway system that would not only connect Brazil's major cities but also tie the vast interior of the nation to its coast in order to deepen economic development.[74]

Politicians, intellectuals, and businessmen looked to the example of how Washington Luís had built the Paulista road network and saw in it an important reason for that state's prosperity. A nationwide highway system would "unleash the [country's] wealth." Good roads "were the most productive way to profit from Brazil's natural wealth."[75] The Amazon and the northeast, two regions that represented hope and despair for Brazil, would be particularly well served by automobility. Roads would bring to fruition "the golden dream of Amazonians moving toward great progress" by finally being able to exploit its abundant natural resources. The Ford Motor Company ran advertisements and sponsored stories about Cândido Mariano da Silva Rondon and his work building telegraph lines and protecting recently contacted indigenous people deep in the Amazon region. Rondon went on record calling for the development of a highway network that would reach from the Amazon region through the Planalto and to the coast, particularly roads that would connect Ford's rubber plantations in Pará to Mato Grosso.[76]

Another line of reasoning called for establishing roads in order to settle important social issues. The divisions between coastal Brazil and the vast interior spaces—particularly, but not exclusively, the northeastern *sertão*—seemed insurmountable in the first decades of the twentieth century. From the coastal point of view, one Brazil was urban and forward-looking and the other insular and superstitious. People in the interior, on the other hand, saw themselves as authentic Brazilians and considered those on the coast to be outsiders who had usurped the monarchy and other worthy traditions.[77] A 1926 government report argued that interior folk "ignore civilized life of today" because of their isolation. The *sertanejos* lacked "a spiritual connection to the rest of the country." Roads would allow these people to participate not only in the broader markets for goods but also in the life of the nation. Contact with urban Brazil and with capitalism would civilize the backwoods Brazilian. Governor Fernando de Mello Vianna of Minas Gerais expressed similar sentiments in a speech to the ACB, arguing: "Our *sertanejos* are lazy because they have been abandoned; our enthusiasm [for modern machines and ideas] has not reached them." He concluded by calling for an accelerated program of road building into the interior.[78] Other analyses of the social impact of highways on the interior emphasized how children would have access to teachers, and the sick to medical care.[79]

Road backers considered themselves modern *bandeirantes*. Some even formed the Club dos Bandeirantes do Brasil to lobby for increased highway construction and to work as private citizens to maintain existing roads. These new *bandeirantes* would rediscover and transform the *sertão* through automobility. The ACB heartily embraced this view of car culture, once referring to the automobile as "the indefatigable, tame and sublime mechanical *bandeirante*."[80]

Throughout the republic (1889–1930), the national government had largely stayed out of the states' economic affairs. Automobility began to challenge this extreme federalism because an increasing number of Brazilians wanted to travel across state lines in their vehicles. Auto enthusiasts increasingly looked to the national government for help in road construction. The federal government did, in fact, finance targeted road building in the northeast through the work of its antidrought public works program (the Inspetoria Federal das Obras Contra as Sêcas or IFOCS) and did the bulk of its work during the presidential administration of northeasterner Epitácio Pessoa (1919–1922). Indeed, one of his first acts as president was to use the federal government to create a regional highway network to spur export agricultural and economic development in the impoverished northeast.[81] But a coordinated national road system required centralized planning and, given the disparate economic positions of the states, federal financing. The Third National Roads Congress held in Rio in October 1924 reaffirmed the broad principles of federalism by asserting that individual cities and towns would work within their states to plan highway networks that would then be connected to those of neighboring states. The roads congress noted, however, that some sort of centralized coordination along the lines of the road building done by the IFOCS in the northeast would be needed. Moreover, road building increasingly embraced strategic concerns that required the military's participation in planning. Marechal Setembrino de Carvalho created a permanent committee to coordinate the army's plans for a national highway system, and three of its colonels participated in the 1924 roads congress.[82]

Roads evangelists argued that no less than the future of Brazil as a modern, unified nation depended on the creation of a comprehensive highway system. The process of planning and building roads would, they argued, reveal unknown areas and create new economic opportunities. Trucks would move goods to and from new markets, and cars would allow a previously unimagined level of social interchange among Brazilians from every region. Alcides Lins, the director of transport and public work in Minas Gerais and the future mayor of Belo Horizonte, summed up this point of view in a speech titled "Highways and Brazilianness." He argued: "It is only by permanently maintaining intimate social and economic relations that it will be possible to foster that strong and uniform national sentiment, which is the efficient coordination of our labors and the eliminator of provincial barriers."[83] It is hard to overstate the novelty of such sentiments. Since its creation as a Portuguese colony, through the empire and over the course of most of the republic, Brazil's regions had been tied together only through the figure of the emperor or juridically in the constitution. Road building and automobility would, for the first time, literally and concretely unite Brazil.[84]

Writing about the importance of roads to Brazil's economic, social, and political development was easy enough. Bringing pressure to bear on government to build highways and roads was a much more complex task. Paulistas faced the fewest obstacles in launching a comprehensive highway program because Governor Washington Luís was one of Brazil's most powerful and vocal roads evangelists. Indeed, before his 1916 election as mayor of São Paulo, he served as the state's secretary of justice and public security and in that role backed the construction of the state's first highway (with convict labor), which connected the city of São Paulo with its major port, Santos. As governor, he took over the private road and dramatically improved it.[85] Washington Luís worked to improve internal transportation within São Paulo and to create highways linking it to neighboring states. He employed the latest road-building technologies from the United States and steadily increased the state's highway construction budget. At the same time, the state expanded the use of convict labor in road construction, claiming that such work was "regenerative," and even made pardons available to some of the best workers among the prisoners.[86] The results were impressive. By the end of his term as governor, the state's primary commercial centers were tied together by highways with steadily increasing traffic loads.[87] São Paulo's highways met roads from Minas Gerais, Paraná, Mato Grosso, and Goiás.[88] The Paulista road network had an additional impact on the state by increasing agricultural land values. As roads connected more small towns to larger markets, the prices for *sitios*, or small farms, rose twentyfold.[89]

The jewel of the state's road system was the São Paulo to Rio highway. Movement between the national capital and São Paulo had initially been possible only through coastal boat travel. The spread of coffee from the state of Rio to São Paulo brought the first railroad, but as São Paulo developed, most of its agricultural output flowed through the port of Santos, thus redirecting traffic from the Rio–São Paulo axis toward the coast. Under Washington Luís, the São Paulo state government quickly completed its portion of the highway, but Rio's section remained to be built until a coalition of Paulista politicians and Rio auto enthusiasts convinced the federal government to fund the rest of route. Although close to 75% of the road was in the state of São Paulo, federal support of the remaining quarter of the construction represented a significant shift in the national government's view of road building. In the past, the federal government had built roads as a component of its work to mitigate the impact of chronic droughts in the northeast. Even that activity, though, was dependent on political patronage from powerful northeasterners such as Epitácio Pessoa. The São Paulo to Rio highway inaugurated a new era of national support for public works. The Federal Ministry of Agriculture, Commerce, and Industry created a set of uniform specifications for roads in Brazil and provided subsidies for state projects that followed these new construction guidelines. This federal intervention had the effect of strengthening the position of the wealthiest states, because it provided subsidies for partially funded projects rather than seed money to help the poorer states open new roads.

Minas Gerais, one of Brazil's wealthiest states, took advantage of this support to dramatically expand its road network. The state Department of Agriculture worked with local municipalities to coordinate construction and plan the statewide system. On the national level, Mineiro Governor Mello Vianna used the ACB to push for a broader Brazilian automobility that would work with other states in standardizing highway construction. The state's major accomplishments in the 1920s were the construction of a highway connecting Belo Horizonte to Rio de Janeiro and a separate road system that tied the northeast of Minas to Bahia and Goiás. Governors attended the opening of roads that connected these states and celebrated the new transportation links as keys to the nation's "prosperity and national security."[90] In other states, auto enthusiasts used a variety of techniques to encourage politicians to support road-building initiatives. In 1922, Recife's *Jornal do Commércio* sponsored an excursion through Pernambuco, Paraíba, and Ceará. The trip was a major public relations success. The adventures of driving a caravan of six cars through some of the roughest sections of the northeast's legendary *sertão* were recounted through serialization and, later, in a book. There were few passable roads, and quite often the cars had to travel on railroad tracks and cross rivers on railroad bridges, but the reporters were pleasantly surprised to find that most large landowners (*fazendeiros*) owned cars and that even small towns had a handful of cars. Still, the sight of the six-car caravan caused a great deal of excitement throughout the *sertão*. The authors of *Through the Northeast* (*Através do Nordeste*) confidently concluded their report by asserting that the only way to "bring civilization" to the northeast was through the broad embrace of automobility.[91]

Local car enthusiasts discussed the need for their states to keep up with São Paulo and Minas Gerais. If that was impossible, they reasoned, the building of new roads would at least increase ties between their states and the more developed areas in Brazil's center-south.[92] As early as 1915, the state government of Goiás recognized the importance of building highway links with São Paulo and Minas Gerais. In the mid-1920s, Goiás used state money to build such roads. In 1926, it had 3,500 kilometers of roads in use and seven new highways in planning stages. Bahia soon appropriated state funds to build roads to Minas Gerais.[93] Mato Grosso, Paraná, Santa Catarina, and Rio Grande do Sul also built new roads in the 1920s that connected their major cities to each other and to São Paulo. At this time, road builders in southern Brazil also began discussing the construction of a highway that would link their markets to Buenos Aires.[94] Although they had significantly fewer resources and could not directly connect their capitals to São Paulo or Rio, northeastern states continued the road-building programs initially started by IFOCS. Pernambuco, Rio Grande do Norte, and Sergipe developed elaborate plans for statewide highway systems, while Amazonian areas such as Pará planned such roads networks for the future.[95]

No single road project occupied auto enthusiasts more than a semiprivate effort to build a road connecting Rio de Janeiro to Petrópolis, Pedro II's summer home. This road would open car travel to Minas Gerais along the route of the old União e Indústria, which connected Petrópolis with Juiz de Fora. More important, however, was the ACB's plan to design and build the road primarily through private means in order to demonstrate the efficacy of such projects to a wary state. In 1917, the Rio state governor Nilo Peçanha had solicited private funds to help build highways to São Paulo and Minas. He petitioned the Light and Power Company that provided electricity and ran the urban trolleys for land grants. Both Minas and São Paulo had used mixed public-private financing to build roads, and the state of Espirito Santo created a new state tax to fund construction. The ACB pushed this idea in the early 1920s as it witnessed Rio falling far behind its neighbors in road construction. Just a few miles beyond the nation's capital, small towns and villages remained dependent on horses and oxen and thus were cut off from the rest of Brazil. By financing and building their own highway, the ACB argued, it could show how important automobility was to the development of urban *and* rural Brazil.[96] Privately built highways usually fail because of the extraordinary costs of such projects. From William K. Vanderbilt Jr.'s private Long Island parkway in the early 1900s to the Mexico City to Toluca toll road in Mexico in the mid-1990s, private highways have overextended planners and disappointed investors.[97] The ACB, however, had no intention of building or operating a toll road to make a profit. Instead, the club's leaders hoped to encourage government officials to embrace automobility and then use public money to extend the area's road network out from the one they privately built. An auto road into Minas Gerais, combined with the coming São Paulo to Rio highway, would open the interior of the state to development by drawing it closer to the city of Rio, especially with the growth of truck farming for the capital. Work began in 1922 with a small federal contribution of 500 contos. The remaining costs were covered through direct donations from businesses and wealthy individuals. The club worked with representatives of the U.S. government and U.S. businesses to advertise the latest techniques in construction and to stress that such a road would prove that motorcars were no longer luxury items but a common form of transportation. The road was inaugurated with great fanfare on 13 May 1926. Even though it was a source of great pride in Rio, the road was not heavily traveled, and U.S. observers considered it to be mediocre in quality.[98]

The completion of the Rio to Petrópolis road soon after the São Paul–Rio highway signaled the beginning of a new era in the relationship between the states and the federal government. After a flurry of road-building activity by the IFOCS from 1919 to 1923, the administration of Arthur Bernardes moved to balance the federal budget and therefore ended federal support for nearly all public works. Washington Luís, on the other hand, translated his experiences as an activist mayor and governor to the national level when he became president in 1926. He believed strongly in the role of government in infrastructure development, and so on 5 January 1927, he signed the Federal Highway Law. This measure included plans for the creation of a national roads system that would have design uniformity throughout Brazil. Most important, however, was the fact that a portion of the duties levied on imported automobiles would be sent to the states to subsidize road construction.[99]

The 1927 Federal Highway Law brought about tangible changes in the ways politicians on the state level thought about and dealt with the national government. The federal government had funded public works in the past but never on such a potentially large scale. The 1927 law encouraged every state to petition the national government for road-building funds. In return for such support, the states had to make their highways part of a national network through a formal planning process and had to adopt uniform construction standards. Such centralized financing and planning ran counter to the republic's long-standing tradition of laissez-faire economics.[100] These very real changes in public policy dovetailed with the new ways people started to think about Brazil as a nation, given this revolution in transportation. The ongoing use of raids and new car races was a tangible expression of that hope. The most common trip was between São Paulo and Rio. Lesdain's 1908 trip had taken a full 34 days. By 1921, Ogden Wilson had made the trip in a Dodge in only 11 days. With ongoing construction of the São Paulo portion of the road connecting the two cities, this raid took less and less time. In 1925, a Buick made the journey in just 66 hours. By September 1926, the raid took only 18 hours and 32 minutes; a few weeks later. a new record of 14 hours, 6 minutes was set. In July 1928, a Studebaker made the trip in only 6 hours and 49 minutes.[101] The most important raid between Rio and São Paulo since Lesdain's first trip, however, was the "*bandeira* Washington Luís" in honor of the Paulista's inauguration as president of the republic in late 1926. The ACB in Rio worked closely with São Paulo's Roads Association (Associação de Estradas de Rodagem) to make sure the road was completed by the inauguration. More than 3,000 additional workers were employed to finish the highway. More than 400 cars made the trip in October, showing the nation Paulista pride and technological (and consumer) sophistication and displaying the increasing interconnectedness of the states of Brazil.[102]

Raids were not confined to Brazil's developed center-south; auto enthusiasts in the northeast traveled from Pernambuco to Ceará and to Alagoas. From Rio and São Paulo, raids frequently went into Minas Gerais, Mato Grosso, and Goiás. In southern Brazil, sportsmen drove from Curitiba in Paraná to Foz de Iguaçú and from Porto Alegre up to Curitiba.[103] Anticipating similar raids in the early 1960s that fanned out from Brasília to all the states' capitals, one raid from Goiás (close to where Brasília would be built 30 years later) to Paraná was described as a trip from "the future Brazilian capital" to the growing south of the nation.[104] At the same time, some sportsmen planned international raids to Buenos Aires and even to La Paz, Bolivia, and Lima, Peru. The trip to Peru was supposedly discussed with General Rondon, who was by this time a national hero for his work in building the telegraph line deep into the Amazon. The Rio to Buenos Aires raid took place, as did trips up from Argentina to various Brazilian cities. The planned journeys to La Paz and Lima were not attempted at this time, given the absence of roads connecting Brazilian cities and their Andean neighbors.[105]

It was in this milieu of using new technologies to remake Brazil as a modern, integrated nation that leading intellectuals, many of whom had personally embraced automobility, proclaimed a cultural revolution with the opening of the Week of Modern Art in São Paulo's Teatro Municipal on 11 February 1922. The great writer and diplomat Graça Aranha opened the festivities by speaking of a cultural rebellion that rejected the simple aping of European cultures. The poet Menotti del Picchia called for the "Brazilianization of Brazil." Writers such as Oswaldo de Andrade and Mário de Andrade and the composer Heitor Villa Lobos worked in new forms with themes of national integration. Their authentic Brazil, however, would not necessarily be completely new. The mere presence of Graça Aranha made clear that this was more cultural evolution than revolution.[106] Still, the themes of the modernist movement closely fit the emerging protodevelopmentalist ideas held by auto enthusiasts.[107] Indeed, the automobile was both a symbol and a tool for the Brazilian modernists.

One trope of the Brazilian modernist movement fit perfectly with the goals of the auto enthusiasts: cultural cannibalism. Writer Oswaldo de Andrade posed the question "Tupí or not Tupí" in his 1928 "Cannibal's Manifesto" (Manifesto Antropófago). He asked this question in what one scholar has referred to as "tropicalized English" to emphasize the melding of the local (Tupí Indians) and the foreign (Shakespeare).[108] His modernist colleague Mário de Andrade (not a relation) took up similar themes in his pathbreaking novel, *Macunaíma*. The Andrades and other modernists invoked cannibalism as an anthropomorphized process of creating a national (or broadly indigenous) culture. Every cultural influence (including imported foreign ideas) would be consumed and regurgitated as a new Brazilian identity. The modernists ultimately proposed a hybrid culture that eschewed nostalgic visions of a supposedly authentic Brazil and critiqued a seemingly unthinking adherence to foreign, particularly French, cultural forms.[109]

As part of their project of cultural cannibalism, a group of intellectuals traveled in a self-described "modernist caravan" from São Paulo into Minas Gerais in 1924 to discover Brazil's past. Given the poor quality of available roads, they went by train and explored only more settled areas in rural São Paulo and Minas. Still, they turned inward toward Brazil's great interior and its colonial past to understand the nation better. In this way, modernist intellectuals and auto enthusiasts—who were not mutually exclusive groups—shared a belief that Brazil's true national identity would be uncovered through the physical interaction of people made possible by modern forms of transportation, particularly automobiles. The *sertão* was to be civilized through contact with the urban populations of the coast, and such contact would humanize the harsh city dwellers and thus create a new, more authentically Brazilian citizen.[110] Modernist intellectuals made explicit how technology was changing Brazil. Although they were much more hopeful about how modernity would transform the country's interior folk than Euclides da Cunha or Lima Barreto, these intellectuals all understood that new forms of communication and transportation were already changing Brazil.[111]

In the 1920s, a consensus of sorts had developed in Brazil's largest cities. Businessmen, intellectuals, and government officials embraced automobility as the tool that would finally unite Brazil and make it a modern nation. Proof of this was the widespread road building throughout the country at this time. The total distance of roads in the wealthier states of the center-south far exceeded that for the rest of the country, but other areas were busy expanding their automobility as well. The divergence in the funding of highway construction between Brazil's two richest cities helps explain both the function of the country's extremely federated system and the challenges that system posed to expanded automobility. São Paulo, the capital of Brazilian entrepreneurial behavior, turned to state funding to break bottlenecks in transportation with an extensive road-building program. Rio de Janeiro, the national capital, first sought to demonstrate the efficacy of highway construction by turning to private money. Before the 1927 highway act, each state thought about the nation in its own terms, and even if its leaders wanted to build highways to connect their major cities to those in neighboring states, they more often than not faced severe fiscal limitations on such projects. Washington Luís set the foundation for thinking in national terms about roads, but given the structure of the federal funding, only the richest states could take advantage of the subsidies. Given the limits of federal support, the unity brought through automobility in the 1920s and into the 1930s could not come from state governments or local entrepreneurs. The intervention of powerful foreign interests would force an initial form of national unification.

CHAPTER 3 | # Americanism and Fordism: The Search for a Brazilian El Dorado

IN 1926, THE NEWSPAPER *A Tribuna* of Uberabinha, Minas Gerais, announced that it was working with local businesses—including Ford Motor Company dealers—to raise funds to erect a statue of Henry Ford. The monument would honor Ford for his role in producing the automobiles used to open the states of Goiás and Mato Grosso. Almost forty years later, the hundredth anniversary of Ford's birth was commemorated by the installation of a bust of Henry Ford in the city of São Paulo.[1] The Ford Motor Company, along with General Motors and to a lesser extent Dodge, Studebaker, and other American automobile manufacturers, not only played a fundamental role in opening Brazil's vast interior spaces for immigrants, businessmen, and the state but also profoundly affected Brazilian society and culture. Transforming consumer culture and recreation, American cars, trucks, and buses became synonymous with Brazilian modernity.

Brazilians adopted aspects of Fordism—particularly the relationship between advanced forms of industrial production and broad-based consumerism—and Americanism without mimicking the United States. Embracing these ideas was part and parcel of the modernist project of nation building. Brazilians took the components of Fordism and American culture that they believed best served their needs and then made them Brazilian.[2] They believed, for example, that broad-based consumerism and the use of advanced technology were key tools for understanding and gaining control over the national territory. These Brazilians did much more than simply imagine a highly developed, industrial nation; they gave

Henry Ford a massive land concession in the Amazon to begin the process of transformation. The area known as Fordlândia was the first sustained attempt to implant modernity in the national interior. In many ways, it was a precursor to the establishment in 1960 of the new national capital, Brasília.

Although Ford's Model T was at first the most common car in Brazil, General Motors' Chevrolets became extremely popular by the mid-1920s. Like the ubiquitous Model T, the Chevy was inexpensive and hardy, which led to its widespread use in both cities and the countryside, and General Motors came to rival Ford as an agent of change. Both brought the ideas and practice of mass production and therefore mass consumption to Brazil. They operated large-scale factories (Figure 3.1) and far-flung networks of dealers. They transformed the nascent advertising industry and made consumer credit widely available. And they also stood as potent symbols of the power of modern corporations to transform society.

Fordism offered the possibility of transforming Brazil not only economically and spatially but also culturally. Too often Fordism is thought of as being nearly synonymous with scientific management or Taylorism

FIGURE 3.1 The General Motors plant in which Completely Knocked Down Units were reassembled into cars. Photo courtesy of the U.S. National Archives.

because Henry Ford is so closely associated with the assembly line.[3] Fordism is more a set of ideas about the relationship between production and consumption than a system of work itself. Henry Ford well understood that there was little point in producing a steadily increasing number of automobiles if the market for those cars was not also expanding. As early as 1909, Ford decided to pay his workers wages above those dictated by the market in exchange for their conscientious work on the shop floor and their commitment to a temperate lifestyle at home, which involved learning to balance home life and work, as well as having private lives monitored for sobriety and marital fidelity by the Ford Sociological Department. Ford hoped the high wages would decrease labor turnover on the monotonous assembly lines and also allow workers to become consumers of the products they made. Over the course of the 1920s and 1930s, workers' unions, politicians, and some industrialists expanded the basic tenets of Fordism into public policy in the United States and parts of western Europe. As a result, the broad ideas of Fordism moved from an employment strategy in the auto industry to a way that advanced capitalist countries organized themselves.[4]

Neither Alfred E. Sloan nor the ideas referred to as Sloanism are as well known as Ford and his legacy, but they profoundly affected twentieth-century capitalism and Brazil in particular. Leader of General Motors from 1923 to 1946, Sloan fundamentally altered the relationship among manufacturing, marketing, and consumerism. Sloanism involves the production of consumer goods that emphasize style over functionality. The marketing of those goods—in the case of Sloan and GM, cars and later domestic appliances such as refrigerators and stoves—downplayed their utilitarian nature and instead accentuated their relationship to the consumer's place in society and stage of life. Sloan developed this strategy at first out of necessity, given the disorganized and disparate nature of General Motors' many brands. He decided to put consumers on an ever-escalating trajectory from the basic Chevrolet through Pontiacs, Oldsmobiles, and Buicks to the ultimate luxury of a Cadillac. Although the Model T symbolized the democratization of consumerism, Sloan and GM's wide variety of highly stylized products represented a key component of modern consumption: the desire to trade up to a more prestigious and expensive model. Fordism and Sloanism, therefore, brought U.S.-style industrialism with methods of production and consumption that promised Brazilians progress and development. Because they were American in origin and broad based in practice, Fordism and Sloanism also seemed to promise political democracy through the creation of a stable working class based in auto factories and an ever-expanding middle class that defined itself largely through what it bought.[5]

The growing presence of the two giant U.S. automakers spread these ideas about consumerism and production. Fords arrived in Brazil during the first decade of the twentieth century and became among the most popular cars of the 1910s as the Model T gained renown for its durability, particularly on the horrible roads outside the downtowns of major cities. An advertising campaign highlighting how the head of Brazil's Indian Protective Service, Cândido Mariano da Silva Rondon, relied on the Model T to navigate Brazil's distant interior deepened popular perceptions about the value and reliability of Fords.[6] Back in Michigan, Ford Motor Company officials noted as early as 1913 that the Model T was making steady inroads among coffee planters because of its reputation for dependability.[7] During the 1920s, Ford and GM vehicles increasingly filled Brazilian streets. Locals began to equate these less expensive autos—particularly Model Ts and Chevrolets—not only with American capitalism but also with democracy itself, because they conflated broad participation in the consumer economy with popular involvement in politics.[8]

The presence of automobiles on Brazil's city streets and rural roads had been a tangible sign of a coming modernity since the first decade of the twentieth century. By the 1920s, the steadily increasing number of cars, trucks, and buses became visible contributions to the sense of change taking place in the country. Industrialists, modernist intellectuals, and others extolled the presence of the Ford and General Motors assembly plants in São Paulo and elsewhere. They saw such factories as mechanisms for transforming Brazil into a modern industrialized nation. They would become training grounds for skilled and disciplined workers and would also affect Brazilian manufacturing by introducing the latest production techniques and by promoting high-quality output.[9]

These were hopeful views. The Ford and GM plants, although impressive, were not complete manufacturing facilities. They were quite literally assembly lines where Brazilian workers rebuilt vehicles produced in the United States and Europe that had arrived in pieces as CKDs.[10] The fact that these cars were not truly manufactured in Brazil was of little significance to most observers. The assembly lines were considered by Brazilians to be equal to the most advanced industrial establishments in the world. The magazine *Auto-Propulsão* called the first factory on Rua Solon in São Paulo a "duplicate" of Ford's facilities in the United States and crowed that "the installation of the Ford assembly line is the same as the creation of a new national industry." The General Motors plant in São Caetano do Sul (a suburb of São Paulo) was lauded as the most modern factory in Brazil, with its assembly line and automatic fire suppression system. The Automóvel Club noted that the auto plants were transforming São Paulo from primarily a coffee-producing state to a major industrial center.[11] Record crowds at the Ford assembly line pavilion at the 1925 Rio auto show revealed the broad appeal of the auto plants beyond modernist intellectuals, industrialists, and state policy makers.

Corporate headquarters in Dearborn insisted that its Brazilian plants be as efficient and clean as any other Ford facility. By the mid-1920s, these included smaller versions of the São Paulo facility in Porto Alegre (1925) in the South, Rio de Janeiro (1927), and even Recife (1926) in the northeast.[12] By 1924, they were assembling roughly 14,000 autos per year. Both Ford and GM expanded their São Paulo facilities in the late 1920s, not only in response to increased demand for cars but also for assembly of truck and bus chassis to be fitted to locally manufactured bodies.[13] This development foreshadowed one of the most important tangible effects fostered by the U.S. auto plants. Beginning in the 1920s and continuing until the full installation of automobile manufacturing in the mid to late 1950s, a steadily increasing number of Brazilian businesses opened to provide parts and services for cars, trucks, and buses.

This new industrial activity became a key component of Brazil's metalworking sector, which expanded dramatically in the 1920s and 1930s. The cutoff of trade with Europe and the United States during World War I had fostered the growth of domestic machine shops, primarily in São Paulo. The profitable coffee economy of the 1920s, as well as dramatic growth in output of textiles and other light consumer goods, increased demand for the tools and light machinery. Many of these small metalworking concerns were flexible enough to move into auto parts or even bus and truck bodies without large infusions of capital and manpower.[14] Moreover, both Ford and GM encouraged local industry to produce auto parts to supplement CKDs from abroad, as well as supply the secondary market of garages and repair shops.[15]

The larger, but less significant, component of this industry focused on building truck and bus bodies to be placed on Ford and GM chassis. This industry thrived because of its low technological requirements (the work was primarily carpentry and simple metalworking) and the high ocean freight expense of sending bus and truck bodies from the United States to Brazil. This reduced the American producers' costs, while giving Brazilian consumers the ability to custom-design buses and trucks. Few cities outside Rio and São Paulo, for example, purchased covered buses; most instead relied on the less expensive open models. Manufacturers like São Paulo's Grassi, which had been in the coach business since 1904, became bus and truck dealers by purchasing chassis from the foreign auto companies and selling the finished products. The existence of this manufacturing and sales network facilitated the entry of International Truck and Chrysler into the Brazilian bus and truck market.[16]

The growth of auto parts manufacturing in the 1920s and 1930s also shaped Brazil's long-term industrial development. The U.S. Department of Commerce's Howard Tewksbury studied the car and auto parts markets in Brazil in the mid to late 1920s and uncovered a burgeoning parts sector that produced high-quality goods. Although U.S.-manufactured replacement parts dominated the market at this time, the quality of bumpers, windshields, springs, radiator caps, and axles impressed Tewksbury. (He was less taken with the quality of locally made pistons and electrical equipment.) Nevertheless, Tewksbury noted the breadth of auto parts manufacturing, as well as the potential for future growth.[17] Some production was done by small shops employing fewer than 20 skilled metalworkers. Other parts were made in large-scale factories. In 1927, for example, São Paulo's Souza Noschese Company built the first all-Brazilian internal combustion engine, using steel from Minas Gerais. In 1928, A. Preses Company built a truck with nearly all Brazilian content (the carburetor and some electrical equipment were imported) capable of hauling seven tons with its four-cylinder, 45-horsepower engine. In Rio, the Fábrica de Engrenagem e Acessórios, owned by Sandi e Sauer, had one of the most advanced metalworking shops in Brazil, boasting that they could fabricate any auto part for any model car.[18] Although in its early stages, this nascent auto parts sector deepened industrial development, stoked national pride, and foreshadowed the economic growth strategies of the 1940s and 1950s. Perhaps most significant of all, the growth of this sector of the economy increased demand for skilled labor.

The image of skilled metalworkers producing auto parts, engines, and even the occasional vehicle was a lot more appealing to Brazilian elites and the growing middle class than the years of worker activism and repression that had followed the 1917 general strike. Widely recognized as the first major industrial worker uprising in Brazilian history, the strike was begun by and filled with young women workers from São Paulo's growing textile sector.[19] Industrialists and government officials responded to worker activism in the 1920s and 1930s with a mixture of repression and attempts to recast workers through changes in production techniques (Taylorism) and education.[20] In other words, they embraced key components of Fordism.[21]

Even though Fordist production often lowered the skill requirements for workers, there was a clear preference for men in automobile plants. The high wages men received in exchange for the monotonous labor on the assembly line was intended to allow them to support their wives and children. Such family arrangements depended on the simple sexual division of labor between men as wage earners and women as nurturers who maintained the home and entered the market only as consumers. Wages that were high relative to those in other industrial settings were a linchpin in the Fordist system not only because they tied workers to the assembly line but also because they allowed families to purchase an ever-widening array of consumer goods. The ultimate Fordist purchase was, of course, the family car.[22]

To pay high wages, industries must be extremely profitable, as Ford was during the 1910s and 1920s. Industrialists in Europe, Japan, and Latin America envied Ford and wanted to adopt many of his company's policies, but they often faced financial limitations.[23] Fordism in Brazil avoided this problem by relying on the great resources of Ford and General Motors. The two American auto companies paid among the highest industrial wages in the country and provided a broad variety of worker training programs. General Motors concentrated on worker education before expanding its production facilities.[24] Ford's industrial training program produced mechanics and metalworkers for companies throughout greater São Paulo. Indeed, Júlio Prestes, São Paulo state governor, commented on visiting Ford's industrial training facilities in 1929 that they were a key component of the ongoing "progress" of the state.[25]

The Ford and GM factories were eagerly welcomed by a broad cross section of Brazilians in contrast to the reactions to large and powerful American corporations in other Latin American nations. Quite often the modernity that these companies brought to Latin American economies so disrupted traditional forms of production and ownership that they ended up fueling anti-Americanism.[26] In Brazil, the U.S. auto companies were seen as necessary instruments of progress. Their factories would transform unruly migrants from the countryside and foreign immigrants into a skilled and disciplined working class that would participate in society through advanced consumerism, as well as through work, and in this way would transform Brazil.[27]

The most significant proponent of such a viewpoint was, of course, Henry Ford himself. Through his voluminous writings, which sometimes singled out Brazil as a country ready for the changes automobility promised, Ford made the case for a car-based modernity. Ford's ideas were well known in Brazil; his business dealings were closely covered in the Brazilian press, his books were quickly translated into Portuguese, and his opinions on a wide range of topics, including his opposition to key components of Franklin Roosevelt's New Deal, were reported.[28] His most significant work, *Today and Tomorrow* (or *Hoje e Amanhã*), argued for an auto-based transformation of Brazil. In its chapter "The Wealth of Nations," Ford described his company's experiences in Brazil as mirroring those of its branches in the United States and Europe, except that Brazilian workers were initially even less prepared for the factory work they soon came to master. The impact on the workers' lives was swift: "Our branch is hardly more than a year old, but already the high wages...are beginning to have an effect. The workers have not yet made much change in their housing conditions but they are buying more clothing, they are buying a few furnishings, and they are saving money.... Soon they will begin to develop more needs, and the process of material civilization will start. The automobile will make a great nation out of Brazil. The natives, though totally unused to machinery of any kind or to discipline of any kind, fell very quickly into the work of assembly and repair."[29]

Brazilians paid a great deal of attention to Ford and his ideas. Newspapers reported on innovations in Ford's factories in the United States, particularly the five-day work week and the eight-hour day. Ford Motor Company executives even attempted in vain to plan a visit to Brazil for Henry Ford.[30] Brazilians came to see Henry Ford as a man of action who used industrial innovation to foster modernity. Even the failed attempt to industrialize the production of rubber in the Amazon was read as more of a daring experiment than an abject failure.[31] Ford's marketing department spread such ideas with the help of several prominent Brazilian intellectuals.

No Brazilian surpassed the writer Monteiro Lobato in support of all things Ford. He translated three of Ford's books and wrote glowing prefaces for the Brazilian editions. In 1926, Lobato wrote a series of articles in the newspaper *O Jornal* about Ford, which were later collected and published in English as *How Henry Ford Is Regarded in Brazil*.[32] According to this booklet, Ford was the single most important agent of positive change on earth. His work was summed up as "THE SUPRESSION OF HUMAN MISERY" (emphasis in the original). He argued that Ford had ended the conflict between labor and capital by fostering a culture of abundance. Lobato noted that Brazil would move forward as a nation only once it fully embraced Ford and Fordism: "Pity it is that we in Brazil live stuck in the mire of last century ideas, rancid and moldy ideas translated from the French. In spite of the amazing advance of the United States, an advance that has placed them in the forefront of the modern world as the fashioners of Humanity's tomorrow, we here continue marking time."[33] Lobato continued in this vein with a short novel published in Portuguese with the mixed-language title, *Mr. Slang e o Brasil*. The book revolves around an extended fictional conversation over a game of chess between a "common man" and an Englishman, John Irving Slang, who lived in Rio. Originally serialized in *O Jornal*, it is an extended analysis of Brazil's potential. The country did not lack hardworking citizens or reasonable goals; it simply did not have the right plan to achieve progress and modernity. Mr. Slang assures his companion that Fordism is the answer to Brazil's problems. In this system, "there are not work categories in industry. There is no job that is more noble than another. Only work.... And because he pays such great wages for eight hours of work...no one refuses or tries to avoid giving eight full hours of hard work—not like in Brazil, eight hours of standing still."[34] Later in the dialogue, Mr. Slang approvingly quotes Ford directly from *Today and Tomorrow* on Brazil's great size and the role automobility will play in its transformation.[35]

Other proponents of Fordism focused on the relationship between consumerism and democracy. Analyses of the United States in the Brazilian press increasingly made this connection, especially with regard to automobiles. One article summed up this thinking with the headline, "The Great Role Automobiles Play in American Democracy." "The automobile eliminated social, commercial, and industrial barriers," it contended.[36] The affordability and dependability of the Model T furthered the association between Fords and democracy. Interestingly, such ideas were hardly isolated to Brazil. The Cuban novelist Félix Soloni refers to the "democratic Ford" in *Merse* (1926). Another Cuban, Rodríguez Acosta, considered the arrival of the Ford (known as "fotingos" on the island) a "true revolution: not only in the trade and industry but in the spirit and relations of people."[37] In the United States, Latin America, and elsewhere, automobile ownership became nearly synonymous with American-style consumer-based democracy, in part because of the efforts of the huge marketing departments at Ford, General Motors, and other American automakers in selling the dream of democratic car ownership.[38] To increase sales, Ford, GM, and other American auto companies worked with Brazilian auto proponents and used new forms of advertising, often associating their companies with the ideals of automobility itself. This early form of branding both strengthened the American presence in the Brazilian economy and sold a particular vision of Brazil that was modern, unified, and forward reaching.[39] In many ways, the American car manufacturers became among the most powerful and persuasive proponents of Brazil's "order and progress."

In the first two decades of the twentieth century, automobile advertisements in Brazil were simple translations of ads from Europe and the United States.[40] This changed during the 1920s, when Ford and GM more or less created the Brazilian advertising business, first through their own in-house departments and later through close collaboration with American firms that opened local branches specifically to service the auto giants.[41] Although some foreign auto companies continued to do little more than use English-language catalogs in the 1920s, an increasing amount of advertising concentrated on educating Brazilian consumers about the abilities of various models while paying close attention to local tastes.[42] By the late 1920s and early 1930s, modernity, national unity, and progress became frequent themes in ads for U.S.-made automobiles, trucks, and buses.

Ford's advertising often highlighted the presence of its São Paulo factory to emphasize its role in bringing modernity to Brazil. Ford proclaimed its role as "an agent of civilization" and openly referred to creating "the world of cars." The Model T worked to transform Brazil, as it had other parts of the world with a "road mentality." Studebaker ads spoke of the need for a car in order to enjoy "modern living" (Figure 3.2).[43] General Motors used its São Paulo factory to closely associate its products with modern industrialism. It sold both luxury and less expensive cars in Brazil and openly advertised

FIGURE 3.2 Studebaker marketing in the countryside: "An Automobile Is Better and Costs Less" than relying on animal transportation. Photo courtesy of the U.S. National Archives.

the idea of giving the owner the opportunity to emulate American tastes and life. The Brazilian Cadillac buyer would share a cosmopolitan consumerism with wealthy Americans, while local Chevy owners would emulate the middle class in the United States.[44] The worldliness of car ownership was emphasized by tying auto culture to American culture broadly and to Hollywood especially, with movie stars often appearing in ads.[45]

Foreign businesses picked up the Brazilian themes of mobility and national unification and promoted their products as patriotic. Ford's advertising department popularized the expression "The Ford goes where nobody is capable of going," and the company sponsored a vast national advertising campaign claiming that General Cândido Mariano da Silva Rondon used a Ford to travel through the interior in his work establishing telegraph lines throughout the nation. One advertisement from 1926 even includes the text of a telegram he allegedly sent from Cuiabá in Mato Grosso to Ford headquarters in São Paulo. He claims to have traveled 1,140 kilometers in only 43 hours in a Ford over rough trails and terrain. Rondon concludes, "I consider Ford one of the benefactors of industrial civilization, a venerable partner in the penetration of Brazil's backlands."[46] In addition to Rondon, Ford also noted that the Brazilian Army relied on its trucks and cars because of their durability. Businesses that transported goods back and forth to the countryside were also said to be among Ford's best customers.[47]

Advertisements for Ford trucks pictured them in the hinterland outside Belém on the Amazon and penetrating the interior of Pernambuco. In addition, Ford tried to sell its tractors as "the most perfect transportation for modern times, in the city and in the countryside, for agriculture and industry." Ford marketed tractors as the ideal expression of industrial modernity because they could be used in urban construction, road building, hauling, and of course, agriculture. Because of their extraordinary versatility, Ford argued that its tractors were capable of obliterating the urban-rural or coastal-interior divide for industrialists and farmers.[48]

General Motors and Studebaker also advertised their cars as tools for unifying the great nation. Many GM ads emphasized nationalist themes and associated its vehicles with Brazil's industrial and agriculture progress. Advertisements in the *Estado de São Paulo* newspaper, for example, depicted the trucks bringing produce from the interior to the city with the tag line "For the provisioning of São Paulo."[49] Studebaker ads frequently mixed urban and rural scenes to highlight the role its cars played in tying together Brazil. Often its advertisements included rural folk, sometimes even Indians, to make the cars seem at home throughout the country (Figure 3.3). As a result, Studebaker's advertising posters were particularly

FIGURE 3.3 Studebaker also brought this popular stunt to its urban marketing. Photo courtesy of the U.S. National Archives.

popular in small towns. Studebaker became even more popular in the Paulista countryside in late 1927, when a group of people decided to play the local lottery with the license plate number from an Erskine automobile depicted on a poster. The winning number brought them (Cr 800$000 or almost $100) and gave Studebaker's advertising a near mythical power in and around that small town.[50]

To further appeal to Brazilian patriotism, Ford used celebrity endorsers, including the country's first national soccer stars (members of 1913 team that had played and won Brazil's first international match, a 2–0 win over Argentina) and the nephew of the former emperor, Dom Pedro II.[51] Foreign oil companies used similar techniques. Esso associated itself with wealthy and powerful Brazilians who gave testimonials about its products. Texaco went even further by sponsoring a series of history-oriented advertisements that highlighted the role of Cabral in discovering Brazil in 1500, the *bandeirantes* in exploring the interior in the seventeenth century, and the modern automobile driver for unifying the nation through road building and driving in the twentieth century.[52] European car companies, on a smaller scale, tried to use similar themes in advertising. Fiat went so far as to publish ads in Italian-language newspapers in Brazil, claiming it was patriotic for an Italian Brazilian to own one of its cars.[53]

Central to these marketing campaigns was the idea that automobility was the key tool in Brazil's quest for progress, though this was broad and somewhat vague. Individual consumers did not often think about the work of manufacturing an automobile and its impact on the national social structure, nor did they imagine a day-to-day role for themselves in opening Brazil's vast interior spaces. To sell cars to individual consumers, the auto companies marketed their products as having much more tangible benefits for individual Brazilians. The U.S. manufacturers sought to dominate the "family car" market and so geared their advertising to idealize American-style suburban living, with a car parked in the driveway of a single-family home.[54]

A key component of American middle-class identity was a new, public status for women. American movies provided glimpses of both flapper culture and new professional roles for women in society. Advertising from U.S. auto companies played into the development of changing ideas about gender in 1920s and 1930s Brazil.[55] Ford claimed women preferred "the comfort and convenience" of its vehicles, since they were designed for "modern women, who are practical and smart." Hudson simply used pictures of women driving cars in familiar locations such as along Rio's beaches. An advertisement for LaSalle autos included a picture of a woman driver and the tag line "Other times, other ways."[56] These ads struck a nerve because women were increasingly seen on the streets of Brazil's major cities driving their own cars. The Automóvel Club in Rio even sponsored a series of races for women. The club openly promoted women driving roadsters and coupes and often included pictures of women behind the wheel on the cover of its monthly magazine.[57]

Reactions to women's driving ranged from nearly messianic support to dread. A 1928 article in the car magazine *Automobilismo* titled "Women and Automobiles" argued that female drivers were part of a broader societal revolution sweeping Brazil. It noted that just as women surely deserved the right to vote, which they would gain in 1934, they should have full rights to drive. Cars had become "a symbol of real civilization" and were indicative of a new modern mentality. Other commentators increasingly associated fashion and cars and frequently pointed to American movie actresses who drove their own autos. Indeed, one car dealer specifically sought out what he referred to as "jazz-girls" as future customers.[58] Other articles in *Automobilismo* severely criticized women as "timid" and "lazy" behind the wheel. Young female drivers were seen as particularly ill prepared to handle a car. One article said that women were fine drivers but that the stress of traffic was ultimately too much for them to bear.[59] No matter what local commentators thought, in the late 1920s and 1930s, Brazilian women who could afford cars bought them. The foreign automobile companies had no interest in abandoning a significant market segment and so encouraged women's driving.

Expanded consumer credit was another innovation from American capitalism that was popularized by the auto companies in Brazil. The weak banking sector, along with the high cost of automobiles, forced the foreign manufacturers to encourage and facilitate financing for new car purchases. Throughout the 1920s, the American producers worked with the U.S. Department of Commerce and local auto clubs to bring down tariffs on imported vehicles and lower the cost of credit for new cars. With more than 80% of new car purchases being financed, the foreign manufacturers had to create a modern system of consumer credit in Brazil. Buyers at first had to have close to 50% of the purchase price in cash and were given about a year to pay off the balance, but competition among car companies led to much more favorable terms. To fight the growing American dominance in the Brazilian market, Fiat offered loans for 75% of the purchase price with 24 to 30 months to pay. Ford was forced to follow with similar promotions. Ford also created special loan arrangements for farmers whose cash flow was more seasonal. Studebaker followed Fiat and Ford, even though it had difficulty matching their terms. All these arrangements were broadly advertised, and Ford created special booklets explaining the new methods of financing purchases. These practices filtered down to the used car market, with local dealers instead of the manufacturers often providing the financing.[60]

Financing not only increased sales but also deepened the myth that car ownership was an integral part of middle-class life in Brazil in the 1920s and 1930s. Although measuring the impact of advertising is an imprecise art, it is clear from the historical record that Brazilians increasingly believed this aspect of auto marketing and thought that car ownership was common among the middle class in cities such as São Paulo and Rio. One internal Ford Motor Company report noted how popular the use of credit was to buy autos in Brazil's vast rural sector: "RC Dun & Co.'s representative advised that they were investigating all applicants for Studebaker of which 50% were not financially responsible which shows no matter how worthless a man is he wants to buy an automobile."[61] The foreign manufacturers did all they could at this time to make their vehicles more affordable, and that, too, played into the idea that car ownership was becoming widespread.[62] By the mid-1920s, quite a few Brazilian commentators simply assumed that the middle class was defined by automobile ownership. Ford and GM promoted such thinking, and Ford began importing its Model Y from England, which was even less expensive than the Model T, to increase sales among middle-class consumers. This led one proponent of automobility to fantasize that Brazilian workers would soon own their cars. One analyst blamed Brazil's weak currency—as opposed to the skewed distribution of income—for the failure of automobility to be even more widespread.[63]

Such sentiments were not limited to auto enthusiasts. In one of the most bizarre examples of believing in widespread automobility in Brazil, the São Paulo city government moved in 1927 to outlaw the parking of Fords and Chevrolets in the city center. The mayor believed that such common and inexpensive vehicles lowered the prestige of the city. Ford and Auto Club leaders, rather than dispute the class nature of Model T and Chevrolet ownership, defeated the measure by arguing that it was antidemocratic.[64] This episode and conflicting reports about auto sales confused matters. In 1926, for example, Ford executives claimed they were not able to build enough cars to meet growing demand. The company opened an assembly line in Recife just to meet expanding demand in the northeast. Any demand Ford failed to meet was happily taken up by Studebaker and GM. In 1929, one analysis claimed that Chevrolets could be found throughout the Brazilian "hinterland."[65] Sober assessments of the Brazilian market, however, continued to show a fairly narrow demand for cars, and comparisons with the United States made this quite clear. According to a 1925 study, Brazil had the highest rate of increase of any country in the world of American auto imports, but it still had only one vehicle for every 650 inhabitants nationwide; the number in the United States was reported to be one for every 6 inhabitants.[66]

The American auto companies not only emphasized modern ideals and patriotism through their ads but also used new methods of communication that symbolically and physically fostered the process of nation building. Radio shows, the use of billboards on new roads and highways, and the publication of Brazil's first nationally circulated magazine, *Cruzeiro*, broadly disseminated information about automobility. During the 1930s, as radio expanded dramatically in Brazil, foreign car, oil, and tire companies used this new form of advertising by sponsoring soap operas and other broadcasts.[67] Billboards reached out into the countryside with new roads, becoming more of a national advertising force.[68] Yet neither radio nor billboards had such an immediate revolutionary impact on Brazilian consumerism as the 1928 publication of *Cruzeiro*. Modeled closely on the American *Life* magazine, this glossy, picture-filled weekly publication focused on national themes from the start to its last issue in 1978. Its national focus and the nationalizing orientation of auto ads combined to push notions of Brazilian unification to new levels.[69]

The American car companies continued to use auto shows, special banquets, and celebrity endorsers to sell their products, but they also began to market automobility in more geographically complicated ways.[70] In the 1910s and early 1920s, most raids were undertaken by "sportsmen" and auto advocates, but as the car companies' marketing departments grew, they quickly became components of advertising campaigns. Success in races and raids demonstrated the durability, handling, and speed of the newest models. They also put cars in front of potential buyers in both the city and the countryside. The Rio to São Paulo raid continued to be the most popular, and it allowed the car companies to publicize the latest record times for the trip. As early as 1921, Standard Oil, Goodyear, Dodge, and other American companies sponsored raids and used the drivers' success in advertisements. The 1921 trip took a full week, but by 1925, a Buick could make it in only 66 hours. A 1926 raid sponsored by Studebaker made the trip in 48 hours, and just a month later, with more bridges opened on the route, a Marmon Motor car set a new record of 18 hours, 32 minutes. By the end of the 1920s, professional race drivers such as Irineu Corrêa were able to make the trip in under seven hours.[71]

The foreign auto companies next sponsored raids beyond the Rio to São Paulo corridor. Studebaker arranged a Santos to Florianópolis raid of more than 3,000 kilometers in 1926, and Ford arranged raids throughout the southernmost state of Rio Grande do Sul. Hupmobile and Ford backed a 5,000-kilometer raid from São Paulo to Buenos Aires.[72] The car companies then recast raids as endurance tests for their vehicles, driving them far into the interior or making a circuit around three cities and running cars until they ceased functioning. One 1929 test kept a Ford Model A engine running nonstop for 202 hours. A few months later, Chevrolet reported that one of its cars operated for a remarkable 1,170 hours without a break. Throughout the 1930s, the foreign auto manufacturers continued to sponsor races to advertise their vehicles.[73]

Ford and GM developed even more creative ways of getting their vehicles before far-flung consumers. At first, they focused on selling cars to rural doctors and even priests in order to have their travels serve as a form of visual advertising.[74] Ford pioneered the practice of creating sales caravans to travel into the rural sector showing off its latest products and making sales along the way. On 25 May 1926, for example, 16 vehicles ranging from Fordson tractors to Lincolns left São Paulo to tour 25 interior towns, often traveling over "roads [that] were no more than dirt paths through the forest." Ford worked with General Electric, Vacuum Oil, Goodyear Tire and Rubber, and other companies to set up mini–sales expositions everywhere the cars traveled. In the evenings, the tractors were used as electrical generators for movie projectors that showed films about the latest developments in consumer goods from the United States. This first caravan lasted 43 days, and Ford estimated that it reached more than 100,000 people. General Motors used similar caravans but included circus acts to make the events even more popular in the small interior towns. The GM circus caravans were enthusiastically welcomed by local inhabitants. Often banners hung over the main street, and local newspapers ran front-page stories on the caravan with headlines such as "Progress has reached town, at last!"[75]

The caravans demonstrated the durability and endurance of the vehicles on the rough interior roads, but they also inverted traditional sales techniques. Rather than have rural elites travel to the capital city to see the latest foreign imports, the foreign manufacturers brought elite consumption directly to the countryside and even delivered their new purchases to buyers.[76] The American companies continued to innovate in urban marketing as well. On the streets of major Brazilian cities, GM paraded its 1927 models covered in white fabric with holes only for the windshields in order to create mystery and excitement about the new line. Sometimes a single, white cloth-covered car would drive in cities or from city to city to pique public curiosity. General Motors succeeded in making the unveiling of its new models a major event. Studebaker used a similar promotion in Porto Alegre and unveiled its new models on 15 November 1926, the anniversary of the founding of the Brazilian Republic. Ford used special parades of new vehicles to help inaugurate new roads throughout Brazil.[77]

American cars were so popular in Brazil and the rest of Latin America by the early 1920s that French manufacturers openly spoke of their industry as being in "ruin." Vehicles from the United States made up 65% of automotive imports in 1923, dominating the market through their high quality and low price, relative to European models.[78] Over the course of the 1920s and 1930s, American vehicles became even more popular with Brazilians. Despite the growing nationalist sentiment during the 1930s, American cars and trucks remained the vehicles of choice. Brazilians showed some pride in efforts to manufacture trucks and buses locally but still had a strong preference for American products.[79] The American car companies' innovative marketing techniques did much more than just succeed in selling their cars; they also sold the ideals of Americanism and automobility. The American automobile companies were foreign corporations that operated throughout the globe as multinationals, yet they were among the most powerful forces in the creation of a modern unified nation out of the disparate and largely unconnected regions of republican Brazil. The largest and most profitable Brazilian businesses in the nineteenth and early twentieth centuries had little or no reach beyond their home regions. Ford, General Motors, and to a lesser extent, Studebaker became the first private enterprises with truly national scope, outweighing even the national influence of the central government. With the exception of military campaigns, the telegraph service, and sporadic public works such as the short-lived antidrought measures of the early 1920s, the government in Rio had little impact on local life throughout Brazil's immense territory.

The most obvious ways American auto companies reshaped the physical, economic, and social geography of Brazil was through their public and private support of road building. The American corporations secretly funded much of the work of the Good Roads Movement and helped plan future highways.[80] In another important unifying move, Ford, GM, and Studebaker set up national dealer networks that became the first businesses with branches throughout Brazil. Moreover, these corporations, particularly Ford, provided the means for transforming the nation's massive rural sector by helping to change the production and marketing of agricultural goods. Finally, and perhaps most significantly, American companies affected the geography of the nation in much less tangible ways. By encouraging automobile transportation into the interior of Brazil, these companies began to alter the mental geography of the nation.

The American car companies pushed road building for two basic reasons. They knew that an expanding road network would spur demand for more cars, trucks, and buses. If automobility remained primarily urban, it would never be widespread in Brazil. The other reason behind the companies' support of road building was that the Americans believed they had a distinct advantage over their European competitors in durable and high-clearance cars that were particularly well suited for Brazil's road areas. The Model T, for example, had handled tough, deeply rutted roads in the rural United States and so could handle many of Brazil's most treacherous routes. Kristian Orberg, a Ford executive in Brazil, recalled, "The car owners soon began to make trips into the interior [in the 1920s], roads or no roads, and tall stories were told about the advantages of this fantastic car [the Model T] which had the reputation of always getting there." Ford's Model A was also popular for its high clearance and ability to handle rough rural roads.[81] American-made trucks were equally successful in Brazil's tough interior. They had been designed for travel throughout the United States, which had thousands of miles of rural roads, many of them as bad as those in Brazil.[82]

The Brazilian structure of the American auto companies had a similar impact on the nation's geography. Ford and General Motors put their headquarters in São Paulo in recognition of that city's growing industrial base and its relationship to automobility. In hindsight, this appears to be an obvious location for the foreign firms, but at the time, Rio was the national capital, a major port, and the center of Brazilian culture. The city of São Paulo had no port (seagoing cargo was unloaded in Santos and driven or taken by train to the state capital) and was much more dominated by locally owned businesses producing goods for the domestic market than by firms involved in foreign trade. The arrival of the foreign auto manufacturers coincided with the birth of the modernist movement in São Paulo and the city's rise to dominance in the Brazilian economy. The Studebaker Corporation recognized this when it decided in 1926 to move its South American headquarters from Rio to São Paulo.[83]

The development of a truly national network of Ford and GM dealers spread these companies throughout Brazil. When Ford first came to Brazil, it sold its cars through two large independent dealers, T. Wright in São Paulo, which became Casa Ford, and Sulford in Porto Alegre. Other importers sold Ford products, but in the 1920s, the company centralized control of sales through wholly owned branch offices. When these proved to be too unwieldy, Ford established a vast national network of dealerships.[84] Successful local sales agents were often granted their own dealerships. Ford had used medical doctors, pharmacists, mechanics, and even priests to sell cars in small towns. One priest was so good that a Ford executive, Kristian Orberg, remembered his exploits three decades later: "I don't know whether he didn't promise his prospects a soft hereafter for any hell the Ford may give them on earth. The fact is he sold a surprising number of cars in his zone."[85]

The dealers used a wide variety of sales techniques to place their vehicles in even the remotest locations. General Motors expanded its presence in the northeast with "traveling men" who went deep into the *sertão* to sell cars and trucks. They often worked with local bankers and businessmen to determine who had the means to make such purchases.[86] Some of the terrain the American companies targeted for sales was so inaccessible that car company executives often had to travel by airplane to organize sales in the interior in the 1930s. All these activities were coordinated with São Paulo offices, but they focused on changing attitudes and consumption habits throughout the previously distant interior spaces. Ford representatives sold the idea of the speed and durability of auto transport over the continued use of oxen and other forms of animal transport. Salesmen arrived in small interior towns in Bahia, Minas Gerais, Mato Grosso, Paraná, and Rio Grande do Sul to give special demonstrations of their vehicles' capabilities. They marketed the idea that auto ownership would fundamentally reshape life in Brazil's interior by giving residents of formerly isolated towns new business and social opportunities. Ford's salesmen were even instructed to rev up their vehicles' engines as much as possible because Fords were louder than other makes and thus seemed more powerful and more capable of handling Brazil's rough interior.[87]

In the remotest locations, such as throughout the Amazonian state of Pará and in the isolated Amazon city of Manaus, cars and trucks were sold primarily by hardware merchants. Sales agents in these locations maintained close ties to their customers after their purchases to provide gasoline, oil, service, and repairs on the vehicles.[88] The U.S. companies pushed service contracts to continue to make profits throughout an auto's lifetime. They used tactics such as guaranteeing "quality" factory parts, as opposed to locally manufactured goods. These local dealers could rely on their monopoly on automotive knowledge to maintain close ties to their customers.[89] The unique nature of automobiles as consumer goods promoted such ongoing ties. As hardy as the Model T and Chevy were, compared with European sedans, they still required extensive service, ranging from brake pad replacements to total engine rebuilds. In rural Brazil in the 1920s and 1930s, the dealers often owned the only fully equipped garages staffed with trained mechanics.

The unique properties of autos as consumer goods also allowed a flourishing used car and truck market to develop in the interior. Urban dealers frequently offered very good prices for trade-in vehicles to spur new model sales. The resulting used car inventories had several positive effects on Brazilian automobility. Dealers sometimes pooled these vehicles for large used car fairs in the cities. Middle-class consumers who could not quite afford new cars had a much easier time purchasing these. Urban dealers also extended their reach into the countryside by marketing used cars in the interior. Often roadmen would drive caravans of used vehicles through small towns and sell their inventory along the way. Used car owners then had to make ties with local dealers for maintenance and other services, effectively broadening the reach of foreign car companies and their dealers.[90]

No matter how effectively the American car companies penetrated Brazil's vast interior with their dealer networks and innovative marketing and sales campaigns, nothing they did was more ambitious than Ford's plans to transform Brazilian agriculture. Ford and the other American auto companies began to notice a sharp rise in demand for trucks in Brazil. With the construction of roads over the course of the late 1920s and 1930s, agricultural producers increasingly replaced rail freight with truck transport. The American companies responded by expanding truck production in Brazil and by building bodies designed specifically for the local market. These were so popular that that ratio of trucks to cars was much higher in Brazil than in most other countries. Brazilians used trucks to literally clear land for agricultural production and roads, including pulling huge tree trucks out of the ground to open land for planting in Paraná and elsewhere.[91] The flexibility of truck transport—as opposed to the fixed routes of trains—allowed new soybean and cotton producers in the south and center-south to compete with more established areas in Brazil and abroad.[92]

Ford dealers pushed the company's tractors by promoting the idea of mechanized agriculture through sales materials hailing the modern and scientific methods of production that tractor use would stimulate. Often borrowing the language of *bandeirantismo*, Ford's advertising spoke of the "Brazilian spirit" of "conquering" new territories and opening new lands to modern agriculture.[93] Between 1919 and 1952, Ford sold 11,661 tractors in Brazil. (Between 1952 and 1959, it sold more than 7,000 more tractors for agriculture and construction work.) Many tractors purchased in the 1920s were used by factory owners as generators during periods of electrical brownouts and blackouts. Ford officials commented that it was much easier selling cars than tractors to Brazilians, even though the tractors seemed to have more practical applications.[94] In the late 1920s, Henry Ford initiated a bold project to forever alter the Amazon by introducing an industrialized form of agricultural production to an area marked by rubber gathering by tappers. To facilitate such production, he attempted to implement the broad outlines of Fordism at rubber plantations he established in the state of Pará (Figure 3.4). Ford constantly sought to deepen the supply integration of his company by purchasing iron mines, building glass works and steel mills, and creating his own fleet of freighters. As early as 1923, Ford and his friend Harvey Firestone discussed the idea of jointly owning a massive plantation to supply their businesses with rubber. When the international price of rubber climbed in the 1920s, in part because of the great expansion of automobility and thus tire manufacture, Ford became receptive to Brazilian offers of a large land concession in the

FIGURE 3.4 Fordlândia and Belterra had U.S.-style housing, roads, and utilities built in the jungle. Photo courtesy of The Henry Ford Museum and Library.

Amazon.[95] Working through the former U.S. consul in the area, William L. Schurz, Ford received a concession on the Tapajós River in the state of Pará. Ford and Paranense officials finalized the deal on 21 July 1927 for 1 million hectares that included a fifty-year tax exemption and gave Ford Motor Company full legal jurisdiction over the land. Ford also retained all mineral and land rights, giving it access to all the lumber there and any oil that might be discovered.[96] The land was not ideal for large-scale rubber production. It was too hilly and sandy and had highly seasonal rainfall patterns. Moreover, Ford's oceangoing fleet could not reach the plantation during several months each year. Consistently hurt by outbreaks of South American leaf blight, this experiment in industrialized agriculture never produced enough rubber to justify its high costs.[97]

Fordlândia, as the initial plantation soon became known, is significant beyond its meager rubber output. In the late 1920s, the granting of this massive land concession brought out Brazilians' divergent views on the role of foreign capital and fairly uniform and positive views of the importance of automobility for national development. At first, Ford seemed to have received extraordinarily favorable terms. All the project's local costs were paid by the São Paulo office with profits from Brazilian auto sales. Ford also received a generous 60% reduction in tariffs on all imported goods destined for the plantation and complete relief from duties on lumber harvested on the land. The incoming governor of Pará, Eurico de Freitas Valle, distanced himself from the terms of the concession and tried to stoke nationalist resentment against Ford.[98] In Rio, where one might expect protests against the potential foreign domination of the Amazon, Ford seemed to have a great deal of support for the project, including that of President Washington Luís, who worked closely with Ford officials to facilitate the deal.[99]

Ford's new venture became Brazil's major news story. Rio's leading newspapers at first praised the land concession. They tended to view the project as more the work of Henry Ford the man than of the company that bore his name (and that was run by his son Edsel).[100] The *Jornal do Brasil* editorialized in October 1927 that Henry Ford's "capital and initiative" were all that were required for the Amazon "to become transformed into an enormous storehouse of numberless products." This editorial warned that Ford's project would face a nationalist critique, but argued that that was little more than "morbid patriotism." The *Jornal do Brasil* concluded by praising Ford: "even though Henry Ford is a businessman, his name is universally known for the nobility with which he conducts his business affairs. Therefore there can be only reason for us to rejoice at the interest which the Valley of the Amazon awakened in him." Rio's *O País*, in an October 1927 editorial titled "New Horizons for the Amazon," praised the "good sense" and "true patriotism" of those involved in making the deal.[101] In February and March 1928, Rio's newspapers began to reflect some of the political maneuvering in Pará. *O Globo* protested that Ford's concession foreshadowed the end of local production in the Amazon, and the previously supportive *Jornal do Brasil* warned again of foreign capital undermining Brazilian sovereignty. Assis Chateaubriand's *O Jornal* took up Ford's cause, equating it with the progress of Brazil. Its editorial took a combative tone in arguing on behalf of the project: "Mr. Ford's enterprise in the Amazon holds so many fascinating possibilities that it would seem difficult to find mentalities so dense as not to be impressed by the possibilities of the dramatic metamorphosis which Ford's enterprise promises to effect in that vast region." The editorial concluded by arguing that such grand projects held out hope for the transformation of the entire Brazilian economy.[102]

The automotive press was even more effusive in its support. *Automobilismo* argued that Fordlândia would become a growth pole that would stimulate the entire region. Highways and railroads would follow, opening the Amazon to even greater economic development. Ford, unlike his Brazilian predecessors, would use "scientific" methods to develop this region. It was not just that his plantations would rekindle the rubber economy; auto enthusiasts believed that Ford's employment practices would stimulate the entire region's economy.[103] When they lobbied for relief from import and export tariffs, Ford men pushed the notion that, while the company would make money, it would at the same time transform the Amazon. The U.S. consul in Pará reported with a good deal of hyperbole that "Mr. Ford considers the project as a 'work of civilization.'...Nothing else will explain the lavish expenditures of money, at least three million dollars in the last sixteen months, in laying the foundation of what is evidently planned to become a city of two or three hundred thousand."[104]

The environmental limitations of the topography and the quality of the soil in the initial grant—the part formally known as Fordlândia—led the company to swap some of this area for more promising land also on the Tapajós. The second plantation became known as Belterra. It was run in exactly the same fashion, but given its more favorable conditions, it was able to produce more rubber than Fordlândia. The initial work on these plantations proved to be much more challenging than Ford's men in São Paulo and Dearborn had imagined. Indeed, they planned these jungle cities without much information about the land or people. Their greatest mistake was the failure to analyze carefully how the rubber trees they planted would fare in a plantation environment, which eventually led to the demise of the project.[105] Still, Fordlândia and Belterra fired the imaginations of Brazilians over the possibilities of using modern technologies to create out of the forest a productive, developed region with a well-educated and democratic workforce that would actively and positively participate in Brazilian society.

The initial construction of Fordlândia revealed the enormity of this project. When first planned, some thought Ford would employ 50,000 laborers to clear the forest. The actual number was much closer to 3,000, which was still a remarkable concentration of workers in the Amazonian jungle.[106] The Ford men sent to the jungle faced great hardships. Their initial equipment consisted of three tractors and two trucks, which they rarely used, given the scarcity of fuel in the jungle. The sawmill that was to provide lumber for construction was in constant disrepair, so most work was done by hand. The brutal environment was the greatest obstacle for these engineers and businessmen. Of the 104 full-time Ford employees sent to set up the jungle city, 30 were listed as sick in an early report. It continued: "NO SCREENS ANYWHERE, no sanitation, no garbage cans, flies by the million, all filth." Shortages of water filters, the absence of ice, and boredom further demoralized the men.[107]

Still, Ford managed to build its jungle city. By 1933, it had 30 kilometers of roads, 10 kilometers of railroad tracks, houses of various sizes, schools, administrative buildings, and a hospital. Fordlândia had 5,000 total residents, 3,000 of whom were directly employed by Ford; 97% were recruited locally. These Brazilians were residents of a new and foreign environment. Ford paved the plantation's roads and provided running water and electricity to workers' houses (Figure 3.5). As the town grew, it added an ice-making facility and cinema, water towers and smokestacks. A 1932 report on Ford's progress noted: "A feeling akin to disbelief comes over the visitor on suddenly seeing projected before him a picture which may be considered a miniature of a modern industrial city."[108] As Fordlândia and

FIGURE 3.5 Consumerism was a key component of Fordism, and workers on the rubber plantations took advantage of the goods available in the company stores. Photos courtesy of The Henry Ford Museum and Library.

Belterra expanded, Brazilians began to discuss the need to build transportation links between these budding jungle cities and the nation's political and industrial capitals, Rio and São Paulo. Although Ford envisioned his plantations exporting their rubber directly to factories in the United States, Brazilians pointed to the growth of tire manufacturing in São Paulo. As a result, the Ford plantations provided the first links between the largely unknown and distant interior and the coast.[109]

Although such ambitious road building through the Amazon would not begin until the 1950s, Fordlândia and Belterra did deliver on their promise to transform the lives of the region's people. At first, Ford faced problems recruiting labor. The original plantation was isolated, and riverboats charged exorbitant fares for travel to Fordlândia. The company refused to cover any of these costs, so the burden on those who were turned away was particularly steep. Early misunderstandings ranging from labor terms to the design of worker housing to the type of food served in the plantation's cafeterias led to tensions, culminating in riots. These initial problems led some to view Fordlândia, and by extension, the later plantation at Belterra, as failures because of labor scarcity and/or instability. However, the company made great progress in transforming labor by bringing Fordism to the jungle.

The plantations relied on a highly specialized division of labor. One salary and wage book from the 1930s lists more than 30 separate professions from rubber planter and assistant rubber planter to blacksmiths, tinsmiths, boilermakers, masons, and pipefitters. From the start, Ford worried about potential labor shortages, and so the company offered extensive training and good wages.[110] When he first planned these plantations, Henry Ford had spoken of providing a $5-a-day wage to the rubber gatherers. Average wages at Fordlândia and Belterra were the highest in the region, although they never reached $5 per day, and may have been the highest agriculture pay in all Brazil. To fight labor turnover, Ford created a well-defined seniority system that increased wages with workers' tenure. By the early 1930s, the company had managed to stabilize its workforce with such wages.[111] Beyond these high agricultural wages, the extensive division of labor and well-defined work rules led to regulated workdays of between 8 and 11 hours, depending on the job, and generally peaceful relations with management.[112]

If creating a stable supply of rubber was the first goal of the Ford plantations, the transformation of the Amazon was the second. Both Henry Ford and his corporation spoke openly of "civilizing" the region by turning local inhabitants into modern citizens. By 1933, 300 children attended school each day and 150 adults each night at Fordlândia's three schools, which were free to students. Pre-school-age children filled its daycare centers. Belterra had five schools (three in the town and two supported by Ford in the outskirts) with 958 students. All the students wore crisp white uniforms and well-shined shoes, free to workers' children. The Fordlândia hospital was making more than 300 consultations per year, with all medical services free to workers and their families. When Ford opened Belterra, it set aside land for growing foodstuffs and pasture land for cattle. Workers could also tend their own gardens around their homes. Belterra, with its 844 houses, was even more elaborate than Fordlândia, which had 229 houses. It included a range of housing facilities from barracks for single men to bungalows for families. Managers lived in large, U.S.-suburban-style houses. All the workers had access to a nine-hole golf course, swimming pools, soccer fields, and movie houses. A Ford Motor Company booklet on the plantations enthusiastically described the new plantation as a modern marvel: "Paved roads, cement walks, comfortable homes, electric lights, telephones—this might be any Midwestern town. But it is Belterra, buried deep in the jungle of Brazil."[113]

Engineers marveled at the accomplishment of building these complex facilities in such an isolated region of the jungle, but the more complicated question was whether these plantations could remake the people of this region into modern Brazilian citizens.[114] The housing facilities were so foreign that some rubber gatherers at first used the installed toilets to clean their feet.[115] The working people of Fordlândia and Belterra soon adapted to their new surroundings, however. Women quickly embraced the system of running water in their homes, and Ford changed the menu in its restaurants to include local dishes after the riots. The company also expanded the offerings in its stores to meet workers' demands for local products.[116]

The plantations not only paid high agricultural wages but also paid in cash. Moreover, Ford ran company stores that provided goods to the workers at discounted prices.[117] One report on this new style of consumerism noted how much women's work had changed. They no long gathered bananas and prepared mandioca to serve with fish they caught in the river. Now they shopped like women in São Paulo, Rio, and American cities: "The section of town given over to shops is particularly animated in the early morning hours. The housewives, who for the first time in their lives know the joys of shopping are to be seen moving from store to store and finally emerging with market baskets of conventional design filled with groceries." In addition to the Ford-run general stores, other merchants moved from Manaus to sell goods in Fordlândia and Belterra. As a testament to the changing buying power and attitudes toward time in this section of the Amazon, a jeweler sold more watches on the Ford plantations than he had ever sold in Manaus.[118]

Beyond making Fordlândia and Belterra economic growth poles, the company also sought to instill a democratic ethos among its workers. Early on, Henry Ford planned to have the plantations' residents elect their own local government officials.[119] The 1930 revolution and the following political upheaval and dictatorship made such elections impossible, but the plans for them demonstrate the important connections between Fordism and democracy in the Amazon. Educated workers with access to health care, high-quality food, and good housing were seen by Ford as capable of operating as modern citizens, and he hoped they would become the templates for all Brazilian working people in both rural areas and the cities. When the dictator Getúlio Vargas visited Fordlândia and Belterra in 1940, he reviewed all the social services at the plantations and made a national radio address from Manaus praising the great progress Ford had made in transforming the lives of Amazonian people. Vargas continued by stating that Ford's labor practices made his social legislation unnecessary.[120]

Throughout the 1930s and early 1940s, the Vargas government emphasized nationalist development and was often critical of other foreign enterprises. When several government officials, such as former labor minister Lindolfo Collor and Pará governor Magalhães Barata, praised the Ford plantations, Foreign Minister Oswaldo Aranha responded in a highly nationalist way by openly criticizing the role of foreign capital in Brazil. In private, however, Aranha apparently assured Ford officials that the company's activities throughout Brazil were highly valued.[121] He did so because the Vargas government had to balance carefully its economic nationalism with the reality that Fordlândia and Belterra offered Brazil previously undreamed-of opportunities to develop the nation's vast interior. Throughout the late 1930s and early 1940s, Brazilians and foreign business executives discussed plans for building large-scale tire factories in the Amazon and using automobility in general to transform the interior of Brazil. The potential benefits Fordlândia and Belterra seemed to offer the nation greatly outweighed popular ideas about the negative aspects of foreign capital.[122]

The many environmental limitations on growing rubber on Amazonian plantations, along with advances in synthetic rubber production during the war, ultimately doomed the Ford experiment. In 1945, when Henry Ford II took over the company, he decided to sell Fordlândia and Belterra to the Brazilian government for only $244,200, which left the company with a net loss of a bit more than $7.8 million. Ford's internal analyses predicted that the Amazon plantations would never produce enough rubber to meet even a small portion of the company's needs and that production costs would continue to be high, given the elaborate social services and free housing there.[123] Fordlândia and Belterra did, however, succeed in firing the Brazilian imagination about the potential of developing the Amazon. Moreover, the company's extensive investment in social services demonstrated how such a concerted effort could potentially make distant interior folk into modern workers and citizens.

Long after the company had sold the plantations, much of the infrastructure remained intact, and local residents continued to praise Ford for his attempt to develop the region. In 1993, Leon Correa Bouillet, the mayor of the area, remarked: "Brazilians are always talking about how foreigners exploit our resources, but our government and people never do anything. Ford built us a hospital; he paid his workers well and gave them good houses. When Fordlândia had a train, the big city, Santarem, was still using oxcarts.... It would be nice if the company would come back."[124]

	Nationalist Development: Getúlio
CHAPTER 4	Vargas and the Integration of Brazil

BEFORE THE FULL IMPACT of the worldwide depression could be felt in Brazil, President Washington Luís had managed to cause a crisis of his own. He upset the traditional power-sharing arrangement between the nation's two most powerful states, São Paulo and Minas Gerais. Rather than allowing a candidate from Minas to run as the Republican Party candidate—which would make him the preordained victor—Washington Luís put forward his Paulista protégé Júlio Prestes as the party's standard bearer.[1] The revolution of 1930 began as a simple regional squabble, with the states of Minas Gerais and Rio Grande do Sul heading a coalition against São Paulo. When Getúlio Vargas, the Riograndense governor, took power on 3 November 1930, no one in Brazil had reason to believe the new provisional president would bring fundamental change to Brazil, yet his rule from 1930 to 1945 and then from 1951 to 1954 inexorably changed the relationship between the national government and the states. Vargas as Brazil's provisional president (1930–1937), dictator (1937–1945), and finally democratically elected populist president (1951–1954) sought to centralize power in Rio and attempted to transform the nature of that power by creating a more activist and interventionist state, often relying on the latest technology to do so. No matter how much he juggled the interests of different groups and even classes according to circumstances, Vargas always maintained a focus on unifying Brazil and fostering a greater sense of nationalism.

In other words, Getúlio Vargas was Brazil's first modernist leader, and as such, he would both rely on and profoundly influence the nation's growing automobility.[2] To some, Vargas was a "populist" oriented toward Brazil's urban poor. To others, he was the first leader to use the national government to foster capital accumulation for ongoing economic development. His critics, including traditional agricultural elites, at first saw shades of socialism in his labor politics, but the establishment of the Estado Novo (New State) dictatorship in 1937 later brought the charge that he was a fascist. Those labels not only miss the mark but also obscure the reality of Vargas's rule. State making, industrialization, and the first stirrings of social welfare were components of a budding Brazilian modernity more than of any formal political ideology.

Technology broadly and automobility in particular offered Vargas the means to make Brazil a modern nation. The problem he faced was that most Brazilians associated these technologies with foreign corporations, particularly American auto companies. Vargas responded by navigating a middle path between embracing the transformative power of technology and beginning to make the automobile more Brazilian. He certainly did not set out to create a national automobile industry, and indeed, its establishment came after his death. He did, however, create much of the necessary legal, physical, and industrial framework for the establishment of Brazil's automobile industry. Perhaps more significantly, he deepened the cultural infrastructure of developmentalism by increasingly tying together automobility, industrialism, and nationalism. No matter how Vargas was defined as Brazil's leader in the 1930s, 1940s, and 1950s, he was consistent in his advocacy of a strong central state that would push national development. Soon after taking office on 3 November 1930, Vargas dissolved Congress and took on executive and legislative authority. He next exercised even greater centralizing authority by closing state and municipal legislatures and councils, and then by removing all state governors, except the new Minas leader, who had supported the revolution. Governors were replaced with federally appointed "interventors" who reported directly to Vargas. He also created new federal organizations with explicitly national, developmentalist orientations, such as the Ministry of Education and Public Health and the Ministry of Labor. Vargas even moved to gain control over the coffee sector, long the purview of the Paulista elite, with the creation of the National Coffee Department (DNC) in 1933.[3]

Many of the ideas behind these moves had been articulated by a group of left-leaning, young military officers grouped in the Club 3 de Outubro. Known as *tenentes*, or lieutenants, these officers often had gained firsthand experiences fighting in Brazil's great interior spaces, both against the millenarian uprising in the Contestado region of Santa Catarina and Paraná in the 1910s and in chasing the so-called Prestes Column of former young officers—including some from the *tenente* movement itself—who went into open rebellion against the state in 1924. These military engagements in the hinterland demonstrated just how little impact the central state had beyond Brazil's largest cities. Local elites often were completely unaware of national politics, and the rural poor were completely disconnected from the nation. These young soldiers also struggled to do their jobs without basic tools, such as adequate topographical maps. The pursuit of the Prestes Column magnified these problems. Captain Luís Carlos Prestes went into open rebellion in October 1924, joining segments of the São Paulo state militia who had rebelled in July. General Cândido Rondon subdued the disaffected soldiers by April 1925, but Prestes and Miguel Costa of the São Paulo militia fled into Paraguay and then reentered Brazil practicing a "war of movement" strategy to avoid capture. They traveled through Mato Grosso, Goiás, and a series of northern and northeastern states until going into exile in Bolivia in 1927. The army relied on rail transport and used the few roads available to them, but chasing a guerrilla force through the interior of Brazil convinced these soldiers that the country needed fundamental change. Inadequate forms of transportation in the interior had to be upgraded, and the disparate state militias had to be brought under national control. Most significant of all, many of these young officers developed a strong critique of Brazil's social structure and argued, in ways that resonated with the ideas of modernist intellectuals, that the rural poor had to be better integrated with the rest of the nation.[4]

The *tenente* uprisings and the Prestes Column affected the ways many who worked with Vargas viewed the nation. Pedro Aurélio Góes Monteiro, who had been the chief aide to the commanding general in the pursuit of the column, became Vargas's minister of war and quickly put all the nation's state police forces under federal command. João Alberto Lins de Barros, a *tenente* from the northeast who had initiated the 1924 rebellion with Luís Carlos Prestes but was not part of the later Prestes Column, became Vargas's first interventor in the state of São Paulo. João Alberto alienated much of the Paulista elite because he was an outsider and because he represented Vargas's drive to centralize authority in Rio. In July 1931, he forcibly ended a strike of about 70,000 industrial workers but guaranteed that the new Ministry of Labor in Rio would meet their "just and reasonable" demands. Although it was a victory for São Paulo's industrialists, the new federally appointed governor and national Ministry of Labor had intervened in the local affairs of Brazil's most powerful state.[5] João Alberto's actions were merely the first for a regime intent on creating a more powerful national government that would directly affect many local affairs.

The creation of assertive national state institutions threatened the power and independence of São Paulo's agricultural and industrial elites. The increasing presence of Rio in the state's affairs led the state's militia and a small group of disaffected army officers to declare themselves in open revolt against the national government on 9 July 1932. The civil war of 1932 lasted for a little more than three months, with São Paulo conceding defeat in early October. Although brief, it had wide-ranging effects on Brazil. São Paulo's rebellion reined in Vargas's ambitious program of concentrating power in Rio. In the aftermath of the war, he devolved many national functions to the São Paulo state government to mollify Paulista elites. São Paulo's industrialists, for example, were largely exempted from control by the national Ministry of Labor. Vargas permitted all industrial relations in their state in the 1930s and 1940s to be directed by the São Paulo Labor Department, which was controlled largely by local factory owners. Socially, the insurgent São Paulo government adopted many of the employment policies brought to Brazil by the foreign auto companies. Paulista elites relied on a number of Fordist policies to maintain industrial production during the war and so learned that they could indeed emulate the great foreign companies in their own factories.[6] The most important lessons from the war, however, were learned on the battlefield. Insurgent São Paulo forces and the federal army increasingly relied on car and truck transport for troop movement and supply. Both sides also used crude tanks in battle.

The conflict demonstrated Brazil's burgeoning reliance not only on automobility itself but also on the American companies that manufactured the vehicles. Elites in São Paulo saw both the promises and limits of local vehicle production during the war. Cut off from imports, the insurgents had to rely on local industry to manufacture armored railcars and tanks. They were also dependent on local machine shops and mechanics to fashion replacement parts for vehicles. At the same time, the federal government in Rio relied on imported trucks for the war effort because it was cut off from the foreign auto companies' São Paulo factories. It is not surprising, therefore, that in the aftermath of the civil war, a steadily increasing number of Brazilian policy makers embraced the idea that they would have to deepen industrial development for strategic, patriotic, and economic reasons by creating a national auto industry (Figure 4.1).

Brazil's military leaders now thought about roads, industry, and development broadly. Unlike the nation's interior, where so many previous battles had been fought, São Paulo had Brazil's most comprehensive network

FIGURE 4.1 Although roads had improved by the 1930s, many were still only dirt. This 1938 scene reveals the difficulties of making the 1,500-kilometer trip from São Paulo to Porto Alegre. Photo courtesy of the General Motors Corporation.

of roads and rail transport. Góes Monteiro confided to Vargas that had the Paulistas taken advantage of their state's extraordinarily well-developed infrastructure to launch an offensive against federal troops, they might have toppled the government in Rio.[7] The juxtaposition of their experiences fighting in the jungles and dense forests of Mato Grosso, Goiás, the Contestado region of Santa Catarina, and Paraná, on the one hand, and in the highly developed state of São Paulo, on the other, convinced military leaders that the Vargas administration should work to make Brazil as a whole more like São Paulo in terms of its economic and social development.[8]

More broadly, Vargas moved away from a program of forced central policy making and control and, instead, worked to bolster a nationalist Brazilian identity through a series of cultural initiatives. These took on many forms, from supporting the arts to a new emphasis on education. Several programs, such as creating a national road-building plan, promoting tourism, and backing the expansion of auto racing, directly advanced the cause of automobility. Indeed, mobility and the physical and cultural unification of Brazil became key themes of Vargas's program for nationalist development.[9] The physical movement of people, through advanced transportation networks, would be required to complement the more ethereal components of Vargas's state making. He encouraged all Brazilians to physically experience the nation beyond their hometowns and states.[10] Although these projects had significant long-term implications for Brazil, they were particularly valuable to Vargas because they did not create the animosity of his early attempts to centralize practically all policy making in Rio.

The promotion of automobility also had an established constituency that eagerly worked with the regime to spread the gospel of broad auto ownership. Vargas reinstituted road building as part of the Federal Drought and Relief Commission, making it Brazil's most effective road-building organization from 1930 to 1941.[11] In 1937, he upgraded the National Highway Commission into the National Highway Department and increased its funding. Overall, Vargas nearly doubled the kilometers of highways and roads in Brazil from 113,329 in 1930 to 208,325 in 1938. Still, only about 15,000 kilometers of these roads were considered usable in all weather conditions.[12] Although Vargas expanded the federal government's role in road building as a part of his broad state making, he never budgeted sufficient funds for the country's transportation needs. In 1940, for example, the federal government allocated U.S. $1,650,000 for road construction and U.S. $550,000 for maintenance. In 1941, the state of Rio spent the same amount ($1.65 million) on roads as the federal government planned for the entire nation. São Paulo, which already had Brazil's best highway system, spent U.S. $10 million on highways, and Rio Grande do Sul, U.S. $3.3 million.[13] The low levels of federal funding kept total road building far below the levels needed to tie together Brazil's massive national territory. An internal General Motors study of the country's infrastructure done in 1941 found that the only roads that could be considered on par with U.S. highways were the São Paulo to Campinas route and the highway connecting São Paulo and Rio. Other roads were of poor quality, and most of Brazil lacked even rudimentary transportation links.[14] Still, Vargas closely associated himself with road building by attending openings and speaking publicly about the importance of such infrastructure for the ongoing development of the country. In lieu of large government expenditures, Vargas at least lent the prestige of his office to the idea of road construction.[15]

Like road building, pleasure driving and tourism had long been promoted by automobile and touring clubs throughout Brazil. In contrast to raids, which were exercises in speed and endurance, the government wanted to promote trips into the interior as a way to instill a love of Brazil among the population.[16] Driving for pleasure out of Rio to the nearby interior combined the agendas of modernists, who sought to increase contact between coastal or European Brazil and the indigenous and *mestiço* populations of the hinterland; car enthusiasts; and the Vargas government, which sought both to foster a broad sense of Brazilianness and to create concrete instruments of national unification. These forces coalesced around the idea of promoting national tourism. The Touring Club of Brazil, with its national headquarters in Rio and state branches in São Paulo, Minas Gerais, Rio Grande do Sul, and Bahia, lobbied Vargas for state aid to advance tourism. The group's leaders spoke of their "patriotic labor" to unify Brazil through tourism. They invoked both Vargas's interest in national unification and the modernist themes of the authentic Brazilian being known only through cultural interchange.[17] The Touring Club specifically tied travel to citizenship, arguing that it sparked curiosity and armed Brazilians with the knowledge they needed to participate in and even intelligently criticize their government.[18] Although in many ways this was little more than self-interested hyperbole, the Touring Club and Automobile Club highlighted two of the most significant issues of the 1930s: national unification and citizenship rights.[19]

In 1932, these clubs and the government launched a campaign to encourage travel to Brazil's northeast with the slogan, "It's necessary to reveal Brazil to Brazilians." In 1936, the focus shifted to the far-south state of Rio Grande do Sul.[20] Local auto and touring clubs in these areas, in turn, promoted Rio de Janeiro as a vacation destination. Not only was Rio a beautiful resort city but also, as the national capital, it was filled with historic sites that every Brazilian should see.[21] Touring clubs provided ready-made itineraries with lists of approved hotels, restaurants, and auto garages and published maps and basic guides for the trips. Beyond these measures and continuing to pressure local, state, and federal officials to build new and better highways, there was little the clubs could do to foster an expanded tourism industry in Brazil.[22]

The national government, however, had the resources and the political interest to do more. The Rio to Petrópolis road became a focal point in this effort in the 1930s, when the federal government made the old mining center of Ouro Preto in Minas Gerais a national heritage site.[23] When the ACB built the Rio to Petrópolis road, it sought not only to tie Rio to Minas Gerais through auto transport but also to encourage Rio's wealthier residents to drive to the old imperial summer residence for leisure. The

Automobile Club did not imagine that it would also play a central role in the development of interstate tourism in the 1930s. By declaring Ouro Preto Brazil's first "national monument" on 12 July 1933, Vargas signaled his interest in promoting an idealized version of Brazilian nationalism. Ouro Preto was not only the wealthy center of Brazil's eighteenth-century gold- and diamond-mining boom but also the location of the nation's best known and most significant anticolonial or protonational uprising, the 1789 Inconfidência Mineira or Minas Conspiracy. In reality, the revolt was little more than an elite rejection of a new tax regime foisted on Brazil from Portugal, but the Vargas administration reinterpreted it as a celebration of nationalism and a strong central state. The Pantheon of the Inconfidentes on the ground floor of Museo da Inconfidência and the Grande Hotel de Ouro Preto were monuments to a modernism, designed by leading lights of the modernist movement, José de Souza Reis and Lucio Costa.[24]

The juxtaposition of Ouro Preto's many baroque churches and general colonial architecture with new, modernist tourist sites highlighted the intimate relationship between the modernist conceit and Vargas's promotion of national tourism. Cars would travel on new roads to Ouro Preto, and then tourists would stay at Lucio Costa's modernist hotel and visit the modernist shrine to the insurgents, while at the same time experiencing the beauty of the town's colonial past. Such experiences, government planners hoped, would foster national pride. The strategy was a bit ahead of its time, for only the well-to-do could afford such vacations in the 1930s, when auto ownership was still quite limited. Although the scarcity of cars kept the vast majority of Brazilians from having such direct tourism experiences, it was significant in promoting domestic travel for elites in lieu of trips abroad to Europe and the United States.

The national government and several state governments worked to improve roads and develop other sites for potential visitors.[25] The primary areas were around Rio and throughout the states of Minas Gerais and São Paulo, which had the best developed road systems and small towns filled with historical sites. The urban centers and small towns of Brazil's center-south also had the nation's highest concentration of car ownership. Brazilians visited the former imperial summer residences of Petrópolis, saw the grand houses of plantations in Teresópolis, and traveled to the beautiful beach community of Paratí.[26] None of these destinations had the same historical and political significance as Ouro Preto, but the increase in traffic to them is proof of the development of the beginnings of national tourism. Several states seized on the opportunities offered by Vargas's interest in domestic travel by working with local auto and touring clubs to create state agencies to promote local tourism. These efforts forced local politicians and business leaders to think about the place of their cities and states within Brazil. Rio Grande do Sul, for example, openly marketed its *gaúcho* culture as both distinct and a fundamental component of the national identity, and Bahia declared itself "the cradle of Brazilian civilization."[27]

The expansion of bus travel at this time aided the development of domestic tourism, but these were the earliest years of such travel. Still, the Vargas administration, various state governments, and auto and touring clubs sought to build a broad sense of Brazilianness by encouraging vacation travel, and in doing so they popularized the sort of mobility that in the past had been associated only with migration, often due to drought and other dire circumstances.[28] Middle-class and elite Brazilians increasingly moved beyond their hometowns and cities to experience their country's history and culture.[29] Tourism did not yet play a significant role in Brazilian life, but Vargas's modernist vision of a unified Brazil provided the framework for the sort of domestic tourism that would flourish with the expanded road building and broader auto ownership of the 1960s and 1970s.[30]

Vargas's use of culture was not limited to elite or middle-class pursuits. Throughout the 1930s, the federal government, for the first time in Brazil's history, took an active role in the promotion of spectator sports.[31] The government focused on soccer, or *futebol*, with the creation of a national council in 1933 to help coordinate play among the new leagues and organize the national team for World Cup competition. As early as the mid-1910s, tens of thousands of fans were attending matches in São Paulo and Rio, and medium and small cities had built stadiums for their local teams. The regime subsidized the 1938 World Cup team's travel to France, and as Brazilian players garnered international respect for their skills and flair, the national government identified itself more and more closely with the sport.[32]

During the Vargas years, auto racing emerged as a modern sport that was regulated, widely reported in the press, and followed closely by a large national fan base.[33] Organized auto sports allowed Brazilians to experience advanced technology and speed, at least vicariously, regardless of whether they could afford a car of their own.[34] Many Brazilians and foreigners raced in competitions throughout the country during this time, but auto racing as a major spectator sport was largely defined by two very different Brazilians, Manuel de Teffé and Francisco "Chico" Landi. Baron Manuel de Teffé von Hoonholtz was the son of Brazil's ambassador to Italy in the 1920s and 1930s. Teffé began racing in competitions against other wealthy sportsmen in Europe. Chico Landi, on the other hand, was born and raised in a modest São Paulo family, and he came to auto racing through his ownership of a local garage. Like Teffé, Landi helped to create the sport of grand prix racing in Brazil.

Teffé's participation in Italian auto races was widely reported in Brazil, where he soon became a well-known proponent of automobility. He argued for both grand prix–style racing and broad car ownership and even for the creation of a Brazilian auto industry. Teffé's racing in Europe stoked nationalist pride among Brazilians and increased local interest in motor sports.[35] When he returned home with European racers in tow, Teffé completely changed the sport in Brazil by bringing it both prestige and organization. Traditionally, auto racing in Brazil involved different classes of cars competing within categories of engine size. Fords, Chevies, Dodges, and Studebakers continued to dominate in these races that used crude tracks or cordoned-off city streets.[36] When grand prix racing debuted in Rio in 1933, it had more in common with European and North American competitions than with the contests that had usually been held in Brazil.[37] The Primeiro Grande Prêmio do Brasil was held in the Gávea section of the city on 3 October 1933. Brazilian and foreign drivers lined up in vehicles by Alfa Romeo, Bugatti, Fiat, Isotta Fraschini, and Mercedes Benz, as well as Ford, Chrysler, and a few others. Drivers referred to the dangerous route as "the Devil's spring board" (*Trampolim do Diablo*), but this only made the race more popular. Teffé won the inaugural grand prix in his Alfa Romeo, covering the 223-kilometer course in 3 hours, 19 minutes, and 25 seconds.[38] The second Rio Grand Prix in 1934 demonstrated the growing national and international appeal of racing in Brazil. The Brazilian Irineu Corrêa won the race that was marked by the death of the Italian Nino Crespi in a spectacular crash and by the presence of the French female racer, Helenice, who not only finished the race but also took time in Rio to pose provocatively, cigarette in hand, on Rio's Leblon beach.[39] Death, sex appeal, and a Brazilian victory made this second grand prix a great success and solidified auto racing's place in the national culture.

The 1934 grand prix also witnessed the momentous debut of Chico Landi, who became perhaps the single most important individual in the development of motor sports in Brazil. Landi was born into a working-class family in São Paulo. He left school at 11 to become a mechanic and later worked for a local Hudson dealership, where he prepared cars for sale. Landi soon developed a taste for giving the new vehicles high-speed tests late at night on the city's streets. Often in trouble with the police, Landi became a local legend for the street races he held against local chauffeurs. At 26, he traveled to Rio for the grand prix and led the race until his car failed with only eight laps to the finish. Although he did not win a grand prix until 1941, he quickly established himself as the most popular driver in Brazil.[40] His fame spread with his participation in races in Argentina and when he became the first Brazilian to race in a European grand prix.[41]

The increasing popularity of motor sports caught Vargas's attention. Although the Automobile Club, along with the Mappin department store, continued to sponsor Rio's grand prix, Vargas lent his considerable prestige to the race not only by attending it but also through the fascination he showed publicly for the racers and their cars. In May 1937, Vargas christened Rio's new track at Gávea and attended, along with 400,000 other spectators, the June 6 grand prix. It was increasingly obvious to Vargas and others that large numbers of Brazilians were attracted to automobile racing. Although its popularity would never rival that of soccer, auto sport had become an important and unique form of popular entertainment in Brazil.[42]

When he reviewed the state of racing, Vargas was particularly impressed by the number of highly competitive Brazilian drivers. Racing promoted the broad agenda of automobility (national progress through mobility and unification wrought through modern technology and consumerism), and it was also a sport without any sense of social or class antagonism. Whereas the best rivalries in Brazilian soccer often reflected racial, ethnic, and other social tensions (as in the classic Flamengo versus Fluminense divide in Rio and the Corinthians versus São Paulo FC in the city of São Paulo), Brazilians cheered the best drivers their country had to offer against a steady stream of skilled foreign competitors. Motor sports fit so well with Vargas's sense of national identity and progress that he began to personally promote races throughout Brazil and even agreed to lend his name to an endurance race that connected every state in the country. The Automobile Club and National Roads Congress organized the first Prova Presidente Getúlio Vargas for May 1939. Vargas also approved a special lottery to fund national road building and new tourist facilities, as well as a new national raceway for the capital. This federal funding helped to pay for motor sports and lent additional stature to racing. Soon, other cities throughout Brazil began work on major new raceways.

Vargas's support, the growth of the international grand prix circuit, and continued funding from car companies encouraged auto clubs throughout Brazil to sponsor new, grand prix–style races in their cities, particularly São Paulo and Porto Alegre. According to a U.S. consular official, more than 600,000 people attended the 1936 São Paulo Grand Prix. During the mid to late 1930s, racing became so popular in the region that it even spread to smaller cities throughout the state of São Paulo. The 1937 Campinas Grand Prix attracted 80,000 fans, and the resort town of Poços de Caldas saw more than 30,000 people turn out for a 50-lap race through its streets.[43] Vargas's promotion of racing, along with the work done by local auto clubs and the foreign car companies, deepened the growing culture of auto sport in Brazil. A U.S. consular official even reported on the new sport of children's racing in motorized toy cars on Rio's city streets: "The only difference between the Brazilians and ourselves is that they permit nine-year olds to drive in miniature cars in a restricted area whereas we license people who drive like nine-year olds to operate cars in public thoroughfares."[44] From children's races to regional contests to the Rio Grand Prix, auto racing captured the Brazilian imagination during the 1930s. Racing became so popular that advocates of a Brazilian manufactured car believed that auto sports would convince public and private interests to support such an industry.[45]

Vargas's support of tourism and motor sports helped push forward the broad tenets of automobility, but such cultural initiatives could accomplish only so much. Over the course of the 1930s, Vargas planned a system of highways that would tie together Brazil's massive national territory. In April 1931, he appointed José América de Almeida the head of a commission that would draft the first General Plan for National Transit. Almeida's commission presented Vargas with a plan to build highways that would connect Rio directly or indirectly with every state capital. Modern roads would also reach from the coast far into the interior, some all the way to the nation's borders.[46] The commission's plans would not be put into effect for several decades, but they were significant nonetheless. Such centralized control over road building represented a major advance in state making.

The establishment of a national highway system (or at least planning for such a system) necessitated the promulgation of unified rules of the road. In the late 1930s and early 1940s, Vargas used the power of the federal government to standardize and expand auto travel in Brazil by writing the first national traffic code. Politically, the new rules allowed Vargas to insert the national government directly in the affairs of cities and states. Practically, the traffic code was a direct response to the ongoing deterioration of life in the cities brought on by the highly disorganized nature of modern transit. Brazilian traffic seemed overly dangerous and chaotic even to those who were used to the tumult of large North American and European cities. When Rudyard Kipling visited São Paulo in 1927, the chaos in its streets and the failure of the authorities to even attempt to regulate it astonished him:

Cars and lorries move everywhere, like electrons in the physics primers.... Traffic—most of the inner streets are one-way—is regulated by policemen with truncheons and notebooks; by superior policeman with larger note-books and a fistful of reins, sitting on the wisest and stillest horses ever foaled; and super-policeman, with ledgers, I think, in charge of green-and-red light-towers. Having done all this they permit traffic to overtake on either side indifferently, and are astonished that the accident-rate does not go down.[47]

As bad as conditions were in metropolitan São Paulo, the city and the state had the most advanced system of auto registration and driver licensing in Brazil, and it had the nation's most detailed set of driving regulations.

The São Paulo government created a special transportation commission in 1934 to review and standardize all local traffic regulations. To further spur Paulista mobility, the state forbade individual municipalities from charging taxes or tolls on motorists passing through towns. With an effective and unified traffic code and no restrictions on travel, Paulista auto clubs and road associations were so proud of these accomplishments that they lobbied other state governments and the federal authorities to follow their lead.[48] When the Touring Club of Brazil, working closely with the federal ministries of justice and transportation, organized the First Transit Week for 23–30 April 1939, it took much of its inspiration from the Paulista experience and focused on the creation of standardized traffic regulations that would modernize transportation throughout Brazil and make its cities' streets safe for pedestrians. Delegates from throughout the country congregated in Rio to compare their states' traffic policies and to begin to craft a national set of standards. Officials from nearly every state spoke of the need to decrease traffic fatalities in the cities, particularly accidents between motor vehicles and pedestrians. Juvenil Murtinho Nobre, president of Touring Club do Brasil and the chair of the conference, noted that in addition to new ways of policing traffic and encouraging better circulation of vehicles in the cities, the gathered delegates should think about ways to create a new, "modern mentality" that would allow people and machines to coexist.[49] During the week of meetings and presentations, police from São Paulo demonstrated the latest traffic-control techniques in Rio's downtown and Largo da Lapa. According to statistics compiled soon afterward, the presence of Paulista police in their crisp uniforms and white pith helmets led to a marked decrease in the number of pedestrian injuries in Rio during their week in service.[50] At the meetings, delegates from São Paulo, Minas Gerais, and Rio Grande do Sul worked to draft a proposed national driving code. They argued for uniform license plates and drivers' licenses. These officials from Brazil's richest and most powerful states also suggested that the individual states should have the right to alter aspects of the national code to meet local conditions and so demonstrated the limits to their centralizing tendencies.[51]

The meetings fulfilled several long-held wishes of Brazilian auto enthusiasts and fit well with the philosophy and style of the Vargas dictatorship. Unlike previous roads congresses and other gatherings sponsored by the national and state auto clubs, Transit Week was not secretly underwritten by foreign car companies or held to get the attention of state authorities. This meeting was sponsored by two federal ministries (Transportation and Justice) and then coordinated by a civic organization (the Touring Club). Its aim was to bring together bureaucrats and police from all the states to craft a national response to the rapid expansion of motorized traffic in Brazil's cities and among its states. By the late 1930s, the presence of a centralizing and modernizing dictatorship finally facilitated the establishment of national policies for using automobiles. Indeed, the National Traffic Code (Decreto-Lei 3651), which Vargas finally decreed on 25 September 1941, was a curious mixture of central state control and broad-based policy making. At 70 pages, it covered all aspects of driving, from education and licensing to parking, road signs, and fines. The law explicitly stated that federal codes would always trump local measures and that cities and states were obligated to bring their traffic regulations into agreement with the new national regulations.[52] Unlike Vargas's labor legislation, which was both widely celebrated and largely ignored, the National Traffic Code's regulations were written in Rio and in fact implemented throughout Brazil.

Extending the federal government's reach into the interior of the nation had been part of Vargas's broad program since the 1930 revolution. In his New Year's Eve address at the end of 1937, Vargas announced the government's support for expanded colonization of the interior and the creation of modern transportation links with those vast lands to bring "the benefits civilization" to all Brazilians.[53] Encouraging such interior settlement, which quickly became known as the "March to the West" (*Marcha para o Oeste*), appealed to long-held ideas about Brazil's future resting with the successful development of its interior spaces.[54] Vargas encouraged the broad settlement of lands in what would become two distinct regions, the center-west (made up of the states of Goiás, Mato Grosso, Mato Grosso do Sul, and Tocantins) and the north (commonly referred to as the Amazon, including what would become the states of Acre, Amazonas, Amapá, Pará, Rondônia, and Roraima).[55] These regions were hardly empty spaces, having been occupied by Indians for thousands of years and by a diverse mix of migrants, runaway slaves, rubber tappers, and others over the course the preceding 400 years.[56] To make Brazil's interior as economically viable as the states of the center-south, especially São Paulo and Minas Gerais, Vargas would have to establish transportation networks that would tie the agriculturally productive parts of the west to interior cities and then connect those regions to São Paulo, Minas, Rio, and other coastal population centers. Beyond the two railroads serving the west from the center-south, however, most travel in the interior continued on colonial-era roads and paths, thus limiting the impact of the ambitious settlement program. Indeed, when an American businessman considered the ambitious goals of the March to the West, he concluded it would fail because there simply weren't roads on which to move people and goods in and out of the region.[57]

With the exception of the National Traffic Code, the first decade of Vargas's rule witnessed the encouragement of broad automobility without the establishment of concrete institutions that would expand actual auto ownership. The onset of World War II and Brazil's participation in it changed that. Brazil's close ties to the United States—the country sent troops to fight in Europe under American command—and the impact of the war itself on strategic planning and on everyday life brought new institutions and industries that helped lay the groundwork for the eventual creation of a national automobile industry and broad-based car ownership.[58] The first and by far the most significant industry spurred on by the war was the Companhia Siderúrgica Nacional (National Steel Company, or CSN), which Vargas created in 1941. A full decade earlier, Vargas as the then-provisional president, spoke forcefully of Brazil's need for a reliable supply of steel: "The biggest problem, one might say the basic problem of our economy, is steel. For Brazil, the steel age will mark the period of our economic opulence." Industrialists had long supported the idea of a domestic steel industry, and it fit in well with Vargas's nationalism and developmentalism, but it was the backing of the military and the coming of World War II that finally led to the building of large-scale production facilities in Volta Redonda, on an abandoned coffee plantation in the state of Rio de Janeiro.[59]

Although planned in strategic terms for the production of armaments and to supply existing industry, the steel mills of Volta Redonda provided a key ingredient for the eventual establishment of a domestic automobile industry. Few associated with the CSN openly spoke in such terms when the plant went into production in 1946, but many people tied to the project privately saw important linkages between Volta Redonda and national auto production (Figure 4.2). When the domestic auto industry began production in the mid to late 1950s, it became a key consumer of CSN steel.[60] Volta Redonda mirrored other aspects of automobility itself. Vargas both satisfied the military's demand that the facility be far from the coast for defense reasons and conciliated the competing interests of Paulista and Mineiro elites by choosing a location convenient to both but in neither state. He also fulfilled a basic tenet of Brazilian modernity, for the CSN brought the latest in industrial production and social relations to a long-decadent coffee region. If the personal mobility of travel into the interior fostered a cultural cannibalism, putting industrialism in a former coffee county would bring the economic modernization and social development implied in modernity.

In its design and operation, the city of Volta Redonda itself invoked automobility. As a state enterprise, the CSN had to embrace the paternalistic

FIGURE 4.2 Although cars remained the most exciting aspect of Brazilian automobility, city dwellers increasingly relied on bus transportation, as in this scene from São Paulo in 1947. Photo courtesy of the General Motors Corporation.

aspects of Vargas's labor legislation. In practice, living and work arrangements in the city went well beyond government policies and took on an openly Fordist orientation. Workers lived in new, specially designed, company-subsidized housing. The public schools were among the best in Brazil, and the city's workers and their children had access to a wide range of social services and recreation facilities. Its medical facilities were state of the art. All in all, Volta Redonda was an industrial, government-sponsored version of Fordlândia and Belterra. Although the rubber plantations and the steel town shared a Fordist conceit in how they organized their workers' lives, Volta Redonda was much more successful than Fordlândia and Belterra, and so it became a much more concrete symbol of the transformative power of automobility for Brazil.[61]

Brazil's wartime work further promoted its industrial development. In 1942, under the auspices of the Lend-Lease Program, the United States helped the Brazilian government establish the Fábrica Nacional de Motores (National Motors Factory, or FNM) in Rio de Janeiro. For strategic reasons, the U.S. military wanted to develop a supply of aircraft engines beyond American manufacturers. Producing 450-horsepower Wright engines fit in well with Brazil's unfolding nationalist developmentalism, especially given the nation's growing industrial base and its long interest in aviation (Figure 4.3). Although the plant did not produce engines in time for use in the war effort, it eventually manufactured trucks under a licensing agreement with Italy's Isotta-Fraschini. The FNM formally incorporated in 1948, with the government holding 99% of its stock. In 1948, it manufactured 50 trucks with at least 30% of their content made in Brazil, and some of their components were fashioned out of steel from Volta Redonda. The truck cabs where completely manufactured locally. When Isotta-Fraschini went bankrupt in 1951, the FNM signed an agreement with Alfa Romeo to build a new, more modern model of truck. Throughout its early years, the FNM emulated a Fordist enterprise as best it could, even maintaining its own farm to provide inexpensive foodstuffs for its employees.[62]

The war also brought about the local manufacture of an extremely important automotive component: the gasogene. This apparatus, which looked like a medium-sized metal trash can with tubes attached, usually fit on the back of an automobile (passenger cars, trucks, and buses) and produced gaseous fuel by partially burning wood, charcoal, peat, and other combustibles. Use of such alternative energy sources was forced on Brazil by the severe wartime gasoline rationing.[63] The situation was so dire in late 1944, for example, that São Paulo had less than a week of diesel fuel for trucks and buses in reserve.[64] The federal government had planned for

FIGURE 4.3 By 1950, the Rio to Bahia highway had reduced the time it took to move people and goods by land between Salvador and the national capital from two months to one week. Photo courtesy of the General Motors Corporation.

gasoline shortages by creating a national commission to study the production and use of gasogenes. The devices quickly became so important for maintaining Brazilian automobility during the war that in 1941 the São Paulo state government regulated the production and sale of the units to prevent price gouging. Slightly less than 10% of all vehicles nationwide used gasogenes during the war, but as many as half the trucks in São Paulo depended on the devices by late 1944.[65] Metalworking shops turned to their manufacture soon after the war began but could not meet the steadily increasing demand. Brazilian factories produced machines for use with foreign-made autos that freed drivers from dependence on oil and helped them maintain their way of life in the face of wartime shortages. Chico Landi's victory in 1944 at São Paulo's new grand prix circuit at Interlagos in a gasogene-powered Alfa Romeo deepened the pride Brazilians had in these locally produced appliances.[66] The rise of manufacturers such as Gasogênio Paulistano, among others, would also play an important role in the ongoing development of São Paulo's auto parts industry, which would soon help usher in the era of domestic vehicle manufacture.[67]

Although exigencies of wartime rationing led to reliance on the gasogene, its use also highlighted a structural weakness in Brazil's budding automobility: the absence of a dependable and affordable supply of oil.[68] As soon as cars, trucks, and buses started to fill the streets of Brazilian cities, the question of whether Brazil might have its own oil reserves loomed large. There was no particular evidence that the nation had oil, but the enormous size of the country and the fact that so little was known about whole regions, particularly the Amazon, led many to believe it must be there.[69] During the Estado Novo, Vargas created the National Petroleum Council to study government's role in regulating exploration and oil refining. Given the insignificant known reserves in Brazil and the revenue stream from taxes on imported oil, there was little incentive to create a state oil monopoly similar to Volta Redonda or even the National Motors Factory.[70] After wartime rationing and with steadily increasing imports of foreign oil, Brazilian consumers used the now open political system to demand that the government do something to guarantee the free flow of affordable gasoline. The administration of President Eurico Gaspar Dutra (1946–1951) faced increasingly vocal calls to take some action to protect the nation from the power of American and British oil companies.[71] Military officers played an important role in debating how the state's role in the economy—this time regarding the exploration, refining, and distribution of oil—affected national security. In April 1947, generals Juarez Távora and Horta Barbosa debated whether the government should limit the role of foreign capital in the oil sector. Barbosa's nationalist position prevailed politically. When Vargas ran for president in 1950, he embraced the popular "The Oil Is Ours" campaign and promised he would restrict foreign activity in the oil sector.[72]

Despite a small 1939 find near Salvador da Bahia, Brazil had no significant known oil reserves when Vargas was elected president in 1950. With a steadily increasing number of cars, trucks, and buses being imported in the aftermath of the war, and with the promise of at least some domestic vehicle manufacture by the FNM, Brazilians worried that oil shortages could derail their national progress. General Arthur Levy expressed this anxiety when he said, "Energy is the motor of development and it is the heart of the national organism and therefore should be [Brazilian]. No one lives with a borrowed heart!"[73] Such views led to a remarkably broad political consensus on behalf of forming a national oil monopoly. Vargas submitted legislation in December 1951 that would have allowed national and foreign capital to combine for some projects, but members of Congress from practically every political party gave the government even more control of private capital.[74] The legislation creating the national oil company, Petrobras, became law in October 1953.[75]

During the first decade after its founding, Petrobras navigated complex politics and changing administrations to become perhaps the second most important component of the government during the 1964–1985 military dictatorship, after the military itself.[76] Vargas had envisioned it as a tool of nationalist development, but it instead became a symbol of nationalism itself. With steel produced at Volta Redonda, trucks from the National Motors Factory, and oil supplied by Petrobras, Brazil had created a great deal of economic integration and could fully embrace the transformative power of automobility. Although the nation lacked an effective network of roads, let alone highways, and the FNM produced few trucks and Petrobras little domestic oil, the nation seemed to have reached the point from which its progress was assured. Given the flurry of activity, Brazilians began to believe that automobility would no longer be tied to dependence on foreign corporations. In addition to having the tools to unify and transform the nation, Brazilians would become truly modern through Brazilian means.

At the same time, the Brazilian and U.S. governments were studying the state of the Brazilian economy and ways to move it forward. The Joint Brazil–United States Economic Development Commission balanced Vargas's nationalism with the North American interest in deepening trade relations with Latin America's largest country. The commission analyzed ways to stem Brazilian inflation, improve its balance of payments, and physically facilitate more trade between the two nations by upgrading local transportation networks.[77] Brazilians focused more on the commission's findings that their nation had made significant strides industrially and had a large and expanding market for consumer goods. They also no doubt noted the report's calls for improved generation of electricity and improved and expanded highways.[78] (See Figure 4.4.) The joint commission provided a template for part of the development program that Vargas had been creating in fits and starts since first coming to power in 1930. Almost a quarter of a century after the revolution of 1930, Brazil seemed to be on the path laid out by modernist intellectuals and auto enthusiasts beginning in the 1910s and 1920s. The most optimistic view of Brazil's situation was of a nation that would be increasingly physically integrated and that would have flourishing agriculture and industry.

Vargas, however, knew better. Although he had done a great deal to further the causes of national economic integration and development, and

FIGURE 4.4 Before the bridge over the Paraguaçu River in Bahia was completed, vehicles were ferried over the water. The expansion of bus travel in the 1950s accelerated internal migration, especially from the northeast to the center-south. Photo courtesy of the General Motors Corporation.

even been a major proponent of automobility, Vargas's accomplishments did not go beyond creating the political, economic, and cultural infrastructure for a budding sense of developmentalism. He also succeeded in dramatically increasing popular expectations about Brazil's future. His program of national political and economic integration was not just supposed to free Brazil from the vicissitudes of export boom-and-bust cycles; it was to make Brazil a powerful nation. But the capital requirements and high levels of technological knowledge necessary to produce steel, explore for and refine oil, and manufacture automobiles forced a new sort of dependence on Brazil. The untenable compromise between nationalist state enterprises and reliance on foreign corporations weighed heavily on Vargas and combined with a series of political scandals to exhaust him. He famously commented on his deteriorating political position: "I have the feeling I am standing in a sea of mud."[79] After dominating Brazilian politics for close to a quarter of a century, the many contradictions of his politics weighed heavily on Vargas. He committed suicide in the Presidential Catete Palace on 24 August 1954.

Vargas left a politically charged suicide note that laid responsibility for nearly all of Brazil's problems on foreign powers—public and private—that would not countenance the independent path he set for the Brazilian people. He wrote, in part, "After decades of domination and plunder on the part of international economic and financial groups, I placed myself at the head of a revolution and won.... I wished to bring national freedom in the use of our resources by means of Petrobras; this had hardly begun to operate when the wave of agitation swelled.... They do not want the Brazilian people to be free."[80] It was not foreign intrigue or intransigence that was causing Brazil's political and economic troubles in the early 1950s. At best, the Vargas years had only begun the process of making Brazil less vulnerable to the swings of the international economy or less dependent on foreign trade. At their worst, Vargas's policies altered the ways Brazil remained a part of the world economy and ultimately made the nation even more dependent on foreign automobile and oil companies.

CHAPTER 5 | # The Multinational Solution: Juscelino Kubitschek and the National Auto Industry

JUSCELINO KUBITSCHEK TRAVELED THROUGHOUT Brazil during his 1955 campaign for the presidency. He wanted to see and be seen in as many different parts of the nation as possible. Whereas previous presidential candidates had achieved geographical unity by picking a running mate from a distant region—usually a political leader from the northeast—Kubitschek, who was widely referred to as "JK," logged some 205,307 kilometers during the campaign, using planes, trains, and automobiles—or river launches and horses where modern forms of transportation were unavailable.[1] In his memoirs, Kubitschek wrote that his platform and then the policies he promoted as president were developed out of this experience of traveling throughout Brazil and listening to its people. JK's own first-hand knowledge of Brazil's poorly developed infrastructure confirmed the comments he heard from people throughout the nation. As a presidential candidate, he realized that only a program of massive public works projects to push forward industrialization and national unity could make Brazil modern. He summarized his vision with the slogan Fifty Years of Progress in Five.[2]

Automobility was central to achieving such progress. In his five years in office (1956–1961), Kubitschek oversaw the creation of a domestic automobile industry through the broad entry of foreign investment, the building of highways that connected distant regions, and the construction of Brasília, the car-dependent, modernist national capital in the interior. Every aspect of this program had deep roots in the national psyche and

Kubitschek's personal experiences. The new president, born in 1902, had grown up in Minas Gerais in an era of economic development and technological innovation. As a young man, JK worked as a telegraph operator to pay for medical school. He later practiced medicine and then traveled to Europe for advanced study in urology. While abroad, Kubitschek began to see the impact of modern technology and economic development on other societies. These experiences, along with his interest in modern medicine, led JK to believe that public and private interests would have to consciously set about transforming Brazil—physically and economically—for its people to become citizens in a modern, capitalist democracy.

The Vargas era had left Brazil with the economic and political infrastructure for the ongoing industrialization of the nation. The 1930s and 1940s had also been an era of expanded automobility and plans for even greater reliance on cars, trucks, and buses for Brazil's ongoing development. Vargas attempted to solve the social question of broad popular incorporation within the polity through state institutions. His suicide marked the end of such top-down attempts to bring the disenfranchised into the system through controlled inclusion in state-sponsored entities. Rather than tamp down Brazilians' dreams of industrialization, democracy, and development, JK fueled the national desire to become modern. He expanded on the existing framework for increased automobility (Volta Redonda, Petrobras, the recommendations of the Joint U.S.–Brazil Economic Development Commission) and tapped into Brazilians' aspirations for consumer goods, such as cars, in crafting his program of "Fifty Years of Progress in Five." He attempted to use a development program to unify the nation physically and culturally and to modernize the economy. In doing so, he sought to foster democracy for the first time in Brazil's history. Kubitschek's program went far beyond a simple attack on existing economic and structural bottlenecks to industrial development. JK attempted to implement a democratic revolution in Brazil without the associated social conflict endemic to such a late form of broad political incorporation. He used developmentalist projects in lieu of immediate political incorporation, hoping that the social and economic transformations brought about—in this case, the creation of a middle class—would smooth the transition to broad electoral participation. Kubitschek hoped to foster such change by altering the nation's spatial, consumptive, and social arrangements. That is, he attempted to radically, but peacefully, transform Brazilian society.

Kubitscheck was a charismatic politician with broad popular appeal. As the mayor of Belo Horizonte and then governor of Minas Gerais, JK used modern planning to expand the generation and distribution of electricity and the building of roads. He even teamed with architect Oscar Niemeyer to create a modern new neighborhood in Belo Horizonte. Kubitschek, perhaps more than any leading Brazilian politician before him, rejected the tenets of laissez-faire capitalism and instead embraced the idea of using the state to plan the development of the nation. After his experiences as mayor of Belo Horizonte, JK commented, "The mayor's office...served to consolidate my belief in planned action, in a Program.... In five years the Minas capital had fifty years of progress."[3] Beyond the broad calls for progress and deepening industrialization, JK's presidential campaign promised to promote automobility. One of his frequent slogans on the campaign trail was More Energy, More Roads! This slogan, like most of Kubitschek's platform, resonated with Brazilians' views of their nation's needs.[4]

Public opinion polling conducted by IBOPE (Brazilian Institute of Public Opinion and Statistics) found that Brazilians of all social classes wanted their government to address the nation's problematic infrastructure. A 1950 study done in Rio Grande do Sul found that the single most important thing the government could do to improve the state was build more roads. Transportation, electrification, and road construction were among the state's residents' most pressing concerns.[5] A nationwide survey in 1951 that focused on transportation issues found that most respondents wanted the government to build roads and facilitate private auto ownership and use. Urban Brazilians, who were more likely to be polled by IBOPE researchers, registered their belief that cars in Brazil were overpriced and that something should be done to rein in the auto companies' excessive profits. Curiously, another survey found that most people thought that luxury car owners (specifically Cadillac drivers) had worked hard and earned and deserved their expensive vehicles.[6] These surveys seemed to indicate that Brazilians wanted government action to make autos more affordable so that hard work and savings could be rewarded through car ownership. Moreover, despite the nationalist rhetoric of the Vargas years and the pride so many had in both the National Motors Factory and the newly founded Petrobras, Brazilians in 1951 and 1952 broadly supported the entrance of foreign companies to help develop the nation. Slightly more than 60% of Cariocas wanted Volkswagen to come to Brazil to build passenger cars (17.2% opposed and 22.2% had no opinion) and an even broader majority (67%) were in favor of U.S. experts and executives coming to Brazil to advance industrialization and modernize agriculture.[7] Brazilians also wanted state work to improve the nation's roads. Sizable numbers of Brazilians held these views in the early 1950s because so many of them had experienced some aspect of automobility. In addition to the constant barrage of car ads they had seen since the 1920s and the rise of auto sports during the 1930s and 1940s, Brazilians were also increasingly traveling to other parts of the country by bus. Although they preferred almost every other form of travel, most Cariocas of all social classes had taken a bus trip to another city by 1951. Indeed, elites relied on intercity bus travel much more than members of any other social class in the early 1950s.[8]

Media reports, like these IBOPE polls, reflected the broad interest Brazilians had in expanding automobility in the early to mid-1950s. The popular newsmagazine *Cruzeiro* commented in a 1953 story that "Brazilians, in general, are divided into two classes: those who *have* a car and those who *want* to have a car." Auto ownership was increasingly listed as one of Brazilians' most frequently registered material aspirations.[9] Brazilians also had a clear preference for American cars. Paulistanos frequently noted their desire to own Chevies and Fords; Cariocas nearly obsessed about the possibility of driving a Cadillac. This fascination with the American luxury brand became known as *cadilaquismo*, and those lucky enough to own the cars were referred to simply as *cadilaquenos*.[10] Beyond their preference for American autos, Brazilians were poised in the mid-1950s to double the nation's purchases of new cars, and the used car market boomed. Although most people focused on buying their own car, urban planners and politicians took note of the nation's need for better highways, the expanded use of trucks and buses for intercity travel, and improved public transportation.[11]

After his long campaign of traveling throughout Brazil and with access to polls showing what the electorate expected of him, Kubitschek was well attuned to people's desires for broad economic development, especially an expansion of automobility. He therefore wasted little time in unveiling the Targets Plan (*Programa de Metas*) that detailed the specific goals that would produce his promised rapid progress. On his first day in office, at 7:00 A.M., Kubitschek met with his cabinet to begin work on formalizing his development proposals. Also on the first day of February 1956, JK created the Development Council to coordinate planning.[12] The Targets Plan expanded on the basic findings of the Joint Brazil–U.S. Economic Development Commission by focusing on bottlenecks in industrial production and transportation and by adding a few key programs that spoke to Brazilian aspirations. In all, there were 30 numbered targets broken down into five sectors (Energy, Transportation, Food, Basic Industries, and Education). Only one concerned a consumer good. Target 27, "The Automobile Industry," called for the manufacture of 170,000 Brazilian vehicles by 1960. The others called for increased rubber production (Target 25), the construction of cold storage warehouses (15), and increases in cement (22) and alkali (23) production. The building of a new, interior capital was listed as a "synthesis goal."[13]

Planning for the creation of the national automobile industry began almost immediately and became the template for work on the other targets. Kubitschek reorganized the working group of advisors on automobiles into the Executive Group on the Automobile Industry (*Grupo Executivo da Indústria Automobilística*, or GEIA). Lucas Lopes, who served as the general secretary of the government's Development Council, told Kubitschek that the GEIA had to act decisively because the market alone would not find "a solution to the automobile problem."[14] The final proposal called for a combination of financial incentives to encourage foreign manufacturers to move production to Brazil. Those companies that did not avail themselves of these incentives faced financial penalties and steep import tariffs on foreign-made vehicles.[15] Manufacturers would continue to receive favorable tariff and sales tax treatment if they managed to shift production to Brazil by 1960. Specifically, they operated under a schedule that called for at least 90% domestic content of autos by July 1, 1960.[16] Initially, GEIA officials emphasized truck and bus construction. A great deal of cargo and tens of thousands of Brazilians already relied on such vehicles for transportation, and a flourishing industry already produced truck and bus bodies. Moreover, production of passenger cars was more complicated, for Brazilian autos would have to compete in terms of styling, features, and reliability with the foreign-made vehicles that had recently been imported.

Ford and General Motors, the dominant foreign manufacturers already in Brazil, quickly shifted to production of trucks and buses in their newly expanded São Paulo facilities (figures 5.1 and 5.2). They did so in response to the findings of the Joint Brazil–U.S. Commission that had called for improved transportation networks to facilitate trade. Ford and GM resisted manufacturing cars in Brazil because they considered that market to be too small. Spokesmen from both companies publicly extolled Kubitschek's program. Ford responded to the GEIA guidelines by submitting a proposal in January 1957 to expand its truck manufacturing by using a recently opened assembly line, in addition to a planned foundry, engine factory, stamping plant, engineering office, and testing grounds. General Motors followed suit and proposed building two truck models with 90% Brazilian content. Mercedes-Benz was soon producing one bus and two truck models in new Brazilian facilities.[17] Ford and GM's decisions to forgo car manufacture, because of the large additional capital such new factories would require and their belief that the Brazilian passenger car market could not

FIGURE 5.1 Juscelino Kubitschek inaugurates Ford's light truck production in São Paulo, 1957. Photo courtesy of the Arquivo Nacional do Brasil.

FIGURE 5.2 Ford light truck factory in October 1957. Photo courtesy of the Arquivo Nacional do Brasil.

sustain local production, surprised many in Brazil and ultimately hurt these two American companies in the 1960s and beyond, when they did build passenger cars in plants in São Paulo. Their miscalculations may have damaged their status in Brazil, but they benefited and deepened the sense of change ushered in by Kubitschek's developmentalism, for new foreign corporations from the United States and Europe would soon redefine Brazilian automobility.[18]

Germany's Volkswagen and America's Kaiser Industries quickly filled the void left by Ford's and GM's reticence. In fact, Henry Kaiser almost immediately took over as Brazil's most vocal foreign proponent of Fordism. Kaiser Industries had prospered during the 1930s and 1940s by building construction projects for FDR's New Deal and victory ships and jeeps for the Allied war effort. In addition to aluminum production and the eventual creation of the first HMO (Kaiser-Permanente), Kaiser Industries owned Willys-Overland Motors, which produced cars, trucks, and, jeeps in Toledo, Ohio. With declining Jeep sales after the war and ongoing problems with the Kaiser-Frazer line of automobiles, Kaiser looked to reduce costs by locating new production facilities in Latin America.[19] In August 1954, Henry Kaiser traveled to Argentina, Colombia, Ecuador, Mexico, Peru, and Brazil to discuss the importance of local automobile production and the benefits Willys-Overland could bring to Latin America. In his speech to São Paulo's industrialists, Kaiser argued that Brazil would advance as a nation only by expanding its highway system and establishing an automotive industry. These developments could take place only if they were broad based, with roads throughout the nation and autos owned by as many Brazilians as possible. Echoing Henry Ford, Kaiser noted that "mass consumption cannot exist without mass purchasing power...without high consumption on the part of the people."[20] Kaiser noted that "the United States, when it finished its expansion in the West, began to build its industrial base," and that Brazil was a "new frontier" that would soon make its leap to a new level of industrial development. After meeting with Getúlio Vargas, Kaiser told the Brazilian press that if he manufactured automobiles in their country, he would do so not only for domestic consumption but also for export to the United States.[21]

Kaiser and his advisors closely studied the Brazilian situation and took note of the nation's long-held interest in having its own automotive industry. When speaking to Brazilian audiences, he invoked familiar themes of national development.[22] Kaiser's primary interest in establishing manufacturing facilities in Brazil, however, was his company's falling rate of profit at home. After reviewing São Paulo's impressive industrial base and skilled workforce, he decided he could eventually transfer production to Brazil as a lower cost country. No matter what Kaiser's motives may have been, members of Brazil's National Confederation of Industries heartily welcomed this proposal to manufacture autos not only for local consumption but also for export to the American market.[23] Neither Ford nor General Motors faced Kaiser's problems in the United States and so had no incentive to move large-scale production facilities to Brazil. Instead, they promised the Brazilian government they would expand truck manufacture there while continuing to assemble cars produced in American factories.[24] Volkswagen, like Ford and GM, at first had little interest in opening large-scale manufacturing facilities in Brazil and instead simply wanted to reassemble vehicles built in Germany. Volkswagen agreed to manufacture a full line of automobiles only after reviewing the economic incentives offered by the Kubitschek administration and the disincentives to continued imports established by the GEIA.[25]

Kaiser Industries immediately took advantage of the financing facilities made available by the Kubitschek government. Kaiser proposed building a forge, foundry, engine plant, stamping facilities, and an assembly line. The company's initial goal was an output of 30,000 Jeeps and station wagons and 10,000 sedans per year. In addition to the 40,000 engines for these vehicles, Willys-Overland do Brasil (WOB) would manufacture another 40,000 for commercial sales and replacements. While Kaiser Industries was exporting old factory equipment for antiquated models to its subsidiary in Argentina, the company planned to build a modern, efficient auto industry in Brazil from the ground up in 14 to 20 months.[26] These new facilities were in addition to WOB's existing factory that reassembled Jeeps produced in the United States. As the company opened new manufacturing facilities in Brazil and built close ties to domestic auto parts firms, the percentage of Brazilian-made content of WOB's Jeeps steadily climbed.[27] In its formal proposal to the GEIA, Willys argued that "any passenger vehicle of modern design, made in Brazil, which is sold at reasonable prices, should have no trouble becoming established in Brazil." It further noted that although there was only one car for every 71 Brazilians, well-priced, high-quality autos could eventually get Brazil to the U.S. ratio of one car per every three Americans.[28]

Even before its new factories produced locally manufactured autos, Willys's cars became the most popular sold in Brazil. Internal company documents noted that the market was ready for these cars, because "Brazilians are very style conscious and strongly favor American products."[29] Sales spiked in 1954 as Brazilians embraced the foreign company that had most enthusiastically taken up domestic production. In addition to stoking national pride, WOB also provided a unique mix of autos that met a broad range of Brazilian tastes and needs. Jeeps and the Rural Willys were marketed as made completely in Brazil for Brazil's challenging terrain. Ads in *Cruzeiro* magazine for the Rural Willys read, "For the first time, a car is sold in Brazil, specially designed for our country and produced in Brazil."[30] The company's sedans included the Brazilian version of the its Aero-Willys, which it marketed as the Itamaraty and the Executivo, and a Renault Dauphine built under license in Brazil.[31] The Dauphine was smaller and less expensive than Willys's other sedans. An internal Kaiser Industries report justifying the deal with Renault argued that "the production of a good small car, saleable at a price within the reach of the growing middle class, is good for Brazil and therefore for the company."[32] Willys marketed its diverse lineup of autos by working closely with the family of Oswaldo Aranha, Vargas's former foreign minister and closest advisor, which had a broad network of dealerships in place throughout the country. With its good mix of products and its dealership network, Willys-Overland do Brasil accounted for 24% of the vehicles of all types—and 52% of cars—produced in 1959.[33]

Volkswagen had first incorporated in Brazil in 1953, with the sole purpose of importing CKDs built in Germany and reassembling them in a plant in Ipiranga, São Paulo. By mid-1957, VW began manufacturing in its new factory in São Paulo's industrial suburb, São Bernardo do Campo. At first, the company built only Kombi vans, but it soon expanded to the VW-1200,[34] which quickly became known as the Fusca.[35] Both the Kombi and the Fusca became ubiquitous in Brazil and soon were manufactured with more than 95% Brazilian-made content. By 1961, Volkswagen was selling more Brazilian-made vehicles than any other manufacturer, including Willys-Overland do Brasil.[36] Although VW and WOB dominated the passenger car business in the late 1950s and early 1960s, a number of other companies manufactured a broad range of automobiles. Germany's DKW formed a joint venture with a Brazilian company known as Vemag (Veículos e Máquinas Agrícolas, S.A.), which had been the local distributor for Studebakers, Packards, and several American tractor manufacturers, to build small sedans, station wagons, and jeeps. The National Motors Factory (FNM) moved beyond trucks by licensing several Fiat-designed cars and the French Simca-Chambord sedan for production in Brazil. In 1960, it launched the JK-2000 compact sedan as an homage to the outgoing president who had installed the national auto industry.[37]

Even though Ford and GM initially focused only on trucks, they, too, dramatically expanded their production facilities in Brazil. Ford built a foundry in Osasco and an engine factory in São Paulo. Although Ford was convinced that it could produce autos more efficiently in its existing U.S. factories and that those vehicles would be more affordable for Brazilians, the company knew that it could not ignore the politics of industrialization. Chairman Henry Ford II told an audience in Dearborn after visiting Brazil and meeting with Kubitschek that "if we want to share in those [Latin American] markets, rich and vast as they will some day surely be ... we are going to have to go in with our capital and tools and know-how and then get the things they want."[38] General Motors opened an advanced die-casting foundry in São Caetano do Sul in 1950. At first, it primarily supplied components for refrigerators sold by the company's Frigidaire division. It later built truck bodies for GM's São José dos Campos factory.[39]

Although the FNM continued to build trucks in its plant near Rio, the vast majority of new factories in the auto sector were opened in the once rural suburbs ringing São Paulo, in São Bernardo do Campo, São Caetano do Sul, and Diadema south of the city and in Osasco to the north.[40] The massive foundries, forges, engine plants, and assembly lines built by the foreign auto companies were the most obvious signs of the growth of this new industrial sector, but growth by auto parts suppliers also had a profound impact on São Paulo. In 1956, IBOPE polled a group of foreign auto company executives and found a deep and growing demand for a wide variety of auto parts. During the decade of the 1950s, the number and size of auto parts suppliers grew steadily. In 1953, for example, Ford trucks used about 2,000 Brazilian-made parts, and by 1958 the company reported that it used more than 3,000 such components. Willys reported similarly impressive growth in the use of Brazilian-made auto parts throughout its vehicle line. The foreign auto companies also spurred the manufacture of new products, such as shatter-resistant glass for windshields. Auto parts manufacturers expanded existing facilities and opened new factories in and around São Paulo that employed a steadily increasing number of workers at highly competitive wages, although still less than workers in the foreign auto plants earned.[41]

The opening of any sort of auto factory was a very public event celebrated in the press. Kubitschek arrived at the opening of a new Willys transmission plant in one of the company's Jeeps. He spoke of how autos were unifying the nation and revealing its great potential. The president said the country would one day soon have cars for all its citizens so that they could move off the coast to settle the nation's massive interior spaces. He concluded his speech: "We must overcome skepticism and negativism, for we are vigorously moving toward the future. Within five years, Brazil will be a great nation; and within twenty years one of the great powers of the world." In a speech opening a new General Motors plant in São José dos Campos, JK declared that cars were the primary factor in the struggle to achieve fifty years of progress in five. The president never hesitated to praise the efforts of the foreign auto companies in transforming the nation. At the opening of that WOB transmission factory, he said: "Willys-Overland is giving admirable examples to Brazil of what this nation can accomplish through the strength and temperament of its sons and through the intelligence of its workers."[42] Other political leaders used factory openings to celebrate the transformation they hoped autos would bring to Brazil. Minister of Transportation Lúcio Meira and 600 invited guests opened a Scania-Vabis diesel engine plant in May 1959. Members of Congress also toured new plants, as did visiting dignitaries such as United Nations Secretary General Dag Hammarskjöld and Mexican president Adolfo López Mateos, which lent an air of international approval to Kubitschek's program.[43]

After the Mexican leader visited the São Bernardo do Campo factory, WOB presented him with a Rural Willys. It was a symbolic gift, because the Brazilian auto industry sought to export its products as well as meet local demand. So, when Chile imported Brazilian Jeeps, the press noted that the auto industry was not only transforming the nation but also differentiating it from the rest of Latin America. Manuel Prado, the president of Peru, made similar comments when he visited the WOB plant and drove in Brazilian-made vehicles during his state visit.[44] The Brazilian government eagerly sought such exports and supported them financially. Not only did the prospect of exporting autos promise to reverse the balance of payments problems that importing cars and other vehicles had caused in the late 1940s and early 1950s but also it elevated Brazil's status in the world. Throughout the twentieth century, automobility had been seen as a tool for unifying Brazil so that the nation could finally meet its great potential (Figure 5.3). Exporting autos, as opposed to coffee and other agricultural products, signaled that perhaps Brazil was reaching its potential even before the interior had been settled and transformed through automobility.[45]

The changes ushered in by the auto industry were broad. Willys opened an engineering center in São Paulo for design work on future models. The other foreign companies soon built their own facilities. These companies also introduced modern planning and accounting divisions and imported the latest computers from IBM to handle administrative tasks.[46] In addition to transforming São Paulo's businesses through contracts and other contact with thousands of local companies, the auto manufacturers also brought real change to other regions. Farmers first gained access to Jeeps

FIGURE 5.3 Studebaker emphasized national unification in its sales practices, including this standard map of Brazil in its showrooms. Photo courtesy of the Studebaker National Museum and Library.

through Ministry of Agriculture subsidies that made them available at cost. Willys continued to work with the government throughout the 1950s to market its autos to farmers and other interior folk. The company actively marketed the Jeep and Rural Willys as perfect for "today's *bandeirantes*," given their toughness and ability to handle Brazil's nearly inaccessible interior.[47] The company also built a second assembly plant in the early 1960s in the northeastern state of Pernambuco specifically for Jeeps and Rural Willys. It sought to counter recent plant expansions by General Motors and Volkswagen and to promote the use of its vehicles throughout the nation, especially in the impoverished northeast.[48]

The physical unification and transformation of the nation had been a central tenet of automobility since at least the 1920s. The dominance of Ford and General Motors for so many years had also tied automobility to American notions of consumerism, the middle class, and even democracy. Yet even with the modern system of financing they introduced in the 1920s, cars, from Model Ts and Chevys to Lincolns and Cadillacs, remained elite possessions. In the late 1950s, Willys and Volkswagen both created extensive credit facilities to make their vehicles more affordable to a steadily increasing number of Brazilians, putting cars within reach of the middle class for the first time in Brazilian history.[49] Auto companies' advertising campaigns, in turn, promoted the theme of broad-based consumerism. One DKW-Vemag ad showed a boy taking a picture of his parents, brother, and cocker spaniel by their station wagon parked in the driveway of their ranch house. Another depicted a family packing up the car for a picnic and included the tag line, "It's a beautiful scene to see!" These very American settings were sold to Brazilians as the pinnacle of modern consumerism even by a German manufacturer that had no presence in the United States. Volkswagen marketed its Kombi van as the ideal family vehicle for doing the shopping, as well as going camping.[50]

With the large-scale entry of foreign auto companies in the 1950s, especially the prominent role played by Willys-Overland do Brasil, ideas about the social and political transformations related to the production and ownership of cars spread. These companies, however, had to balance the positive aspects of their status as foreign—particularly in how they represented American notions of consumerism and a middle-class lifestyle—with Brazilian nationalist pride in their burgeoning domestic industry.[51] Willys managed this contradiction by marketing itself as a separate, Brazilian company and not a foreign subsidiary of Kaiser Industries. First and foremost, WOB did this by selling equity in the company to Brazilians. Even though a close reading of internal Kaiser Industries documents reveals that this was a public relations fiction that also aided Kaiser's domestic balance sheet, Brazilians took great pride in their ability to own a part of a national auto producer. At first, shares were distributed to a few powerful bankers and politicians through Oswaldo Aranha's son Vavau, who was the president of Willys-Overland do Brasil. Kaiser quickly realized that he could take advantage of spreading Brazilian nationalism by selling as much as a 50% stake in the Brazilian operation to Brazilians, and so by the early 1960s, there were more than 50,000 individual Brazilian investors in Willys-Overland do Brasil. Kaiser even provided 10% discounts on new car purchases to shareholders. In a 1961 company publication highlighting its Brazilian ownership, WOB included photos of nine shareholders, including a student, machinist, dentist, barber, civil engineer, and military man, among others. In addition to stoking nationalist pride and encouraging shareholders to buy the company's cars, there was one additional benefit to this scheme: As a Brazilian-owned company, Willys could receive government loans for factory expansion, worker training, and other programs.[52] The stock offering also allowed the company to present itself as Brazilian.

In internal corporate documents, Willys management noted that it was well positioned on the issue of economic nationalism and that the company should support Petrobras in the face of foreign, primarily American, criticism of the state oil monopoly. Indeed, when Chrysler Motors considered licensing several models for production by WOB, it did so because Willys "was publicly identified in Brazil as a Brazilian company."[53]

To succeed, Kubitschek's developmentalism had to maintain a careful balance between promoting the fortunes of the foreign auto companies and nurturing the strong sense of economic nationalism first fostered by Vargas and expressed through public support for Volta Redonda and Petrobras. Although JK, Brazilian industrialists, and the public at large all viewed the auto sector through the lenses of economic development and national pride, the foreign corporations focused on profits. At first, they even sought to import components because they were so dissatisfied with locally made auto parts.[54] Ford and GM had long ago learned to market their products and even their presence in ways that stoked nationalist pride; Willys, VW, and the other new auto companies quickly learned the value of such practices.

Over the course of the 1950s, Brazilians became more and more comfortable about buying cars produced by Brazilian workers in the foreign-owned auto factories, and they increasingly saw this industry as their own. At this time, Ford put more Brazilians in visible management positions (Figure 5.2), and WOB's leadership appeared to be under local control, even though in reality they reported directly to Kaiser corporate headquarters in Oakland, California.[55] The auto industry also focused its marketing on nationalist themes of economic development. As they always had, the car companies emphasized the role autos would play in the physical unification of the nation. During the Kubitschek years, these companies broadened their appeal by focusing their advertising on the idea that Brazil had entered a new era of dynamism and optimism brought on by the achievements of the Targets Program. General Motors explicitly marketed the idea of autos ushering in a better age for Brazil with the slogan Tomorrow's World Begins Today. The success of the auto industry even became a focal point for advertisements for all sorts of consumer goods, from radios to toothpaste.[56] Increasingly, the auto industry seemed to hold out the real possibility that Brazil was on the cusp of becoming, if not an equal to the United States in terms of industrialization, at least a nation more advanced than the rest of Latin America. São Paulo was finally becoming the "new Detroit" that modernists had imagined in the 1920s.[57]

Perhaps the most profound change the auto companies brought to Brazil was the creation of a new working class. Brazilian elites had long been concerned by the racial makeup of the majority of the population. Their view that people of color were not only inferior to whites of European heritage—hardly a unique perspective in the nineteenth and much of the twentieth centuries—but also the central cause of Brazil's status as a nondeveloped country led to a wide variety of policy initiatives, from subsidized European immigration to a broad embrace of eugenics.[58] At first, the rise of industry in São Paulo held out hope for elites who believed that European immigrants and their families working in factories would be a recognizable part of a civilized society, unlike the "superstitious" interior folk of the Canudos and Contestado uprisings. But years of strikes and other industrial actions challenged the validity of this facile urban-rural divide for many elites. Despite repression and some minor attempts at co-optation by industrialists and state intervention in the unions beginning in the 1930s, industrial workers in São Paulo and other major cities continued to launch increasingly disruptive strikes.

With the resumption of at least nominally civilian rule after the 1945 ouster of Getúlio Vargas, São Paulo's industrial workers increasingly used illegal strikes and direct negotiations with employers to increase their wages and improve conditions at work. The strikes were often broad, public events that shut down the city for weeks at a time. Not only did they violate the letter and spirit of Brazil's labor code, which forbade strikes and called for wage and other industrial disputes to be settled through state-sponsored mediation in labor courts, but also the strikes shook Brazilians' faith in the power of modern industry to transform workers into orderly and productive citizens. Strikers often took to the streets, marching through São Paulo's city center, where they might clash with police. Other worker uprisings involved the destruction of buses and trolleys in São Paulo and Rio. Politicians, business leaders, and many in the urban middle class were further put off by the fact that so many of the industrial strikes in São Paulo were openly led by women workers from the city's textile mills. In the years immediately preceding the establishment of the national automobile industry, gender anxieties had joined fears about class and race in shaking many Brazilians' faith in the positive power of modern industry to transform poor Brazilians into what they considered to be responsible citizens.[59]

The auto industry seemed to offer a way out of this predicament. Extensive training of people with little or no previous factory experience, high industrial wages, and far-reaching benefits packages would give the foreign auto companies the opportunity to create new, modern Brazilians who would embrace the ideals of hard work, loyalty to their employers, and consumerism. Unlike work in the nation's textile factories or nationally owned metalworking shops, laboring in the auto plants brought Brazilians into contact with the latest industrial equipment. Brazilian autoworkers were no longer relegated to only reassembling cars built abroad and shipped as CKD units. The auto companies sent foremen abroad for training not only on the latest machines but also in worker management. The foreign manufacturers coordinated some industrial training with SENAI, the National Service for Industrial Training, but mostly relied on their own experiences in the United States and Europe for molding workers.[60]

The foreign auto companies initially worried that although wages were low in Brazil, so was productivity, thus making the cost of labor potentially higher there than in U.S. and European factories. The auto companies therefore established elaborate training programs for everything from work in foundries and on the engine assembly line to secretarial duties in accounting and other offices. Ford expanded its existing training programs and included a special literacy program and even English lessons. Ford technicians from the United States set up courses for instruction in specialized areas in the factories. The company provided this training for both employees already working in the assembly facilities and for new hires.[61] Willys quickly created a comprehensive education program for workers in all its factories. Classes were kept to 15 or fewer students. Formal instruction took place in classrooms near the shop floor, and then the new employees received hands-on training in the factories. Willys also provided literacy and other instruction because so many of its workers were new to the industrial sector and had had little formal education before arriving at the plant. At Willys, men made up the vast majority of factory workers; women were trained to do clerical work.[62]

Underlying the rhetoric about the transformative power of work in the auto factories were the highest working-class wages and best benefits available in Brazil. Training and experience determined wage levels, but even the lowest paid assembly line workers (who made up a quarter of the labor force in the auto sector) earned significantly more than the vast majority of other urban laborers in the 1950s and early 1960s. Positions in the paint shop brought 30% higher wages than work on the line. Those who fashioned machine tools or who worked in the quality-control section earned almost double the income of those on the line. General Motors do Brasil noted that by the early 1960s, the auto factories provided a "high employment level...a praiseworthy quality of life and the highest per capita income in the country."[63] In addition to the highest industrial wages in Brazil, the foreign auto companies also provided comprehensive benefits. Ford do Brasil had been offering its workers health care at work and medical and accident insurance since 1937 with far better benefits than the plans created by the Vargas government. Ford dramatically expanded its health care services as it built new industrial facilities over the course of the 1950s. According to Ford's employment manual, all workers received access to company run infirmaries, dentists, and barbers. They could eat at subsidized company restaurants and take industrial and literacy classes. Workers were automatically enrolled in Ford's sporting club and given access to a wide variety of athletic facilities. The company practiced a central tenet of Fordism by selling Ford vehicles (along with Philco radios and televisions) at a discount and with company financing available to its workers. Those employees who did not yet have their own cars could get around São Paulo and its industrial suburbs on either company-owned or subsidized buses.[64]

The development of this skilled group of workers became a source of great pride for many in Brazil. The news magazine *Visão* proclaimed, for example: "In Brazil we have machines and factories that are as efficient as those in any other part of the world and the Brazilian worker is as productive as any other." Advertisements for Brazilian-made cars and trucks highlighted the role of national labor in building the machines that would finally unify the country, such as one for Scania-Vebis engines with three men working on an engine over the caption "Integrated in Our Progress."[65] Foreigners stoked Brazilian pride by publicly raving about the high skill levels and great productivity of this new workforce. When Henry Ford II visited his company's Brazilian facilities, he made a point of discussing the great impact industrial training had had on the country's workers. Ford went so far as to claim that Brazilian autoworkers had the same skills as their North American counterparts.[66] Executives from Mercedes-Benz also commented on the ways the men in the country's auto factories served as the vanguard of the new, highly skilled Brazilian worker. Friederich Schultz-Wenk, the head of Volkswagen do Brasil, said his workers were "as good or better than German workers." Schultz-Wenk noted that VW's Brazilian facilities were nearly identical to its German factories and bragged that Brazilian-produced cars were good enough to export to the United States.[67]

An internal report to the WOB Board of Directors also took note of the fact that most of these workers were new to industry: "It is with pride that we can affirm that, in spite of the fact that the great majority of our employees had little or no previous training or experience in the automotive field, work standards and production per man hour are the equal of those in other countries with generations of industrial training."[68] Increasingly, Brazilians came to view the auto factories as sites for the transformation of interior folk into modern citizens. National road building was a key component of Kubitschek's developmentalism, and by the late 1950s, people from throughout Brazil, but especially the northeast, had migrated to São Paulo to look for work. They traveled the new highways on the backs of flatbed trucks (known as a *pau de arara* or "macaw's perch") equipped with a rod to hang onto. No job in metropolitan São Paulo was more desirable than one in the foreign auto factories. Second in value was a position with a nationally owned auto parts company.

Brazil's most widely read magazine, *Cruzeiro*, reported in 1959 that "the workers and technicians [in the auto factories] are men from every state: Amazonenses, Gaúchos, Cariocas, Cearenses, etc. They are the Brazilian hands and minds that are giving our nation a technical culture...for us and our children and grandchildren." Auto plants, *Cruzeiro* argued, represented the "optimism of our future."[69] One report on these new workers highlighted the ways that the auto industry was finally instilling a modern ethos in Brazilians. *Quatro Rodas*, the new glossy car magazine, looked at how migration from the countryside to the new auto plants in São Bernardo do Campo was filling the factories with young men eager to learn new skills. Although some came from industry, most came directly from agriculture, and for them "the change was extreme: coming from cattle ranches, coffee farms, cotton, tobacco, and sugar plantations to auto manufacture." João Avelino Pires, for example, arrived from the northeastern state of Bahia as a 21-year-old with no skills. He began as a watchman at the Willys Jeep plant and worked his way up to a position as a manager of the fire control office. *Quatro Rodas* also chronicled the life story of a *caipira* from Taubaté in the interior of São Paulo who migrated to the city to look for work. Without any previous factory experience, he rose from being a helper on the shop floor to managing 35 men in a section of a foundry. Like João Avelino Pires, this young man was transformed by his experiences in the auto plants.[70]

The reality of skill levels and the nature of that transformation are, of course, more complex than the beliefs trumpeted by these magazines.[71] There is some irony in a society's celebration of autoworkers' advanced industrial skills, given the role of Henry Ford's original assembly lines in de-emphasizing technical expertise in the production of cars.[72] Brazilian autoworkers did not possess skills that lent their industry a comparative advantage over American and European manufacturers, but they did require enough industrial education to make them costly to replace. The foreign auto companies' high wages and comprehensive benefits also dissuaded these workers from seeking other employment. Moreover, they quickly came to occupy a unique social space in that they represented Brazil's progress and modernity. Although previous groups of industrial workers had used labor mobility and factory-specific skills to bid up wages and improve work conditions, they did not have autoworkers' prestige. That status was derived not only from employment by foreign companies in labor seen as skilled but also because these men had received industrial training and a wage high enough to allow many of their wives and partners to stay out of the wage labor market. As new arrivals from the rural sector, they were also free of any taint, in the eyes of the larger society, from association with either Communist or populist unions and politicians. In other words, jobs in the foreign auto plants not only made these men into a new class of workers, they also made them Brazil's labor elite.[73]

The auto companies defined modern and forward-looking workers in ways that served corporate interests and, at the same time, appealed to many Brazilians of all social classes. Volkswagen declared that "in a modern factory there is also room for women." While men operated huge stamping equipment, women sewed seat cushions. Despite this traditional sexual division of labor, VW described all its employees as "modern workers."[74] The sexual division of labor elevated male laborers over women workers and so reassured many after the massive, women-led general strikes of the mid-1940s and early 1950s. Indeed, their very appearance and self presentation reassured many Brazilians. The foreign-owned plants required workers to wear uniforms in the factories; foremen in some sections wore ties.[75] The foreign executives in charge of these facilities valued order and cleanliness on the shop floor and believed that industrial training and discipline were the keys to high productivity and profitability. An inspection of Willys's Brazilian plants by an American-based corporate official concluded: "The whole operation had a feeling of soundness. The plant was clean, the tempo was very good, and the morale was high. I think you should be very proud of your organization."[76] Kubitschek's targets, foreign investment, and internal migration seemed to hold the key to solving Brazil's social problem by finally attaining the "order and progress" initially promised by the founding of republic. The auto factories produced cars that Brazilians wanted to own and workers they seemed to respect—and at the very least did not fear.[77]

By the early 1960s, somewhere between 600,000 and 700,000 Brazilians worked in the auto sector. Their presence and high pay and extensive benefits led different newspapers and magazines to refer to São Paulo as the Detroit, Birmingham, Wolfsburg, and Turin of Brazil. The city's industrial suburbs grew and prospered along with the auto plants, as migrants from throughout the country made their way there.[78] All the foreign manufacturers followed Ford's lead and offered their employees cars at discounted prices with special financing. Volkswagen even helped workers buy houses with discounted mortgages and other assistance.[79] The wages and benefits so outpaced anything else available to poor and working-class Brazilians that a position in the auto factories became nearly synonymous with social mobility. The press frequently wrote about autoworkers owning not only their own cars but also modest homes. In the case of Willys, many were also depicted as being modest shareholders as well. Indeed, WOB made much of the diverse backgrounds of its workers and the ways they could all advance. Its in-house news organ, *Noticiário Willys*, profiled workers such as Josué Porfirio, who had migrated from work on a plantation to find a position in the auto sector. Masaaki Kyomem was born in Hiroshima, Japan, and came to Brazil as a child. He received his industrial training at Willys, where he worked as a machine operator. José Santos Ramos from Aquidabâ in the northeastern state of Sergipe came to São Paulo in 1948 and eventually found a position in a WOB stamping plant. With help of Willys, he bought his own car and house, where his wife raised their two children.[80]

Social mobility, stay-at-home mothers, and consumerism make up the dominant themes of these stories. José Soares de Oliveira Irmão, for example, came to São Paulo from a small town in the northeastern state of Bahia. After seven years at Volkswagen, he was able to buy his own car and house, which he filled with appliances sold at a discount at the company store. Whether the worker was raised in a *favela* (urban slum) or on a plantation, he almost always had a car. and his wife did not work outside the home.[81] Luiz Inácio Lula da Silva, who rose from birth in rural Pernambuco to work in a factory to prominence as a labor leader to the presidency of Brazil, recalled how affluent autoworkers seemed to be in the early 1960s: "At that time, the people in automobile industry got something like ten raises a year. They were the elite—they had houses, they were the first to buy televisions, the first to buy cars. I saw the people at VEMAG pass, because it was close to where I lived, at Christmastime, loaded down with boxes of toys for their kids."[82] There were several obvious reasons the foreign auto companies offered such comprehensive benefits: to remain competitive in the local labor market, because they offered similar compensation in their home countries, and because such benefits were a more predictable and potentially less costly way to compensate employees in the inflationary environment of this era. The end result was the creation of a new working-class elite that seemed to be more interested in social mobility and consumerism than in labor militancy.

During the founding and this initial phase of growth for the auto sector, workers had little reason to turn to either São Paulo's grassroots factory commission movement or the populist or Communist unions.[83] Not only was their total compensation much higher than that available in any other industry but also their bosses so distrusted the government-run industrial relations system that they often avoided the labor courts and instead granted inflation adjustments before workers could file requests. Foreign auto executives rightly saw the entire government labor bureaucracy as essentially political, and so they worried about the tendency of populist governments to side with workers in wage disputes. (They did not, of course, object to the military regime that came to power in 1964 using that same structure to discipline workers who rejected the companies' later wage demands.)[84] High wages and extensive benefits not only brought labor peace but also continued to attract new job seekers from throughout Brazil.

The vast majority of Brazilians (88.5% of those polled in 1959) believed the foreign auto factories were playing the lead role in strengthening the Brazilian economy and nation.[85] In 1960, the press reported favorably on Volkswagen's impact in the "economic emancipation of Brazil."[86] This broad popular approval of the presence of these multinational corporations stands in stark contrast to Vargas's nationalistic "The Oil Is Ours" campaign of the early 1950s and calls into question facile descriptions of nationalism and anti-imperialist sentiments in Latin America. Willys and the other auto producers did much to encourage Brazilians to see them as domestic versions of successful foreign corporations, no doubt diminishing the nationalistic critique of their presence. But such broad public support for the foreign auto companies also demonstrates how the productive side of capitalism (i.e., modern factories with good jobs that manufacture popular products) was welcomed throughout Latin America, while the more obviously exploitative aspects of this economic system (e.g., extractive industries and financial speculation) often engendered harsh opposition in the region. Perhaps the most important factors in their acceptance were that they provided the tools for Brazilians to achieve long-held national dreams and they shaped those tools to local tastes. In other words, the foreign auto companies refashioned themselves as Brazilian.[87]

Kubitschek was not insensitive to nationalism, even though the success of the auto industry seemed to put it on the back burner politically. His targets had always stressed the development of the nation, and nothing combined the symbolic and literal promises of republican ideals of "order and progress" more than the establishment of the new, interior capital, Brasília. Although it was of the highest priority to JK, moving the national capital out of Rio and off the coast for ostensibly developmentalist reasons had long been a dream of an extraordinarily diverse group of politicians, from the eighteenth-century Portuguese prime minister the Marquis of Pombal and the protorepublican revolutionary Tiradentes to the early-nineteenth-century naturalist and statesman José Bonifácio and the historian-diplomat Francisco Adolfo de Varnhagen. Although the republican 1891 Constitution granted Congress the right to move the capital from Rio and a handful of twentieth-century leaders endorsed the idea, the creation of Brasília did not gain legitimacy until Kubitschek made it a central component of his 1955 presidential campaign.[88] He argued that having a new national capital in the interior would finally draw Brazil's diverse regions together, making a stronger whole. He referred to this process as "integration through interiorization," which entailed stimulating colonization along the new highways that would emanate from the capital to the nation's major cities. Beyond the basic economic impact of the move off the coast, Brasília would draw together the cultures of coastal, outward-looking Brazil with the more insular perspectives of the nation's interior folk, not unlike Fordlândia.

Although building the new national capital in the interior was to become the centerpiece of Kubitschek's developmentalism, it was the one part of his platform that did not initially have broad public support. In 1952, IBOPE studied public views about the ongoing March to the West. More Brazilians (45% in Rio and 44% in São Paulo) preferred that the government focus its attention on fixing problems on the coast than on developing Goiás and Mato Grosso.[89] Rio's residents were particularly resistant to the idea of losing the national political capital to a new, planned city in the interior. In 1951 and 1952 (i.e., before JK's campaign for president), only a third of respondents from Rio supported moving the capital. In 1955, when the idea of building Brasília began to gain currency throughout the country, fully 70% of Rio's residents opposed moving the capital. Close to 60% of Paulistas supported the move by 1956.[90] As the city was being built, attitudes in Rio became more positive regarding the new capital. On the eve of Brasília's 1960 opening, a large majority of Cariocas did admit that the new capital would greatly aid in the development of the nation's interior. By January 1961, a broad survey of Brazilians throughout the country found that most believed the new capital would play the leading role in the transformation of the interior.[91]

In his first year in office, JK created the New Capital Urbanization Company (*Companhia Urbanizadora da Nova Capital*) to coordinate Brasília's construction. Work began in 1957, and Kubitschek inaugurated the new city on 21 April 1960. He turned to Lúcio Costa for the city's master plan and Oscar Niemeyer for its signature buildings. These veterans of modernist architecture, who called upon both the ideas of Le Corbusier and their own experiences in the Brazilian modernist movement, created an urban space that sought to remake the nation's people into modern, democratic citizens and that was a breathtaking monument to their country's ambitions.[92] A brochure for the project described the uniformity of the apartments (within the *superquadras*) and the fact that space was made available according to a family's size rather than its income. Such arrangements were a key component of Brasília's mission to remake the population: "And because of this distribution [of space according to need not wealth] and the inexistence of social class discrimination, the residents of a *superquadra* are forced to live as if in the sphere of one big family, in perfect coexistence.... And thus is raised, on the plateau, the children who will construct the Brazil of tomorrow, since Brasília is the glorious cradle of a new civilization."[93] Automobility was a key component of this egalitarian utopianism. Each apartment came with a garage for the family's car, and the city's design of sweeping boulevards and few sidewalks discouraged pedestrian traffic.

Brasília represented an experiment in state Fordism that attempted to stimulate working-class consumerism by offering the highest wages in the nation and broad benefits within a structure of utopian egalitarianism.[94] Consumerism, particularly car ownership, became the centerpiece of this plan. The ideal of personal freedom (of movement, at least) embedded in driving one's own car became closely associated with broader notions of freedom and democracy. When Kubitschek spoke of national development, he conflated the ideas of economic modernization with social, cultural, and political modernism. He hoped that by doing so, his government would create a peaceful political transformation of Brazil through the incorporation of the poor and working class who now had a stake in the system. He sought no less than to finally democratize Brazil. In some significant ways, the experiment succeeded. In many ways, it failed.

Kubitschek was unequivocal in his belief that development was the key prerequisite for democracy. In his 1956 message to Congress, the president asserted that the development envisioned by his program would "consolidate a free and powerful nation." Throughout his administration, JK spoke forcefully of the connection between the economic goals of his targets program and political freedom. In 1958, he said, "The economic situation of Latin America must improve if democracy is going to survive.... Today, economic development is inseparable from the concept of collective security and it constitutes the necessary condition to protect our liberty."[95] He also did not mind admitting that he wanted Brazil to at least reproduce the success of the United States in the creation of a consumer-oriented capitalist democracy. Still, Kubitschek made a careful distinction between wanting to emulate the United States and becoming dependent on it.[96] Unlike the auto sector, Brasília was built with only domestic inputs. As the synthesis target, the new capital emphasized the nationalistic component of the administration's drive to implant democracy through developmentalism.[97]

Completing work on Brasília played a central role in Kubitschek's plans. It is hardly surprising that clear majorities of Brazilians doubted the ability of the government to achieve "50 years of progress in 5."[98] Brazil had never had a powerful or effective central state, even during the Vargas dictatorship, and the idea that an administration would be competent enough to plan, build, and inhabit a new city in the nation's interior was far-fetched indeed. Kubitschek knew that opening Brasília would not only provide the template for a new sort of Brazilian citizen and spur growth of the interior but also demonstrate the efficacy of the central state. Inaugurating the new capital on time made almost any project seem feasible and greatly increased the general Brazilian sense of hopefulness about the future.[99] That optimism reflected long-held beliefs about the power of technology, especially automobility, to unleash Brazil's latent power. Kubitschek sometimes spoke of this aspect of his program in religious tones, asserting that "the struggle in defense of the style of life we have adopted, our Christian character, our love of liberty and democracy, requires that Brazil utilize and transform its mineral reserves and its raw materials."[100]

Brasília opened on time. The builders relied on the manual labor of an army of workers to fashion the city's broad boulevards and erect its modernist government offices and residential *superquadras*. Despite its celebration of automobility and futuristic appearance, unskilled laborers built the city with little help from bulldozers, backhoes, and dump trucks. Brasília's inaugural ceremonies on 21 April 1960, deliberately timed for a national holiday, ignored this incongruity and instead celebrated the city's uniquely Brazilian modernity. Kubitschek carefully blended history, mythology, and a sense of hope in the opening of the new capital.[101] At the inaugural, Brazil's poet laureate Guilherme de Almeida spoke of the symbolic transfer of the capital from Rio to Brasília and raised the modernist themes of blending the interior and the coast and the indigenous and the foreign to craft authentic, forward-looking Brazilian citizens. He said, in part: "Now and here is the Crossroad Time-Space, Road which comes from the past and goes to the Future, road from the north, from the south, from the east and from the west, road traversing the centuries, road traversing the world: now and here all cross at the sign of the Holy Cross."[102]

Kubitschek emphasized the importance of mobility and national unity by starting the inaugural before formally opening the city with the Caravan of National Integration. Caravans of Brazilian-made vehicles simultaneously left Porto Alegre, Rio de Janeiro, Cuiabá, and Belem. Caravan leaders were referred to as "modern pioneers" (*bandeirantes modernos*), and each road was a "road of progress" (*caminho de progresso*). Every domestically produced vehicle was draped with an English-language banner proclaiming "Made in Brazil." Benjamin Rondon, son of the great explorer, traveling on the new Belém-Brasília Highway, referred to it as "the dorsal fin of the New Brazil."[103]

One photo in the *Cruzeiro* story on the Caravan depicts a new Brazilian-made Kombi driving near a man herding cattle down a road. The photo's caption, "Two Eras, Two Styles," captured the Caravan's spirit. Just as the 1920s modernists hoped to foster a new Brazilian identity by combining the authentic, indigenous interior folk with the cosmopolitan, coastal urban dwellers, the Caravan provided the means to finally unite the two Brazils. The *Cruzeiro* report noted that significant numbers of Brazilians were "lost" in the *sertão* and Amazon region and that roads and nationally manufactured automobiles would lead to their "discovery" and integration into the new nation.[104] The national media increasingly celebrated the idea that the new capital and the new national auto industry were the two keys to Brazil's future. Brasília brought about a new sense of mobility, change, and development that would unleash the nation's true potential as a great regional and perhaps even world power. With the opening of the new capital, Brazilians not only shed their skepticism about the project but also became near euphoric over its possibilities. In March 1960, 73% of Cariocas approved of moving the capital from their city to Brasília, and 85% believed the new city would positively contribute to developing the interior. In January 1961, 62% of Cariocas said they believed Brasília would bring benefits to the entire country, and 80% said that JK's targets had successfully "accelerated national progress."[105]

The new modernist capital and a steady stream of Brazilian-made cars were the most glamorous and public symbols of Kubitschek's developmentalism (Figure 5.4). The hard work of national integration, however, was being accomplished through the more modest aspects of automobility:

FIGURE 5.4 Juscelino Kubitschek speaking at the Clube Militar in Rio on 21 July 1959 and detailing how the expanded national road network has unified Brazil. Photo courtesy of the Arquivo Nacional do Brasil.

road construction and the expanded use of trucks throughout the economy. After World War II, the government in Rio finally turned its attention to highways by building key links such as the Via Dutra between São Paulo and Rio and BR-4, which connected Rio to the northeastern state of Bahia. More than 10,000 workers were required to pave BR-4, which replaced the São Francisco River as the main north-south transportation route from the center-south to Bahia and beyond. The government built other major highways connecting São Paulo and Belo Horizonte, such as the BR-55, which dramatically improved the Minas capital's commerce with coastal Brazil. The opening of BR-2, linking Curitiba (the capital of Paraná) and São Paulo, so increased ties between the southern states and São Paulo and Rio that it was openly referred to as the "Road of National Integration."[106] At the same time, states built spurs from these major highways connecting secondary cities to their capitals. Still, a 1955 analysis of Brazil's highway system (i.e., paved parkways capable of supporting high-speed travel) revealed a dismal situation. Latin America's largest nation had only 2,000 kilometers of high-quality paved highways, while the American protectorate of Puerto Rico (which is geographically smaller than the Brazilian state of Alagoas) had 4,000 kilometers, and the island of Cuba had 3,735 kilometers. Brazil's highway network paled in comparison with those of most Latin American nations.[107] Most Brazilians were well aware of this problem and wanted the government to build highways and so create a national transportation network.[108]

At first, Kubitschek set a target of an additional 3,000 kilometers of paved highways, which he quickly increased to 5,800 kilometers. By September 1960, JK's administration had built 5,611 kilometers of highways, concentrating on routes that tied Brasília to various state capitals.[109] The Belém-Brasília road, for example, had been planned as a north-south access highway in the 1947 National Highway Plan. Work on what became BR-14 began in May 1957. Less than two years later, in late January 1959, two teams made up of more than 5,000 workers met up in Açailândia, Pará, finally linking—through Brasília—São Paulo, Rio, Minas, and the rest of the center-south of Brazil by road to Belém, at the mouth of the Amazon River. By tying the coast to the interior and the north with the south, the Belém-Brasília highway did more than any other public or private initiative to begin to fulfill the promises of automobility. The national media openly referred to the highway's role in uniting the "two epochs, two styles" of the two Brazils.[110] But even this construction masked the limited transportation links in Brazil's interior. In 1962, Kaiser Industries studied the cost effectiveness of flying 40,000 metric tons of iron ore per day 300 miles versus the construction of a rail spur. In the final analysis, rail construction and transport turned out to be only slightly more cost effective than air travel, highlighting how the limited road system was a serious bottleneck in the Brazil economy.[111]

The center-south, however, significantly expanded its highway capacity. The Via Dutra connecting Rio and São Paulo quickly became Brazil's most traveled highway. By 1960, it handled about 1.5 million vehicles per year (25 years later, it would have 17 million). Private cars used this high-speed route, completing the trip in between five and six hours, compared with Count Lesdain's 1908 trek of 34 days. Increasingly, people of all social classes relied on buses of various levels of comfort to travel between Brazil's two largest cities. Along the way, they passed by fast-food restaurants, gas stations, motels, and small factories. As important as personal travel was for the developing sense of mobility, trucks came to dominate traffic on this highway as corporations built industries along the route. The Dutra most profoundly affected the town of São José dos Campos, which before the 1950s, had largely been known as a small village where people went for tuberculosis treatments. By the 1980s, it had more than 300 industrial establishmenta, including facilities for General Motors do Brasil, Ericsson,

Embraer, and Petrobras. The highway also spread industrial development in those sections of São Paulo and Rio through which it passed.[112]

The auto companies highlighted the use of trucks and tractors in tying the coast to the interior and further fostering modernity by transforming agriculture. The media frequently reported, with prodding from the advertising departments of the auto companies, the ways trucks were changing the Brazilian economy. Cargo could now be moved from Porto Alegre in the southernmost state of Rio Grande do Sul to Fortaleza in Ceará in the northeast. Truck transport began to alter transportation axes by tying together regions that had been dependent on river systems. Roads and trucks allowed areas dependent on the east-west flow of the Amazon, for example, to move goods south toward Minas, São Paulo, and Rio.[113] Ford's marketing emphasized themes of national integration and new forms of commerce through expanded truck transportation. One ad of fishermen packing fish into a Ford truck near the ocean had the caption, "Fresh Fish for Belo Horizonte!" More dramatically, Ford organized yet another caravan of its trucks to travel deep into the interior in 1960. Seven Brazilian-made F-600 trucks went from the factory in São Paulo to Brasília. They then motored up the Brasília-Acre highway (BR-29) to great acclaim along the way. The caravan completed its trip in Porto Velho, the capital of Rondônia and the home of the famous Madeira-Mamoré Railroad.[114]

Beyond marketing and advertising stunts, Brazilians increasingly used jeeps, trucks, and tractors to gain control over the nation's vast interior. *Cruzeiro* noted that jeeps "make their own road." Their durability and versatility made them obvious symbols of the *bandeirante* spirit. Willys-Overland in the United States reported, for example, that pioneers christened a new town on the Paraná River "Toledo," in honor of the jeep's hometown. Jeeps opened new areas to agricultural production that were then developed through the extensive use of tractors.[115] Although much of the mythology around opening Brazil's interior focused on the Amazon, a great deal of new agricultural production in the 1950s and 1960s took place in the three most southern coastal states, Paraná, Santa Catarina, and Rio Grande do Sul.[116] As land in this region was increasingly devoted to growing soybeans for export, farmers used tractors for field preparation and harvest and then trucks to move the crop. The agricultural sector in this rapidly growing region became more and more dependent on automobility. Ironically, the promises of industrialism and modernity came to fruition on farms producing for export.[117]

The transformation of agriculture was concentrated in the more prosperous center-south states, while the northeast continued to suffer. Kubitschek responded to this disequilibrium by establishing the Superintendency for the Development of the Northeast (*Superintendência para o Desenvolvimento do Nordeste*) or SUDENE in 1959. He chose Celso Furtado, Brazil's foremost economist, to lead this effort.[118] This new, massive government agency was formed in response to a devastating drought in the region in 1958. Reports of the human and physical devastation in the northeast were widely reported in the national media. Of particular concern, beyond the immediate human misery, were the large-scale migrations of people looking for work in the cities, using the newly inaugurated highway system to travel to Brazil's center-south states.[119] Kubitschek was confident he could use the same tools he had employed in building Brasília and installing the auto industry to encourage industrial development in this region.[120] SUDENE's results were at best mixed and, compared with JK's other programs, a failure in the eyes of many. Still, the agency remained a part of the government into the twenty-first century and so stands as a testament to Kubitschek's belief in the power of the state to create both technological and spatial fixes to Brazil's historic problems.[121]

With the opening of Brasília, Kubitschek met or exceeded the various goals he had established in his Targets Program. Mundane but important basic industries such as cement and steel experienced dramatic increases, not only in output but also in capacity. No matter, overcoming economic bottlenecks in basic materials production did not inspire Brazilians.[122] The new national capital and the domestic auto industry were the most popular and exciting signs of Brazil's and JK's success. Indeed, Kubitschek closely followed the progress of the new auto sector. At the start of his term, only the inefficient Fábrica Nacional de Motores produced vehicles in Brazil, and its trucks were not widely used. In November 1960, the National Development Council reported to the president: "The automobile industry has become the leader of Brazil's industrial economy." Ten large-scale factories manufactured vehicles; 1,200 small, medium, and large factories built auto parts. Employment in this sector climbed from 15,000 in 1957 to an estimated 128,000 for 1961. The approximately 142,500 units built had between 90% (trucks) and 95% (cars and jeeps) domestic content. Moreover, the multinational corporations producing these vehicles had differing degrees of Brazilian ownership. Ford, General Motors, Volkswagen, and a few others were predominantly foreign owned, but Mercedes-Benz do Brasil and Simca do Brasil were approximately half German and French ownership and half Brazilian. Vemag, WOB, FNM, and Scania-Vabis had mixed ownership, with foreigners holding a controlling interest.[123]

The Development Council further reported to JK that the government's great success in exceeding the original production goals for autos made Brazil Latin America's leading industrial power. The First Automobile Exhibit, held in São Paulo from 26 November to 11 December 1960, celebrated this new economic and industrial prowess. Although there had been auto shows in Brazil since 1923, this event was restricted to Brazilian-made autos and dubbed the "First Exhibit" because it marked the beginning of a new era of industrialism and modernity.[124] The nation no longer aspired simply to produce vehicles and parts; it also began the transition to an export platform of such manufactured goods. Brazil sent VWs to Mexico and DKW-Vemags to Spain. And although the export of cars to Paraguay might not do much to stoke nationalist pride, selling auto parts to the United States (for use in Ford vehicles) separated Brazil from the rest of Latin America, at least in the eyes of its own citizens.[125]

The dramatic expansion of automobility under Kubitschek had an immediate and long-lasting impact on the Brazilian economy. It also had a less tangible but highly significant impact on how Brazilians viewed the present and their future. An IBOPE survey of more than 4,300 residents of Rio and São Paulo conducted in August and September 1959 revealed that these urban Brazilians embraced the ideals of automobility with an enthusiasm that had been in previous eras reserved for only the most active members of the nation's various auto clubs and associations. Almost everyone polled (93%) was aware of the new auto industry and the role JK played in its establishment, and 89% believed this new industry was the decisive factor in pushing forward "national development." More than three quarters of those polled thought the auto industry could not have been established without foreign capital, and a similarly large majority (87%) believed the government concessions were required to get the industry going. Brazilians were so enthusiastic that 77% believed that the country needed even more large vehicle factories to satisfy demand. Although they saw prices as high, they believed there was a large domestic market for cars and trucks. Moreover, a solid majority of people polled viewed Brazilian-made cars as being of equal quality to those manufactured in the United States and Europe.[126]

The seemingly smooth installation of the auto industry, with its modern facilities and well-compensated and trained workers, along with the opening of Brasília, reassured Brazilians that their future was bright. It seemed in 1960 as if Kubitschek had indeed delivered 50 years of progress in only 5. The national government succeeded in crafting and executing a plan to modernize the Brazilian economy and promote modernist ideals such as national unification and social mobility through its developmental-ism. More than these accomplishments, JK had demonstrated the efficacy of coherent state direction of the economy through a structured partnership with foreign and domestic businesses. His administration seemed to take a giant step toward modernity without the anxiety so often associated with it. Normally a messy and contingent process, Brazilian capitalism seemed organized and predictable. Whether it was state Fordism or the develop-mentalist policy prescriptions from the UN's Economic Commission for Latin America (CEPAL), Kubitschek's plan allowed Brazil to make a sud-den and successful leap into modernity. What few realized in the halcyon days of Brasília's inauguration was that the economic modernization and social modernism of the 1950s did not produce a stable and predictable path toward a geographically, politically, and economically unified nation. Deep divisions remained, and Brazilian modernity would prove itself to be unstable and contingent in ways that few of Kubitschek's admirers could have predicted.

CHAPTER 6

From Technocrats to Democrats: Automobility and Citizenship

F IVE YEARS OF JUSCELINO Kubitschek's dynamic administration left Brazilians filled with optimism about the future of their country. New Brazilian-made cars, modern highways, and an interior national capital were the most obvious signs that Brazil was on the cusp of greatness. Its modern transformation was obvious on 31 January 1961, the day Jânio Quadros, the young São Paulo governor, was sworn in as Brazil's new president. Kubitschek had taken the oath of office among Rio de Janeiro's Belle Epoque–era government buildings. When Quadros, who had turned 44 years old just days before the inaugural, took the oath in Brasília, the new modernist capital's streets were filled with VW Fuscas, Willys sedans, and JKs.[1] The autos' presence, along with the smooth political transition from one popularly elected president to the next, seemed to prove that Kubitschek had accomplished 50 years of progress in only 5. The nation now manufactured cars, trucks, and buses (Figure 6.1). New highways connected distant regions and tied Brazil together for the first time in its history. Production of cement, steel, glass, and other industrial inputs had surged, as had the generation of electricity. Socially, Kubitschek's program seemed on the surface to have fostered social peace among urban workers and to have created mechanisms for transforming the rural poor into modern citizens, primarily through migration to São Paulo, where recent arrivals might work in the growing auto industry or live in Brasília.

Quadros was at first seen as a young and vigorous change of pace for Brazilian politics. Foreign auto executives viewed him as a political ally

FIGURE 6.1 American General Motors executives inspecting the advanced tool and die facilities in Brazil in 1963. Photo courtesy of the General Motors Corporation.

but worried about his interest in expanding trade with the Soviet Union and its allies and with China. Quadros did little to dispel these fears when he traveled to Cuba to meet with Fidel Castro in March 1960 in the midst of the presidential campaign. There was also concern about the fact that his candidate for the vice presidency (which was voted on separately from the president), Milton Campos of the conservative UDN, had lost to João Goulart of the populist PTB.[2] In terms of domestic policy, though, foreign businesses were pleased that Quadros worked closely with Roberto Campos and other conservative economists. More specifically, the foreign business community hoped Quadros would provide a bulwark against what they saw as a rising tide of militancy from labor and the left.[3] In the 1940s and 1950s, Brazilian industrialists had differentiated among populists (tied to the Ministry of Labor), members of the Brazilian Communist Party (PCB), and independent activists tied to factory commissions and neighborhoods.[4] In the late 1950s and early 1960s, American and European auto executives did not have enough experience in Brazilian industrial relations to understand the nuances of labor organizing and politics. The leaders of Ford, GM, Willys, Volkswagen, and other multinationals tended to conflate and confuse populist and communist labor leaders as "demagogues," and so these businessmen considered all strikes as political. They had deliberately sought out recent arrivals from the rural sector to whom they could provide industrial training and insulated them from established labor and political organizations by building factories in São Paulo's new industrial suburbs.

Jânio Quadros was ill prepared for the political complexities he faced as president. He reacted to the high inflation wrought by the borrowing JK used to fund his extensive developmentalism by first altering the exchange rate regime so drastically that prices for wheat and oil doubled. He next adopted strict monetary controls, as suggested by the International Monetary Fund (IMF), and renegotiated some of the government's foreign debt. Although many supported the idea of such a broad-ranging stabilization program, Quadros's economic policies alienated business and labor in the short term and seemed to be little more than a form of economic obedience to foreign interests, particularly the IMF. Internationally, Quadros not only continued to court Castro but also openly discussed reestablishing diplomatic relations with the Soviet Union, which had been severed in 1947, and flirted with establishing a closer relationship with China. None of those moves decreased popular dissatisfaction with his economic stabilization program, but they did alienate Brazilian conservatives, including many in the UDN. Quadros reacted to his increasing unpopularity by simply resigning the presidency on 25 August 1961, after only eight months in office.[5]

Quadros's shocking resignation left control of the government in the hands of João Goulart, widely known as "Jango." Brazilian and foreign business leaders had long distrusted Goulart, considering him a populist demagogue who at best resembled Vargas and at worst the former Argentine leader, Juan Perón. The fact that Jango was in China on a goodwill mission when Quadros resigned only heightened conservative fears of what a Goulart administration might bring. His political opponents at first hemmed Jango in by reducing his presidential powers through congressional intervention. Although he recovered full executive power in January 1963, Goulart's ascension to the presidency and the anxiety it engendered among businessmen and the leadership of the army foreshadowed the military coup of 1 April 1964.[6]

To make matters worse, Jango had few of the skills required to navigate the complex politics of the early 1960s. He also faced the nearly impossible task of trying to satisfy Brazilians' high expectations in the aftermath of Kubitschek's extraordinarily successful term. Jango was left without any obvious developmentalist initiatives to claim as his own. Instead, he faced high popular expectations about the ability of the national government to move the country forward, but in an environment of both high inflation and a large foreign debt. He at first attempted an economic stabilization program that brought immediate sacrifices, particularly to workers and the poor, but would take time to have a positive impact on the economy. Goulart quickly abandoned economic orthodoxy as he sought to solidify his political base. No matter which way Jango turned, however, he faced an increasingly polarized polity. On his left, a dizzying array of parties and movements challenged the status quo, while Goulart's conservative opponents looked to the military for relief.[7]

Two aspects of this political quagmire distinguished it from prior crises. First, the intensity of the left-right political polarization reflected changes in Brazil and throughout the hemisphere. Brazil's looming political showdown between its populist-left president and his conservative critics and their allies in the military played out in the shadow of the Cuban revolution.[8] That fact highlighted the other new component of Brazilian politics in the early 1960s: the presence of the rural poor. Castro and his 26th of July movement had succeeded in seizing power through a rural insurgency. Brazil had had a long tradition of rural upheaval, including sporadic rural labor organizing in the 1940s, but with the example of Cuba in many people's minds, combined with the construction of highways linking the interior to the coast and the impoverished north and northeast to the nation's center-south region, the specter of rural protest felt more dangerous and uncomfortably close to Brazil's urban elites and middle class.[9] Kubitschek had created SUDENE specifically to obviate such rural discontent and migration, but bus, truck, and car travel had accelerated rural to urban movement in the late 1950s and early 1960s. Moreover, the growth of new media, such as television, heightened awareness of this trend among urban Brazilians. The triumph of automobility in unifying huge sections of Brazil had also fostered a great deal of anxiety among urban Brazilians. By the early 1960s, it seemed as though urban Brazilians—particularly elites and members of the rising middle class—had discovered the downside of cultural cannibalism.

As popular anxiety grew, leaders of the so-called moderate wing of the military hierarchy decided to overthrow the Goulart government and institute a dictatorship that would endure for 21 years. The coup and dictatorship had deep roots in Brazil's political history, with its fragile balance between civilian rule and military intervention.[10] The threat of Cuban communism and the overall terms of the cold war in Latin America gave this history a new vocabulary and urgency. It also led to the careful and behind-the-scenes intervention of the U.S. government in Brazilian politics. The Johnson administration closely monitored the tensions between Goulart and the military hierarchy, and it also offered support for the coup itself. The anti-Goulart military leaders worried that a large-scale mobilization would require a great deal of motor and airplane fuel that might not be available, so the U.S. government arranged to have a number of Navy and private tankers available off the Brazilian coast in the event of such shortages.[11] Unlike previous coups, when armies marched on Rio de Janeiro, this time the military understood it had to extend its control throughout the nation. The army knew it could easily seize Brasília, but the generals realized that they would have to control far-flung but now increasingly integrated regions of the nation, from the Amazonian north and coastal northeast to the far south. The highly mechanized Brazilian military had itself become dependent on automobility and so was forced to marshal all the petroleum it could in the run-up to the coup.

From the time early auto enthusiasts first proposed using cars, trucks, and buses to integrate the nation, they had thought little about the potential downside of their fervent embrace of technology and even modernity. Few of the intellectuals, industrialists, or state policy makers had considered that the sort of changes they sought—from national integration through large-scale road building in the interior to the altering of urban spaces—might bring about social upheaval and environmental degradation. The aggressive proponents of making Brazil modern failed to consider that annihilating space through time would, among other things, draw the nation's rural poor to the cities. Auto enthusiasts and modernizing politicians had not thought about the ways that breaking with Brazil's past would engender anxiety throughout society. As the promise of automobility began to bear fruit in the latter part of the twentieth century, Brazilians also confronted its pitfalls. Developmentalism had failed to foster a broad-based democracy in Brazil by the 1960s. The 21-year military dictatorship would, paradoxically, create many of the preconditions for the eventual development of a truly open polity. This was most clearly expressed by the rise of the autoworkers as a key political actor in Brazil's process of democratization in the late 1970s and throughout the 1980s.

The military's quick seizure of power in some ways marked Kubitschek's developmentalism as a failure. Although he had achieved the material aspects of his program, the social and political goal of creating a stable citizenry was not in evidence in 1964. The advent of the military dictatorship, rather than celebrating the good wages and the concomitant consumerism of autoworkers, cracked down on unions and squeezed wages. The auto industry was no longer seen as a tool for transforming the nation's poor into a viable middle class. The generals and technocrats who ran Brazil during the dictatorship continued to embrace automobility, but in a much more narrowly defined way. They still believed that using cars, trucks, and buses to integrate the nation geographically was one of Brazil's greatest tools for making itself into a modern nation, but their focus was much more economic than social. Rejecting the Fordist ideal, these technocrats concentrated on the ways the auto industry could be central to economic expansion. Trucks and buses would grow in importance as more and more people and freight relied on them to travel the nation's steadily expanding network of highways. Cars would be marketed to Brazil's existing middle class and sold for export. Automobility also had important strategic implications for the military government, as many generals viewed road building first in terms of the armed defense of the nation itself and only secondarily as a tool for deepening the economic development of the interior.[12]

Military men at first tended to focus on the strategic and economic implications of Brazil's growing network of highways and roads. Beginning in the mid-1950s, about 250,000 people migrated each year into the nation's interior frontier on the new highway system. The Belém-Brasília highway and other roads to and from the nation's new capital facilitated the movement of people and goods into the Amazon region.[13] When the auto magazine *Quatro Rodas* sent a correspondent on the BR-29, between Brasília and the Amazonian state of Acre, in 1962 he reported on the extreme isolation of the region and how being cut off from coastal Brazil had kept the area impoverished. Rubber tappers told the reporter they lived under the "law of strongest" and that they often killed Indians who tried to keep them from their harvest. The Brasília-Acre highway would not only bring a larger population to Rondônia's small capital, Porto Velho (which had only 51,049 inhabitants in 1962), but also help transform the entire region.[14]

By the mid-1960s, the Belém-Brasília highway (BR-14) functioned as the main link between Brazil's north and south. A well-developed highway system already connected São Paulo, Rio, Belo Horizonte, and other major cities in the center-south to the new national capital. The opening of BR-14 made auto travel possible to and from the far south of Brazil and the mouth of Amazon on the north coast. Although the vast majority of its 2,000 kilometers were not paved, the highway supported two private bus lines that traversed its length at 80 kilometers per hour in the dry season.

In rainy weather, the highway became treacherous and often impassable. Although seasonal conditions limited its effectiveness, the highway opened new, national markets for São Paulo's industrial goods and provided new supplies of raw materials and food to the developed center-south.[15] One American media report noted that "Mercedes...and Alfa-Romeo's churn up dust and waddle through mud, carrying everything from elevators and TV sets north and bringing back tropical fruits and other products, or running empty." The report continued by commenting on the social and cultural impact of the road: "By putting the remote Amazon region in overland contact with the country's industrial south, it is sparking new life in the one-half of Brazil virtually untouched by progress." *Manchete* magazine echoed not only this American view but also the ideas of Brazil's early modernist intellectuals when it reported that such highways "shorten distances and allow people to understand each other better."[16]

Brazil's growing highway system also dramatically expanded personal mobility. In just its first year, the Belém-Brasília highway provided a route for about 100,000 people to migrate from the crowded coast to small interior towns. Government planners and economists rarely considered the idea that these new roads would also allow rural migration to Rio, São Paulo, and other coastal cities when interior conditions deteriorated.[17] They also gave little thought to the ways many interior folk would react to being more closely tied to the rest of the nation. Urban Amazonians shared these conceits. Residents of Belém (the capital of the state of Pará on the Atlantic coast) and Rio Branco (capital of Acre, located near the borders of Peru and Bolivia) both wanted the government to concentrate its development program on road building. In Belém, 45% of the 300 people polled named roads as the number one government priority, followed by 23% who favored public health programs. Its extreme isolation led 75% of the 200 polled in Rio Branco to favor roads over all other government programs. All these urban Amazonians believed that better transportation links would make the region "more Brazilian." These interviews reveal the distinction not between coastal and interior Brazil or between the center-south region and the north or Amazonia, but rather a divide between those who had embraced modernity and those who had not. Indeed, the polling data show that the poor in Belém and Rio Branco had an even greater belief in the importance of roads to their cities than middle-class and elite residents.[18]

Road-building and other development projects initially held little interest for the military government of Castello Branco (1964–1967). In the years immediately after the coup, the generals and their technocrat allies concentrated on bringing down government spending to fight inflation. Rather than put additional money into programs such as Kubitschek's SUDENE that sought to industrialize the impoverished northeast, the military government tried to stimulate the national economy by focusing on the more prosperous and industrial center-south region.[19] Civilian economists tied to the military regime advocated budget cutting and shrinking the government's presence in the national economy. Many army officers, however, had long dreamed of remaking Brazil physically and socially. From Rondon's building of the telegraph into the Amazon to the *tenentes'* support for Vargas to the founding of the Superior War College (*Escola Superior de Guerra*, or ESG) in 1949, military men looked to play a leading role in the economic and social development of the nation, with a special emphasis on building Brazil's infrastructure.[20] Their control over the national government afforded them the opportunity to reshape Kubitschek's developmentalism. They could focus on the physical unification of the nation through large-scale construction projects that would not only serve national security, broadly defined, but also tie Brazil together geographically. Such national integration would spur further economic growth and allow internal migration and colonization of the Amazon region.[21] Although plans for such projects spoke to their economic and security goals, the officers who supported them seemed to have absorbed components of the old modernist dream of socially and racially transforming the nation by uniting the coast and the interior.

In 1965, the Castello Branco administration embraced aspects of developmentalism over its early commitment to fiscal restraint and created the National Highway Plan, which involved paving existing roads and building new highways. Even though about 4,000 kilometers of roads were paved each year from 1965 to 1970, the government's initial roads program was limited in scope.[22] The military government next initiated Operation Amazon in 1966 to coordinate the economic development of the region (including road building) among state, domestic, and multinational capital. The program relied on a series of tax incentives and other measures similar to those offered by SUDENE.[23] The main impetus for a major program, however, came in the form of another devastating drought in the northeast in 1970. When President Emílio Garrastazú Médici (1969–1974) toured the affected areas in Pernambuco and noted that that tens of thousands of refugees from the drought-stricken interior were migrating to its capital, Recife, and other coastal cities that could not support them, he decided to institute a broad development program that would tie Brazil's two problematic regions together. He called this "the solution to two problems: men without land in the Northeast and land without men in Amazonia."[24] With new government resources available due to a robust economy (the so-called Brazilian miracle of the late 1960s and early 1970s), the Médici government crafted the National Integration Program (*Programa de Integração Nacional*, or PIN). It had three basic components. The government would irrigate an additional 40,000 hectares in the northeast and also create special export corridors in the region. Most significantly, the PIN would open the interior and link it to the coast through the construction of the Transamazonian Highway. The highway would lead, in the words of the military government, to the "gradual occupying of empty spaces." It would also facilitate internal migration to "reduce the regional differences existing in the country's unbalanced development." Of equal importance were the strategic components of road building in the Amazon. According to Médici, without a viable road network, the Amazon would be "vulnerable to foreign seizure, gradual denationalization, or exploitation by domestic enemies."[25]

Médici formalized the PIN in October 1972, although road construction had begun more than a year before that. At the plan's formal inauguration, Médici announced that for the first time in its history, the government was "tying together Brazil from north to south and east to west." Minister of Transportation Col. Mario Andreazza added that once all the PIN roads had been built, Brazilians would be able to fill the Amazon region with people.[26] Every time elites thought about controlling and/or transforming the interior to further capitalist development, expand the state, or solve an environmental crisis, they did so in terms of remaking it in the image of the nation's coastal cities and agricultural settlements. They gave little or no thought to existing environmental or social conditions or the legacy of previous attempts to colonize Brazil's vast interior spaces.[27] Although the road building of the 1960s and 1970s would not bring about rebellions or other mass political movements, this new push into the Amazon had a profound impact on the social structures and ecosystems of the nation's interior.

Military planners imagined a series of modern, paved highways that would finally fulfill the Amazon's promise as a major source of national wealth and pride. Economic development would follow the Transamazonian Highway, providing opportunities to migrants who would settle on small plots and larger agrobusinesses that would be able to more efficiently exploit the land. The technocrats who engineered the highway were not unaware of the project's underlying political goals. Beyond the stated need to develop the interior, the military regime was also interested in creating a stable rural population and providing a safety valve for urban discontent. The 1964 coup had been more than a simple reaction to the disorganized and seemingly leftist politics of the Goulart government; it was also a reaction to the organizing and protest activities of the rural poor in Brazil's northeast. The creation of new economic spaces in the Amazon would, the regime imagined, alleviate social and political tensions in the rural sectors of Pernambuco and Bahia without having to redistribute land held by the region's elites. Beyond that political calculus, the technocrats behind these policies understood that opening new lands to agricultural production while keeping large landholdings intact would increase productivity and, in theory, lower domestic food prices (to the benefit of all, but particularly urban labor) while also potentially providing increased export earnings. In theory, opening the Amazon to such colonization had few costs and many benefits.

Once built, much of the Transamazonian Highway, although impressive in its scope, was not paved and often was unusable during periods of heavy rain. Moreover, the original 8,000-kilometer road was scaled back to 4,800 kilometers, thereby connecting Pará and Amazonas and not reaching its original end point on the Peruvian border. The road (BR-230) did connect to a series of other Amazonian highways that effectively linked the region's northern tier (the Perimetral Norte) and the south through Cuiabá to the Santarém highway. The existing Belém-Brasília highway then served as a sort of spine that integrated the new highway system. When the Transamazonian was inaugurated on 30 August 1972, its military planners looked with great pride at the extensive road system they hoped would unify the region, limit domestic social and political disturbances, and protect Brazil from foreign intrigue along its northern borders.[28]

The construction of side roads off these major highways intensified the impact the new highways had on the Amazon region. To facilitate development along these new highways, the government created a new agency, the National Institute for Colonization and Agrarian Reform, or INCRA (*Instituto Nacional de Colonização e Reforma Agrária*). It would be the primary agent in the settlement of migrants on new plots of land along the Transamazonian Highway and other new interior road projects. In its first five years of operation, INCRA sought to settle 100,000 families from Brazil's northeast in towns called *agrovilas*. Each *agrovila* would house 48 to 64 families and would be built about every 10 kilometers along the highway. These would be tied to *agrôpoles*, which were set 100 kilometers apart and had administrative power over the *agrovilas*. The largest settlements (with upwards of 20,000 inhabitants) were to be the *rurôpoles*, which would be regional commercial and administrative centers every 200 kilometers. Its master plan called for a total of 1 million families (or about 5 million people) to be similarly resettled along the Transamazonian. These dense settlements would provide community life for the relocated families, who would have title to plots of land for planting subsistence crops and some marketable staples (e.g., beans and corn). This experiment in "rural urbanism" was a dismal failure. The colonists disdained the settlements and often moved their houses out of them to their farms. Moreover, the government never fully funded the project, and it soon lost coherence. Money for INCRA became increasingly scarce as the impact of the 1973–1974 oil shocks began to be felt in Brazil. Expensive fuel also affected the colonists' decision making. The high cost of transporting their crops to markets made production of higher margin commodities such as coffee and cacao increasingly attractive. These embedded costs helped to doom this development scheme and led to the transition to livestock grazing on many of the INCRA farms.[29]

Auto-dependent settlement along the Transamazonian Highway had one more significant limitation that profoundly affected the program and the region itself. The technocrats who developed the multitiered system of settlements and towns approached the region as a blank slate upon which to craft a new interior society. The design of lots and their allocation did not take into account local environmental conditions, the requirements of different crops, or even the impact of differing levels of access to transportation (some lots were on the main roads, others far from them). The regime's rural urbanism promoted intensive agriculture and the marketing of crop surpluses over newly built roads and highways through the imposition of a spatial organization that was alien to the environment and the needs of the colonists. Such high-modernist planning had brought mixed results to new cities such as Brasília, but urban spaces by definition radically transform the land on which they are constructed. Agricultural settlements, as Henry Ford and the agronomists at Fordlândia and Belterra had learned in the 1930s and 1940s, cannot thrive or even survive in complex ecosystems like those of the Amazon region without careful consideration of the agricultural suitability of the land. The government's system of geometrically identical plots of land clustered together made more sense in planning documents in Brasília than on the ground along the Transamazonian Highway.[30]

As technocrats attempted to use road building and other aspects of automobility to bring order to interior spaces, the increasing presence of cars, trucks, and buses reconfigured existing urban spaces throughout the country. New roads connecting rural areas to cities brought a modern ethos to previously isolated parts of the nation (Figure 6.2). Small towns along the Dutra between Rio and São Paulo quickly experienced the problems of being along one of Latin America's most advanced highways. By 1960, more than 1.5 million vehicles used the Dutra per year. (By 1985, more than 17 million traveled it annually.) Although the highway connected the nation's two leading cities, much of the area it covered had been rural and largely unconnected to urban culture before the road opened in 1951. In the 1960s and 1970s, this region grew dramatically, with São José dos Campos in São Paulo becoming the home to the Brazilian Aerospace Center, as well as a major General Motors factory. Later, Embraer (the airplane manufacturer) and a host of other national and multinational corporations built factories there. This rapid rate of economic development brought about a culture

FIGURE 6.2 General Motors do Brasil's vehicle, engine, and transmission manufacturing facility in São José dos Campos. The creation of massive factories on former coffee plantations by the 1960s reveals the complex integration of urban and rural Brazil at this time. Photo courtesy of the General Motors Corporation.

clash between those who had lived in the area long before the highway opened and the new residents used to the fast pace of travel and life of the 1960s and 1970s. The Dutra became famous for speeding cars and trucks colliding with horses and other animal forms of transportation. In 1960, there were 1,700 accidents on Dutra. The number of accidents continued to rise during the decade as factories, gas stations, fast-food restaurants, and other businesses opened along its route.[31]

Road building and the arrival of a Willys manufacturing facility in the northeastern city of Recife in the 1960s were marketed to the Brazilian public as tools for unifying the nation and bringing the prosperity of the center-south to the region. As early as 1962, Edgar Kaiser had begun planning a Willys manufacturing facility in the northeast "to make a valuable contribution to its industrial development." The factory in Jaboatão, 12 miles outside Recife, opened in July 1966 with more than 3,000 dignitaries in attendance. Willys promised that the Jeep facility would dramatically increase the standard of living of Recife's population. The Willys factory employed close to 500 locals, who received extensive industrial training and literacy education. These workers were to be the first of many *nordestinos* who would benefit from automobility's transformative power. Other workers in this poor and largely agricultural region would have similar opportunities, as the Jeep manufacturing facility spurred other industrial enterprises to open nearby.[32]

Willys, along with the Brazilian media, did all it could to promote the idea that this factory would bring prosperity and modernity to Pernambuco. The state was heavily dependent on agriculture; its primary crop was sugarcane, which afforded planters little pricing power. Moreover, it had been a focal point for the landless movement in the years leading up to the 1964 coup and so had been one of the most violently suppressed in the aftermath of the military takeover. Willys and its allies argued that a modern industrial sector would remake Recife and the sugar plantations in the coastal lowlands (*zona da mata*). Auto factories might also discourage the ongoing migration of Pernambucanos to São Paulo and other southern cities. The public relations campaign around the Willys factory included photos of Dom Helder Câmara, the Archbishop of Olinda and Recife, driving the first Jeep produced in the state and advertisements extolling the new automobile-based links between the northeast and the Amazon, as well as to the rest of Brazil. The factory in metropolitan Recife eventually manufactured Jeeps, the Rural Willys, and a pickup truck version of the Jeep.[33]

Roads also transformed the interior of Paraná in the south. Highway construction connecting Porto Paranaguá on the coast and the far interior brought with it a dramatic expansion in coffee production and exports beginning in the late 1950s. Less than 20 years after being founded, for example, the town of Maringá in northwest Paraná had more than 135,000 inhabitants.[34] New highways also transformed existing urban areas, such as São Paulo and Rio. With the ongoing expansion of BR-101, which runs north-south all the way from Natal in Rio Grande do Norte to Porto Alegre in Rio Grande do Sul, Brazil experienced a surge in internal migration, as poor people from the northeast made their way to the economically vibrant center-south.[35] During the years of rapid expansion in the 1950s and 1960s, São Paulo's population growth was largely fueled by internal migration, not only from the nearby rural sector but also from Brazil's northeast.[36] The major cities of Brazil's center-south had long been shaped culturally, economically, and politically by migrants from the rural sector. What was new in the 1960s and 1970s was the high number of people who had come from great distances. Their steadily growing presence increased anxiety among the largely white middle class and urban elites.[37]

New arrivals from the rural sector, no matter what their ethnic and racial makeup, were but one new facet of life in Brazil's rapidly growing, automobile-dependent cities in the 1960s and 1970s. Cars, buses, and trucks altered—often beyond recognition—the cities' social and physical geography. With the steadily increasing number of migrants filling Rio de Janeiro's favelas in the 1950s and 1960s, conservative politicians used middle-class and elite fears about the presence of so many poor people of color to their advantage. Rio's conservative governor Carlos Lacerda (1960–1965) actually launched a "war on the favelas." Although more rhetorical than real at first, Lacerda used army troops after the 1964 coup to forcibly remove poor residents from their homes. Again in the late 1960s, the government removed *favelados* and destroyed their homes. The large number of migrants from the northeast and the increasing availability of bus transport from cities' burgeoning peripheries to work in the city distinguished the 1960s and 1970s from previous eras. The mobility of Brazilian society brought seemingly distant social problems from the countryside to the city.[38]

Automobility brought even more profound social, spatial, and political changes to São Paulo. The advent of bus transportation beginning in the 1920s and accelerating in the 1940s, along with a system of rent control, encouraged the city's working-class and poor residents to build homes and shantytowns on São Paulo's periphery.[39] As private bus companies worked with real estate interests to open new areas far from the center of town, and the city instituted a major renovation and road reform, São Paulo spread out over the 1940s and 1950s. Although middle-class and elite

Paulistanos increasingly relied on their own cars to commute to work, go shopping, or take the family on a vacation in Santos or Guarujá along the coast, the working class and poor became completely dependent on bus transportation. Workers' dependence on multiple buses to commute from their now far-flung homes became a problem during World War II and was brought to national awareness in 1947 during a series of riots to protest high fares and poor service.[40] The city's poor and working class became even more dependent on buses over the course of the 1960s and 1970s, as government policies and social practice encouraged even more settlement along São Paulo's growing outskirts. The concentration of recent migrants in new shantytowns on the periphery obscured the city's social and racial transformation during the years of the military dictatorship. By 2000, São Paulo and other cities in Brazil's center-south had become much more racially and culturally diverse as a result of rural to urban and north to south migration along the nation's new highway system.[41]

Highways literally filled Brazil's largest metropolis with more cars, trucks, and buses than the city could handle. The majority of freight trucks traveling north-south in Brazil actually passed through the city because the major highways that connect the northeast to Paraná, Santa Catarina, and Rio Grande do Sul do not connect to a beltway around São Paulo.[42] Traffic on the two main in-town highways, the Marginal Pinheiros and the Marginal Tietê (both technically part of SP-015), has played an important role in the spatial development of the city and the steadily deteriorating conditions of life there because São Paulo's roads and highways became increasingly inadequate for the expanding megalopolis's own traffic. Over the course of the 1960s and 1970s, the metropolitan area became even more dependent on automobility. The military government's tax and mortgage policies encouraged middle-class and elite home ownership in more central neighborhoods. This, in turn, further encouraged the growth of working-class and poor communities on the city's periphery. With such spatial development, the number of cars registered in São Paulo grew from about 63,000 in 1950 to 415,000 in 1966, to 1.4 million in 1993.[43]

In addition to the impact of land prices, the opening of new bus lines, and government tax policies, cultural, social, and political factors also shaped metropolitan São Paulo and its relationship to autos. The U.S.-style car culture had always appealed to Brazil's auto enthusiasts. Over the course of the 1960s, young men in São Paulo drag-raced through the streets of the Morumbi neighborhood, drive-through restaurants and other enterprises opened, and one entrepreneur, in an obvious attempt to copy California's car culture, opened a Mexican restaurant with ample parking.

Real estate developers built large-scale auto-dependent projects such as the city's first American-style indoor mall, Shopping Iguatemi, which opened on 28 November 1966. Although residential construction grew vertically throughout the 1970s and 1980s, the city did not become more densely populated or less dependent on automobiles and buses. Middle-class and elite Paulistanos increasingly moved out of single-family homes and into high-rise condominiums, primarily in response to real and perceived threats of increased crime on the city's streets. Such closed condominiums in neighborhoods such as Morumbi and Vila Andrade were not intended to be part of a new downtown development with shops within walking distance of residences. They included supermarkets (some of the largest, with 100 checkout lanes, were known as hypermarkets) and malls that depended on private automobile transportation and so actively discouraged life on the streets.[44]

The ultimate expression of these trends came in the 1970s with the opening of the Alphaville suburban development in the nearby *municípios* of Barueri and Santana do Paranaíba, northwest of the city of São Paulo. Named to connote "the first among cities," the massive commercial and residential area quickly became home to businesses and wealthy and middle-class Brazilians who no longer wished to navigate life in the rapidly expanding megalopolis.[45] Although seemingly self-contained, the gated residential communities and office buildings were all closely connected to the city of São Paulo. Most residents commute to work on the Castelo Branco Highway (SP-280), and the corporations in Alphaville's office parks do a great deal of business in the metropolitan area. Rather than being autonomous, Alphaville relies on automobility for its connections to greater São Paulo. Internally, it is also highly auto dependent. Alphaville's affluent residential communities are home to an extremely high rate of motor vehicle accidents, probably because so many of the area's teenagers are given cars by their parents.[46] Despite these limitations, Alphaville was considered a highly successful suburban development. Smaller scale versions of this community have been developed by Alphaville Urbano, its parent company, in Campinas, São José dos Campos, and Ribeirão Preto in the state of São Paulo, in Curitiba, Londrina, and Maringá in Paraná, and in other locations throughout Brazil, spreading the ideal of suburban sprawl and increased dependence on automobility.[47]

São Paulo's urban development followed market impulses and valued automobility as a way to transport the working class and elites from their far-flung housing on the periphery and in modernistic suburbs, respectively. Curitiba, Paraná's capital city, relied instead on government-mandated urban planning to come to terms with the changes wrought by both auto-mobility and its rapidly expanding population in the 1960s and 1970s. One of the reasons Curitiba so successfully integrated automobility was that the city's leaders had embraced urban planning before its streets were flooded by motorized vehicles. Donat-Alfred Agache of the French Society for Urban Studies (*Societé Française des Urbanistes*, SFU) prepared plans for several Brazilian cities, but Curitiba was the one that implemented at least some of his recommendations. The high cost of comprehensive urban renewal limited the impact of the Agache Plan, but Curitiba's political and business leaders had in their possession a careful analysis of their urban space and experience working with planners. Both became invaluable in the 1960s, when once sleepy Curitiba's population approached 500,000.[48] In response to requests for a new plan in the mid-1960s, an architect at the Federal University in Curitiba, Jaime Lerner, proposed limiting the city's sprawl, protecting its historic district, and controlling downtown traffic in part by putting in place a comprehensive system of public transportation. The city took up Lerner's Curitiba Master Plan in 1968.[49] It closed some roads to motor vehicles and created a series of pairs of one-way streets to move traffic in opposite directions. The city also created a complex system of buses that reduced congestion and rationalized movement throughout Curitiba.[50] The city continued to update its transportation system in the 1980s with the implementation of the Integrated Transportation Network (*Rede Integrada de Transporte*), which relies on a bus rapid-transit system with so-called Speedybuses. This program required the manufacture of special articulated vehicles. Volvo built these 270-passenger, uniquely designed buses that utilize specially built covered bus stops. Then, in the 1990s, the city installed a traffic radar system that automatically photographs the license plates of speeding cars. The citation process is completely auto-mated. Such planning made Curitiba Brazil's most livable large city.[51]

Curitiba is an exceptional case. Brazil's capital and secondary cities more often followed the example of São Paulo's elite and middle-class sub-urban sprawl, with the concomitant explosive growth of poor communi-ties along the cities' peripheries in the 1960s and 1970s. This deepening reliance on car and bus transportation, along with the dramatic growth of intercity bus and truck transport, left the nation particularly vulnerable to increases in the world price of oil. By 1974, when the price of crude oil quadrupled, Brazil imported 80% of the oil it used. The administration of Ernesto Geisel (1974–1979) had sought to maintain the impressive 10% growth rate of the years of the so-called economic miracle from 1968 to 1973. So much of that growth had been fueled by imports of capital goods and energy that the 1973–1974 oil price shock threatened to derail the economy. Higher input costs that would squeeze the balance of payments would not only slow growth but also potentially spur inflation. Geisel responded with a series of measures, from promoting nuclear energy to expanding hydroelectric capacity. To address the high cost of imported oil for Brazil's growing dependence on automobility, Geisel directed Petrobras to expand off-shore exploration, and he initiated an alternative fuels program based on alcohol.[52]

Refining ethanol, made primarily from sugarcane and less so from manioc, was a near-perfect long-term solution to Brazil's need for a domestic source of automotive fuel.[53] Building large-scale refineries to produce enough ethanol to meet the needs of Brazil's steadily increasing fleet of cars would require a massive investment in a new industry. (Trucks and buses continued to use diesel fuel refined from petroleum.) Accordingly, Geisel introduced the Alcohol Program (*Programa Nacional de Álcool* or *Proálcool*) on 14 November 1975. Within a decade, *álcool* production quadrupled; by 1996, Brazil had 352 refineries (246 in the center-south and 106 in the northeast) producing ethanol. The first cars and light trucks manufactured to run entirely on ethanol came to market in 1979, and sales of these vehicles grew steadily over the course of the 1980s.[54] With these new Brazilian-designed and -manufactured cars, the *álcool* program reinvigorated the national auto industry, which had slumped in the aftermath of the oil price shock. The move from a gasoline-ethanol mix that existing engines could handle to cars that ran only on *álcool* boosted auto sales beginning as early as 1980. The car companies pumped up nationalist pride in their vehicles and extolled the positive impact they would have on the economy and environment, for ethanol is said to produce less harmful pollution than gasoline.[55]

Proálcool solved a broad array of the military government's problems, beyond the high cost of imported oil. Sugar prices had been in a long, steady decline, but demand for ethanol created an entirely new market for Brazil's growers. The alcohol program therefore had the added benefit of spurring development in the rural sector broadly, particularly in the impoverished northeast. Although the sugar areas around Campinas in São Paulo benefited from the establishment of refineries, the most dramatic impact from ethanol was in the northeast, especially in states such as Pernambuco. The steady growth of the *álcool* industry over the course of the 1980s did more to transform the economy around Recife than the Willys plant that had opened to such fanfare in 1966. Moreover, investment in such sugar areas had an important political benefit: Many of the military regime's staunchest political supporters represented the rural sector, especially in the northeast. (During most of the 21-year military dictatorship, a form of electoral politics operated, with civilian members of Congress and governors chosen in voting that was heavily circumscribed by a wide variety of shifting regulations imposed by the regime.) As the military moved toward opening politics and eventually returning to the barracks, its leaders sought new ways to bolster their civilian allies. *Proálcool* proved to be an effective tool in those efforts.[56]

The dramatic rise in oil prices, however, had truly shocked the Brazilian economy. Beyond the loss of foreign exchange and the growing external debt, the oil shock revealed one of the central, if never before recognized, flaws of the country's developmentalism. Brazil's political and business leaders had embraced state-supported industrialization since the 1930s as a way to break the country's dependence on agricultural exports and to make the nation more independent from external economic forces. The thriving auto sector seemed to mark Brazil's transition toward a less dependent economic status. The oil shock quickly revealed the flaw in such thinking by showing how automobility had made Brazil dependent on certain key foreign inputs. The *álcool* solution limited the impact of this new dependence by providing a native technological fix to a serious problem. Moreover, by solving a problem of automobility through reliance on the agricultural sector's oldest export commodity, sugar, the regime ultimately embraced the modernists' dream of uniting rural and urban Brazil.[57]

Auto enthusiasts, industrialists, and government officials had longed dreamed of selling Brazilian-made cars, trucks and buses abroad. Exports of auto parts at first outpaced foreign sales of cars, trucks, and buses, but over the course of the 1960s and early 1970s, Brazilian-based manufacturers increased vehicle sales throughout Latin America.[58] In addition to the financial benefits, such sales bolstered national pride and served to separate Brazil from the rest of Latin America and the developing world. Moreover, exports became increasingly important to the auto sector during the dictatorship because, unlike its civilian predecessors, the generals did not seek to expand middle-class consumption to Brazilian workers but instead focused on expanding exports of manufactured goods.

By the early 1970s, automobile production had become the centerpiece of Brazil's rapidly expanding industrial sector. The annual growth rate in production of transportation equipment far outpaced any other component of the economy from 1967 to 1977.[59] By 1980, manufactured goods made up more than half of all of Brazil's exports, even though the agricultural output had increased since the inception of the national auto industry.[60] Although the export of other industrial products, from armaments to airplanes, contributed to the growth of advanced manufacturing in Brazil, autos led this dynamic sector of the economy. By the early 1970s, Volkswagen, Ford, and General Motors dominated production and sales of cars, trucks, and buses. Mercedes-Benz, Scania-Vebis, and the Fábrica Nacional de Motores also manufactured trucks and buses for the expanding markets that followed the military's road building in the northeast and into the Amazon.[61] The foreign corporations did much more than simply manufacture vehicles in Brazil. In 1969, Ford opened a massive research and design center in São Bernardo do Campo. In late 1968, General Motors introduced its first Brazilian-designed model, the Chevrolet Opala. Perhaps the most illustrative example of the new place of the auto sector in the Brazilian economy came in 1974, when GM inaugurated the Cruz Alta Proving Grounds in Indaiatuba, São Paulo, on land that had once been a coffee plantation.[62]

In 1976, a state-of-the-art Fiat factory on the outskirts of Belo Horizonte (in the town of Betim, Minas Gerais) produced the Fiat 147 (a three-door hatchback), the first Brazilian car fueled exclusively by ethanol. Unlike the national legislation JK used to force foreign manufacturers to put plants in Brazil, the Mineiro governor, Rondon Pacheco, negotiated a series of concessions with Fiat president Giovanni Agnelli in Turin for the building of the Betim plant. From the 1970s through late 1980s, Fiat's Betim plant employed about 12,000 and built about 800 cars a day. At the beginning of the twenty-first century, Fiat employed about 17,000 workers in Minas Gerais and manufactured about 1,800 cars per day for both domestic and export markets, making it the company's most productive facility.[63] The rise of Fiat demonstrated the structural and spatial maturity the auto sector had achieved by the late 1970s. The Betim factory was built far from São Paulo's industrial suburbs and manufactured primarily small, energy-efficient passenger cars that could compete for market share at home and abroad. Indeed, the arrival of Fiat signaled the beginning of a new phase for Brazil's auto industry.

At about the same time the Brazilian government reinvigorated car sales with *Proálcool*, multinational car companies embraced the notion of the "world car."[64] The auto companies developed these cross-platform vehicles as a response to deteriorating rates of profit. The growing success of Japanese cars in the United States, when world oil prices remained high in the 1970s, led the American auto companies to look to their European and South American operations (especially in Brazil) to provide expertise in the design and manufacture of small, fuel-efficient vehicles. The perceived financial synergies in a cross-platform world car added to their appeal, along with the increased leverage over workers in higher wage settings (e.g., the United States and Western Europe) who could be replaced by moving operations to Brazil, Mexico, Argentina, South Africa, and elsewhere. Although the world car strategy grew out of problems in the American industry, it represented a triumph for the Brazilian auto sector. Ford plants in and around São Paulo produced an Escort model that shared components with the same car sold in the United States and Great Britain. In 1985, Volkswagen even exported Brazilian-made Fuscas to the United States as Beetles, before the model's complete redesign in 1994 and reintroduction in 1998.[65] The auto companies marketed the idea that Brazilian-made cars were increasingly popular throughout the world. One VW advertisement from 1981 shows a Passat in a wooden crate marked "Made in Brazil." The text notes that the quality of locally made VWs was so high that the Passats sold in the United States and Germany used Brazilian engines. Fiat's advertising in 1982 featured Brazilian-made vehicles on the streets of Paris outside Dior, Maxims, and near a variety of monuments. Perhaps the most historically interesting aspect of Brazil's role in world car production was its shipment of vehicles as completely knocked down units (CKDs) to other Latin American countries.[66]

Although the automobile was invented in France and the first car brought to Brazil was a Peugeot, conquering the American market would be the surest sign of the maturity of Brazilian manufacture. In late 1985, Volkswagen do Brasil announced that it would challenge the dominance of small Japanese sedans in the United States by exporting the Brazilian-made Parati and Voyage to America and selling them there as the VW Fox. Factories in São Bernardo do Campo and Taubaté (both in São Paulo state) had new robotic welders installed to increase quality for export. Indeed, Volkswagen needed three years to make the 2,000 changes in the gasoline-powered Fox that were necessary to pass U.S. safety and environment standards. The promotional campaign in the United States, which included a Super Bowl ad, did not mention that the Fox was made in Brazil, but back in its home country, the Voyage and Parati were marketed as being good enough to be sold in America. Billboards and magazine ads featured the cars parked in famous locations, from Wall Street to the Golden Gate Bridge.[67] Other car companies and parts makers likewise boasted of Brazilian technological prowess and the skill of the nation's workers. From components for cars made in Japan, the United States, and Europe to the motors running Boston's subway, Brazilian autos and parts were by the 1980s an important part of the ongoing process of globalized trade.[68]

Ironically, the VW Fox, despite the marketing campaign, did not sell well in the United States, while the Mexican-made Beetle became popular and trendy in the United States, Europe, and Japan.[69]

One of the planners' goals when they established the national auto industry was to protect Brazil from its insecure status in the international economy as a commodity producer. Auto factories would, they believed, lessen the nation's dependence on the international prices for coffee, sugar, and other commodities. And Brazil would no longer exhaust its foreign exchange on imports such as cars; instead, it would produce value-added manufactured goods for export. The 1973–1974 oil shock showed that broad automobility brought its own vulnerabilities to the international economy. Then, increasing globalization in the 1970s and 1980s, exemplified in the development of world cars, laid bare the false promise that advanced industrial production would somehow insulate the Brazilian economy from external forces. Autos had long before the creation of world cars become commodities; the interchangeability of production facilities for common platforms only made that fact more obvious.[70] Brazilian manufacturers could either expand domestic consumption within a protected market, as proposed by Kubitschek and his planners, or emphasize exports, relying on their comparative advantage as a low-cost producer. Although the initial supporters of JK's targets believed the Brazilian auto industry could do both these things, the military and its technocratic allies emphasized exports and middle-class consumption over expanding the internal market through a more equitable distribution of income. Indeed, during most of the dictatorship, real wages for workers fell, and income distribution became more skewed toward the wealthy.[71]

During the dictatorship, car ownership remained an important marker of being middle class, but automobility no longer provided an opening to the middle class for segments of Brazil's poor. Although Brazil had the greatest number of cars in South America in the mid-1960s, it had a much lower incidence of car ownership than Uruguay, Argentina, and Venezuela. In 1960, about half of 1% (0.57%) of Brazilians owned a car. By 1980, the number had climbed significantly but was still small at only 5%.[72] Even though auto ownership remained a luxury throughout the 1960s and into the 1970s, research on consumer habits showed that Brazilian car buyers were most sensitive to price. In greater Rio de Janeiro, for example, they preferred less expensive models that were fuel-efficient. Even among the wealthiest Brazilians surveyed, only a quarter of them used their cars to commute to work. The vast majority (69% in one survey) of urban Brazilians used buses for their commute.[73] Car ownership was also regionally skewed at this time. A study of national trends found that 63% of all Brazilian cars were in the center-south region, with São Paulo state accounting for 37% of all the country's vehicles.[74]

That did not dissuade manufacturers from marketing car ownership as an integral part of a modern Brazilian lifestyle. Indeed, households with cars frequently sought a second vehicle. Marketers noticed this trend in the early 1970s, and by 1981, women sought drivers' licenses at nearly the same rate as men in São Paulo. Women's car purchases represented a middle-class or elite economic status, but they also spoke to women's increasing sense of freedom and mobility.[75] Unlike previous eras, when driving was held out as a unique marker of modern womanhood, the car companies now sold the idea of equality through automobility, which dovetailed with the growing feminist movement among middle-class and elite women. Although not discussed in advertising, by this time automobility contained an element of sexual freedom. Both women and men could frequent so-called drive-in motels that existed for sexual rendezvous, as opposed to tourism and travel.[76] In Brazil, driving and auto ownership did not so much contribute to women's growing sense of independence; instead, they were markers of the changes enveloping society at this time.

Regardless of whether they owned an automobile, Brazilians increasingly embraced the broad car culture that had developed since the Kubitschek administration. Auto shows continued to attract big crowds, and magazines such as *Quatro Rodas* grew in popularity. Beginning in 1965, the magazine even began publishing national tourist guides for Brazilians. Still, nothing promoted automobility better than the growth of racing.[77] The auto companies continued to sponsor raids, races, and endurance challenges, as they had in the late 1950s and early 1960s. The Willys team raced in other South American countries, and Volkswagen ran a Rio-to-Bahia rally featuring its vehicles.[78] As the sport matured, more cities built their own tracks and promoted everything from soapbox derbies for kids to kart and stock-car races. Rio Grande do Sul opened the Autódromo Municipal de Guaporé in December 1969 and the Autódromo Internacional de Tarumã Viamão in November 1970. At about the same time, Brasília, Goiânia, and Rio inaugurated new tracks, and the old facility in Fortaleza was updated.[79]

Despite all the institutional support for the sport, the growth in popularity of racing in this era was personified in the career of one man, Emerson Fittipaldi. Earning international renown, Fittipaldi twice won the Indianapolis 500 (1989 and 1993) and won world championships in both Formula One (1972 and 1974) and CART (1989).[80] Fittipaldi was born in 1946 in São Paulo to a family of racing enthusiasts. Both his parents raced, and his father, Wilson, was a popular motor sports journalist who helped stage the first 1,000-mile endurance race in Brazil in 1956. Emerson's older brother, Wilsinho, drove Formula One and even owned a race team. At age 19, Emerson won the Prêmio Victor as the best young driver in Brazil. Over the course of the 1970s, he was the most prominent of a group of young Brazilian drivers (including Nelson Piquet, Bird Clemente, Luisinho Pereira Bueno, José Carlos Pace, Alex Dias Ribeiro, and Ingo Hoffmann) who came to prominence competing in Europe.[81] Fittipaldi's and his generation of racers' celebrity was a source of national pride, and this group of drivers cemented the place of motor sports in Brazil.[82]

The rise of Ayrton Senna to prominence in the 1980s transformed Brazilian auto racing from the realm of sport to that of mythology. Senna's professional record is impressive enough. In 162 races, he had the poll position (first at the start) 65 times. He won the Monte Carlo Grand Prix five times in a row (1989–1993) and six times in all. All Formula One drivers are highly skilled and brave, but Senna was held out as particularly talented and daring. The legend is that he had begun racing when he was four years old. He won the South American Kart Championship at age 17 and soon after went on to Europe to begin his adult career.[83] On the Formula One circuit, Senna's skill, particularly in tough conditions, gained him a broad following at home and abroad. Despite his hard-charging style, Senna was quite literally the only driver to stop in the midst of races to help rescue drivers from wrecks.[84] Still, it was his winning ways that made him so popular. The man who said, "Being second is to be the first among the losers" was the number one–ranked driver in the world three separate times in a 10-year career in Formula One. (He took two second places, one third, and three fourths; his worst finish was ninth place.)

After his tragic death in 1994 on the track of the San Marino Grand Prix, much of what Senna had done and said was magnified, as a sports hero became a national legend and a symbol of Brazilian modernity. He represented some of the ways that automobility put the nation on the world stage. Exports of inexpensively made cars, trucks, and buses stoked nation pride as Brazil made the transition from being a primarily agricultural producer to an industrial powerhouse, but competing in the United States and Europe in the most technologically sophisticated automobiles ever built made Senna an example of what Brazilians hoped to become. The public fascination with Senna's life transcended his massive public funeral, when all traffic was supposed to stop throughout the nation for one minute. In the months after his death, the news that Senna had been secretly donating large sums of money to children's charities only increased his popularity.

In the 12 years after his death, the Ayrton Senna Foundation donated more than $80 million to a wide variety of children's causes.[85] Even posthumous news of his extramarital affairs added to the Senna myth. The children's television personality Xuxa, one of Brazil's biggest stars, not only admitted to having had a relationship with Senna but also made a public spectacle of purchasing his personal Audi.[86]

The ongoing spread of automobility in the 1960s, 1970s, and 1980s had more than a direct economic impact or a broad cultural appeal. It profoundly affected Brazil in ways auto enthusiasts had never discussed. The environmental degradation of huge portions of the Amazonian rain forest and other interior spaces connected by roads to the coast or other urban areas was only the most obvious negative consequence of the triumph of Brazilian automobility. Destruction of the forest cover in the Amazon region accelerated in the 1970s and 1980s. By 1977, 96.5% of the forest remained, but that number dropped to 90% in 1990, and then to 86% in 2000.[87] Moreover, even with the less harmful exhaust produced by cars burning ethanol, exhaust pollution dramatically decreased the standard of living for urban Brazilians. The steady growth in the number of autos at the end of the twentieth century also brought dramatic increases in the number of traffic accidents and fatalities. These negative consequences of increased dependence on automobility, especially combined with the increasing city sprawl and suburbanization, were constant reminders of the costs of having given the internal combustion engine a central role in everyday life.[88]

No matter how successful automobility had become during the dictatorship, the vast majority of Brazilians still did not have the means to purchase a car. This primarily affected the people who built Brazilian autos. Kubitschek's dream of transforming these workers into middle-class consumers had been crushed by the 1964 coup. The military took control of 409 unions nationally. That move, a new strike law in 1964, and the ongoing repression of perceived and real opponents of the regime sent a clear message to all working people that the corporatist industrial relations system, through which disputes over wages and work conditions were to be settled, had once again become a tool to spur industrial production, rather than a means to promote social justice or even to provide a living wage (Figure 6.3). Over the course of much of the 1960s and 1970s, wages for industrial workers failed to keep up with inflation.[89] Despite the crackdown on Brazil's official unions, in 1968, dissident workers launched a series of strikes in foreign-owned metalworking establishments. The strike in São Paulo's industrial suburb of Osasco in July 1968 bypassed the established corporatist labor relations system and sought direct bargaining with

WILLYS OVERLAND DO BRASIL S.A.
ANNUAL REPORT
FISCAL YEAR ENDING JUNE 30, 1965

WORK, ORDER AND PROGRESS

FIGURE 6.3 After the 1964 military coup, work in auto factories was no longer easily associated with upward mobility and democracy. The Willys Annual Report for 1965 emphasizes "Work, Order and Progress." The report was published in English as well. Photo courtesy of the Bancroft Library, University of California at Berkeley.

employers. Strikes, student protests, and the growth of an armed guerrilla movement combined to give the most conservative elements of the military the authority to crack down even more on civil society. The repression that followed the announcement of Institutional Act 5 included torture of regime opponents. Not only were worker activists included among lists of such opponents but also rumors spread throughout São Paulo that individuals tied to the foreign auto companies supported and may have participated in the torture.[90]

Despite the crackdown, workers in metropolitan São Paulo's auto factories continued to organize informally. In the early 1970s, they were particularly concerned with the impact inflation was having on the value of their wages. These workers also worried that the government was understating the real rate of inflation, and so wage adjustments made through the Labor Courts would not keep up with the actual increase in their cost of living. Since the mid-1950s, however, workers in São Paulo had had a tool for collecting and analyzing wage and cost-of-living data. Formed in the aftermath of 1953's "Strike of the 300,000," the Inter-Union Department of Statistics and Socioeconomic Studies or DIEESE (*Departamento Intersindical de Estatísticas e Estudos Sócio-Econômicos*) provided unions with reliable data for negotiations with employers and in the Labor Courts. In the authoritarian context of the early 1970s, Brazilian workers could argue that inflation was, in fact, higher than the regime claimed, but they had few tools for making the real numbers part of wage adjustments. In 1973, for example, the government said that inflation had been 15%, but DIEESE's numbers showed a rate of between 20 and 25%. The regime's technocrats failed to calculate how Brazil's integration into the world economy might affect this debate. The World Bank, for one, had a strong interest in knowing Brazil's real rate of inflation and saw enough in the data to question the official figures. In July 1977, after making their own analysis, World Bank economists claimed that inflation had been 22.5% in 1973, thereby calling into question all the regime's economic figures, lending prestige to DIEESE, and providing Brazilian workers a new rallying cry for organizing and protest activities.[91]

Autoworkers responded over the course of the next year by organizing within their factories to directly push their employers to raise wages. At first, their decision to strike was barely noticed. As the work stoppages grew in size during May 1978, the strikes became a focal point for many in Brazil. The media portrayed the strikers and their demands in a positive light, which greatly aided both the immediate strike and the ongoing transformation of the labor movement. Favorable press coverage also fit with currents of elite thinking about autoworkers and their role in Brazilian society overall and specifically in the gradual political opening the military had begun in the mid-1970s, which was known as the *Abertura* (or Opening). When the May 1978 strikes began, the elite press openly discussed the justness of the workers' cause. Industry's *Gazeta Mercantil* noted that most businessmen admitted that the nation's workers—even the elite autoworkers—were woefully underpaid.[92] *Veja*, Brazil's leading newsmagazine, reported that many in São Paulo viewed the industrial relations system as a vestige of the worst period of the dictatorship and thought there should be direct negotiations between workers and their employers.[93] The highly respected *Jornal do Brasil* editorialized that Brazil's striking autoworkers were no different from their counterparts in the United States and Europe. Strikes and direct negotiations for higher wages were a standard component of advanced capitalist societies. To further make this point, the press reported that the United Auto Workers had pressured Ford do Brasil to negotiate with the strikers, and industrial relations experts from both Ford and Volkswagen began direct bargaining sessions with the workers' factory commissions.[94]

The following week, Mário de Almeida wrote an influential editorial in *Veja* titled "The Deconstructed Myth." In it, Almeida argued that striking automobile workers represented Brazil's "new working class" that was ready for democracy "after three quarters of a century of industrialization." He continued by describing the strikers and their leaders as "moderates" who had done their best to limit the influence of extremists on the left. In the final analysis, Almeida wrote that Brazil's working people were ready to be full participants in the *Abertura*, as this era of political opening was known.[95] That same week, *Veja* added in another editorial that students and left intellectuals should leave the strikers alone to settle things in direct negotiations with their employers and not intervene. This point of view meshed perfectly with the evolving culture of the strike movement, which operated through an almost hyperdemocratic practice and openly disdained nonworkers (particularly intellectuals) who tried to speak for the movement.[96]

Of even greater significance than the editorials supporting the strikers as democratic were reports that various military and police officials shared this point of view. Officials from the Ministry of Labor were leery of direct negotiations and suggested that they might need to intervene, perhaps violently, to force adherence to the law. Some São Paulo police and military officials, however, saw the strikers as peaceful and feared an armed presence would change that. General Dilermando Monteiro opposed police action and was satisfied that "mature" workers and unionists, such as Luiz Inácio Lula da Silva, would act in the best interests of the strikers. He added that employers were "showing good sense" in ignoring the strike laws and negotiating directly with their workers.[97] The press framed the 1978 strike as workers and employers negotiating peacefully, just like their counterparts in the United States and Europe. Segments of the military and police supported this development, while the Ministry of Labor continued to embrace the antiquated corporatist structure.[98]

Although the autoworkers did not receive such nearly universal support in later strikes in 1979 and 1980, they continued to be painted by key actors in Brazil and beyond as the embodiment of modern, capitalist, democratic workers. Nowhere was this belief more widely held than among the very individuals with whom the strikers negotiated: the directors of industrial relations departments at the major foreign auto companies. Diogo Clemente, Ford do Brasil's director of industrial relations, said after the late 1970s and early 1980s strikes, that the nation's autoworkers were well ahead of the rest of society, particularly industry, in understanding how direct contract negotiations were a fundamental component of a democratic capitalist society. Clemente explained: "In the negotiating of a legitimate labor contract [without the government involved] we create democracy for this country, which is fundamental for its survival."[99] Emanuele Sessarego, the chief of Italian tire maker Pirelli's industrial relations department, argued in May 1978 that Brazil's labor laws were antiquated and did not fit in with the *Abertura* or even just normal employer-employee relations. Edmir de Freitas Garcez, who directed the Human Relations Department at Ford do Brasil, recalled that all his negotiations with Lula and union activist Jair Menaguelli in São Bernardo do Campo took place "in an atmosphere of absolute respect." Phillip Caldwell, the president of Ford in the early 1980s, explained that he was expanding the company's investments in Brazil because of the quality of workers there. He said the Brazilian strikes and negotiations were no different from those in other countries.[100]

The auto companies seized on the fact that autoworkers organized themselves in factory commissions as proof that they were embracing democratic ideals.[101] Ford's industrial relations people worked closely with the commissions. Volkswagen do Brasil attempted to create company factory commissions but soon learned to negotiate with the workers' real representatives. Paulo Pizarro, the president of Brazil's Association of Industrial Training, argued that factory commissions increased workers' stake in the success of the firm. He saw them as local expressions of democracy on the shop floor and a way to keep workers focused on wage and work issues, as opposed to the sorts of political concerns unions had taken up in the past.[102] Even when some military men, most notably President João Figueiredo (1979–1985), called for cracking down on Lula and the factory commissions in 1980, executives in the foreign auto sector continued to work with the metalworkers through the commissions.[103] Analysis conducted in the mid-1980s shows that the majority of industrialists who opposed working with factory commissions and who saw them as political institutions did not have such organizations in their firms. Those businesses with the commission structure valued them as tools for increased worker-management communication.[104]

In addition to their experiences in dealing with businessmen and industrial relations executives, the autoworkers benefited greatly from comparisons with other unionists. Brazilian industrialists favorably contrasted the autoworkers to populists and communists. Criticism of these autoworkers by the Communist Party leaders on the one hand and by populist politician Leonel Brizola on the other furthered the popular impression that these workers were moderates. The workers' allies and opposition during the April 1980 strikes clarified this situation for most of civil society.

São Paulo's progressive archbishop, Cardinal Paulo Evaristo Arns, publicly supported the striking workers, while the Communist Party loudly called for their return to work.[105] Years after this initial wave of strikes in São Paulo's automobile factories, industrial relations executives and business leaders in the auto sector continued to note that the workers who went on to make up the rank and file of the Workers' Party (*Partido dos Trabalhadores*, or PT) were quite distinct from their predecessors. Industrial relations experts noted in their primary journal, *Tendências do Trabalho*, that there were two broad sets of ideological and intellectual influences on Brazilian labor: On the one hand, there was the Communist/Populist block tied to the Partido Communista Brasileira (PCB) and Ministry of Labor. Although often bitter rivals, these groups shared a belief in the corporatist system and found a home in the mainstream opposition party of the early 1980s, the Brazilian Democratic Movement Party (Partido do Movimento Democrático Brasilerio, or PMDB). Opposing these often corrupt unionists of the right and left (known as *pelegos*) were the workers in the Central Única dos Trabalhadores (CUT) and PT. Although seen as having ties to some far-left groups (e.g., the Maoist PC do B and academic Trotskyists), they were mostly coded as "authentic unionists" with the support of the Catholic Church.[106] In 1992, Francisco José Marcondes Evangelista wrote in *Tendências do Trabalho* of the stages the Brazilian working class had gone through. The PT was seen as breaking the iron grip of corrupt unionism (*peleguismo*) and opening the way for democratic unionism that focused on wages and work conditions.[107]

During the long military dictatorship, Brazil's automobile workers occupied a unique social space. They were a privileged and to some extent revered segment of the working class whose patterns of consumption made them appear to be part of Brazil's growing middle class.[108] Long before the May 1978 strike at the São Bernardo do Campo Scania plant, these workers were seen by many in Brazilian society as different from previous groups of strikers. Who they were, the ways they behaved, what they sought, and who opposed them became tangible reasons the strikers were seen as representatives of a new, democratic Brazil. Unlike populists and communists, the autoworkers did not discuss taking state power. They did not seek out political alliances with middle-class or elite groups. They explicitly called for the state to exit from industrial relations and openly rejected political ties to established parties.[109] The end result of this orientation was the founding of the workers' own party, the PT.[110] The fact that these strikers were overwhelmingly male (indeed, having a beard was a key outward symbol of one's status as autoworker at this time) and the primary wage earners in what were read as traditional families gave the strikers further legitimacy. Where and how they struck and protested—peacefully in their factories or in *futebol* stadiums they had arranged to use—also signaled their interest in focusing on wage and work issues over more obviously political questions. They did not march symbolically through the center of town or move to São Paulo's central Praça da Sé to demand state intervention in their industrial disputes. They focused first and foremost on their factories to push for better wages and improved work conditions. In addition to their own behavior, the strikers were fortunate to be opposed by the Communist Party and some populist leaders.[111] These enemies made the autoworkers seem not only palatable but also attractive to many industrialists, the elite press, and the general public.

When the Brazilian media celebrated the 30th anniversary of the establishment of a national automobile industry in 1986, they noted the nation's pride in producing automobiles and even exporting cars and auto parts throughout the world. The media also took note of the auto sector's most enduring new product: the new Brazilian worker. These workers possessed specialized skills and had a new orientation toward their employers. According to auto company executives, these new workers were the forefront of a new "employer-employee relationship" and "a new labor consciousness."[112] Most of the autoworkers were "new" in many senses of the term. In Ford's São Bernardo do Campo plant, more than 70% of the workers were 38 years old or younger. A clear majority (67.9%) came from families who had worked exclusively or mostly in agriculture. Only 15.7% of these workers came from families with no direct ties to the rural sector.[113] Indeed, they were the very people modernist intellectuals, industrialists, and state policy makers had hoped would be socialized into citizenship through work in Brazil's automobile factories.

The strikes of the late 1970s and early 1980s revealed the contours of their socialization. They took their citizenship rights very seriously. The workers' deeply held belief in democracy inside their unions and throughout society shaped their actions and how they were perceived by civil society and segments of the state. The democratic practice of the new unionism meant that working-class politics in greater São Paulo would be seen as fundamentally new. Perhaps most significantly, they no longer seemed threatening to other segments of society. These workers had a clear ideological orientation, and it was very different from the perceived image of Brazilian workers gleaned from populist and communist rhetoric. Close analysis of data from 1983 to 1985 of attitudes held by 13,638 Ford workers in plants in São Bernardo do Campo and Ipiranga by the noted sociologist Leôncio Martins Rodrigues demonstrates how different the PT's supporters were from the popular view of labor in the past.[114] These Ford workers supported their unions and factory commissions and believed they were the best means for improving wages and conditions on the shop floor.[115] Support for their own institutions did not, however, translate into opposition to their employer. When asked to respond to the assertion "When the company gains, workers lose out," clear majorities disagreed. They explicitly said that they benefited from Ford's success.[116] Interestingly, these workers also rejected nationalist claims about foreign corporations. Few (10.2% in São Bernardo do Campo, 2.4% in Ipiranga) believed conditions at work would be better if Ford were Brazilian-owned. Majorities (São Bernardo do Campo, 54.1%; Ipiranga, 77.2%) said conditions would be worse or equal. Huge majorities (77.8% in São Bernardo do Campo and 70.4% in Ipiranga) claimed they would be in worse shape if Ford were government-owned.

Populists and communists had always agreed on a nationalist politics that demonized foreign, particularly U.S.-based, corporations. Moreover, these two groups had placed their faith in the Ministry of Labor and its corporatist industrial relations system. Ford workers rejected this political orientation. They accepted, and in many ways benefited from, the presence of multinational corporations. Employees in greater São Paulo's automobile factories were among the best compensated workers in Brazil. They had the highest incidence of home and car ownership of any group of workers in the nation. They also tended to own refrigerators, television sets, and other consumer goods. Brazilian automobile workers were not so much a labor aristocracy as they were a vanguard for labor. These workers were the consumers and citizens imagined by the industrialists and state makers who had pushed for the creation of domestic automobile industry. Unlike their counterparts in the United States and Europe, however, Brazilian autoworkers did not allow acceptance of and participation in the capitalist system to become quiescence. During the *Abertura* and the civilian administrations that followed the military regime's end in 1985, autoworkers continued to articulate an aggressive working-class politics that called for the deepening of Brazilian democracy and a more equitable distribution of the fruits of the capitalist system. They became the active citizens of a consumer-based capitalist democracy anticipated by intellectuals, industrialists, and state makers, but they articulated politics never imagined by those elites.

There is no shortage of irony in the role that 21 years of military dictatorship played in transforming Brazil's autoworkers into some of the nation's most important proponents and practitioners of democracy. In the years immediately after the coup, military leaders and their technocratic allies abandoned Kubitschek's goal of transforming the country's poor into middle-class citizens and instead destroyed unions, tortured opponents, and held down wages to increase the rate of profits. When these workers organized and struck during the *Abertura* for the wages they had always assumed due to those who manufactured autos, they tapped into Brazilian ideas about modernity, technology, consumerism, and even democracy. They became an important symbol of Brazil's success in transforming itself over the course of the twentieth century into a unified and economically developed nation that seemed to be on the brink of establishing a pluralistic capitalist democracy. Autoworkers in and around São Paulo had helped bring about many of the dreams and hopes of early auto enthusiasts, modernist intellectuals, and state makers.

Epilogue: Tropical Modernity in a Globalized Space

THE MILITARY HAD PLANNED a smooth transition out of power through the *Abertura*, but the actual process of regime change and democratization was chaotic, confusing, and completely unpredictable. An indirect election for president on 15 January 1985, held by the legislature, was supposed to guarantee the presidency to one of the military's civilian allies, but the opposition party, the PMDB, and dissidents from the military-affiliated PDS joined together to make Tancredo Neves, a vocal opponent of the dictatorship, Brazil's first civilian leader since the 1964 coup. The evening before the scheduled March 15 inaugural, Neves was taken to the hospital to treat a severe stomach illness. After a series of operations and declarations of good health, the president-elect died on 21 April. José Sarney, a former member of the promilitary PDS who had run on the ticket with Neves, became the unlikely leader of a newly democratic Brazil.

Civil society, from the women's movement to progressive sectors of the Catholic Church and particularly autoworkers in the newly constituted Workers Party (PT), had helped push the military from power and bring about the election of Neves and Sarney. These groups next focused their attention on writing a constitution for the newly democratic Brazil. Begun in 1986 and completed in 1988, it was a curious mix of broad civil rights and economic nationalism. A reaction to the authoritarian rule of the military, the constitution granted illiterates the right to vote. It also provided for the creation of consumers' rights and special rights for the young, and it included an expansive civil code. Violations of Brazilians' civil liberties could now be punished severely. The 1988 Constitution did not, however, roll back the role of the state in the economy, which had grown dramatically during the dictatorship. It even explicitly guaranteed that Petrobras would remain a state enterprise.[1]

After more than a century, political liberalism finally seemed to trump economics in Brazil. The extraordinary success of automobility was partially responsible for this new balance. Autoworkers' organizing and strike activities helped to define how Brazilian democracy would operate in the postdictatorship period, with its emphasis on unfettered popular organizing outside the old corporatist labor structure. Paradoxically, the auto sector's accomplishments limited the appeal of the economic neoliberalism that was sweeping the region in the 1980s.[2] The unique partnership of multinational, local, and state capital had built large-scale foreign-owned auto factories, parts manufacturers, and an extensive alternative energy complex based on ethanol. The success of these programs in the eyes of many Brazilians obviated the need to alter the balance of public and private investments in the economy.

The late 1980s were a period of political hope and economic disorder. While Brazilians celebrated their new democracy, the weak Sarney government tried to stem the dizzying rate of inflation, which was 416% in 1987, and mollify angry consumers and producers.[3] Shunning the sort of neoliberal solutions being pushed by Washington at this time, Sarney instead instituted a heterodox policy that froze prices before wages were initially increased and then frozen. The plan's structure at first stimulated consumer demand and seemingly controlled inflation. But Sarney's program soon fell apart, with inflation reaching 1,038% in 1988. The plan's promises of economic stability and the broad public belief that democratic politics would provide the solutions to Brazil's problems led to high expectations that Sarney could not meet.

The 1989 presidential election became the first forum for debating ways to fix these problems. Former autoworker and trade unionist Luiz Inácio Lula da Silva and a previously unknown northeastern politician, Fernando Collor de Melo, faced each other in the final round of voting, after receiving the most votes out of the 22 registered candidates. Lula supported the maintenance of protectionism for industry and a vibrant state presence in the economy. Collor de Melo increasingly embraced neoliberal solutions for fighting inflation and reigniting economic growth that seemed to be so successful in Argentina, Chile, and Mexico in the late 1980s. After gaining the presidency, Collor de Melo quickly lowered tariffs on many imported goods, including foreign-made automobiles. Although the president left office because of an extensive financial scandal, economic policy continued in the neoliberal vein. The 1994 election of one-time Marxist sociologist turned moderate Paulista senator, Fernando Henrique Cardoso, cemented the so-called Washington Consensus of eliminating trade and investment barriers.[4] Cardoso had made his reputation as the finance minister who finally tamed inflation, which had reached an annual rate of 2,489% in 1993. By 1997, the rate was only 4%.[5]

Lowering or even eliminating import restrictions and tariffs was a key component of Cardoso's anti-inflation strategy. Foreign-made goods were often cheaper and better made than Brazilian products. The automobile industry, although owned by multinational corporations, was undercapitalized and did not use the latest, most competitive technologies in either its factories or its products. Competition would bring needed change to the industry and, in the long run, make Brazilian cars more attractive on the foreign market. The multinationals had the resources to retool their Brazilian facilities, but the impact of the newly opened markets reached beyond the big producers. Auto parts makers faced inexpensive imports, and the ethanol industry now had to compete with increased use of petroleum because imported vehicles had gasoline-powered engines.[6]

Low inflation and growing consumer confidence helped auto sales recover from the economic downturn of the late 1980s and early 1990s. Throughout the Cardoso years, car ownership grew as a marker of middle-class success in Brazil. Indeed, owning the latest model separated the affluent from the merely middle or upper working class. Driving an imported car, particularly a Honda or Toyota, was an important status symbol for the rising middle class in the late 1990s and early 2000s.[7] The increased foreign and domestic investment of the Cardoso years also benefited road building and other key parts of Brazil's infrastructure. During the 1980s, roads inside and between the country's leading cities had deteriorated at a rapid rate. A sinkhole in Rio de Janeiro, for example, swallowed a VW whole, and the highways in the nation's center-south became notorious for potholes that easily disabled vehicles.[8]

Increased public investment in infrastructure and the net inflow of capital, along with the privatization of telecommunications and much of the electricity supply, further stimulated the economy during the Cardoso years, but in ways that exposed Brazil to the vicissitudes of the international economy. Indeed, by 1998, Brazil fell victim to a world financial crisis that had begun in Asia.[9] Cardoso won a second presidential term just as the impact of this crisis was being felt in Brazil, and he spent much of his final years in office trying to contain it. With the 2002 presidential election on the horizon, Brazilians expressed support for Cardoso's skill as a leader but increased skepticism about the value of neoliberal economic solutions.

In this atmosphere, Lula's fourth presidential campaign resonated with a majority of Brazilians. The former autoworker and trade unionist took office on January 1, 2003, and was overwhelmingly reelected in October 2006. Indeed, Lula's life story, as well as his administration, makes up part of automobility's extraordinary role in the development of Brazil's modernity. Lula himself was born into poverty in the northeastern state of Pernambuco. As a young boy, he spent 13 days on the back of a flatbed truck (*pau de arara*) on his way to São Paulo. At age 12, he began working in menial jobs, but he later gained access to job training through the industrial education institute, SENAI. He then gained employment in the metalworking and automotive industries as a mechanic and lathe operator. As an activist and then leader of the union representing autoworkers in São Paulo's industrial suburbs, Lula became a prominent proponent of both basic labor issues (better pay and transparent and open unions) and the establishment of a vibrant democracy in place of Brazil's long military dictatorship. A founding member of the Workers' Party (PT), Lula was elected to Congress in 1986 and ran unsuccessfully for president three times before winning that office in 2002.[10]

Despite fears expressed by conservative commentators and politicians in the United States and Europe, Lula's government maintained stable rates of economic growth and low inflation, while continuing to welcome foreign investment.[11] Moreover, his most prominent program was the establishment of the Family Stipend Program (*Bolsa Família*), which provided the rough equivalent of wages earned by working children to families whose children maintained high attendance records at school and updated vaccination records. By 2008, more than 11 million families had benefited from this program. Mirroring the sort of education and health programs previously offered only by Brazil's largest employers, as pioneered by the foreign auto companies and some forward-looking Paulista industrialists, the *Bolsa Família* is part of a continuum of ideas about the social, economic, and political refashioning of the Brazilian population.[12] This program, along with a robust economy based on expanding both agricultural and industrial output during his presidency, quickly began to benefit the poorest Brazilians. Careful research of incomes, living conditions, and consumerism throughout society showed that by 2007, more than 23 million Brazilians had moved from the lowest income categories (labeled D and E) into the lower middle class, or category C. Indeed, by December 2007, more than 70% of Brazilians lived in their own houses.[13]

Lula was elected on a platform that called, in part, for a modification of the extreme economic liberalism of his predecessor, Fernando Henrique Cardoso. Lula and the PT argued that Brazil could have both free market capitalism and government regulation of economic and social conditions. Such regulation, combined with the *Bolsa Família* and other policies, made up a sort of state Fordism that Brazil had never before experienced. Placed within the context of a century of automobility, this state role in the economy makes a great deal of sense. That is, probably the two most important issues in twentieth-century Brazilian politics were: First, how should the nation incorporate its entire population into formal politics? In other words, should Brazil be a democracy? Second, what role should the state play in shaping the economy? Since the mid to late nineteenth century, leading Paulistas had embraced some level of state support for agriculture, and segments of the state's elites supported tariffs and other measures to encourage early industrialization. But through the presidential administration of Washington Luís, economic liberalism and laissez-faire policy making dominated in Brazil. Vargas and Kubitschek embraced different levels of state planning in the economy, but they did not succeed in creating a democratic polity, and the military dictatorship was explicitly antidemocratic.

The election of an autoworker to the Brazilian presidency at the beginning of the twenty-first century was an unexpected outcome of the nation's long struggle to become modern. Lula's life story, his coalition, and his governing style mirrored key aspects of Brazil's twentieth century and have been, like modernity itself, highly contingent and unpredictable. Although the nation was physically unified by roads and other forms of communication by the time he took office, Brazil continued to face important issues related to its massive size and its legacy of intense regionalism. Lula's 2006 reelection revealed the ongoing regional divide and its legacy of racism, as some of the president's opponents in São Paulo and elsewhere in the nation's center-south region derided the president and his supporters as uneducated northeasterners. Mass e-mails calling for the richer, whiter center-south to secede from the poorer and less economically developed northeast made their way around cyberspace during the campaign. The e-mails blared, "The Solution Is to Separate!!!" (Epilogue Figure 1). The country was depicted as divided in half, with the center-south run by Lula's opponent, Geraldo Alckmin, and the north and northeast controlled by Lula.[14]

Lula's presidency represented both the triumph of Brazilian national unity and its ongoing challenges. Other aspects of automobility have affected Brazil in equally complex ways. In late July 1999, for example,

A SOLUÇÃO É SEPARAR!!!

JÁ QUE ELES QUEREM TANTO...

ELES FICOM COM
ELE...

NÒS COM
ELE...

EPILOGUE FIGURE I Despite the significant transformation of Brazil, the 2006 presidential election recalled the cultural and economic aspects of the nation's regionalism. An anonymous anti-Lula e-mail declares "The Solution Is to Separate." E-mail in possession of the author.

truck drivers launched an extraordinarily successful four-day strike to protest high fuel costs and government fees. About 700,000 truckers shut down national commerce by refusing to transport everything from fuel to food and including all manner of goods. Trucks transported 63% of Brazilian goods at that time, so the strike's impact was felt quickly throughout the nation. Truckers dramatized the impact of their strike by parking their vehicles on key highways to close off all other traffic. For four days, a 400-kilometer traffic jam of parked trucks clogged the Dutra between São Paulo and Rio. The strike ended only when President Cardoso threatened to use violence to break it up and also agreed to freezing tolls, lowering the points system for traffic offenses, and providing new resources to fight highway robberies.[15] The truckers' stoppage showed that along with the highly integrated national economy of the late twentieth century, Brazilian development was also quite fragile. Disgruntled truckers could bring almost the entire economy to a standstill, and they ended up with most of their demands met, even though the president had used the threat of force.

Automobility again proved less of a panacea for all the nation's ills and more just another mundane aspect of late-twentieth-century life in Brazil when Ford announced in July 1999 that it would close its iconic

Ipiranga plant in São Paulo. The much less industrial northeast state of Bahia offered Ford significant tax incentives to move some production facilities to Camaçari. Workers responded by striking, but they could not prevent the move and soon returned to work. The loss of jobs to the less developed, lower wage northeast brought home to São Paulo's autoworkers the reality that although they had among the best industrial jobs in Brazil, their employment was not necessarily secure. Moreover, news of the Camaçari factory broke at about the same time that McDonalds Comércio de Alimentos Ltda (or McDonalds Brasil) overtook Volkswagen do Brasil as the nation's largest private-sector employer, challenging the facile assumptions many Brazilians had held throughout the twentieth century that industrialism, foreign enterprises, and particularly the manufacture of automobiles would transform both the nation and its people. At the beginning of the twenty-first century, Brazil's successful industrialization left it vulnerable to many of the same economic forces that had brought deep economic contractions to the auto industry in Michigan, Indiana, and elsewhere in the United States.

Another change in Brazil's car industry in the early twenty-first century undermined old assumptions about the role of automobility in the nation's economic development. The multinational corporations had increasingly looked at production in South America as key to their overall profitability. Fiat's Minas factory, for example, was the company's most productive and profitable. Ford and VW in Argentina and Brazil had earlier tried to raise their rate of profit by creating a special automobile free-trade zone called Autolatina. Founded in 1987 and dissolved in 1995, VW held 51% of the holding company's stock and produced cars, and Ford, with its 49% share, was responsible for truck production. Relying on so-called badge engineering, Autolatina turned out cars and trucks under both the VW and Ford brand names but never succeeded in achieving significant cost savings, largely because of the undercapitalized Argentine facilities. Such attempts to alter production and sales were fruitless, and Brazil became an increasingly frustrating market for foreign manufacturers. Worker assertiveness and weakening demand left the auto companies scrambling for profitability at the end of the twentieth century.[16]

After the failure of Autolatina, VW and Ford next turned to a radical reengineering of the entire concept of the automobile factory, using Brazil for experiments in manufacturing techniques and labor relations. Volkswagen built a new truck and bus plant in rural Resende in Rio de Janeiro state, far from its existing facilities in São Paulo. It was the first automobile manufacturing facility of its kind in the world, for Volkswagen owned and operated the factory building, but each segment of production was controlled by subcontractors.[17] This so-called modular production facility—which was later emulated by Boeing and Airbus—freed VW from contentious wage negotiations with line workers because they were employed by the subcontractors. Ford quickly followed with the 2001 inauguration of its Camaçari plant in Bahia, which executives at corporate headquarters in Dearborn, Michigan, labeled the model for future plants. At Camaçari, Visteon, Lear, and 20 other suppliers conducted actual component manufacturing before assembling Ford vehicles. By 2007, this "simultaneous supply chain" employed more than 9,000 workers from more than two dozen companies, including Ford.[18] Volkswagen's Resende and Ford's Camaçari factories were just two of the new, state-of-the-art automobile plants built in Brazil in the late 1990s and early 2000s. All were constructed far from the manufacturing center of metropolitan São Paulo and relied on advanced manufacturing schemes that sought to blunt the power of the nation's autoworkers' unions. The multinational auto companies built these plants not only for Brazil's growing domestic market but also for export. They hoped that the factories' new, innovative designs and decentralized labor relations would make Brazilian production among the most efficient and profitable in the world.[19]

Toyota anticipated the marketing of Brazilian-made Corollas in the United States with print advertisements in leading magazines, such as *Newsweek* and *Time*. The two-page ads featured a coffee farmer on one page and on the other a declaration that "the people of Brazil produce the world's best coffee and soon some other great ways to get to work in the morning."[20] The text continued by noting that the Corolla would soon be manufactured in a new plant in São Paulo. The ad inadvertently noted one of the unintended consequences of Brazil's successful industrialization: the transformation of the automobile into a commodity. The Honda Civic and Toyota Corolla had become the late-twentieth-century versions of Ford's Model T and GM's Chevy. They were mass-produced, highly reliable, and relatively inexpensive industrial commodities.[21] By the end of the twentieth century, Brazil was one of the world's leading industrial nations, and its auto sector played a central role in domestic manufacture and the structure of multinational automobile companies.[22] And yet, the very success of this aspect of automobility left Brazil highly vulnerable to oscillations in the international economy; indeed, it may have become even more vulnerable than it had been in the previous century.

Automobility unquestionably played a central role in Brazil's economic modernization. Its place as a tool of cultural and political modernism was not always as obvious. The automobile companies, from the advent of the Model T in 1908 onward, associated owning and driving a car with a new sense of personal freedom. Henry Ford himself successfully combined consumerism and work to define a new sort of citizenship. The claims of advertisers and the reality of car ownership, which remained extremely limited until the late 1950s, did not always correspond. As much joy and heartache as car ownership or bus travel brought Brazilians, perhaps the most significant personal transformations wrought by automobility had more to do with the manufacture and presence of cars, trucks, and buses than their use. The creation of a new working class, with its modern and democratic identity, represented the high point of Brazilian automobility's impact on culture and politics in the twentieth century. The deforestation of huge swaths of the Atlantic forest and Amazon region represented one of its low points. The interminable traffic and choking pollution in the nation's largest cities, particularly São Paulo, Rio de Janeiro, and Belo Horizonte, are more than just another cost of economic modernization. They also mitigate or even retard the positive cultural and political components of Brazilian modernity.[23]

Brazilian modernity has been neither an utter triumph nor unmitigated tragedy. The struggle to be modern shaped twentieth-century Brazil, but often in ways modernists, state makers, auto enthusiasts, and others could never have imagined. So many of these people thought of modernity as some sort of virtuous state of being that would finally usher in Brazilian progress by providing its literal and figurative tools. What they failed to understand was that the nature of modernity is contingent and frequently in flux. There was no glorious end point of a developed, peaceful, and modern Brazil at the close of the twentieth century. Automobility had succeeded in finally unifying the interior with the coast and the rural with the urban. It has obliterated the notion of the "two Brazils." In its place, it left a unified nation with effective and functioning lines of communication but one that was a much more complicated, variegated, and globalized space than the Brazil into which Santos Dumont brought the nation's first car.

Introduction

1. Edvaldo Pereira Lima, *Ayrton Senna: Guerreiro de Aquário* (São Paulo: Brasiliense, 1995); and Christopher Hilton, *Ayrton Senna* (Somerset: Patrick Stephens, 1994), 8–22. All the quotes are from *Los Angeles Times*, 10 May 1994.

2. Brazil is so large that all the nations of Europe, from Iceland to Ukraine, fit comfortably within its borders. This geographical enormity is well depicted in map form in E. Bradford Burns, *A History of Brazil*, 3rd ed. (New York: Columbia University Press, 1993), 14.

3. Throughout this book I refer to the United States as "America" and people from the United States as "Americans." This is common both in the United States (my home) and in Brazil (the subject of this study and, in some ways, my second home). Many Latin Americans, particularly in Mexico and the Caribbean basin, object to these terms applying only to the United States, but given the subject of this book, I have chosen to use those terms that are most commonly applied in the United States and Brazil.

4. Henry Adams wrote the first chapter of the first volume (of six total volumes) of his *History of the United States of America* (1889) on the issue of transportation in the settlement and expansion of the United States. Moreover, George Washington, James Madison, and Alexander Hamilton all supported an active state role in the creation of national transportation links for the United States. See Sarah H. Gordon, *Passage to Union: How the Railroads Transformed American Life, 1829–1929* (Chicago: Ivan R. Dee, 1996), 13–14; John F. Kasson, *Civilizing the Machine: Technology and Republican Values in America, 1776–1900* (1978; New York: Hill & Wang, 1999), 33–36; and Joseph S. Wood, "The Idea of a National Road," in Karl Raitz, ed. *The National Road* (Baltimore: Johns Hopkins University Press, 1996), 93–122.

5. Although these railroads were primarily tied to the export economy, they stimulated economic growth and provided key regional transportation links that Brazil did not have. See John Coatsworth, *Growth against Development: The Economic Impact of Railroads in Porfirian Mexico* (DeKalb: Northern Illinois University Press, 1981).

6. Thomas J. Misa, *Leonardo to the Internet: Technology and Culture from the Renaissance to the Present* (Baltimore: Johns Hopkins University Press, 2004), 118–121.

7. Patricia Seed, *Ceremonies of Possession in Europe's Conquest of the New World, 1492–1640* (Cambridge: Cambridge University Press, 1995), 140. The quote is from the original grant. See pp. 100–148 for Seed's illuminating analysis of Portuguese seafaring technology and practice.

8. Thomas E. Skidmore, *Brazil: Five Centuries of Change* (New York: Oxford University Press, 1999), 1–27.

9. See Bertha K. Becker and Claudio A. G. Egler, *Brazil: A New Regional Power in the World Economy* (Cambridge: Cambridge University Press, 1992), on the population's concentration on the coastal escarpment. The settlement pattern, however, should not obscure the fact that Brazilians have inhabited the interior since the colonial era. In addition to Quilombos and Indian villages, large portions of the *sertão* were occupied in the seventeenth and eighteenth centuries. It is important to note the different regional effects of these settlement patterns. Minas Gerais became one of the nation's wealthiest states through agriculture and later industry in the aftermath of the mining boom. See Douglas Cole Libby, *Transformação e Trabalho: Em Uma Economia Escravista, Minas Gerais no Século XIX* (São Paulo: Brasiliense, 1988); and Marsall C. Eakin, *Tropical Capitalism: The Industrialization of Belo Horizonte* (New York: Palgrave, 2002). The rubber economy, however, did not spur additional growth in the Amazonian states and territories. See Barbara Weinstein, *The Amazon Rubber Boom, 1850–1920* (Stanford, Calif.: Stanford University Press, 1983).

10. On the scope of rail transportation through 1930, see Steven Topik, *The Political Economy of the Brazilian State, 1889–1930* (Austin: University of Texas Press, 1987), 93–128; Julian Smith Duncan, *Public and Private Operation of Railways in Brazil* (1932; New York: AMS Press, 1968); and William Summerhill, *Order against Progress: Government, Foreign Investment and Railroads in Brazil, 1854–1913* (Stanford, Calif.: Stanford University Press, 2003). Summerhill details the impact of railroads in lowering freight costs and therefore having a positive impact on economic development. Summerhill may overstate the impact of railroads, given Brazil's great size and the difficulty of constructing lines. For a careful comparison of national communications and transportation networks, see Claudio A. G. Egler, "Dinâmic Territorial Recente da Indústria no Brasil: 1970–1980," in Bertha K. Becker et al., eds. *Tecnologia e Gestão do Território* (Rio de Janeiro: UFRJ, 1988).

11. On the Companhia União e Indústria, which built and maintained the turn-pike, see Sérgio de Oliveira Birchal, *Entrepreneurship in Nineteenth-Century Brazil: The Formation of a Business Environment* (New York: St. Martin's Press, 1999).

12. On the figure of Pedro II in this regard, see Lilia Moritz Schwarcz, *As Barbas do Imperador: D. Pedro II, um Monarca nos Trópicos* (São Paulo: Companhia das Letras, 1998); and Roderick J. Barman, *Citizen Emperor: D. Pedro II and the Making of Brazil, 1825–1891* (Stanford, Calif.: Stanford University Press, 1999). On Brazilian exceptionalism, see Emília Viotti da Costa, *The Brazilian Empire: Myths and Histories* (Chicago: University of Chicago Press, 1985). The case of nineteenth-century Brazil is an ideal example of the sort of nationalism analyzed by Benedict Anderson in that it was more a product of language and imagination than of concrete territoriality and centralized juridical domination. See *Imagined Communities: Reflections on the Origin and Spread of Nationalism*, rev. ed. (London: Verso, 1991). Gopal Balakrishnan offers an important critique of Anderson that focuses on the need to ana-lyze sites of contestation, particularly open warfare in defining national-ism. The strength of Balakrishnan's argument for some parts of the world (e.g., Europe) only confirms the applicability of Anderson for Brazil. See "The National Imagination," in Gopal Balakrishnan, ed. *Mapping the Nation* (London: Verso, 1996), 198–213.

13. See Euclides da Cunha, *Os Sertões* (1902; Rio: Paulo de Azevedo, 1938). Da Cunha's fascination with the role of place, space, and object in the unfold-ing of history is well analyzed in Nicolau Sevcenko, *Literatura como Missão: Tensões Sociais e Criação Cultural na Primeira República* (São Paulo: Brasiliense, 1983), 130–160. De Cunha is famously, and perhaps unfairly, lampooned as the "nearsighted journalist" who observes the uprising through bro-ken glasses in Mario Vargas Llosa's *La Guerra del Fin del Mundo* (Caracas: Biblioteca Ayacucho, 1981).

14. Demétrio Magnoli, *O Corpo da Pátria: Imaginação Geográfica e Política Externa no Brasil, 1808–1912* (São Paulo: UNESP, 1997), 79–131. Becker and Egler, (*Brazil: A New Regional Power*, 16–41) argue that weak national integration forced the central state to rely on regional landowners for control of the terri-tory. This precluded the development of "nationality" and instead led to the creation of "stateness" based on an archipelago of unconnected agricultural areas—each with its own lines of communications to Europe.

15. On the close connection between the accumulation of knowledge and state making, see Charles Tilly, *Coercion, Capital, and European States, A.D. 990–1992* (Oxford: Blackwell, 1990); Anderson, *Imagined Communities*, 163–185; and James C. Scott, *Seeing Like a State: How Certain Schemes to Improve the Human Condition Have Failed* (New Haven: Yale University Press, 1998), 53–83.

16. Henri Lefebvre, *The Production of Space* (Oxford: Blackwell, 1991). For elab-orations of Lefebvre's categories that have informed this work, see David

Harvey, *The Condition of Postmodernity* (Oxford: Blackwell, 1990), 211–259; and Derek Gregory, *Geographical Imaginations* (Oxford: Blackwell, 1994), 70–205. The quote is from the IHGB *Revista*, cited in Magnoli, *O Corpo da Pátria*, 96. On the IHGB's tendency to focus on certain aspects of colonial history in order to create a mythologized European heritage for Brazil, see Lilia Moritz Schwarcz, "Os Guardiões da nossa História Oficial: Os Institutos Históricos e Geográficos Brasileiros, *Textos IDESP* 9 (1989).

17. Caio Prado Junior, *Formação de Brasil Contenporeneo* (São Paulo: Livraria Martins, 1942); and Sérgio Buarque de Holanda, *Caminhos e Fronteiras* (Rio: José Olympio, 1957). See also João Capistrano de Abreu, *Caminhos Antigos e Povoamento do Brasil* (1889; Rio: Sociedade Capistrano de Abreu, 1960).

18. The creation of the national telegraph service played an extremely important role in unifying the nation but did not allow for the movement of people or goods. On this key development, see Todd A. Diacon, *Stringing Together a Nation: Cândido Mariano da Silva Rondon and the Making of Brazil, 1906–1930* (Durham, N.C.: Duke University Press, 2004). On the broad cultural and economic impact of the telegraph in general, see Tom Standage, *The Victorian Internet: The Remarkable Story of the Telegraph and the Nineteenth Century's On-Line Pioneers* (New York: Walker, 1998).

19. On the various agendas embedded in the city's master plan, see James Holston, *The Modernist City: An Anthropological Critique of Brasília* (Chicago: University of Chicago Press, 1989).

20. For a cogent analysis of commercial air travel as quintessentially modern, see Thomas J. Misa, "The Compelling Tangle of Modernity and Technology," in Thomas J. Misa et al., eds. *Modernity and Technology* (Cambridge, Mass.: MIT Press, 2003), 1–30. In the late twentieth century, Brazil's Empresa Brasileira de Aeronáutica or Embraer came to dominate production of regional jets. See Roberto Bernardes, *EMBRAER: Elos entre Estado e Mercado* (São Paulo: FAPESP, 2000); and "The Little Aircraft Company That Could," *Fortune*, 14 November 2005.

21. This episode is detailed in Chapter 2. Despite this fact, science and technology have not been widely considered in analyses of Brazil. Exceptions to this trend include Nancy Leys Stepan, *Beginnings of Brazilian Science: Oswaldo Cruz, Medical Research, and Policy, 1890–1920* (New York: Watson, 1981); Simon Schwartzman, *Formação da Comunidade Científica no Brasil* (São Paulo: Nacional, 1979); and Milton Vargas, ed., *História da Técnica e da Tecnologia no Brasil* (São Paulo: UNESP, 1994).

22. Boris Fausto, *A Concise History of Brazil*, Arthur Brakel, trans. (Cambridge: Cambridge University Press, 1999), 137–138.

23. On the differences between Lamarckian eugenics embraced in Brazil and the more rigid racial system of the United States, see Nancy Leys Stepan, *"The Hour of Eugenics": Race, Gender and Nation in Latin America* (Ithaca, N.Y.: Cornell University Press, 1991), 46–55, 153–169. Richard Graham's *Britain*

and the Onset of Modernization in Brazil, 1850–1914 (Cambridge: Cambridge University Press, 1968) remains the best work on the impact of positivism on the late empire and its implementation during the republic. On Emperor Pedro II's fascination with the technological progress of the United States in the 1870s, see Schwarcz, *As Barbas do Imperador*, 357–407. For a stimulating work that ties Brazil's nineteenth- and twentieth-century fascination with technology and progress, see Francisco Foot Hardman, *Trem Fantasma: A Modernidade na Selva* (São Paulo: Companhia das Letras, 1991).

24. Leo Marx, *The Machine in the Garden: Technology and the Pastoral Ideal in America* (New York: Oxford University Press, 1964); and Kasson, *Civilizing the Machine*. In *American Technological Sublime* (Cambridge, Mass.: MIT Press, 1994), David E. Nye, argues convincingly that this transition was so thoroughgoing that by the latter part of the nineteenth and early twentieth century, the American attraction to the natural sublime had been transferred to technology.

25. Ken Alder, *Engineering the Revolution: Arms and the Enlightenment in France, 1763–1815* (Princeton, N.J.: Princeton University Press, 1997).

26. Donald Reid, *Paris Sewers and Sewermen: Realities and Representations* (Cambridge, Mass.: Harvard University Press, 1993); and Gabrielle Hecht, *The Radiance of France: Nuclear Power and National Identity after World War II* (Cambridge, Mass.: MIT Press, 1998). For the complicated French relationship to automobility, see Kristin Ross, *Fast Cars, Clean Bodies: Decolonization and the Reordering of French Culture* (Cambridge, Mass.: MIT Press, 1995). On a uniquely French attempt to bridge automobility and mass transit, see Bruno Latour, *Aramis, or The Love of Technology* (Cambridge, Mass.: Harvard University Press, 1996).

27. Gyan Prakash, *Another Reason: Science and the Imagination of Modern India* (Princeton, N.J.: Princeton University Press, 1999).

28. Physicist Alvin M. Weinberg is often credited with coining this term. See his *Reflections on Big Science* (Cambridge, Mass.: MIT Press, 1967), 141; and Weinberg, "Can Technology Replace Social Engineering?" in Albert H. Teich, ed. *Technology and Man's Future* (New York: St. Martin's, 1972), 27–35. In his memoir, Weinberg notes that the phrase may have been used by Richard Meier, a Berkeley, California, city planner, before he embraced it. See *The First Nuclear Era: The Life and Times of a Technological Fixer* (New York: American Institute of Physics, 1994), 150–152. People often reveal their enthusiasm for technology and its transformative powers at world's fairs and other exhibits of the latest machines and gadgets. See Thomas P. Hughes, *American Genesis* (New York: Viking, 1989), 295–351; and David E. Nye, *Electrifying America: Social Meaning of a New Technology, 1880–1940* (Cambridge, Mass.: MIT Press, 1990), 368–379.

29. Without knowledge of the environmental impact of auto exhaust, which was at that time heavily weighed down by lead as a gasoline enhancement,

many residents of New York, London, and other major cities hoped cars would end the reliance on horses and thus decrease the impact of animal dung on urban life. See Clay McShane, *Down the Asphalt Path: The Automobile and the American City* (New York: Columbia University Press, 1994), 41–56, 103–124. Airplanes, it was argued, would increase social intercourse and thus beget peace. See Stephen Kern, *The Culture of Time and Space, 1880–1918* (Cambridge, Mass.: Harvard University Press, 1983), 242–247. The Germans had a less peaceful view of aviation, but they did consider the zeppelin a key tool of national unification. See Peter Fritzsche, *A Nation of Fliers: Aviation and the Popular Imagination* (Cambridge, Mass.: Harvard University Press, 1994), 9–58.

30. David Harvey describes the spatial fix in terms of uneven geographical development created by capitalism. Expansion, usually in the form of advanced capitalist societies extending their reach into new markets, is the common attempt at a spatial fix to solve the internal contradictions of a capitalist crisis. See Harvey, *The Limits to Capital* (Chicago: University of Chicago Press, 1982), 431–438.

31. Benjamin S. Orlove, ed. *The Allure of the Foreign: Imported Goods in Postcolonial Latin America* (Ann Arbor: University of Michigan Press, 1997); and Arnold J. Bauer, *Goods, Power, History: Latin America's Material Culture* (Cambridge: Cambridge University Press, 2001).

32. For a theoretical treatment of this topic in Latin America that focuses on Mexico, see Néstor García Canclini, *Consumers and Citizens: Globalization and Multicultural Conflicts*, George Yúdice, trans. (Minneapolis: University of Minnesota Press, 2001). For a detailed historical analysis of the politics of consumer citizenship in post-1945 America, see Lizabeth Cohen, *A Consumer's Republic: The Politics of Mass Consumption in Postwar America* (New York: Knopf, 2003).

33. The introduction of automobiles affected other cultures in similarly profound ways. On Germany, for example, see Wolfgang Sachs, *For the Love of the Automobile: Looking Back into the History of Our Desires*, Don Reneau, trans. (Berkeley: University of California Press, 1992).

34. This now famous dictum is from Marx's *Grundrisse*. This notion is much more fully developed in terms of geography in David Harvey, "The Geopolitics of Capital," in Harvey, *Spaces of Capital: Towards a Critical Geography* (New York: Routledge, 2001), 312–344.

35. For a careful critique of this perspective, see Enrique Dussel, "Eurocentricism and Modernity," *Boundary 2* 20:3 (Autumn 1993): 65–76. Fernando Coronil's thought-provoking study of twentieth-century Venezuela reveals the complexity of how European notions of modernity helped to shape (or misshape) politics. See Coronil, *The Magical State: Nature, Money, and Modernity in Venezuela* (Chicago: University of Chicago Press, 1997).

36. V. I. Lenin's *Imperialism, the Highest Stage of Capitalism: A Popular Outline* (1917; Peking: Foreign Language Press, 1965) should be read in conjunction with Francis Fukuyama, *The End of History and the Last Man* (New York: Free Press, 1992), as well as Samuel Huntington, *The Clash of Civilizations and the Remaking of the World Order* (New York: Simon and Schuster, 1996).

37. A provocative analysis of the idea of European technological domination and how it defined the idea of cultural superiority can be found in Michael Adas's *Machines as the Measure of Men: Science, Technology, and Ideologies of Western Domination* (Ithaca, N.Y.: Cornell University Press, 1989). An early view of the awe inspired by such machines is Henry Adams, *The Education of Henry Adams* (1918, New York: Oxford University Press, 1999), 318. For this phenomenon in nineteenth-century Brazil, see Hardman, *Trem Fantasma*. For a similar fascination that existed in mid-twentieth-century India, see Prakash, *Another Reason*.

38. Although Marshall Berman rejects a predetermined, linear path of progress and understands the contingent nature of modernity, his work still focuses on Europe and the United States. See Marshall Berman, *All That Is Solid Melts into Air: The Experience of Modernity* (New York: Simon and Schuster, 1982). Niklas Luhmann, *Observations on Modernity*, William Whobrey, trans. (Stanford, Calif.: Stanford University Press, 1998), studies much more successfully the contingent nature of modernity.

39. Gilberto Freyre, *Order and Progress: Brazil from Monarchy to Republic*, Rod W. Horton, trans. (New York: Knopf, 1970), was both attracted to and repelled by such markers of modernity as the railroads and Santos Dumont's flights. European imperial powers used the level of science and technology in African and Asian societies as a way to evaluate their peoples. See Adas, *Machines as the Measure of Men*. On the relationship between technology and U.S. imperialism, see Michael Adas, *Dominance by Design: Technological Imperatives and America's Civilizing Mission* (Cambridge, Mass.: Harvard University Press, 2006).

40. Other Vargas-era laws (e.g., his labor legislation and promulgations) are often cited as having had a significant impact on the growth of central state power, but those measures were rarely enforced beyond the national capital of Rio de Janeiro. See Joel Wolfe, "The Faustian Bargain Not Made: Getúlio Vargas and Industrial Labor in Brazil," *Luso-Brazilian Review* (December 1994): 77–95.

41. Developmentalism fit well with modernization theory, as is detailed in chapter 5. For a basic definition of modernity that argues that its two basic components are economic modernization and cultural and political modernism, see Marshall Berman, "All That Is Solid Melts into Air: Marx, Modernism and Modernization," in *Adventures in Marxism* (New York: Verso, 1999), 91–152.

42. Lewis Mumford, "Authoritarian and Democratic Technics," *Technology and Culture* 5 (1964): 1–8; and Langdon Winner, *The Whale and the Reactor: A Search for Limits in an Age of High Technology* (Chicago: University of Chicago Press, 1986), 19–39.

Chapter 1

1. Alberto Santos Dumont, *My Airships* (New York: Century, 1904), 34–37; Fernando Hippólyto da Costa, *Santos-Dumont: História e Iconografia* (Belo Horizonte: INCAER, 1990), 24–25; Paulo Cesar de Azevedo et al, *O Século do Automóvel no Brasil* (São Caetano do Sul: Brasinca, 1989), 10; *Quatro Rodas*, September 1960, 53–54; and Peter Wykeham, *Santos Dumont: A Study in Obsession* (London: Putnam, 1962), 30–31.

2. This is a curious example of the intimate connection between Santos Dumont's exploits and challenges to notions of space and time. Santos Dumont wanted to be able to track time without losing use of his hands in flight. On changing perceptions of time and space related to modernity, see David Harvey, *The Condition of Postmodernity* (Oxford: Blackwell, 1990), 201–283; and Stephen Kern, *The Culture of Time and Space, 1880–1918* (Cambridge, Mass.: Harvard University Press, 1983).

3. Santos Dumont, *My Airships*. The Wright Brothers 17 December 1903 Kitty Hawk flight was unwitnessed and unreported for roughly three years. The Wright Brothers' claims were not broadly accepted as true in the United States until about 1908. See Roger E. Bilstein, *Flight in America: From the Wright Brothers to the Astronauts* rev. ed. (Baltimore: Johns Hopkins University Press, 1994), 12–15. The Brazilian government supported Santos Dumont's flight as the first until after the deaths of all the principles. See, for example, Aluizio Napoleão, *Santos Dumont e a Conquista do Ar* (Rio: Imprensa Nacional, 1941).

4. Giberto Freyre, *Order and Progress: Brazil from Monarch to Republic*, Rod W. Horton, trans. (1962; Berkeley: University of California Press, 1986), 277.

5. Freyre, *Order and Progress*, 277–278. For a cogent analysis of Freyre's anti-modernism, see Jeffrey Needell, "Identity, Race, Gender, and Modernity in the Origins of Gilberto Freyre's Oeuvre," *American Historical Review* 100:1 (February 1995): 51–77.

6. Jeffery Needle's *A Tropical Belle Epoque: Elite Culture and Society in Turn-of-the-Century Rio de Janeiro* (Cambridge: Cambridge University Press, 1987) remains the classic study of elite patterns of consumption at this time. See, especially, pp. 156–177. See also Rosa Maria Barboza de Araújo, *A Vocação do Prazer: A Cidade e a Família no Rio de Janeiro Republicano* (Rio: Rocco, 1993). On this type of consumption in general, see Kristin Hoganson, "Cosmopolitan Domesticity: Importing the American Dream, 1865–1920," *American Historical Review* 107:1 (February 2002): 55–83.

7. Warren Dean, *The Industrialization of São Paulo, 1880–1945* (Austin: University of Texas Press, 1969); Wilson Cano, *Raízes da Concentração Industrial em São Paulo* (São Paulo: T. A. Queiroz, 1983); and Stanley Stein, *The Brazilian Cotton Manufacture: Textile Enterprise in an Underdeveloped Area, 1850–1950* (Cambridge, Mass.: Harvard University Press, 1957). Even the best new economic history, concentrating on cliometrics, continues to focus solely on production, especially in the export sector. See, for example, William Summerhill, "Railroads and the Brazilian Economy before 1914," *Journal of Economic History* (June 1996). Some works have focused on the political and cultural dynamic of Latin America's economic policy making (especially regarding "development"), but often in terms that privilege post-1945 politics over long-held cultural and social beliefs dating from the nineteenth century. See, for example, Arturo Escobar, *Encountering Development: The Making and Unmaking of the Third World* (Princeton, N.J.: Princeton University Press, 1995).

8. Vergniaud Calazans Gonçalves reports that Tobias de Aguiar drove São Paulo's second car in 1898. He does not name the type or origin of the vehicle, but it resembled Santos Dumont's car. See *Automóvel no Brasil, 1893–1966* (São Paulo: Editora de Automóvel, 1966), 7–8.

9. *Automóvel Club*, "O Primeiro Autómovel que Trafegou no Rio," February 1930; Maria Chamberelli de Oliveira, *Achegas à História de Rodoviarismo no Brasil* (Rio: Memórias Futuras, 1986), 29–31; Paulo Cesar de Azevedo et al, *O Século do Automóvel no Brasil*, 13. A widely held myth about the first auto accident is detailed later.

10. The complete list includes multiple vehicles for a few of the richest Paulistas: Placa 1 (P1) Conde Francisco Matarazzo, P2 Dr. Walter Seng, P3 Antônio Prado Junior, P4 Persano Pacheco e Silva, P5 Conde Eduardo Prates, P6 Coronel Piedad, P7 "uma empressa" (an unidentified business), P8 Antônio de Souza Queiroz, P9 Dr. Edgard de Souza, P10 Família Matarrazo, P11 Cav. De Vivo, P12 Antônio Prado Junior, P13 Família Sérgio Meira, P14 Antônio Prado Junior, P15 Dr Baeta Neves, P16 major Molinari. See *Quatro Rodas*, September 1960, 53–54.

11. Paulo Cesar de Azevedo et al, *O Século do Automóvel*, 14.

12. *Quatro Rodas*, December 1961, 118; September 1962, 80; and January 1966, 43. The 1962 article argues that Lanat's vehicle may have been Brazil's third automobile.

13. Paulo Cesar de Azevedo et al, *O Século do Automóvel*, 14; and *Revista do Automóvel*, September 1955, 45.

14. The car's fame as the city's and state's first was long-lived. Indeed, *gaúcho* political elites, including Borges de Medeiros, used the vehicle in a variety of ceremonies during the first decade of the twentieth century. The use of the car for political ceremonies was so widespread that it could be seen as a form of political graft.

15. Luiz Fernando Andreatta and Paulo Roberto Renner, *Automobilismo no Tempo das Carreteras: Em Especial no Rio Grande do Sul* (Porto Alegre: Metrópole, 1992), 12.

16. *Estado de São Paulo*, 1 March 1903. This is similar to worries about the dangers of early railroads in the United States. See Sarah H. Gordon, *Passage to Union: How the Railroads Transformed American Life, 1829–1929* (Chicago: Ivan R. Dee, 1996), 56–76.

17. Paulo Cesar de Azevedo et al, *O Século do Automóvel*, 18; *Automobilismo*, August 1928, 33.

18. *Auto-Propulsão*, February 1917. The number of cars in Rio by year was 1903, 6; 1905, 12; 1906, 66; 1907, 99; 1908, 111; 1909, 173; 1910, 615; 1911, 1,239; 1912, 2,369; 1913, 2,588; and 1914, 2,533.

19. Richard M Morse, *From Community to Metropolis: A Biography of São Paulo, Brazil* (Gainesville: University of Florida Press, 1958), 178–198; and Teresa A. Meade, *Civilizing Rio: Reform and Resistance in a Brazilian City, 1889–1930* (University Park: Pennsylvania State University Press, 1997), 75–101. Because Belo Horizonte, the new planned capital of Minas Gerais, opened in 1897, it did not require major reform in this era. Its streets were, however, designed for horse-and-carriage traffic and thus made later driving in the city particularly perilous. On the Mineiro capital, see Eliana de Freitas Dutra, ed., *BH: Horizontes Históricos* (Belo: C/Arte, 1996). For a synthetic analysis of the changing structures of Brazil's major cities, see Flávio Villaça, *Espaço Intra-Urbano no Brasil* (São Paulo: Studio Nobel, 1998).

20. *Bulletin of the Pan-American Union*, November 1911, 915; Reginald Lloyd, *Twentieth-Century Impressions of Brazil: People, Commerce, Industry, and Resources* (London: Lloyd's Great Britain Publishing Co., 1913), 963.

21. Jorge Americano, *São Paulo naquele Tempo, 1895–1915* (São Paulo: Saraiva, 1957), 198–199. See Clay McShane, *Down the Asphalt Path: The Automobile and the American City* (New York: Columbia University Press, 1994), 118–119, 176–177 for early fears in the United States over the impact of automobiles on the health and welfare of urban children.

22. Ernani Silva Bruno, *História e Tradições da Cidade de São Paulo* (Rio: José Olympio, 1954), 3:1081–1082; and *Automóvel Club*, February 1930.

23. Like all consumer-oriented technologies, the automobile had to become more reliable and luxurious to capture its initial market of wealthy individuals. See James J. Flink, *The Automobile Age* (Cambridge, Mass.: MIT Press, 1988), 15–26, on this era of innovation in automotive technology. See also McShane, *Down the Asphalt Path*, 125–133.

24. *Motor Age*, 31 December 1903, and *Cycle and Automobile Trade Journal*, 1 March 1903. Gonçalves (*Automóvel*, 10) reports that the Santos Dumont car was produced in limited quantities, and none was exported to Brazil. It was a car of its era and did not resemble Santos Dumont's first Peugeot.

25. L. E. Elliott, *Brazil: Today and Tomorrow* (New York: Macmillan, 1917), 127.

26. *Fon-Fon!* 22 June 1907 and 13 July 1907.

27. Paulo Cesar de Azevedo et al, *O Século do Automóvel*, 27 on Rio. For São Paulo, see Paul Walle, *Au Pays de l'Or Rouge: L'Etat de São Paulo (Brésil), Ses Ressources, ses Progrés, son Avenir* (Paris: Augustin Challenel, 1921), 56–73.

28. Lloyd, *Twentieth-Century Impressions of Brazil*, 495. See also Elliott, *Brazil: Today and Tomorrow*, 127.

29. Affluent Brazilians who did not quite have the means to purchase a car often hired one for special occasions. See *Sportman*, June 1906, 12; *Auto-Propulsão*, April 1915 and January 1917; and *Auto-Sport*, 1 December 1912, 411. Americano details the different levels of cars of hire from simple to luxury. See *São Paulo naquele Tempo*, 81–82, 202.

30. Americano, *São Paulo naqule Tempo*, 202; Paulo Cesar de Azevedo et al, *O Século do Automóvel*, 17; and *Fon-Fon!* 17 August 1907 (photos).

31. U.S. Department of Commerce and Labor, Bureau of Manufacturers, Special Consular Reports #53, *Foreign Markets for Motor Vehicles* (Washington, D.C., 1912), 40–42.

32. *Bulletin of the Pan American Union*, November 1911, 1001–1002; "The Automobile in South America," *Bulletin of the Pan American Union*, September 1913, 337, 333. This article also claimed that "a thousand miles up the Amazon at Manaus there are more than 80 automobiles, some of them have indeed penetrated the jungle to bring out rubber." It is, however, highly unlikely that autos made there were into the interior of Amazonas to load recently gathered rubber.

33. *Auto-Sport*, 1 October 1912 (the inaugural issue), 23 on cars in Rio; 78–83 on European and U.S. sports, fashions, and architecture; 1 November 1912, 220 on Paris police cars; 15 October 1912, 125 for the quote on development and early circulation figures.

34. *Auto-Sport*, 1 November 1912, 220, 222–223; 15 October 1912, 125.

35. *Auto-Propulsão*, February 1915; January 1917; March 1917.

36. Quoted in Paulo Cesar de Azevedo et al, *O Século do Automóvel*, 27.

37. On the proliferation of these new goods, see Nicolau Sevcenko, "A Capital Irradiante: Técnica, Ritmos e Ritos do Rio," in Nicolau Sevcenko, ed. *História da Vida Privada no Brasil, Vol. 3: República: da Belle Époque à Era do Rádio* (São Paulo: Companhia das Letras, 1998), 513–619; and Flora Süssekind, *Cinematógrafo de Letras: Literatura, Técnica e Modernização no Brasil* (São Paulo: Companhia das Letras, 1987). On early magazine and newspaper advertising, see Ricardo Ramos, *História da Propaganda no Brasil* (São Paulo: USP, 1972), 17–20.

38. Quoted in Paulo Cesar de Azevedo et al, *O Século do Automóvel*, 14.

39. Süssekind, *Cinematógrafo de Letras*; Sevcenko, *Orfeu Extático na Metrópole: São Paulo Sociedade e Cultura nos Frementes Anos 20* (São Paulo: Companhia das Letras, 1992); and Sevcenko, *Literatura como Missão: Tensões Sociais e Criação Cultural n Primeira República* (São Paulo: Brasiliense, 1983).

40. Süssekind, *Cinematógrafo de Letras*, 17–28.

41. *Fon-Fon!* 13 April 1907. The cover of the second issue, likewise, included such a drawing. See *Fon-Fon!* 20 April 1907.

42. Süssekind, *Cinematógrafo de Letras*, 65; *Fon-Fon!* 21 November 1908 and 20 June 1908.

43. Lloyd, *Twentieth-Century Impressions of Brazil*, 594.

44. *Estado de São Paulo*, 5 March 1908.

45. *Automobilismo*, August 1928, 33.

46. *Brazilian-American*, 11 December 1920, 3; Paulo Cesar de Azevedo et al, *O Século do Automóvel*, 17; Ford Motor Company Archives (FMCA), Expansion Overseas, Brazil. Kristian Orberg Reminiscences.

47. Paulo Cesar de Azevedo et al, *O Século do Automóvel*, 18.

48. Oliveira, *Achegas à História*, 29.

49. Paulo Cesar de Azevedo et al, *O Século do Automóvel*, 18, 20.

50. The monopoly over technical knowledge held by drivers and mechanics in New York City in the first decade of the twentieth century led to great social tensions between employers and employees. See Kevin Borg, "The 'Chauffeur Problem' in the Early Auto Era: Structuration Theory and the Users of Technology," *Technology and Culture* 40:4 (October 1999): 797–832.

51. Gasoline supplies were quite tenuous in both Rio and São Paulo (and thus no doubt in smaller cities and towns in Brazil) well into the 1910s. The small number of locations in Rio and São Paulo where gasoline was sold drove up prices and led to frequent shortages. See *Auto-Propulsão*, March 1915 and April 1915. See also Americano, *São Paulo naquele Tempo*, 68.

52. *Fon-Fon!* 1 June 1908; *Brazilian American—Motor Supplement*, 1926, 5; and Bruno, *História e Tradições da Cidade de São Paulo*, 3:1249–1250. The ACB was founded by members of Rio's Club dos Diários. Like all of Rio's social clubs, the ACB had political as well as social aims. See Needell, *A Tropical Belle Epoque*, 82–115.

53. Lloyd, *Twentieth-Century Impressions*, 647.

54. Clubs and auto centers opened in Salvador in 1918; Juiz de Fora, M.G. and Santos, S.P. in 1919; and Rio Preto, S.P. in 1920. *Auto-Propulsão*, March 1918, 15 May 1919, and December 1920.

55. *Estado de São Paulo*, 1 March 1903.

56. *Auto-Propulsão*, October 1915.

57. Getúlio Vargas created the first national transportation code in 1941 as part of his overall program to unify the nation.

58. *Brazilian American*, 20 November 1920, 12.

59. "Os Desastres de Automóvel no Rio," *Auto-Propulsão*, September 1920.

60. Clay McShane, for example, details the extraordinarily crowded streets of Manhattan around 1900. Indeed, New York City was so filled with decaying manure from animal traffic that the automobile was considered a sort of environmental cleanup machine. See *Down the Asphalt Path*, 122.

61. *O Vehiculo*, 1 June 1907; *Fon-Fon!* 15 June 1907 and 28 December 1907; *Quatro Rodas*, January 1966, 44.

62. *Auto-Propulsão*, May 1915; *Brazilian-American*, 23 October 1920, 19–20; and Bruno, *História e Tradições*, 3:1081.

63. Bruno, *História e Tradições*, 3:1085.

64. This account is from the *Revista de Automóveis*, November 1955, 1. For similar versions of the story, see *Revista de Automóveis*, September 1955, 45–47; *Quatro Rodas*, September 1960, "Automóvies de um Tempo Feliz," 54 and January 1966, 42; Paulo Cesar de Azevedo et al, *O Século do Automóvel*, 13; Gonçalves, *Automóvel*, 7–8; and Oliveira, *Achegas à História*, 29–31. Some accounts claim the car was an eight-horsepower Serpollet (*O Século do Automóvel*); others argue it was a Panhard et Levasor (Oliveira).

65. Patrocínio and Bilac were men of the nineteenth century. Patrocínio is most remembered as an abolitionist. Bilac was Brazil's most accomplished practitioner of the Parnassian school of poetry, an extremely formal style of expression that would later be rejected by Brazil's modernists.

66. Census taking in general is a fundamental part of state making, and the fascination with measurement is an aspect of modernity.

67. *Brazilian American*, 7 May 1921. Mexico was not included in the comparison. The decade-long revolution no doubt profoundly affected consumption at all levels, but especially the purchase of luxury items such as motorcars.

68. *Auto-Propulsão*, 1 December 1919, May 1918, June 1917, and December 1920.

69. Before it was a division of General Motors, the Chevrolet Motor Company produced an inexpensive, light car designed specifically to compete with Ford's Model T. The company was established by General Motors founder William C. Durant (after he had been pushed out of his initial management role at GM) and Louis Chevrolet. After General Motors purchased Chevrolet, it continued to produce inexpensive models for the division that bore its name. See Alfred P. Sloan Jr., *My Years with General Motors*, rev. ed. (New York: Doubleday, 1990), 3–10.

70. *Ford Times*, March 1912, 199; December 1912, 101. See also Mira Wilkins and Frank Ernest Hill, *American Business Abroad: Ford on Six Continents* (Detroit: Wayne State University Press, 1964), 56.

71. Morgan to Kenneth deLara Brisbee, Youngstown, OH, 25 July 1914, Record Group (RG) 84, Rio Post 865.15, U.S. National Archives (USNA); Rio Consul General to Ambassador (Morgan), Re: Pope Manufacturing, 23 September 1914, RG 84 Rio Post 865, USNA; Studebaker Corporation to U.S. Embassy Rio, 19 November 1914, RG 84 Rio Post 865.15, USNA; Winston Six Motor Car Co. (Cleveland) to Morgan, U.S. Ambassador, Brazil, 19 November 1914, RG 84 Rio Post 865.15, USNA. The U.S. Commerce Department's Bureau of Foreign Trade soon established a separate Office of Automotive Exports to handle these and similar matters.

72. Howard Tewksbury, *The Automotive Market in Brazil* (Washington, D.C.: U.S. Government Printing Office, 1930), 9–13. By 1929, Brazil was the third most important market for U.S. truck exports, and the fifth most significant for U.S. cars.

73. *Auto-Propulsão*, August 1918 and November 1920.

74. Tewksbury, *The Automotive Market*, 23, 160–161. Statistics on auto ownership cited previously rely on purchase records, not auto registrations.

75. *Bulletin of the Pan American Union*, September 1910, 523, and February 1911, 348; *Auto-Propulsão*, 1 December 1919 and July 1916. Private road building was beyond the means of even the richest individuals. William Kissam Vanderbilt Jr. constructed a private highway on Long Island in 1906 but could not afford to maintain it. See Tom Lewis, *Divided Highways: Building the Interstate Highways, Transforming American Life* (New York: Penguin, 1997), 29–31.

76. Todd A. Diacon, "Private Power and Public Action: A Case Study of State and Society Relations in the Brazilian Old Republic." Paper presented to the 56th annual meeting of the Southern Historical Association, New Orleans, November 1990.

77. *Auto-Sport*, 15 October 1912, 130–131. On the joys of car touring in and around Rio, see *Bulletin of the Pan American Union*, January 1913, 22–24.

78. *Ford Times*, February 1913, 223.

79. Such an advertisement is reproduced in *Quatro Rodas*, January 1966, 121.

80. *Auto-Sport*, 1 December1912, 472. On the first rubber boom, see Barbara Weinstein, *The Amazon Rubber Boom, 1850–1920* (Stanford, Calif.: Stanford University Press, 1983). The dream of a second rubber boom associated with domestic automobile production and consumption played a key role in the huge land grants behind the creation of Fordlândia and Belterra.

81. Goodyear Tire and Rubber, New York, NY to U.S. Embassy, Rio de Janeiro, 24 May 1915, RG 84 Rio Post 860, USNA; *Auto-Propulsão*, April 1921, 14 and May 1921, 5. On the calls for alternative fuels, see *Auto-Propulsão*, June 1915, November 1915, and December 1915.

82. *Auto-Propulsão*, May 1915 and September 1915.

83. Joel Wolfe, *Working Women, Working Men: São Paulo and the Rise of Brazil's Industrial Working Class, 1900–1955* (Durham, N.C.: Duke University Press, 1993), 7–10. This hope ignored the technological innovations necessary to compete with European and, later, U.S. automobile manufacturing. The 1910s and 1920s were a period of rapid technological change in the auto industry. See John B. Rae, *The Road and Car in American Life* (Cambridge, Mass.: MIT Press, 1971), 40–59.

84. *Auto-Sport*, 15 October 1912, 179–180; and *Auto-Propulsão*, 1 April 1919. A fascinating account of women's struggle to gain full access to driving in the United States is Virginia Scharff, *Taking the Wheel: Women and the Coming of the Motor Age* (Albuquerque: University of New Mexico Press, 1991).

85. *Fon-Fon!* 17 August 1907 and 21 September 1907; *Brazilian American*, 24 January 1920, 12; Araújo, *A Vocação do Prazer*, 328–329, 379–386.

86. The introduction of the railroad and telegraph provided the first opportunity to think along these lines. For a thoughtful analysis of the cultural impact of these changes, see Francisco Foot Hardman, *Trem Fantasma: A Modernidade na Selva* (São Paulo: Companhia das Letras, 1991). Sevcenko (in *Orfeu Extático na Metrópole*) provides as excellent analysis of the post–World War I period and the challenges it brought to Brazil.

87. *Correio da Manhã*, 18 February 1908, 19 February 1908, 21 February 1908, and 23 February 1908; and *Fon-Fon!* 7 March 1908. See also Paulo Cesar de Azevedo et al, *O Século do Automóvel*, 23.

88. Santos Dumont had participated in an 1897 raid from Paris to Amsterdam. The first great U.S. raid was a 1903 San Francisco to New York raid, which took 63 days. See James J. Flink, *The Automobile Age* (Cambridge, Mass.: MIT Press, 1990), 32; and Curt McConnell, *Coast to Coast by Automobile: The Pioneering Trips, 1899–1908* (Stanford, Calif.: Stanford University Press, 2000).

89. *Correio da Manhã*, 10 March 1908.

90. *Correio da Manhã*, 10–11 March 1908.

91. A mechanic rode in the car to maintain the flow of fuel and oil to the engine. Early motorcars had gravity-fed fuel systems and splash oilers that were incapable of meeting the demands of raids and racing. See Robert Casey, "The Vanderbilt Cup, 1908," *Technology and Culture* 40:2 (April 1999): 361.

92. *Correio da Manhã*, 10–11 March 1908; *Estado de São Paulo*, 12, 14, and 27 March and 5 and 7 April 1908. The *Estadão*'s reporting included excerpts from the local *Correio do Cruzeiro*.

93. *Estado de São Paulo*, 11–12 April 1908.

94. *Estado de São Paulo*, 20 March 1908.

95. *Brazilian American*, 23 February 1924, *Motor Supplement*; Bruno, *História e Tradições*, 1082; Ciro Dias Reis, *Salão de Automóvel: Trinta Anos de História* (São Paulo: 1990); *Ford em Revista*, March 1967; and *Mundo Motorizado*, April 1958, 5. On an early São Paulo to Jundiahy raid, see *Estado de São Paulo*, 25 March 1908.

96. *Auto-Propulsão* closely reported on these raids. See February 1915, March 1915, July 1915, July 1916, August 1916, September 1916, and October 1918.

97. On early racing, see Flink, *The Automobile Age*, 30–31. On racing and experiencing modernity, see Robert C. Post's provocative study of drag racing, *High Performance* (Baltimore: Johns Hopkins University Press, 1994). On speed as a component of modernity itself, see Marshall Berman, *All That Is Solid Melts into Air: The Experience of Modernity* (New York: Penguin, 1988); and Kern, *The Culture of Time and Space*.

98. *Estado de São Paulo*, 27–28 July 1908; *Fon-Fon!* 8 August 1908. See also Oliveira, *Achegas à História*, 29–31; Andreatta and Renner, *Automobilismo no Tempo*, 11; and Paulo Cesar de Azevedo et al, *O Século do Automóvel*, 24.

99. *Gazeta de Notícias*, 4 September and 20–21 September 1909; *Correio da Mahnã*, 20–21 September; and Oliveira, *Achegas à História*, 29–31. In addition to the ACB, the state of Rio de Janeiro and the local industrialist Visconde de Moraes sponsored the race.

100. *Correio da Manhã*, 19 September 1909.

101. Summerhill, "Railroads and the Brazilian Economy;" and Julian Smith Duncan, *Public and Private Operation of Railways in Brazil* (1932, New York: AMS Press, 1968). This was fairly common of Latin American transportation links. Lines throughout the Argentine pampas ran to Buenos Aires, but did not connect to each other. Mexico's rail system tied its productive areas to the U.S. The geography and colonial development of Brazil made this tendency much worse in Brazil than elsewhere in the hemisphere.

102. Gonçalves, *Automóvel*, 7. The study was published in 1896 during Campos Sales's gubernatorial term. Two years later, he was elected president of Brazil.

Chapter 2

1. The nineteenth-century scholar João Ribeiro commented: "Brazil was an archipelago of human islands with almost no intercommunication." Paraphrased in José Maria Bello, *A History of Modern Brazil, 1889–1964*, James L. Taylor, trans. (Stanford, Calif.: Stanford University Press, 1966), 13. Judy Bieber, in her study of the São Francisco region of Minas Gerais, notes that mail service between that area and Ouro Preto, some 650 kilometers, took more than two months in the 1830s. See Judy Bieber, *Power, Patronage, and Political Violence: State Building on a Brazilian Frontier, 1822–1889* (Lincoln: University of Nebraska Press, 2000), 188.

2. Warren Dean, *With Broadax and Firebrand: The Destruction of the Brazilian Atlantic Forest* (Berkeley: University of California Press, 1995), 207–210; E. Bradford Burns, *A History of Brazil*, 2nd ed. (New York: Columbia University Press, 1980), 201–202; L. E. Elliott, *Brazil: Today and Tomorrow* (New York: Macmillan, 1917), 125; and Ernani Silva Bruno, *História e Tradições da Cidade de São Paulo*, 3 vols. (Rio: José Olympio, 1953), 3:977–980.

3. Work on Belo Horizonte began in 1897, so the new state capital of Minas Gerias had wide, well-paved boulevards, but it was not designed specifically for auto traffic.

4. Mira Wilkins interview with Juvenal Waegle, 14 November 1961, Mira Wilkins personal archive, Florida International University (hereinafter MWFORD).

5. International Bureau of American Republics, *Brazil: General Descriptive Data Prepared in June 1909* (Washington, D.C.: Government Printing Office, 1909), 33, 36–37; and *Bulletin of th Pan-American Union*, March 1911, 562. Government funds subsidized roads suitable for autos in Rio Grande do Sul and Minas Gerais; wagon roads were to be built with these funds in Paraná and the Acre Territory.

6. *Auto-Sport*, 15 October 1912, 126–127.

7. This was particularly important, given the Brazilian belief that immigration would whiten and so change the population. See, among others, Thomas E. Skidmore, *Black into White: Race and Nationality in Brazilian Thought* (1974; Durham, N.C.: Duke University Press, 1993).

8. Afonso de Escragnolle Tauney, *Ensaio de Carta Geral das Bandeiras Paulistas* (São Paulo: Companhia Melhoramentos de São Paulo, 1926), helped to foster a new myth of *bandeirantismo*. For a critique of Tauney, see John M. Monteiro, *Negros da Terra: Indios e Bandeirantes nas Origens de São Paulo* (São Paulo: Companhia das Letras, 1994).

9. On the ACB's early attachment to road building, see *Fon-Fon!* 1 June 1908. For a detailed description of the elite background of Rio social clubs in the late nineteenth and early twentieth centuries, see Jeffrey D. Needell, *A Tropical Belle Epoque: Elite Culture and Society in Turn-of-the Century Rio de Janeiro* (Cambridge: Cambridge University Press, 1987), 64–77.

10. *Auto-Propulsão*, October 1916 and November 1916.

11. Automóvel Club de São Paulo, *Annuário de 1919* (São Paulo: 1919), 107; and *Auto-Propulsão*, December 1920.

12. On the need to coordinate Brazil's growing auto clubs, see *Auto-Propulsão*, 15 May, 1919, and 1 August 1919. On the Centro Automobilistica do Estado da Bahia, see *Auto-Propulsão*, March 1918. On the Rio Preto club in the northeast of São Paulo, see *Auto-Propulsão*, December 1920.

13. *Auto-Propulsão*, March 1918.

14. *Auto-Propulsão*, February 1918.

15. *Brazilian American*, 6 February 1926, 27; and 20 March 1926, 21.

16. In the United States, the Grange (or National Grange of the Patrons of Husbandry) quickly translated its advocacy of rural road building for free mail delivery into support for automobile roads. See, among others, Stephen B. Goddard, *Getting There: The Epic Struggle between Road and Rail in the American Century* (Chicago: University of Chicago Press, 1994), 48–49, 62–63.

17. On rural support for the Brazilian good roads movement, see *Estrada de Rodagem*, January 1922, 14; September 1922; October 1922; June 1923; and December 1923; *Boas Estradas,* June 1924 and October 1926, 5. See also Richard Downes, "Autos over Rails: How U.S. Business Supplanted the British in Brazil, 1910–28," *Journal of Latin American Studies* 24:3 (October 1992): 551–583.

18. Benedict Anderson's path breaking work on "imagining" the nation is often invoked by scholars who study almost any aspect of nationalism. The ways people thought about the nation as a precursor for centralizing action by the state do have a great deal of resonance for Brazil throughout the twentieth century, as we shall see throughout this book. For Anderson's original analysis, see Benedict Anderson, *Imagined Communities: Reflections on the*

Origin and Spread of Nationalism, rev. ed (New York: Verso, 1991). A careful analysis of Anderson's use of Latin American history can be found in Claudio Lomnitz, "Nationalism as a Practical System: Benedict Anderson's Theory of Nationalism from the Vantage Point of Spanish America," in Miguel Angel Centeno and Fernando López-Alves, eds. *The Other Mirror: Grand Theory through the Lens of Latin America* (Princeton, N.J.: Princeton University Press, 2001), 329–359.

19. One of the most interesting analyses of this small but influential movement is Tania Regina de Luca's, *A Revista do Brasil: Um Diagnóstico para a (N)ação* (São Paulo: UNESP, 1998).

20. On the opening of the Ford factory, see Mira Wilkins and Frank Hill, *American Business Abroad: Ford on Six Continents* (Detroit: Wayne State University Press, 1964), 93–95.

21. General Motors do Brasil, *70 Years of History* (São Paulo: Prãemio Editorial, 1995), 12; and Howard Tewksbury, *The Automotive Market in Brazil* (Washington, D.C.: Government Printing Office, 1930), 41–50.

22. Memorandum, Gregory H. Eickhoff to H. Smith, Chief Automotive Division, Bureau of Foreign and Domestic Commerce, 16 July 1928, RG 151, USNA; Tewksbury, *The Automotive Market in Brazil*; and *Auto-Propulsão*, October 1920.

23. A number of scholars have noted that census taking in general plays an important role in state making and is a fundamental component of modernism. See, for example, Margo J. Anderson, *The American Census: A Social History* (New Haven, Conn.: Yale University Press, 1988), 83–85; Patricia Cline Cohen, *A Calculating People: The Spread of Numeracy in Early America* (Chicago: University of Chicago Press, 1982), 224–225; Theodore M. Porter, *Trust in Numbers: The Pursuit of Objectivity in Science and Public Life* (Princeton, N.J.: Princeton University Press, 1995); and James Scott, *Seeing Like a State: How Certain Schemes to Improve the Human Condition Have Failed* (New Haven, Conn.: Yale University Press, 1998), 11–52.

24. *O Automóvel*, March 1925, 27–28; *Automobilismo*, November 1926, 46.

25. Memorandum, Long (São Paulo) to Department of Commerce, DC, 12 March 1928, 532 Automobiles, RG 151, USNA.

26. The statistics comparing cities are spotty at best, but analyses by Howard Tewksbury of the U.S. Department of Commerce and by activists in the Good Roads Movement in Brazil show that the Federal District had 2,865 passenger cars in 1919; there were 3,316 in the city of São Paulo that year. By 1926, the state of São Paulo was home to 30,612 of Brazil's 61,317 registered automobiles. See Tewksbury, *The Automotive Market in Brazil*, 62; *Boas Estradas*, September 1925, 7–13; and *Brazilian American*, 2 October 1926, 27. These numbers are highly suspect and do seem to undercount the local and national totals. The magazine *Automóvel Club* reported in its June 1927 edition that Brazil had 121,000 motor vehicles, with 54,010 in the state of

São Paulo. The *Annuário de 1929* (p. 336) of the Automóvel Club claimed that the state of São Paulo alone was home to 145,057 passenger cars and 148,257 trucks.

27. *Automóvel Club*, July 1925, 44–45; *Brazilian American*, 7 March 1925, 30; *Brazilian Business*, November 1925, 13; and Tewksbury, *The Automotive Market in Brazil*, 41–50. See also Studebaker National Museum, Studebaker Corp. Archives, photo collection, Photographs of Araraquara, 1920s.

28. Limeira had 16 private cars and 4 auto taxis; Tiete had 24 automobiles, 3 of which could be rented. *Brazilian American, Motor Supplement*, vol. 3, 1921.

29. Special Circular #122, Automotive Division, Bureau of Foreign and Domestic Commerce, 531, RG 151, USNA; "O Primeiro Automóvel que Entrou en Goyaz," *Auto-Propulsão*, 1 October 1919; and George T. Colman, "The Good Roads Movement in Brazil, 1921–1922," *Brazilian American, Motor Supplement*, 1922.

30. Colman, "The Good Roads Movement in Brazil, 1921–22."

31. Afraino Corrêa, "Tempo do Landolé," *Revista de Automóveis*, July 1955, 1.

32. "O Primeiro Automóvel," *Automóvel Club*, May 1927.

33. *Brazilian American*, 30 July 1930, 5–7.

34. Bruno, *História e Tradições*, 3:1081; Archibald Forrest, *A Tour through South America* (New York: Pott, 1913), 304; and Paul Adam, *Les Visages du Brèsil* (Paris: P. Lafitte, 1914), 124.

35. "Bulletin of the American Chamber of Commerce in São Paulo," in *Brazilian American*, July 1926, 4–5; *Automobilismo*, September 1926, 32, and May 1928, 27–34. See also photo "Hand Operated Traffic Light and Jay Walkers, Avenida São João" in "Brazil Cities and Towns" in RG 151-FC, 10-E USNA; and "Praça da Sé Filled with Autos" in "Brazil Buildings," RG 151-FC, 10-C, USNA.

36. *Automobilismo*, August 1928, 32; and September 1928, 17–18; and *Auto-Sport*, 28 February 1927.

37. *Brazilian American*, 20 October 1923, 28; 1923 Anniversary issue; 19 December 1925, 23; and 9 January 1926, 16. "Fortaleza Carnival," 20 February 1928, FC 10-E, RG 151 USNA; Tewksbury, *The Automotive Market in Brazil*, 79–87.

38. "Annual Report for Brazil 1919," January 1920, 24, Public Record Office (PRO), Foreign Office 371/4435.

39. Antônio de Alcântara Machado, *Brás, Bexiga, e Barra Funda* (1927; São Paulo: Imprensa Oficial do Estado de São Paulo, 1982).

40. *Estado de São Paulo*, 13 February 1924.

41. *Automobilismo*, April 1928, on the architectural changes, particularly discussions of the U.S.-style house and two-car garages. See also *Boas Estradas*, June–July 1926, 11.

42. On the changes in gender in the 1920s, see Susan K. Besse, *Restructuring Patriarchy: The Modernization of Gender Inequality in Brazil, 1914–1940*

(Chapel Hill: University of North Carolina Press, 1996); and Joel Wolfe, *Working Women, Working Men: São Paulo and the Rise of Brazil's Industrial Working Class, 1900–1955* (Durham, N.C.: Duke University Press, 1993), 23–39.

43. *Automóvel Club*, May 1925. On women and cars in the United States and the challenge the new technology held for gender, see Virginia Scharff, *Taking the Wheel: Women and the Coming of Motor Age* (Albuquerque: University of New Mexico Press, 1991); and Robert Staughton Lynd and Helen Merrell Lynd, *Middletown: A Study in American Culture* (New York: Harcourt Brace, 1959), 136–141.

44. *A Cigarra*, 15–31 March 1929; and *A Noite*, 26 April 1929. I thank Susan Besse for these citations and for pointing out to me the importance of cars to beauty pageant contestants in 1920s Brazil.

45. *Automobilismo*, February 1927, 18–19, and April 1928, 20–21; *Auto-Propulsão*, September 1920; *Automóvel Club*, July 1926; *Brazilian American*, Special Fourth of July Issue, 1926; *Automóvel Club*, December 1925, 31–35; and July 1927; and Tewksbury, *The Automotive Market in Brazil*, 20. The unique driving style of Rio's residents is detailed and lampooned in Priscilla Ann Goslin, *How to Be a Carioca: The Alternative Guide for the Tourist of Rio* (Rio: Twocan Press, 1992).

46. Tewksbury, *The Automotive Market in Brazil*, 57–58.

47. *Brazilian American*, 12 April 1924, 11.

48. The statistics on the Western Hemisphere are from *Automóvel Club*, June 1925, 18. The United States had the most vehicles (15,452,855) followed by Argentina, Brazil, Cuba (26,875), and Mexico (24,985). The comparison with small European countries is from *O Automóvel*, May 1925, 12.

49. *Boas Estradas*, September 1926, 13–14. The extraordinarily high auto ownership in the United States has been noted by people throughout the world. One fascinating example is how the movie *The Grapes of Wrath* was viewed outside the United States. Despite the crushing poverty of Okies like the Joad family, even the poorest of the poor in the United States owned cars and trucks. John B. Rae comments on this in *The Road and the Car in American Life* (Cambridge, Mass.: MIT Press, 1971), 144–146.

50. *O Automóvel*, March 1925, 27–28; *Automóvel Club*, May 1925 and January 1929; and *Automobilismo*, November 1926, 46; June 1926, 26.

51. The embrace of "the latest scientific inventions" is noted in *Automobilismo*, March 1928, 21–23. The relationship between an active street life in the time before automobiles and after is analyzed as a key component of modernity in Marshall Berman, *All That Is Solid Melts into Air: The Experience of Modernity* (New York: Viking Penguin, 1988).

52. *Automóvel Club*, June 1926, 22; January 1929; *Auto-Sport*, 28 February 1927; and Memorandum Cremer (Rio de Janeiro) to Department of Commerce, DC, 18 April 1928, 531 Autos, RG 151, USNA.

53. Tewksbury, *The Automotive Market in Brazil*, 3–5; and *Automobilismo*, November 1927, 27.

54. *Automobilismo*, February 1929, 39, and September 1926, 37; Memorandum Cremer (Rio de Janeiro) to Department of Commerce, DC, 18 April 1928, 531 Autos, RG 151, USNA; and Linda Lewin, *Politics and Parentela in Paraíba: A Case Study of Family-Based Oligarchy in Brazil* (Princeton, N.J.: Princeton University Press, 1987), 90, 93.

55. J. Simão da Costa provides a clear example of this perspective in *Brazilian American Motor Supplement*, vol. 3, 1921. Most countries, including those in western Europe, faced differing degrees of this very problem. Only the United States had broad automobile ownership at this time.

56. On the similarities among the various western European car groups and the American Automobile Association, see James J. Flink, *The Automobile Age* (Cambridge, Mass.: MIT Press, 1988), 27–28.

57. Automóvel Club do Brasil, *Annuário de 1929* (Rio: 1929), 12–21; *Automóvel Club*, August 1925, 21–23, and December 1926, 5.

58. The Minas club continued to meet in the old building of the elite Club Central in Belo Horizonte. On this and other auto associations and their ties to the ACB, see *Automóvel Club*, August 1926, September 1926, and October 1926.

59. Cremer (Rio) to DC, 30 December 1927, Bureau of Foreign and Domestic Commerce, 531, RG 151, USNA; *Automóvel Club*, December 1926. See also Richard Downes, "Autos over Rails: How U.S. Business Supplanted the British in Brazil," *Journal of Latin American Studies* 24:3 (1992): 551–583.

60. On the use of glass and lighting by the new department stores, particularly in Chicago and Philadelphia, see William Leach, *Land of Desire: Merchants, Power, and the Rise of a New American Culture* (New York: Vintage, 1993), 39–70.

61. The best single source on U.S. backing for the marketing of automobility in Brazil is Downes, "Autos over Rails." See also *Final Report of the Commissioner General, 1922–23*, 2 vols., Records of the Commission Representing the U.S. at the Brazilian Centennial Exposition, Records of International Conferences, Commissions, and Expositions, RG 43, USNA. Todd Diacon graciously shared this report with me.

62. *Final Report of the Commissioner General, 1922–23*, 2 vols., 2:293–294; 2:333–334; 1:203; Records of the Commission Representing the U.S. at the Brazilian Centennial Exposition, Records of International Conferences, Commissions, and Expositions, RG 43, USNA. On the centennial itself, see Marly Silva da Motta, *A Nação Faz 100 Anos: A Questão Nacional no Centenário da Independência* (Rio: CPDOC, 1992).

63. *O Automóvel*, 1 December 1923; *Brazilian American*, 18 October 1923, 18, and 20 October 1923, 28; *Brazilian American Motor Supplement*, 23 February

1924; and Ciro Dias Reis, *Salão de Automóvel: Trinta Anos de História* (São Paulo: 1990).

64. Telegram, Connell, SP to DC, 1 July 1924; and Embry, SP to Toledo Chamber of Commerce, 13 August 1924, Automobiles 531, Bureau of Foreign and Domestic Commerce 531, USNA; *Brazilian American*, 4 October 1924, 37; 18 October 1924, 16–18; and 25 October 1924, 34.

65. *Automóvel Club*, November 1925, 34; *O Auto-Illustrado*, January 1926; *Brazilian American*, 24 October 1925, 30, and 14 November 1925, 29. The quote is from *Brazilian American*, 25 October 1924, 24.

66. *Automóvel Club*, August 1925, 32–37.

67. *Automóvel Club*, April 1925; May 1925; July 1925, 42; August 1925, 27–29; September 1925, 16, 36–37; *O Automóvel*, May 1925, 7; July 1925, 22–26; Ambassador Morgan (Rio) to Nelson Pinto, First Secretary Automóvel Club do Brasil, Rio Post 860.7, RG 84, USNA; *Brazilian Business*, September 1925, 18; Automóvel Club do Brasil, Photo Album of Primeira Exposisão de Automoveis, Rio 1–16 August 1925, photo #1632. For truck demonstrations, see also photos 1554–1556.

68. The auto show was closely covered by Rio's press. See, for example, *Correio da Manhã*, 1–16 August 1925. See also *Noicias Ford do Brasil*, November 1958, 405; Ford do Brasil, *A Ford no Brasil*, 8; and Wilkins and Hill, *American Business Abroad*, 147.

69. It should be pointed out that work on the assembly line in American factories did not require a great deal of skill.

70. *Automobilismo*, September 1926, 27.

71. *Correio da Manhã*, 2 August 1925; *Boas Estradas*, September 1927, 266.

72. On Pernambuco, see *Automóvel Club*, December 1925, 42. On Rio Grande do Sul, see, *Auto-Sport*, 28 February 1927; *Automobilismo*, January 1927, 19–20; June 1927, 27; July 1927, 24–25, 32; Cremer (Rio) to Smith (DC), 11 January 1929, 531 Autos, RG 151; and Ford Brasil, *A Ford no Brasil*, 8.

73. *Automóvel Club*, May 1927; General Motors, *70 Years of History*, 19; and *Noticias Ford do Brasil*, November 1958, 5.

74. "O Interesse do Rio Grande do Sul na Atuação do Governo Federal na Expansão Rodoviária," Arquivo Oswaldo Aranha, CPDOC; and "Apreciação Resumida uma Atuação do Governo Federal com Referência ao Desenvolvimento Rodoviário Nacional," Arquivo Oswaldo Aranha, CPDOC.

75. *Auto Sport*, 7 October 1926, 3; *Correio Paulistano*, 3 November 1929; *Automóvel Club*, July 1925, 12. See also *Automóvel Club*, July 1925, 4, and December 1926; and *Auto-Propulsão*, 1 June 1919. Other writers went even further, arguing that road building was the single most important work Brazil faced in the 1920s. A sampling of such sentiments can be found in *Automobilismo*, October 1927, 14–15, 29, and September 1928, 19; *Automóvel Club*, August 1925, 20, 42–44; September 1925, 12; and December 1926; and *Brazilian American*, 27 February 1926, 19.

76. "A Febre das Estradas de Rodagem Chegam ao Amazonas," *Auto-Propulsão*, 1 June 1919. General Cândido M. S. Rondon, "Santarem-Concepcion," *Automóvel Club*, September 1929.

77. The bifurcated nature of Brazilian society was exaggerated by critics at this time in ways that ignored the complexity of both urban and rural people, but this division resonated with Brazilians throughout the twentieth century. The classic analysis of this is presented in Jacques Lambert, *Os Dois Brasis* (São Paulo: Editora Nacional, 1967).

78. Comissão de Finanças, "Um Projecto Visando a Constucção de Estradas de Rodagem," *Automóvel Club*, December 1926. On Mello Vianna, see *Automóvel Club*, August 1925, 53–54.

79. "The Good Roads Movement in Brazil, 1921–1922," *Brazilian American Motor Supplement*, 1922. *Automóvel Club*, September 1929 and April 1932.

80. The quote is from *Automóvel Club*, August 1927. On the Club dos Bandeirantes, see *Jornal do Brasil*, 16 February 1927; *Auto Sport*, 23 September 1926, 3, and 7 October 1926, 1; and *Automóvel Club*, November 1928, 12.

81. Lewin, *Politics and Parentel in Paraíba*, 91–92. See also *O Mundo Ford*, June 1934, 22–23, for a discussion of the role of truck transport in Pernambuco.

82. *Automóvel Club*, August 1925, 42–44; April 1925.

83. "O Rodoviarismo e a Brasilidade," *Automóvel Club*, August–September 1929.

84. A handful of the writings on this include *Boas Estradas*, November–December 1926; *Automobilismo*, September 1927, 14; September 1928, 19; and May 1929, 24–25; *Auto-Sport*, 30 December 1926; *Brazilian American*, 18 April 1925; *Brazilian American Motor Supplement 1922*; *O Auto* (Rio Grande do Sul), June 1926; and *Automóvel Club*, April 1925; August 1925, 44; September 1926; and August 1927.

85. On Washington Luís and roads in general, see Americano, *São Paulo neste Tempo*, 79, 380–382. On his first 1906 adventure with Antônio Prado Junior, see *Automóvel Club*, December 1925, 38. The Santos to São Paulo road was built by a private corporation (the Empresa Autoviaria Paulista), but with Washington Luís's assistance, was able to use public lands. See *Bulletin of the Pan American Union* (October 1912, 824) for details of the beginning of the project.

86. Arquivo Privado Washington Luís, Arquivo do Estado de São Paulo, 188.04.45; *Brazilian American*, 5 March 1921, 11; and *Brazilian American Motor Supplement*, 1922.

87. *Brazilian Business* (March 1926, 9) reports that the São Paulo to Santos road had more than 600 cars daily, the São Paulo to Campinas about 400 daily, Campinas to Prata, 360, and Campinas to Itú, 280.

88. *Brazilian Business*, March 1926, 33, *Automóvel Club*, March 1925; *Brazilian American*, 23 December 1922, 40; and *O Automóvel*, February 1924.

89. *Bulletin of the Pan American Union*, July 1924, 718. See also *Brazilian Business*, March 1926, 17; and *Brazilian Highway Development* (São Paulo: Departamento de Estradas de Rodagem, 1944), 1.

90. *Brazilian Business*, March 1926, 15–16, and 7 August 1926, 29; *Automóvel Club*, August 1925 and July 1926; *Bulletin of the Pan-American Union*, May 1924, 504; and *O Automóvel*, July 1924, 7–9. This latter system reinvigorated the colonial-era transportation network along the São Francisco River.

91. Interestingly, they argued that the railroad would not be able to meet the region's needs and so its leaders should begin a major campaign of road building. See *Através do Nordeste* (Recife: Officinas Graphicos do Jornal do Commercio, 1922).

92. On U.S. support of these efforts, see Cremer (Rio) to DC, 29 May 1928, RG 151, 531 Automobiles, USNA; Smith (DC) to Tewkesbery (Buenos Aires), 22 June 1928, RG 151, 531 Automobiles, USNA; and Pierrot (Rio) to DC, 1 June 1929, RG 151, 531 Automobiles, USNA.

93. *Auto-Propulsão*, August 1915; *Boas Estradas*, May 1926, 8–9, 20; June–July, 1926, 5–8; March 1926, 6–9.

94. *Boas Estradas*, June–July 1926, 5–8; February 1926, 8; *Automóvel Club*, July 1927; *Brazilian American*, 18 September 1920, 9; and *Brazilian American Motor Supplement*, 1922.

95. *O Automóvel*, January 1923 and June 1925, 22–23, 25; *Boas Estradas*, February 1926, 9; Automóvel Club do Brasil, Photo Album, Primeiro Exposição de Automóveis, Rio de Janeiro, 1925, photo #1641; and *Brazilian American*, 21 October 1922.

96. *Auto-Propulsão*, 15 January 1915, October 1915, November 1915, and March 1917; *Brazilian American*, 15 January 1921, 5–9, 46–50. See also *Auto-Propulsão*, April 1920, for a discussion of the impact of a railroad strike on the economy and the ways truck traffic could protect Brazilian producers in the future.

97. On Vanderbilt's road, see Lewis, *Divided Highways*, 29–30. On the Mexican toll road and its terrible return for investors, see "Mexico's Toll Road Not Taken," *New York Times*, 22 February 1993. The San Joaquin Hills Corridor, a mixed public and private project connecting San Juan Capistrano and Costa Mesa in Orange County, California, may be a profitable exception to this rule.

98. *Boas Estradas*, August 1926, 10–11, 20, 22–24; *Automóvel Club*, June 1925, 12–15, 19, and May 1926; *Brazilian American*, 18 September 1920, 29; 23 October 1920, 30; 17 March 1923, 7; 25 October 1924, 16–17; and 27 September 1924, 29; *Brazilian American Anniversary Issue 1924*; *Brazilian American Motor Supplement 1922*; General Motors Corporation, *Economic Survey of Brazil*, 1:158; and Schwarz (Rio) to Owen, Chief of Automobile Division (DC), 7 March 1925, RG 151 Bureau of Foreign and Domestic Commerce, Automobiles 531, USNA. The dangers of the Rio to Petrópolis highway were so well known that Alfred Hitchcock made mention of them in his 1946 film *Notorious*.

99. Howard Tewksbury, *Motor Roads in Brazil* (Washington, D.C.: Government Printing Office, 1931), 12, 80; and Tewksbury, *The Automobile Market*, 5–8.

100. Steve Topik has convincingly argued that the laissez-faire nature of the Brazilian state was exaggerated in *The Political Economy of the Brazilian State, 1889–1930* (Austin: University of Texas Press, 1987), but Washington Luís's roads policies did represent a new level of central state intervention and activism.

101. *O Estado de São Paulo*, 5–10 September 1925; *O Automóvel*, September 1925, 6–7; *Brazilian Business*, November 1925, 14; May 1926, 10; *Automobilismo*, October 1926, 5–6; November 1926; January 1927, 31; and August 1928, 30; *Auto-Sport*, 7 October 1926; *Boas Estradas*, October–November 1925, 21–44; *Brazilian American*, 9 October 1926, 18; and Long (SP) to DC, 31 January 1927, RG 151, 531 Automobiles, USNA.

102. *Automóvel Club*, August 1926 and September 1926; *Automobilismo*, September 1926, 5; *Boas Estradas*, January 1927, 3–20; *Brazilian American*, 21 August 1926, 25; and *O Estado de São Paulo*, 27–28 October 1926.

103. *Auto-Propulsão*, March 1920 and September 1919; *Boas Estradas*, March 1926 and April 1926; *Automobilismo*, March 1927, 18; October 1927, 20–23; and April 1928, 16–18; and *Automóvel Club*, July 1925, 37.

104. *Automóvel Club*, July 1927.

105. *O Automóvel*, June 1924, 5–6, 24, on the raid to Buenos Aires. On the hoped-for La Paz and Lima adventures, see *Automóvel Club*, February 1926, 18, and October 1926.

106. Roberto Schwarz, "Brazilian Culture: Nationalism by Elimination," in Schwarz, *Misplaced Ideas: Essays on Brazilian Culture*, John Gledson, trans. (London: Verso, 1992), 1–18. On the close relationship between the modernists and São Paulo's traditional elite families, which often provided salons for sharing ideas, see Joan Rosalie Dassin, "The Politics of Art: Mário de Andrade and the Case of Brazilian Modernism, 1922–1945" (Ph.D. diss., Stanford University, 1974).

107. Nicolau Sevcenko, *Orfeu Extático na Metrópole: São Paulo Sociedade e Cultura nos Frementes Anos 20* (São Paulo: 1992). On the Week of Modern Art, see Amálio Pinheiro et al., *A Semana de Arte Moderna: Desdobramentos, 1922–1992* (São Paulo: 1992).

108. Doris Sommer, *Foundational Fictions: The National Romances of Latin America* (Berkeley: University of California Press, 1991), 138.

109. Néstor García Canclini sees Brazilian modernism as part of the trajectory toward Latin American "hybridity." See *Hybrid Cultures: Strategies for Entering and Leaving Modernity*, Christopher L. Chiappari and Silvia L. López, trans. (Minneapolis: University of Minnesota Press, 1995).

110. The modernists' fascination with modern forms of travel in general and the automobile in particular was not new for Brazilian intellectuals. An entire generation of writers, such as Lima Barreto and Monteiro Lobato, who were

never identified with modernism, embraced automobility as both a symbol of Brazil's future and a tool for its transformation.

111. On the impact of technology on Brazilian writing, see Flora Süssekind, *Cinematógrafo de Letras: Literatura, Técnica e Modernização no Brasil* (São Paulo: Companhia das Letras, 1987). On this theme in U.S. literature, see Leo Marx, ed., *The Pilot and the Passenger: Essays on Literature, Technology, and Culture in the United States* (New York: Oxford University Press, 1988). For an interesting analysis of the impact of information technology and the Internet on writing and the arts, see George P. Landow, *Hypertext 2.0: The Convergence of Contemporary Critical Theory and Technology* (Baltimore: Johns Hopkins University Press, 1997).

Chapter 3

1. *Brazilian American*, 12 June 1926; Ford do Brasil, *A Ford no Brasil*, 10. See also David L. Lewis, *The Public Image of Henry Ford: An American Folk Hero and His Company* (Detroit: Wayne State University Press, 1976), 488.

2. This may seem to be a bit of contradiction, given how Ford and American culture have been viewed as essentially homogenizing. This interpretation stems from a cursory reading of Antonio Gramsci's famous analysis in "Americanism and Fordism," in *Selections from the Prison Notebooks*, Quintin Hoare and Geoffrey Nowell Smith, eds. and trans. (New York: International Publishers, 1971), 277–318. Careful analysis of the appeal of Americanism in Germany and Japan in the 1920s, however, reveals that it did not lead to dramatic cultural changes. It did usher in changes in production and, to a lesser extent, consumption. See Mary Nolan, *Visions of Modernity: American Business and the Modernization of Germany* (New York: Oxford University Press, 1994) and William M. Tsutsui, *Manufacturing Ideology: Scientific Management in Twentieth-Century Japan* (Princeton, N.J.: Princeton University Press, 1998).

3. Scientific management, which is also frequently referred to as Taylorism, involves the systematization of work regimes in order to maximize output per worker. Assembly line work, such as that in meatpacking and later automobile factories followed the dictates of scientific management. Ford did introduce assembly line production to Brazil as early as 1919. Harry Braverman's *Labor and Monopoly Capital: The Degradation of Work in the Twentieth Century* (New York: Monthly Review, 1974) puts Taylorism into a broad historical and economic context. Even the best work on Fordism in Brazil presents it as little more than a form of industrial production without analyzing the fundamental role of consumption to this ideology. See Barbara Weinstein, *For Social Peace in Brazil: Industrialists and the Remaking of the Working Class in São Paulo, 1920–1964* (Chapel Hill: University of North Carolina Press, 1996).

4. For an analytically rich interpretation of the operation and fall of Fordism in the United States and Western Europe, see David Harvey, *The Condition*

of Postmodernity: An Enquiry into the Origins of Cultural Change (Oxford: Blackwell, 1989).

5. The limited literature on the rise and status of the middle class in Latin America focuses on how employment in professions differentiated this new class from the working class. Where and how middle-class Latin Americans lived, and especially what they aspired to own, have not received adequate analysis. Works that begin to study these issues include David Parker, *The Idea of the Middle Class: White-Collar Workers and Peruvian Society, 1900– 1950* (University Park: Pennsylvania State University Press, 1998); Brian Owensby, *Intimate Ironies: Modernity and the Making of Middle-Class Lives in Brazil* (Stanford,Calif.: Stanford University Press, 1999); and Maureen O'Dougherty, *Consumption Intensified: The Politics of Middle-Class Daily Life in Brazil* (Durham, N.C.: Duke, 2002).

6. Interview with Dumont Villares of Ford do Brasil in the private archive of Mira Wilkins, Florida International University (hereinafter MWFORD), November 13, 1961; *Noticias Ford do Brasil*, June 1959, 4; and *Ford em Revista*, 2nd Trimester 1961.

7. Sales gains were correlated with profitable coffee crops. See *Ford Times*, August 1913, 461.

8. *Automobilismo*, September 1927, 14; *Brazilian American*, 7 November 1925, 40; and General Motors do Brasil, *General Motors do Brasil: 70 Years of History* (São Paulo: Prãemio Ed., 1995), 12.

9. The most influential proponent of this point of view was Roberto Simonsen. See Weinstein, *For Social Peace*, 66–78. See also Luiz Werneck Vianna, *Liberalismo e Sindicato no Brasil* (Rio: Paz e Terra, 1976), 71–77. This discussion foreshadowed open debates by Paulista industrialists in the 1950s about the need to have foreign auto companies in Brazil. See Carin Adis, *Taking the Wheel: Auto Parts Firms and the Political Economy of the Industrialization of Brazil* (University Park: Pennsylvania State University Press, 1999) and Helen Shapiro, *Engines of Growth: The State and Transnational Auto Companies in Brazil* (Cambridge: Cambridge University Press, 1994).

10. The most complete analysis of this process remains Mira Wilkins and Frank Hill, *American Business Abroad: Ford on Six Continents* (Detroit: Wayne State Press, 1964). On how CKDs were manufactured, shipped, and remanufactured, see Kristian Orberg interview, 7 November 1961, MWFORD.

11. *Auto-Propulsão*, January 1921; *Automobilismo*, December 1929, 33; *Automóvel Club*, December 1929. In January 1920, Ford rented out a former skating rink for its first foray into reassembling CKDs. It later built the three-story plant on R. Solon, eventually adding a fourth floor. See Wilkins and Hill, *American Business Abroad*, 93–95.

12. Wilkins and Hill, *American Business Abroad*, 147–148. General Motors only operated the São Paulo area factory in the 1920s and 1930s. It had similar facilities in Buenos Aires and Montevideo.

13. Ford Motor Company Brazil (FMC Brazil), Orberg to Roberge, 21 May 1936; FMC, 880 Box 2, Orberg Memo, 15 March 1932; interview with Sven Neilsen, 16 November 1961, MWFORD; *Automóvel Club*, August 1925, 40; Wilkins and Hill, *American Business Abroad*, 257.

14. Flávio Rabelo Versiani, *A Década de 20 na Industrialização Brasileira* (Rio de Janeiro: IPEA/INPES, 1987), 81–84.

15. Kristian Orberg interview, MWFORD, 7 November 1961; and General Motors, *Seventy Years of History*, 9–11.

16. Howard Tewksbury, *The Automotive Market in Brazil* (Washington, D.C.: Government Printing Office, 1930), 30–31; Memo Embry (Rio) to Hoepli (DC), 18 February 1924, Bureau of Foreign and Domestic Commerce, Automobiles 531, RG 151, USNA; FMC Brazil, Orberg to Roberge, 21 May 1936; and *Manchete*, 16 July 1966, 112–113.

17. Tewksbury, *The Automotive Market in Brazil*, 17–21.

18. Tewksbury, *The Automotive Market*, 30; *Automóvel Club*, August 1927; and *Auto-Sport*, 26 August 1926, 12–13.

19. I have detailed the origins of the 1917 general strike in São Paulo and its impact on worker organizations and ideology in Wolfe, "Anarchist Ideology, Worker Practice: The 1917 General Strike and the Formation of São Paulo's Working Class," *Hispanic American Historical Review* 71:4 (November 1991): 809–846.

20. Weinstein, *For Social Peace*, remains the best work on industrial training, although she fails to place these programs into their proper gendered context. On the attempts to police sexuality during this period, see Margareth Rago, *Do Cabaré ao Lar: A Utopia da Cidade Disciplinar: Brasil, 1890–1930* (Rio: Paz e Terra, 1985).

21. The works of Ford and Gramsci reveal the gendered nature of the new style of production and consumption. See, for example, Gramsci, "Americanism and Fordism," 294–301; and Henry Ford, *My Life and Work* (1922; Salem, N.H.: Ayer, 1987). On the gendered nature of Fordism at Ford in the United States, see Martha May, "The Historical Problem of the Family Wage: The Ford Motor Company and the Five Dollar Day," *Feminist Studies* 8:2 (Summer 1982): 399–424; and Wayne A. Lewchuk, "Men and Monotony: Fraternalism as a Managerial Strategy at the Ford Motor Company," *Journal of Economic History* 53 (December 1993): 824–856. Laura Lee Downs touches on the gendered nature of Fordism in interwar France in her *Manufacturing Inequality: Gender Division in the French and British Metalworking Industries, 1914–1939* (Ithaca, N.Y.: Cornell University Press, 1995), 259–264. For an analysis of how American copper companies attempted to make male workers less radical by encouraging domestic life and marital stability, see Thomas Klubock, *Contested Communities: Class, Gender, and Politics in Chile's El Teniente Copper Mine, 1904–1951* (Durham, N.C.: Duke University Press, 1998).

22. In post-1945 America, this became the dream of purchasing two cars: one for husbands to drive to work and the other—preferably a station wagon—for wives to use to transport children and to go shopping. For a fascinating analysis of the post-1945 U.S. consumer culture, see Lizabeth Cohen, *A Consumers' Republic: The Politics of Mass Consumption in Postwar America* (New York: Knopf, 2003).

23. For Japan, see Tsutsui, *Manufacturing Ideology*, 66–67. On Great Britain, see Downs, *Manufacturing Inequality*, 287–288. In Brazil, industrialists in the 1920s had both profitable and difficult years, but the metalworking shops that made auto parts and truck and bus bodies often did not have the sort of capital available to provide high wages. On labor mobility in São Paulo as a strategy to seek out good wages, see Wolfe, *Working Women, Working Men*, 33, 43–44.

24. General Motors do Brasil, *70 Years of History*, 19–22. Interestingly, GM also trained young women workers at this time, but not in advanced industrial production.

25. Interview with Sven Nielsen, 16 November 1961, MWFORD; and *O Mundo Ford*, March 1929, 14. Ford focused on industrial training in part because it feared that the quality of work in its Brazilian facilities was not up to corporate standards. See Report by K. Orberg to Edsel Ford, 25 September 1926, Acc. 6, Box 446, FMC. Júlio Prestes was technically the "President of the State of São Paulo." The office was the equivalent of a governor.

26. Thomas F. O'Brien details this process throughout much of Latin America in his *The Revolutionary Mission: American Enterprise in Latin America, 1900–1945* (Cambridge: Cambridge University Press, 1996). For a nuanced account of the complex impact of the modernity brought by U.S. companies in Cuba, see Louis A. Pérez Jr., *On Becoming Cuban: Identity, Nationality, and Culture* (Chapel Hill: University of North Carolina Press, 1999).

27. The foreign auto companies did not displace domestic manufacturers; they complemented them in the growing industrial sector of São Paulo. The strength of the domestic industrial base facilitated the smooth entry of the foreign companies in the 1920s. On the local manufacturing sector, see Warren Dean, *The Industrialization of São Paulo, 1880–1945* (Austin: University of Texas Press, 1969); and Wilson Cano, *Raízes da Concentração Industrial em São Paulo* (Rio: Difel, 1977).

28. This included Ford's support for the dissemination of his infamous *The International Jew* in many languages. After protests in the United States, Ford limited the book's distribution in the Americas, but in 1932, more than 5,000 German-language copies were distributed in Porto Alegre with Henry Ford's name prominently displayed on the book jacket. See Lewis, *The Public Image of Henry Ford*, 148.

29. Henry Ford, *Today and Tomorrow* (New York: Doubleday, 1926), 262–263.

30. *Automobilismo*, December 1926, 32; *Auto-Sport*, 30 March 1927; "Kristin Orberg Reminiscences," Ascension 65 FMC Oral History Section, May

1956, 35; *O Mundo Ford*, November 1933, 11. There is no evidence that Henry Ford ever traveled to Brazil.

31. Lewis, *The Public Image of Henry Ford*, 188. The rubber experiments in Fordlândia are detailed later.

32. Monteiro Lobato, *How Henry Ford Is Regarded in Brazil*, Aubrey Stuart, trans. (Rio: Companhia Editora Nacional, 1926).

33. Monteiro Lobato, *How Henry Ford Is Regarded in Brazil*, 5, 18.

34. Monteiro Lobato, *Mr. Slang e o Brasil*, in *Obras Completas de Monteiro Lobato* (São Paulo: Brasliense, 1959), 8:71.

35. Monteiro Lobato, *Mr. Slang*, 88–89.

36. *Brazilian American*, 7 November 1925, 40. See also, *Automobilismo*, September 1927, 14. Analyses of advertising in Brazil frequently point out that consumerism, especially the purchase of American autos, was a fundamental aspect of being modern. Those studies neither define *modernism* nor analyze the place of democracy in being modern. See, for example, James P. Woodard, "Marketing Modernity: The J. Walter Thompson Company and North American Advertising in Brazil, 1929–1939," *Hispanic American Historical Review* 82:2 (May 2001): 257–290; and Owensby, *Intimate Ironies*, 110–117.

37. The latter quote is from Rodríguez Acosta's *Sonata Interrumpida*. Both cited in Louis A. Pérez Jr., *On Becoming Cuban: Identity, Nationality, and Culture* (Chapel Hill: University of North Carolina Press, 1999), 336–337.

38. No work about the United States more succinctly depicts the growth of popular automobility in the 1920s than Robert S. Lynd and Helen M. Lynd, *Middletown: A Study in Contemporary American Culture* (New York: Harcourt Brace, 1929). The French fascination with American automobility was more of a post-1945 phenomenon. See Kirsten Ross, *Fast Cars, Clean Bodies: Decolonization and the Reordering of French Culture* (Cambridge, Mass.: MIT Press, 1995). On autos in Britain, see Sean O'Connell, *The Car in British Society: Class, Gender, and Motoring, 1896–1939* (Manchester, England: Manchester University Press, 1998).

39. For a fascinating and polemical account of the growth of branding during the twentieth century, see Naomi Klein, *No Space, No Jobs, No Logo: Taking Aim at the Brand Bullies* (New York: Picador, 2000).

40. Good examples of this can be found in *Estado de São Paulo*, 23 February 1908. The advertisement for the Reo automobile simply provides the technical aspects and prices of the three models available.

41. The first Brazilian agency is said to be São Paulo's Castaldi and Benneton, which opened in 1913. This company primarily worked on placing print ads in magazines and on the sides of buses. See Ricardo Ramos, *História da Propaganda no Brasil* (São Paulo: USP, 1972), 25–30. On the U.S.-based firms, see Woodard, "Marketing Modernity."

42. Ramos, *História da Propaganda*, 31, 67; Tewksbury, *The Automotive Market*, 33–35; and Gregory H. Eickhoff, Trade Commissioner (Rio) to H. O. Smith,

Automotive Division, Bureau of Foreign and Domestic Commerce (DC), 16 July 1928, RG 151, 531 Automobiles, USNA.

43. *Automóvel Club,* August 1925, 39–41; *O Mundo Ford,* May 1939, 7; *Brazilian American,* 9 May 1925, 5; *Brazilian American Fourth of July Supplement,* 1936, n.p.

44. This is an example of how Sloanism worked in practice. On GM selling U.S.-style modernity, see Woodard, "Marketing Modernity," 270–274, 277. On cosmopolitanism and consumerism, see Kristin Hoganson, "Cosmopolitan Domesticity: Importing the American Dream, 1865–1920," *American Historical Review* 107:1 (February 2002): 55–83.

45. *Auto-Sport,* 15 December 1926 and 30 December 1926. Advertisements also highlighted the technical and safety aspects of various brands of vehicles, but these ideas did not receive the same prominence as did Hollywood stars. See *Automobilismo,* June 1926, 3–4; and *Brazilian American,* 6 November 1926, 15.

46. The telegram ad appears in *Automobilismo,* September 1926, 33. See also General Cândido M. S. Rondon, "Satnearem-Concepcion," in *Automóvel Club,* August–September 1929; and Ford do Brasil, *A Ford no Brasil,* 8; and *Cruzeiro,* 18 April 1953, 93.

47. *Brazilian American,* 11 July 1925, 5; 13 December 1924, 20; and Embry (Rio) to DC, 8 February 1924, Bureau of Foreign and Domestic Commerce, 531 Autos, RG 151, USNA.

48. *O Mundo Ford,* January 1939, 14; *Ford News,* 15 August 1926; and *Brazilian American,* 11 July 1925 and 18 July 1925, 3. Henry Ford was personally fixated on the importance of the tractor, which he is said to have invented, as the key link between the modern automobile-based world and his own idealized rural past. This is one of the primary themes of Robert Lacey, *Ford: The Men and the Machines* (New York: Ballantine, 1986).

49. Quoted in Woodard, "Marketing Modernity," 277. See also General Motors do Brasil, *70 Years of History,* 27.

50. Taylor (DC) to Howard S. Welch, Export Manager Studebaker Corporation, South Bend, IN, 29 February 1928, Bureau of Foreign and Domestic Commerce, 531 Autos, RG 151, USNA; Smith (DC) to Long (SP), 21 February 1928, Bureau of Foreign and Domestic Commerce, 531 Autos, RG 151, USNA; Long (SP) to DC, 27 January 1928, Bureau of Foreign and Domestic Commerce, 531 Autos, RG 151, USNA. See also photograph of man on horse on top of Studebaker car in RG 151-FC-10A, Brazil Advertising, USNA.

51. *O Mundo Ford,* August 1934, 27; May 1936, 14; and June 1936, 28.

52. *O Mundo Ford,* September 1936; October 1936, 3; and May 1937, 27.

53. Green (SP) to DC, 9 August 1930, Bureau of Foreign and Domestic Commerce, 531 Autos, RG 151, USNA.

54. Hupmobile advertised itself as providing "family cars" as early as 1915. See *Auto-Propulsão,* July 1915. On suburban living, see *O Mundo Ford,* June

1940, 6. Neighborhoods such as the Jardins, and Higeonópolis in São Paulo, which were dominated by such single-family houses, were developed during the 1920s and 1930s.

55. On the increase in the use of women in car ads in Brazil, see Ramos, *História da Propaganda*, 28–31. For a broad analysis on changing gender ideologies during this period, see Susan K. Besse, *Restructuring Patriarchy: The Modernization of Gender Inequality in Brazil, 1914–1940* (Chapel Hill: UNC Press, 1996). On women and driving in the U.S., see Virginia Scharff, *Taking the Wheel: Women and the Coming of the Motor Age* (Albuquerque: UNM Press, 1992).

56. *O Mundo Ford*, August 1934, 8–9; September 1934, 10–11; and July 1934 cover photo of a woman driving a coupe. For the Hudson ad, see RG 151m FC11-A, USNA; Woodard, "Marketing Modernity," 275.

57. Jackson (Rio) to DC, 11 August 1927, RG 151 Bureau of Foreign and Domestic Commerce, 531 Automobiles, USNA; *Automóvel Club*, September 1925, July 1925, and October 1925.

58. *Automobilismo*, July 1928, 19; October 1926, 17, 35, 45; *Automóvel Club*, May 1925; and *O Mundo Ford*, February 1939, 19.

59. *Automobilismo*, April 1927, 20–21; September 1927, 22.

60. Tewksbury, *The Automotive Market*, 24–29; *Brazilian Business*, March 1926, 4–5; *Automobilismo*, June 1926, 24; October 1928, 32–34; November 1928, 43; Pierrot (Rio) to DC, "Conditions in Local Automobile Trade," 12 August 1929, RG 151, 531 Autos, USNA; SP to Dearborn, 8 July 1927, FMC International Division 49:16; Montevideo to Dearborn, 4 March 1927, FMC International Division, 49:16; Orberg (SP) to Dearborn, 12 September 1929, FMC International Division, 49:16; Board of Directors Report 18 March 1924, Studebaker Corporation, Minute Books 1920–1933, Studebaker Archives.

61. SP to Dearborn, 2 December 1926, FMC 49:16.

62. The U.S. companies focused on lowering import tariffs and local fees. When these measures failed, manufacturers lowered prices by as much as 25% to increase market share. See Schwarz (Rio) to DC, 6 April 1925; Owen (DC) to Embry (Rio), 9 July 1925; Schwarz (Rio) to Director Bureau Foreign and Domestic Commerce, Automobiles Division, 9 May 1922; Pierrot (Rio) to DC, 3 July 1929; Rio to DC 17 December 1929; Schwarz (Rio) to Owen (DC), 7 March 1925; and Seth B. Robinson Jr., White Trucks & Buses, Cleveland, OH, to Bureau of Foreign and Domestic Commerce, 25 June 1927, RG 151 Bureau of Foreign and Domestic Commerce, 531 Automobiles, USNA.

63. *Brazilian American Motor Supplement 1925*, vol. 3; "O Brasil e o Automobilismo," *Brazilian American Motor Supplement 1924*; "Automoveis e seus Donos," *Brazilian American Motor Supplement*, 18 April 1925; *O Mundo Ford*, March 1933, 11; Wilkins and Hill, *American Business Abroad*, 244–245.

64. *Automobilismo*, February 1927, 26. The São Paulo city government had unsuccessfully tried to ban motorcycles in 1915 because of the negative images they held. See *Auto-Propulsão*, April 1915.

65. Embry (SP) to Taylor (DC), 15 January 1926; Pierrot (Rio) to DC, 13 October 1926, RG 151, Automobiles 531, USNA; *Brazilian Business*, May 1925, 13; June 1925, 8; "The Automobile Business in Brazil," 25 October 1924, 5–9; "O Automóvel no Brasil," *Automobilismo*, February 1929, 35; and Tewkesbury, *The Automotive Market*, 13.

66. Gregory H. Eickhoff to H. O. Smith, 16 July 1928, RG 151, 531 Automobiles, USNA; *Brazilian American*, 23 May 1925, 12; *Brazilian Business*, February 1925, 26–27; April 1925; March 1926, 11, 29. For one of the few non-statistical accounts that reports most urban middle-class Brazilians rode the trolleys and could not afford to own automobiles, see Earl Chapin May, "The Land of the Bandeirantes: São Paulo the Chicago of South America," *Travel*, May 1924.

67. Ramos, *História da Propaganda*, 38–43. On the growth of radio into a national medium during the 1930s, see Brian McCann, *Hello, Hello Brazil: Popular Music in the Making of Modern Brazil* (Durham, N.C.: Duke University Press, 2004), 19–39.

68. Ramos, *História da Propaganda*, 36; *O Mundo Ford*, July 1939, 16.

69. Ramos, *História da Propaganda*, 31–36. On *Cruzeiro's* flamboyant founder, Francisco de Assis Chateaubriand, and his magazine, see Fernando Morais, *Chatô: O Rei do Brasil* (São Paulo: Compahnia das Letras, 1994). Although *Cruzeiro* was the first truly national magazine in Brazil, literary and political journals, including *Fon-Fon!* and *A Revista do Brasil,* did speak to national issues. On the latter, see Tania Regina de Luca, *A Revista do Brasil: Um Diagnóstico para a (N)ação* (São Paulo: UNESP, 1998).

70. See Ford Motor Co. *Circular*, July 1925, January 1928, and February 1928; and *O Mundo Ford*, February 1933, 8–10, 12–17, on intensified use of traditional marketing.

71. *Brazilian American*, 30 July 1921, 5, 24, 28–29; 17 September 1921, 17, 30–31; 31 July 1926, 26; 14 September 1926, 18; 9 October 1926, 18; *O Automóvel*, September 1925, 6–7; *Brazilian Business*, November 1925, 14; *Auto-Sport*, 7 October 1926; 14 October 1926, 12; *Automobilismo*, October 1926, 5–6; November 1926; January 1927, 31; August 1928, 30.

72. *Auto-Sport*, 30 September 1926, 16; *O Mundo Ford*, August 1936, 26; *Brazilian American*, 4 July 1924. Auto enthusiasts planned raids between São Paulo and New York and between São Paulo and Detroit but could not arrange car company backing, probably because of the huge cost and unlikely success of such trips. See *Brazilian American*, 15 May 1926, 25; 21 August 1926, 13.

73. *Automobilismo*, August 1929, 38; October 1929, 36–37; August 1926, 21–25; *Auto-Sport*, 19 August 1926, 2, 20–23; *Brazilian American*, 10 July 1926, 14; August 1926, 3.

74. "Orberg Reminiscences," Accession 65, Oral History Section, FMC.

75. *Automobilismo*, August 1926, 36–37; *Brazilian American*, 17 July 1926, 25; *Bulletin of the American Chamber of Commerce of São Paulo*, August 1926, 4; *Automóvel Club*, September 1926. Ford used similar caravans in Spain and the Middle East. See *Ford News*, 1 June 1925 and 22 May 1925; and General Motors do Brasil, *70 Years of History*, 23, 39.

76. Interview with Francisco Salles Cesar, Porto Alegre dealer since 1920s, 10 November 1961 MWFORD; Long (SP) to DC, 31 January 1927, RG 151, 531 Automobiles, USNA; *Automobilismo*, February 1931, 10.

77. *Automobilismo*, January 1927, 12–16; August 1927, 16; *Auto-Sport*, 30 December 1926 and 30 January 1927; General Motors do Brasil, *70 Years of History*, 24–25; Studebaker photo, RG 151, Brazil Motor Vehicles, FC 11A, USNA; interview with Sven Nielson, 16 November 1961, MWFORD; *Brazilian American*, 9 October 1926, 16.

78. Paris to DC, 24 August 1923, RG 151, 531 Automobiles, USNA. See also *Jornal de la Marine Marchande*, 9 August 1923, 891. On the percentage of autos from the United States, see *Automóvel Club*, September 1925, 25.

79. SP to DC, 5 March 1923, RG 151, 531 Automobiles; Pierrot (Rio) to DC, 16 March 1926, RG 151, 531 Automobiles; Pierrot (Rio) to DC, 4 June 1930, RG 151, 531 Automobiles, USNA; General Motors do Brasil, *70 Years of History*, 19; Paulo Cesar de Azevedo et al., *O Seculo do Automóvel no Brasil* (São Caetano: Brasinca, 1989), 20.

80. On support for the Good Roads Movement, see "Orberg Reminisces," Ascension 65 FMC Oral History Section, May 1956, 24.

81. "Orberg Reminisces," 65 Ascension FMC; interview with Kristian Orberg, 7 November 1961, MWFORD; interview with Alexendre Hornstein, 8 November 1961, MWFORD. These Ford executives noted that the European cars exported to Brazil tended to be low-riding luxury models that could not handle rural roads. Dodge Brothers cars were similarly discussed as ideal for Brazil, given their design for bad roads. See *Automóvel Club*, May 1925.

82. Dwight Eisenhower wrote about the horrible condition of American roads during World War I after his service in the famous 1919 cross-country military caravan. It took 62 days to make the trip, which had an average speed of five miles per hour, given the horrible roads and paths used. That experience no doubt played some role in his support for building an interstate highway system in the United States. See Tom Lewis, *Divided Highways: Building the Interstate Highways, Transforming American Life* (New York: Penguin, 1997), 89–90, 104, 156.

83. Richard P. Monsen (SP) to Studebaker do Brasil (SP), 15 July 1927, Minutes Book, Studebaker do Brasil; Export Sales Manager, South Bend, IN to Foreign Offices, 27 August 1927, Export Books 1928, Studebaker Archives; *Brazilian American*, 22 May 1926, 32. The U.S.-based tire companies began

production in Rio in the 1910s but soon relocated to São Paulo as well. See *Bureau of the Pan American Union*, October 1912; *O Mundo Ford*, November 1939, 29.

84. Interview with C. Marinelli and Alexendre Hornstein, 8 November 1961, MWFORD; Wilkins and Hill, *American Business Abroad*, 108–109.

85. "Orberg Reminiscences," Ascension 65 FMC Oral History Section, May 1956, 14.

86. On GM's activities, see memo, K. Orberg to Edsel B. Ford, September 1926, Ascension 6, Box 446, FMC; interview with Paul Anderson, 13 November 1961, MWFORD.

87. E. A. Evans, Manager São Paulo to Dearborn, 9 September 1920, 572 Box 16, FMC; Porto Alegre to Dearborn, 31 December 1927, Foreign Branches 33:22, FMC; SP to Dearborn, 30 January 1928, Foreign Branches 33:22, FMC; SP to Dearborn, 10 October 1930, 49:16, FMC; Orberg (SP) to Dearborn, 7 August 1930 49:16, FMC; Brownstein to J. C. Younkins, 10 December 1934, MWFORD; interview with Juvenal Waegte, 14 November 1961, MWFORD; interview with Humberto Monteiro (assistant manager, Ford São Paulo), 8 November 1961, MWFORD; *Ford News*, 15 August 1926; *Brazilian American*, 15 July 1922, 27.

88. Minter (U.S. Consul, Pará) to American Used Car Co., San Francisco, CA 8 November 1927, 531, RG 151, USNA; interview Juvenal Waegte, 14 November 1961, MWFORD; interview Paul Anderson, 13 November 1961, MWFORD.

89. Manager Export Sales, South Bend, IN to Studebaker Foreign Offices, 27 August 1927, Export Books, Studebaker Archive; Cremer (Rio) to Smith (DC), 18 May 1929, 532, RG 151, USNA; interview Paul Anderson, 13 November 1961, MWFORD; *Noticias Ford do Brasil*, November 1958, 5; Tewksbury, *The Automotive Market*, 35–38; Wilkins and Hill, *American Business Abroad*, 145–146, 244.

90. SP to Dearborn, 23 November 1926, 49:16 FMC; Long (SP) to DC, 27 August 1927, 531 Automobiles, RG 151; Long (SP) to DC, 12 March 1928, 531 Automobiles, RG 151; Tewksbury, *The Automotive Market in Brazil*, 23, 58–61, 160–161; *Automobilismo*, March 1927, 12; September 1927, 28; October 1927, 25–27.

91. Interview with Humberto Monteiro (assistant manager, Ford São Paulo) 16 November 1961, MWFORD; *O Mundo Ford*, June 1933, 38; September 1936, 16–17.

92. *O Mundo Ford*, January 1934, 12–13, 22–23; June 1936, 7, 18–19; July 1936, 22–23; August 1936, 12.

93. "A Mecanização Agrícola," *O Mundo Ford*, June 1933, 11; *Brazilian American*, 16 May 1925, back cover.

94. *Noticias Ford do Brasil*, November 1958, 5; *40 Anos Crescendo com o Brasil* (São Paulo: Ford do Brasil, 1959); and FMC Circular, 14 March 1925; 8 April

1925. On the chronic electricity shortages in São Paulo in the early to mid-1920s, see Wolfe, *Working Women, Working Men*, 42.

95. For a detailed account of Ford's Amazon venture that puts it in the context of Ford's business practices and ideology, rather than Brazilian history, see Greg Grandin, *Fordlandia: The Rise and Fall of Henry Ford's Forgotten Jungle City* (New York: Metropolitan Books, 2009). The most complete analysis of the environment problems at the Ford plantations can be found in Warren Dean, *Brazil and the Struggle for Rubber: A Study in Environmental History* (Cambridge: Cambridge University Press, 1987), 67–86. For a work that concentrates on the politics of the concession, see John Galey, "Industrialist in the Wilderness: Henry Ford's Amazon Venture," *Journal of International Studies and World Affairs* 21:2 (May 1979): 261–289.

96. In 1930, the U.S. Consul in Pará reported that Ford had signed a contract with Standard Oil to explore some of these areas. See Drew (Pará) to Munro, Memorandum on Compahnia Ford do Brasil, 27 June 1930, Rio Post 860.2, RG 84, USNA.

97. Dean analyzes Ford's output relative to the rubber produced by small holders in Sumatra. The Ford properties, at the height of their productive capacity in 1944, produced half as much rubber as Sumatra's peasants. See Dean, *Brazil and the Struggle for Rubber*, 97–98. Dean also argues convincingly that the Ford venture was an environmental failure. Previous studies asserted that labor problems were the primary problem. For this point of view, see Galey, "Industrialist in the Wilderness"; Joseph A. Russell, "Fordlandia and Belterra, Rubber Plantations on the Tapajos River, Brazil," *Economic Geography* 18 (1942): 141–142; and Barbara Weinstein, *The Amazon Rubber Boom, 1850–1920* (Stanford, Calif.: Stanford University Press, 1983), 32.

98. Minter (Pará) to Rio, 10 October 1927, Rio Post 860.2, RG 84; Morgan (Rio) to Secretary of State, DC, 17 October 1927, Rio Post 860.2, RG 84; Pará to DC, 22 April 1929, Rio Post 860.2, RG 84; and Jackson (Rio) to DC, 15 January 1929, Rio Post 860.2, RG 84, USNA. The local intrigue was complex. The governor at the time of the initial deal, Dionísio Bentes, received a payment for his support. That fact and other details were leaked to the local press by a disaffected and uncompensated associate of the original syndicate. Bentes sought to protect himself from the appearance of impropriety by blocking Ford's initial work on the plantation. His successor intensified this activity. Dean, *Brazil and the Struggle for Rubber*, 73.

99. Oz Ide (Rio) to Clifford B. Longley (Dearborn), "Brazilian Rubber Project," August 1927, FMC 301:2; and Oz Ide (Belém, Pará) to Longley (Dearborn), 10 September 1927, FMC 301:2. Dean (*The Struggle for Brazilian Rubber*, 72–73) misses Washington Luís's support for the project and argues that the advent of the Getúlio Vargas government in 1930 led to a change in Rio's orientation toward development. In this case, beliefs in the transformative power of automobility trumped long-standing political perspectives.

100. Part of this confusion is understandable, given the fact that the Ford Motor Company was privately held at this time.

101. The translations of these editorials are from the U.S. Embassy in Rio. See Rio to DC Dispatch, 17 October 1927, Rio Post 860.2, RG 84, USNA. The originals can be found in *Jornal do Brasil*, 13 October 1927; and *O País*, 13 October 1927.

102. *O Globo*, 29 February 1928; *Jornal do Brasil*, 29 February 1928; *O Jornal*, 28 February 1928; Morgan (Rio) to Secretary of State (DC), 2 March 1928, Rio Post 860.2, RG 84, USNA.

103. *Automobilismo*, March 1928, 31; April 1928, 17–18; December 1929, 34, 36; and *Automóvel Club*, November 1929.

104. Drew (Pará) to Rio, 14 February 1930, Rio Post 860.2, RG 84, USNA. By 31 March 1930, Ford had reportedly spent $31,498,711.74 on the project. See Memorandum on Companhia Ford do Brasil, 27 June 1930, Drew (Pará) to Munro, Rio Post 860.2, RG 84, USNA. For other reports on Ford as a "civilizing" force in the Amazon, see *O Mundo Ford*, March 1934, 29; John Minton, U.S. Consul, Pará, to Secretary of State (DC), 22 July 1927, Rio Post 860.2, RG84, USNA; Morgan (Rio) to Secretary of State, 16 August 1927, Rio Post 860.2, RG 84, USNA; and Morgan (Rio) to Secretary of State, 17 October 1927, Rio Post 860.2, RG 84, USNA.

105. This is the primary critique presented by Dean.

106. Charles Wagley, *Amazon Town: A Study of Man in the Tropics* (New York: Knopf, 1964), 64–99; and Weinstein, *The Amazon Rubber Boom*, 5–34.

107. *Automobilismo*, August 1927, 34; Wilkins and Hill, *American Business Abroad*, 170–174; and untitled report from Boa Vista, 1928 FMC 301:2.

108. "Information Referring to the Operations of 'Ford Industrial do Brasil,'" 1933, MWFORD; *The Rubber Age*, 10 April 1932; *The Ford Times*, March–April 1942, 34–36.

109. On growth of tire manufacturing, see *O Mundo Ford*, February 1939, 24. No less an authority than Rondon called for roads from Mato Grosso to the Ford plantations on the Tapajós. See *Automóvel Club*, September 1929. See also *O Mundo Ford*, June 1934, 22–23.

110. Salary and Wage Schedule, Rubber, FMC, Acc 38, Box 64; *The Planter*, January 1931; *The Rubber Age*, 10 November 1927; *The Ford Times*, March–April 1942, 36–37.

111. The initial turnover rate was estimated to be 20–27% per month. Drew (Pará) to Rio, 14 February 1930, Rio Post 860.2, RG 84, USNA; *The Rubber Age*, 10 April 1932, 22; *O Mundo Ford*, May 1934, 29; and interview with Silvino da Silva, former employee of Ford Industrial do Brasil, 18 September 1961, MWFORD.

112. Companhia Ford Industrial do Brasil, *Index to Facts and Figures*, 1933, MWFORD, Acc. 390, Box 86. Changes in work routines and the structure

of the day created this labor peace. See Mary A. Dempsey, "Fordlândia," *Michigan History* (July–August 1994): 24–33.

113. "Information Referring to the Operations of 'Ford Industrial do Brasil,'" MWFORD; *The Ford Times*, March–April 1942, 34–36; August 1944, 3–5; photo of Fordlândia, FC 11-G, Brazil—Rubber, and accompanying dispatch N. 738, 31 May 1938, "Activities of Cia. Ford Industrial do Brasil," RG 151, USNA; Ford Motor Company, *The Ford Rubber Plantations* (Dearborn, Mich.: Ford Motor Co., 1942); H.C. Deckard, "The Ford Rubber Plantations, 1928–1940," FMC Acc. 1756, Folder 1; *Business Week*, 26 February 1944; and Dempsey, "Fordlândia," 24–33.

114. Edward J. Cleary, "An Engineer's Role on a Rubber Plantation," *Engineering News-Record*, 9 March 1944, 96–105.

115. Dempsey, "Fordlândia," 30–31.

116. Companhia Ford Industrial do Brasil, Index to Facts and Figures, 1933, 2, 6, FMC Acc. 390, Box 86; *The Rubber Age*, 10 April 1932, 20–21.

117. Interview with Silvino da Silva, 18 September 1961, MWFORD; *Business Week*, 26 February 1944. Paying such captive employees (i.e., workers in isolated enclaves) in cash and providing discounts at the company store sharply contrasts with the experiences of miners and others who were paid in scrip and often overcharged in such company stores.

118. *The Rubber Age*, 10 April 1932. Modern groceries were relatively new throughout Brazil in the 1930s and 1940s. See, for example, "Effect of Changes in Retail Trade on the Standard of Living of the Masses in São Paulo," 6 December 1942, São Paulo Post 850, USNA. The broad sale of watches contrasts sharply with initial worker rejection of the 6:00 A.M. to 3:00 P.M. work hours at Fordlândia that led to the smashing of a time clock. When worker shifts were changed to lessen labor during the hottest hours of the day, workers made peace with timekeeping.

119. *Indian Rubber World*, 1 February 1932; *O Mundo Ford*, January 1936, 8–9; *Engineering News-Record*, 9 March 1944, 105.

120. Getúlio Vargas, *Diário* (Rio: Siciliano, 1995), 2:343; "The Ford Rubber Plantations, 1928–1940," FMC Acc. 1756, folder 1; *O Mundo Ford*, November 1940, 8–10; Wilkins and Hill, *American Business Abroad*, 180. It is fair to say that Ford's plantations probably came closer to Vargas's goal of employer-supplied social services than any other workplace in Brazil. Indeed, throughout the 1930s and 1940s, few Brazilian companies came close to offering all the services required by law. For the limited nature of such services in São Paulo, Brazil's industrial heartland, see Wolfe, *Working Women, Working Men*, 70–93. See also Weinstein, *For Social Peace in Brazil*, 84–113.

121. Wilkins and Hill, *American Business Abroad*, 174.

122. Drew (Pará) to Munro, Memorandum on Campanhia Ford do Brasil, 27 June 1930, Rio Post 860.2, RG 84, USNA; *O Mundo Ford*, July 1936, 21;

November 1939, 7, 29; Wilkins and Hill, *American Business Abroad*, 167. Several of these sources reported plans by Firestone Tire and Rubber to open a large Amazon-region factory.

123. *The Rubber Age*, December 1945; Wilkins and Hill, *American Business Abroad*, 183.

124. *Los Angeles Times*, 9 March 1993.

Chapter 4

1. For most of the twentieth century, the presidency alternated between the coffee-producing state of São Paulo and Minas Gerais, which was well known for its dairy industry. This led to the so-called politics of *café com leite* (coffee with milk) that was finally ended by Washington Luís's decision to promote a fellow Paulista for the presidency. For a fairly complete history of the politics of this era, see Boris Fausto, *A Concise History of Brazil* (Cambridge: Cambridge University Press, 1999), 148–197.

2. Scholars have commented on the influence of cultural modernism on aspects of Vargas's program and on his centralizing tendencies, but he has not been explicitly singled out as Brazil's first truly modernist leader. The term is used here in reference to his connections to both economic modernization and cultural modernism. That is, the Vargas era sought to bring modernity to Brazil, although he rarely defined it in such an explicit way. The single best work on the ties between cultural modernism and the regime is Daryle Williams, *Culture Wars in Brazil: The First Vargas Regime, 1930–1945* (Durham, N.C.: Duke University Press, 2001). For a study that concentrates on remaking the economy during this era, see Marcelo da Paiva Abreu, *O Ordem do Progresso: Cem Anos de Política Econômica Republicana* (Rio: Campus, 1990).

3. The Ministry of Labor would soon become the Ministry of Labor, Industry, and Commerce, reflecting Vargas's embrace of a corporatist governing structure for the industrial sector of the Brazilian economy. For a fascinating analysis of the rise of the federal educational bureaucracy, see Jerry Dávila, *Diploma of Whiteness: Race and Social Policy in Brazil, 1917–1945* (Durham, N.C.: Duke University Press, 2003).

4. Todd Diacon, "Searching for a Lost Army: Recovering the History of the Federal Army's Pursuit of the Prestes Column in Brazil, 1924–1927, *Americas* 54:3 (January 1998): 409–436; Diacon, "Bringing the Countryside Back In: A Case Study of Military Intervention as State-Building in the Brazilian Old Republic," *Journal of Latin American Studies* 27:3 (October 1995): 569–592; Frank D. McCann, "The Formative Period of Twentieth-Century Brazilian Army Thought: 1900–1922," *Hispanic American Historical Review* 64:4 (November 1984): 737–765; and Michael L. Conniff, "The Tenentes in Power: A New Perspective on the Brazilian Revolution of 1930," *Journal of Latin American Studies* 10:1 (May 1978): 61–82.

5. Joel Wolfe, *Working Women, Working Men: São Paulo and the Rise of Brazil's Industrial Working Class, 1900–1955* (Durham, N.C.: Duke University Press, 1993), 50–62.

6. Wolfe, *Working Women, Working Men*, 58–68; and Barbara Weinstein, *For Social Peace in Brazil: Industrialists and the Remaking of the Working Class in São Paulo, 1920–1964* (Chapel Hill: University of North Carolina Press, 1996).

7. Frank D. McCann, *Soldiers of the Patria: A History of the Brazilian Army, 1889–1937* (Stanford, Calif.: Stanford University Press, 2004), 333–34. See also Jens R. Hentschke, "From 'Order and Progress' to 'National Security and Economic Development'—The Origins of Brazil's 1969 National Security State," *Justiça e História* 4:7 (2004): 211–258.

8. Mc Cann, *Soldiers of the Patria*, 334. Paulistas had long held the view that Brazil could advance only if it modeled itself on their successful model. Mário de Andrade claimed in "Guerra de São Paulo" that "São Paulo had become too great for Brazil.... Brazil has not yet become a civilization [whereas] São Paulo was a European Christian civilization with the mentality, the climate, the cosmopolitanism, the resources of a European Christian civilization." Quoted in Barbara Weinstein, "Racializing Regional Difference: São Paulo versus Brazil, 1932," in Nancy P. Appelbaum et al., eds. *Race and Nation in Modern Latin America* (Chapel Hill: University of North Carolina Press, 2003), 237.

9. The single best work on these cultural programs is Williams, *Culture Wars in Brazil*. An insightful analysis of the cultural components of the Vargas years can be found in a book written during the Estado Novo. See Karl Loewenstein, *Brazil under Vargas* (New York: Macmillan, 1942), 285–314.

10. Studies of tourism in Latin America usually focus on the how North Americans and Europeans experienced the region. See, for example, Nancy Leys Stepan, *Picturing Tropical Nature* (Ithaca, N.Y.: Cornell University Press, 2001); and Mary Louise Pratt, *Imperial Eyes: Travel Writing and Transculturation* (New York: Routledge, 1992). There is little written on the promotion of internal tourism as a form of state making. One exception is Loewenstein, *Brazil under Vargas*, 297–304. On tourism and national identity in the United States and Europe, see Marguerite S. Shaffer, *See America First: Tourism and National Identity, 1880–1940* (Washington, D.C.: Smithsonian, 2001); and Wolfgang Sachs, *For the Love of the Automobile: Looking Back into the History of Our Desires*, Don Reneau, trans. (Berkeley: University of California Press, 1992).

11. This program focused road building in the states of Ceará, Bahia, Rio Grande do Norte, Piauí, and Paraíba. *Motor*, January–February 1941.

12. "Report of the American Technical Mission to Brazil," vol. 2, January 1943, Part 4, 27–32, USNA; American Brazilian Association, *News Bulletin*, 15 August 1940; General Motors Corporation, General Motors Overseas Operations, *Economic Survey of Brazil* (São Paulo: General Motors, 1943), vol. 1, 158; "Brazilian Highways," unpublished manuscript, University of Wisconsin Land Tenure Center, BR 95, NR; *Motor*, January–February 1941.

13. "Brazilian Highways." Bahia budgeted $252,000 and Paraíba $55,000. Despite the low funding, Bahia created an elaborate statewide road-building plan. See *Cruzeiro*, 16 March 1940, 43–45, 52.

14. General Motors, *Economic Survey of Brazil*, 1:159–160, 2:37.

15. Getúlio Vargas, *Diário* (Rio: Fundação Getúlio Vargas, 1995), 2:201–202, 215–216; American Brazilian Association, *New Bulletin*, 20 November 1940 and 20 April 1942.

16. Not only was auto ownership heavily skewed to wealthy Brazilians in the 1930s but participation in raids often required sponsorship by a foreign auto company and/or possession of more than one car.

17. 16 March 1934, Touring Club do Brasil to Ministério da Justiça, Assuntos Políticos, Box 154 Pro: 2137/34, Arquivo Nacional (AN). The letter made a specific request that the Touring Club be made a "utilidade pública" (similar to a nonprofit enterprise) and thus avoid having to pay taxes. This request was denied, but the federal government did work closely with the Touring Club to promote tourism throughout Brazil.

18. "O Problema Turística Nacional," *Touring*, January 1936.

19. Citizenship had been so narrowly construed during the republic that Vargas sought to inculcate a broad sense of political participation through a series of new state institutions, especially urban labor unions. Néstor García Canclini has argued that consumerism displaced political citizenship in Latin America, but in the case of Brazil, consumerism as a path to citizenship largely predates real political incorporation. See Canclini, *Consumers and Citizens: Globalization and Multicultural Conflicts*, George Yúdice, trans. (Minneapolis: University of Minnesota Press, 2001). On labor and citizenship, see Angêla Castro Gomes, *A Invenção do Trabalhimso*. On its limits in practice, see Joel Wolfe, "The Faustian Bargain Not Made: Getúlio Vargas and Industrial Labor in Brazil" *Luso-Brazilian Review* (December 1994): 77–95. On education policy under Vargas and its role in the development of citizenship, see Dávila, *Diploma of Whiteness*, esp. 155–191. One of the central themes of Williams's *Culture Wars in Brazil* is the use of state patronage in the arts to foster a broad sense of citizenship.

20. *Touring*, May 1936; *Jornal do Commércio* (Recife), 3 April 1936.

21. *Jornal do Brasil*, 25 March 1936; *Correio do Povo* (Porto Alegre), 26 January 1936.

22. As late as 1942, there was no tourist guidebook in any language available for Brazil. Loewenstein, *Brazil under Vargas*, 303–304.

23. It is now a World Heritage Site as designated by UNESCO.

24. Williams, *Culture Wars in Brazil*, 123–124, 130–132. See also *O Museu Inconfidência* (São Paulo: Banco Safra, 1989). On the Inconfidência, see Rubim Santos Leao de Aquino, *Um Sonho de Liberdade: A Conjuração de Minas* (São Paulo: Ed. Moderna, 1998); and Kenneth Maxwell, *Conflicts*

and Conspiracies: Brazil and Portugal, 1750–1808 (Cambridge: Cambridge University Press, 1973).

25. Car travel to and from Ouro Preto remained precarious in the early 1930s, and the Automobile Club argued for improved roads from Belo Horizonte to increase local tourism. See *Automóvel Club*, April 1932.

26. *Touring*, January 1936.

27. *Touring*, April 1936; June 1936. The federal government, working with the Sociedade Anônima Viagens Internacionais, also sought to promote auto-based tourism by foreign travelers. Road trips throughout various regions of Brazil are detailed in *Travels in Brazil* (Rio: SAVI, 1939).

28. Graciliano Ramos's *Vidas Secas* (1938; São Paulo: Martins, 1973) remains the archetypal novel in this genre.

29. It was at this time that Claude Lévi-Strauss, serving as a professor at the Universidade de São Paulo, traveled by car from the Paulista capital into the Amazon to conduct his fieldwork on the local inhabitants. The trip, which led to the eventual publication of his *Triste Tropiques* (John and Doreen Weightman, trans.; New York: Modern Library, 1973), is memorialized in *Saudades de São Paulo* (São Paulo: Companhia das Letras, 1996). This journey far exceeded the tamer forms of popular auto-based tourism of the 1930s, but it did foreshadow the coming of eco-tourism in the 1980s and 1990s. For an informed if somewhat cynical view of this latter form of tourism into Brazil's vast interior, see Geoffrey O'Connell, *Amazon Journal: Dispatches from a Vanishing Frontier* (New York: Dutton, 1997) and Candace Slater, *Entangled Edens: Visions of the Amazon* (Berkeley: University of California Press, 2002), 17–20.

30. Systematic national tourist guides geared toward drivers did not appear until this later period. The well-known *Quatro Rodas* series debuted in 1965, for example.

31. Amusements and mass entertainment were recent developments in urban Brazil. Attendance at movies grew steadily throughout the late 1910s and throughout the 1920s. See Ernani Silva Bruno, *História e Tradições da Cidade de São Paulo* (Rio: José Olympio, 1954), 3:1237, 3:1296; Wolfe, *Working Women, Working Men*, 30.

32. G. J. Bruce, *Brazil and the Brazilians* (London: Methuen, 1915), 258–259; Alex Bellos, *Futebol: Soccer the Brazilian Way* (New York: Bloomsbury, 2002), 30–40. On the military dictatorship's use of soccer and its close identification with the successful World Cup teams of the 1960s and 1970s, see Janet Lever, *Soccer Madness* (Chicago: University of Chicago Press, 1983).

33. Allen Guttmann delineates modern sports from early competitions with seven criteria: secularism, equality (i.e., participation is open all), bureaucratization (the existence of governing bodies), specialization, rationalization (through rules), quantification (statistics), and the obsession with

records. See *Games and Empire: Modern Sports and Cultural Imperialism* (New York: Columbia University Press, 1994). Michael Mandelbaum, in his *The Meaning of Sports: Why Americans Watch Baseball, Football, and Basketball and What They See When They Do* (New York: Public Affairs, 2004), argues that team sports are by definition modern and that they help define modernity itself.

34. Perhaps the most insightful commentary on how spectators experience auto racing and the symbolism it holds for them, and how that differs from being a fan of other sports, is Tom Wolfe's reporting on stock car racing in North Carolina, "The Last American Hero Is Junior Johnson, Yes!" *Esquire* (March 1965). Wolfe argues that stock car racing in the 1950s and 1960s not only focused on cars as symbols of liberation and mobility (especially in post-1945 South) but also offered the perfect mix of the mundane and the dangerous: "Here was a sport not using any abstract devices, any bat and ball, but the same automobile that was changing a man's own life, his own symbol of liberation, and it didn't require size, strength and all that, all it required was a taste for speed, and the guts."

35. *Revista de Automoveis*, November 1955, 9–11; *Automóvel Club*, February 1929, November 1929, and May 1930; *Automobilismo*, February 1929, 45.

36. *O Mundo Ford*, March 1933, 30; April 1933, 19; November 1933; August 1934, 22.

37. The first race referred to as a grand prix was organized by the Automobile Club de France in June 1906. A 1922 race at Monza in Italy was the first grand prix held outside France. Soon the term was used for races in 1924 in Belgium. In 1924, motor clubs from around the world formed the Association Internationale des Automobile Clubs Reconnus, which had a commission to regulate international motor sports competitions. For a race to be considered a grand prix, it had to meet the requirements set out by this body.

38. *Estado de São Paulo*, 3 and 5 October 1933; *O Mundo Ford*, November 1933; *Supplemento da Revista Automóvel Club*, September 1972; *O Globo*, 9 March 1983.

39. *Estado de São Paulo*, 2 Ocober 1934; *O Globo*, 9 March 1983;

40. Another factor that established Landi as Brazil's premier racer of this era was the tragic death of Irineu Corrêa, the 1934 grand prix's winner, in a fatal crash on the first lap of the 1935 Rio Grand Prix.

41. Landi is considered the first Brazilian driver to race in a European grand prix even though Teffé took fifth in the 1938 grand prix in Berne, Switzerland. This distinction is often made because Teffé was seen as an expatriate, whereas Landi was a Brazilian hero. After he retired from racing, Landi led the sport in key administrative roles.

42. Many athletic feats bring on a sense of awe in spectators, but auto racing combined that awe with the exhilaration many felt when they encountered large, technologically advanced machinery. Wolfe, "The Last American Hero

Is Junior Johnson," and Jeff MacGregor, *Sunday Money: Speed! Lust! Madness! Death! A Hot Lap around America with Nascar* (New York: Harper Collins, 2005). Two studies that tie the sense of awe fans have toward spectator sports to national pride are Mandelbaum, *The Meaning of Sports*, and Franklin Foer, *How Soccer Explains the World: An Unlikely Theory of Globalization* (New York: Harper Collins, 2004).

43. Childs (Rio) to DC, 151 531, 23 October 1937, USNA; and *O Mundo Ford*, May 1936, 29. On the early history of Paulista grand prix racing, see also *Supplemento a Revista Automóvel Club*, No. 10, September 1972. On racing in Rio Grande do Sul, see *Jornal do Brasil*, 30 September 1972.

44. Mattix (Automotive-Aeronautics Trade Division) DC to Allen, American Automobile Association, DC, 3 February 1938, 151, 531 USNA.

45. See, for example, *Motorista*, November 1937, 13; *Motor*, January–February 1940, 10–11; September–October 1941, 18–19, and May–June 1943, 74; and General Motors do Brasil, *70 Years of History* (São Paulo: Präemio Ed., 1995), 107. The relationship between the presence of a racetrack and the importance of a city was noted as early as 1931. See "O Rio Precisa o seu Autodromo," *Automóvel Club*, August–September 1931.

46. José América de Almeida, *O Ciclo Revolucionário do Ministério da Viação* (Rio: 1934); Cresó Coimbra, *Visão Histórica e Análise Conceitual dos Transportes no Brasil* (Rio: Ministério dos Transportes, 1974), 178–180.

47. Rudyard Kipling, *Brazilian Sketches* (New York: Doubleday, Doran, 1940), 68. Kipling wrote this brief book in 1927, but it was first published in 1940.

48. *O Mundo Ford*, September 1933, 14; September 1934, 23; and February 1934, 30–31.

49. *Correio da Manhã*, 16 March, 17 March, 21 April, and 23 April 1939.

50. *Correio da Manhã*, 28 April, 9 May, 10 May, and 12 May 1939. The rate of pedestrian injuries and fatalities as a result of auto accidents in Brazil was far higher than in Europe and the United States, where most auto accidents occurred between two or more vehicles. See Eduardo Alcântar Vasconcellos, "Strategies to Improve Traffic Safety in Latin America," paper presented to the World Bank Workshop on Urban Transport Strategy, Santiago, Chile, 6–9 November 2000.

51. *Correio da Manhã*, 28 April and 29 April 1939. The Paulista delegates knew well the limited capacity of the central state to implement federal laws throughout the nation.

52. República dos Estados Unidos do Brasil, *Coleção das Leis de 1941, Vol. 5: Atos do Poder Executivo, Decretos-Leis de Julho a Setembro* (Rio: Imprensa Nacional, 1941), 335–405. Local and state police had the primary responsibility for upholding the national traffic code until 1964, when, as a consequence of the military coup, the military police took control of traffic regulation. Vasconcellos, "Strategies to Improve Traffic Safety in Latin America."

53. Getúlio Vargas, *A Nova Política do Brasil* (Rio: José Olympio, 1938), 5:124–126. A recent translation of Vargas's address excludes explicit mention of the March to the West without explanation. See Robert M. Levine and John J. Crocitti, eds., *The Brazil Reader: History, Culture, Politics* (Durham, N.C.: Duke University Press, 1999), 186–189.

54. Vargas, *A Nova Política*, 5:124–126.

55. The military regime encouraged the establishment of a formal regionalization of the country. See Instituto Brasileiro de Geografia e Estatística, *Panorama Regional do Brasil* (Rio: IBGE, 1967). See also Bertha K. Becker and Claudio A. G. Egler, *Brazil: A New Regional Power in the World-Economy* (Cambridge: Cambridge University Press, 1992), 55–81.

56. On the direct impact of the March to the West on indigenous peoples, see Seth Garfield, *Indigenous Struggle at the Heart of Brazil: State Policy, Frontier Expansion, and the Xavante Indians, 1937–1988* (Durham, N.C.: Duke University Press, 2001), 23–65. On the tendency of the Portuguese and later Brazilian governments to conceptualize the interior as empty spaces, see John Monteiro, *Negros da Terra: Índios e Bandeirantes nas Origens de São Paulo* (São Paulo: Companhia das Letras, 1994).

57. Both the Goiás Railroad and the Noroeste Railroad were overburdened and failed to reach beyond the capital cities of Goiás and Mato Grosso. On the weak transportation links between these areas and the center-south that continued into the 1950s, see *The Development of Brazil: Report of the Joint Brazil–United States Economic Development Commission* (Washington, D.C.: Institute of Inter-American Affairs, 1954), 117–119, 151–153. On the limited prospects of the March to the West, see American Brazilian Association, *News Bulletin*, 15 August 1940.

58. The best work on Brazil's participation in World War II is still Frank D. McCann's *The Brazilian-American Alliance, 1937–1945* (Princeton: Princeton U. Press, 1973). See also Antônio Pedro Tota, *O Imperialismo Sedutor: A Americanização do Brasil na Época da Segunda Guerra* (São Paulo: Companhia das Letras, 2000).

59. A British blockade prevented European steel from reaching Brazil, and the United States was increasingly focusing on war production even before the attack on Pearl Harbor. The confluence of events behind the founding of the CSN is detailed in John D. Wirth, *The Politics of Brazilian Development* (Stanford, Calif.: Stanford University Press, 1970), 71–129. Vargas is quoted in E. Bradford Burns, *A History of Brazil*, 2nd ed. (New York: Columbia University Press, 1980), 456.

60. Benedicto Heloiz Nascimento, "Política e Desenvolvimento Industrial numa Economia Dependente: Formação da Indústria Automobilística Brasileira" (PhD diss., Universidade de São Paulo, 1972); and Helen Shapiro, *Engines of Growth: The State and Transnational Auto Companies in Brazil* (Cambridge: Cambridge University Press, 1994), 40. Steel production began in 1946 at

Volta Redonda and reached 646,000 tons of output by 1955; it doubled output by 1963. See Burns, *A History of Brazil*, 427.

61. On the strong presence of the federal Ministry of Labor in Volta Redonda, see Oliver J. Dinius, "Defending *Ordem* against *Progresso*: The Brazilian Political Police and Industrial Labor Control," in Jens R. Hentschke, ed. *Vargas and Brazil: New Perspectives* (New York: Palgrave MacMillan, 2006): 173–205.

62. José Ricardo Ramalho, *Estado-Patrão e Luta Operária: O Caso FNM* (Rio: Paz e Terrra, 1989), 31–57; Shapiro, *Engines of Growth*, 62–63; John J. Crocitti, "Vargas Era Social Policies: Malnutrition during the Estado Novo 1937–45," in Hentschke, ed. *Vargas and Brazil*, 155.

63. Brazil had mixed sugar-based ethanol into gasoline as early as the 1920s. In 1942, Vargas created the Sugar and Alcohol Institute to promote ethanol production and use by making its mixture with gasoline mandatory. Although this slightly diminished fuel shortages, it had no impact on motorists who had switched to gasogenes. See *Pesquisa Fapesp*, April 2006.

64. On the gasogene in São Paulo during the war, see Roney Cytrynowicz, "Guerra sem Guerra; A Mobilização do 'Front Interno' em São Paulo durante a Segunda Guerra Mundial, 1939–1945" (PhD diss., Universidade de São Paulo, 1998). On gasogene use, see also Christian Brannstrom, "Was Brazilian Industrialization Fueled by Wood? Evaluating São Paulo's Energy Hinterlands, 1900–1960," unpublished manuscript. On gas rationing during the war, see Jorge Americano, *São Paulo Atual: 1935–1962* (São Paulo: Melhoramentos, 1963), 253.

65. Although they helped preserve scarce gasoline stocks, gasogenes' impact on Brazil's forests was significant. See Brannstrom, "Was Brazilian Industrialization Fueled by Wood?"

66. Cytrynowicz, "Guerra sem Guerra," 91. Interlagos was built in 1938–1939 by developers who could not build houses on a track of land they had purchased south of the city. Instead, they created a grand prix–style circuit, based on the design of New York's Roosevelt Field, on the land.

67. The role of the auto parts sector in the establishment of the domestic auto industry is well analyzed in Caren Addis, *Taking the Wheel: Auto Parts Firms and the Political Economy of Industrialization in Brazil* (University Park: Pennsylvania State University Press, 1999).

68. Energy has been a long-term problem affecting Brazilian industrialization and urbanization. For a historically based analysis of the environmental degradation brought on by Brazil's reliance on wood as a fuel source, see Christian Brannstrom, "After the Forest: Environment, Labor, and Agro-Commodity Production in Southeastern Brazil" (PhD diss., University of Wisconsin–Madison, 1998).

69. There is some irony in the fact that the large oil reserves found in Brazilian territory in the twenty-first century have been offshore and not deep within the Amazon region.

70. On the role of import taxes on oil, see Wirth, *The Politics of Brazilian Development*, 133–136.

71. The years immediately after the end of World War II witnessed price spikes for oil, as postwar reconstruction and the booming U.S. economy increasingly relied on the smooth flow of petroleum. In fact, crude oil prices doubled between 1945 and 1948. Within Latin America, domestic demand increased in the context of ongoing urbanization and industrialization and increased state control over oil production. Although created in 1938, Mexico's PEMEX grew dramatically in the late 1940s, and successive Venezuelan regimes increased control over domestic production and export. See Fernando Coronil, *The Magical State: Nature, Money, and Modernity in Venezuela* (Chicago: University of Chicago Press, 1997), 107–138; and Daniel Yergin, *The Prize: The Epic Quest for Oil, Money, and Power* (New York: Free Press, 1993), 278–279, 433–437, 409.

72. Maria Augusta Tibirica Miranda, *O Petroleo É Nosso: A Luta contra o "Entreguismo" pelo Monopolio Estatal, 1947–1953* (Petrópolis: Vozes, 1983); Wirth, *The Politics of Brazilian Development*, 160–183; and Laura Randall, *The Political Economy of Brazilian Oil* (Westport, Conn.: Praeger, 1993), 9–12.

73. Quoted in Randall, *The Political Economy of Brazilian Oil*, 10.

74. Even the usually conservative, anti-Vargas União Democrática Nacional supported the idea of nationalizing foreign-owned refineries in 1953. See Thomas E. Skidmore, *Politics in Brazil, 1930–1964*(New York: Oxford University Press, 1967), 98.

75. Originally spelled Petrobrás, the name formally changed to Petrobras in 1971 in accordance with spelling and accent changes mandated by the Brazilian Academy of Letters in that year.

76. Randall (*The Political Economy of Brazilian Oil*, 21–50) details Petrobras's political maneuvering and the dramatic growth of its power within the federal government.

77. *The Development of Brazil: Report of the Joint Brazil–United States Economic Development Commission* (Washington, D.C.: Institute of Inter-American Affairs Foreign Operations Administration, 1954). This study came on the heels of the Dutra administration's SALTE (for *Saúde, Alimentação, Transportação, Energia* or Health, Food, Transportation, Energy) plan, which was essentially a five-year plan for the allocation of resources. Although a failure, it did point the way toward increased state study and planning for resource allocation and development. See Skidmore, *Politics in Brazil*, 71, 87, 94.

78. *The Development of Brazil*, 9–13, 90–92, 154–185.

79. The most significant crisis the regime faced was the attempted 5 August 1954 assassination of Vargas's most vocal critic, Carlos Lacerda (which led to the death of an air force officer), by one of the president's bodyguards. Vargas also faced soaring foreign debt, high inflation, increasing unemployment, and balance of payments problems. See Maria Celina S. D'Araújo, *O Segundo*

Governo Vargas, 1951–1954: Democracia, Partidos, e Crise Política (Rio: Zahar, 1982); and Skidmore, *Politics in Brazil*, 127–142.

80. *Estado de São Paulo*, 25 August 1954.

Chapter 5

1. Juscelino Kubitschek, *Meu Caminho para Brasília, Vol. 3: A Escalada Política* (Rio: Bloch, 1976), 372. His vice-presidential candidate, João Goulart from Rio Grande do Sul, was chosen for his popularity with the unions and his ties to Vargas through the Labor Party (PTB), not for geographical balance.

2. Kubitschek, *Meu Caminho para Brasília, Vol. 3: A Escalada Política*, 153. This claim is largely political rhetoric. Kubitschek's program really grew out of the recommendations of the Joint U.S.–Brazil Economic Development Commission and of a think tank, Instituto Superior de Estudos Brasileiros (ISEB). For an analytically rich discussion of JK's policies, see Katherine Sikkink, *Ideas and Institutions: Developmentalism in Brazil and Argentina* (Ithaca, N.Y.: Cornell University Press, 1991).

3. Juscelino Kubitschek, *A Marcha do Amanhecer* (São Paulo: Importadores de Livros, 1962), 25.

4. Instituto Brasileiro de Opinião Pública e Estatística (IBOPE), *Boletim das Classes Dirigentes*, 24–30 November 1954.

5. IBOPE, "Pesquisas Especiais, Levantamento das Aspirações do Povo de Porto Alegre, 1950," IBOPE, Arquivo Edgard Leuenroth (AEL), UNICAMP. The only "problem" considered worse than transportation was the high cost of living, which would be brought down by decreasing the freight costs of foodstuffs with the development of a more complete road network.

6. IBOPE, *Boletim das Classes Dirigentes*, nos. 31–40 1951, 1–7 July 1951; nos. 10–20 1951, 25 February–3 March 1951; nos. 41–50 1951, 14–20 October 1951.

7. IBOPE, *Boletim das Classes Dirigentes*, nos. 41–50 1951, 26 August–1 September 1951; "O Carioca e os Técnicos Americanos," 13–19 April 1952. The wealthiest respondents supported foreign capital at the highest rate (72.5%), and the poorest at the lowest rate (52.4%). There was also a preference for foreign capital in agriculture and oil exploration over industry.

8. IBOPE, *Boletim das Classes Dirigentes*, nos. 21–30 1951, 6–12 May 1951: 78.7% of all men and 57.0% of all women had made such a trip; 90% of upper-class respondents, 77% from the middle class, and 57% of the poor/working class had taken a bus between cities.

9. *Cruzeiro*, 25 April 1953, 7 (emphasis in the original); *Revista de Automóveis*, April 1955, 17.

10. *Revista de Automóveis*, April 1955, 17; May 1954, 2–3.

11. *Noticias Ford*, May 1954, 1; *New York Times*, 18 October 1954; *Revista de Automóveis*, December 1954, 46; June 1954, 23; March 1955, 26–27.

12. For an outstanding analysis of Kubitschek's Targets Plan that puts this program in the broader context of post-1945 Latin American political economy, see Sikkink, *Ideas and Institutions*, 122–170. See also Claudio Bojunga, *JK o Artista do Impossível* (Rio: Objetiva, 2001), 401–417.

13. Sikkink, *Ideas and Institutions*, 136–137. Presidência da República, Conselho do Desenvolvimento, *Programa de Metas. Tomo 1: Introdução* (Rio: Gráfica Editora Jornal do Comércio, 1958), 11–13.

14. Conselho do Desenvolvimento (CD), Grupo Executivo da Indústria Automobilística, Processo 53, Lucas Lopes to Juscelino Kubitscheck, 19 April 1956, CD 45, Arquivo Nacional (AN). See also Lucas Lopes, *Memória do Desenvolvimento* (Rio: CPDOC, 1991), 161–205. There are several very good accounts of the creation and operation of the GEIA. See Helen Shapiro, *Engines of Growth: The State and Transnational Auto Companies in Brazil* (Cambridge: Cambridge University Press, 1994); Ramiz Gattás, *A Indústria Automobilística e a Segunda Revolução Industrial: Origens e Perspectivas* (São Paulo: Prelo, 1981); Caren Addis, *Taking the Wheel: Autos Parts Firms and the Political Economy of Industrialization of Brazil* (University Park: Pennsylvania State University Press, 1999); and Sikkink, *Ideas and Institutions*, 134–138. These studies focus on policy and provide the important economic background for decision making about the installation of the auto industry. They do not, however, provide the historical and cultural context of Brazilians' desire to have an auto industry as a component of their modernity.

15. The government instituted a foreign exchange auction system that helped to finance some of the development program. Imports of machinery for the production of vehicles were exempt from this exchange regime. Auto producers were also exempt from sales taxes, and certain vehicles (e.g., trucks, buses, and jeeps) were exempt from sales taxes.

16. Plano de Metas #27 Indústria de Automóveis, Conselho de Desenvolvimento to Presidência da República, CD74, Arquivo Nacional (AN). The schedule was as follows:

Deadline	%Trucks	%Jeeps	%Utility Vehicles	% Cars
12/31/56	35	50	40	—
7/1/57	40	60	50	50
7/1/58	65	75	65	65
7/1/59	75	85	75	85
7/1/60	90	95	90	95

17. Mira Wilkins and Frank Ernest Hill, *American Business Abroad: Ford on Six Continents* (Detroit, Mich.: Wayne State University Press, 1964), 416–417.

18. "As dificuldades que o Brasil atravessa são um "pic-nic," 8 October 1956, Plano de Metas, CD 74, AN; GEIA, "Relatório do Grupo de Trabalho sobre Fixação de Normas a Serem Adotadoas pela Indústria Automobilística,"

17 October 1957, CD 45, AN; and U.S. Department of Commerce, *Foreign Commerce Weekly*, 10 September 1956. Trucks and, to a lesser extent, buses were key components in JK's plan to improve transportation. The focus on trucks followed closely the recommendations of the Joint Brazil–U.S. Commission, but cars were the symbolic centerpiece of Kubitschek's program. See, for example, Plano de Metas #27 Indústria de Automóveis, Conselho de Desenvolvimento to Presidência da República, CD74, AN. Even the U.S. media took note of the growing importance of cars in Brazil's economic development. See *Business Week*, 2 March 1957.

19. Elizabeth A. Cobbs, *The Rich Neighbor Policy: Rockefeller and Kaiser in Brazil* (New Haven, Conn.: Yale University Press, 1992), 205–209.

20. "Henry J. Kaiser on Industrial Development Tour Sees Vast Opportunities in L.A.," speech transcript, Henry Kaiser papers, 141:16, Kaiser Industries (KI), Bancroft Library (BL). Kaiser gave some version of this speech throughout Latin America. His São Paulo speech was widely covered in the Brazilian press. See *Estado de São Paulo*, 20 August 1954; *Diário de São Paulo*, 20 August 1954; *Gazeta*, 20 August 1954; and *Folha de Manhã*, 20 August 1954.

21. *Diário de São Paulo*, 20 August 1954; *Correio da Manhã*, 18 August 1954; and *Globo*, 17 August 1954.

22. Part of the briefings prepared for Kaiser before he left the United States included translations of Brazilian studies of the ways creating a national automobile industry would have significant forward and backward linkages for the economy. See, for example, "Translation of Lucio Meiras, 'Development of the Automobile Industry in Brazil,'" Henry Kaiser Papers, 139:13, KI, BL.

23. Henry Kaiser and Robert C. Elliott to Edgar F. Kaiser and E. E. Trefethen Jr., 15 August 1954, HK 139:1, KI, BL; Henry Kaiser and Robert C. Elliott to Edgar F. Kaiser and E. E. Trefethen Jr., 16 August 1954, HK 85/61c, KI, BL; telegram Henry Kaiser to Tefethen, 12 August 1954, HK 139:1, KI, BL; and *Estado de São Paulo*, 18 August 1954.

24. *Revista de Automóveis*, July 1954; *Noticias Ford do Brasil*, December 1954, 4–5; March 1955, 4; June 1959, 1–4; and Wilkins and Hill, *American Business Abroad*, 414–418.

25. Shapiro, *Engines of Growth*, 78–81, 98–104. It is perhaps not surprising that Kaiser and Volkswagen, two industrial concerns that had worked closely with their respective national governments, had an easier time with the statist model of 1950s Brazil than did Ford and GM. See Moniz Bandeira, *O Milagre Alemão e o Desenvolvimento do Brasil* (São Paulo: Ensaio, 1994), 113–143. On this tendency in Europe, see Simon Reich, *The Fruits of Fascism: Postwar Prosperity in Historical Perspective* (Ithaca, N.Y.: Cornell University Press, 1990).

26. "Proposal of Kaiser Motor Company for Establishing an Automotive Manufacturing Company in Brazil," 8 November 1954, HK 139–4, KI,

BL; Jim McCloud to Edgar Kaiser, 18 November 1954, Edgar Kaiser (EK) 85/61c, KI, BL; *Hanson's Latin American Letter*, 23 October 1953.

27. Domestic content increased by 10% from late 1954 to late 1955, and more Brazilian-made parts were incorporated by WOB. See *A Gazeta*, 2 December 1954, and *Revista de Automóveis*, November 1955, 52. On WOB's purchases forcing Brazilian suppliers to improve their products' quality, see "Convite de Willys-Overland do Brasil, S.A.: 'A Indústria Nacional,'" 1954, HK 139:1, KI, BL.

28. "Proposal of Kaiser Motor Corporation for Establishing an Automotive Manufacturing Company in Brazil," Book 2, HK 291:17, KI, BL.

29. T. A. Bedford, VP to Edgar Kaiser, "Brazilian Automotive Industry," 23 December 1954, EK 85/61c, KI, BL. The memo notes that Brazil was Latin America's most promising market. On WOB's evolving product lineup, see *Quatro Rodas*, September 1960, 9.

30. A copy of the ad was included in Pearce to Edgar Kaiser, 26 October 1959, EK 146:3, KI, BL.

31. Cable Hickman to Edgar Kaiser, 17 September 1954, HK 83/42c, 139:1, KI, BL; Oswaldo G. Aranha to Edgar Kaiser, 13 February 1958, EK, 145:35, KI, BL. The Dauphine was designed by Amédée Gordini and sold as the Renault R1090, or simply the Gordini, in France. WOB came close to building a number of Chrysler models (a Plymouth sedan and Dodge pickup truck) under license as well. The deal to do so was even reported in the U.S. press (*Newsweek*, 20 January 1958), but it eventually fell apart. See "Points to Discuss with Chrysler," 3 November 1957, EK 85/61c, KI, BL; and telegram Lloyd Cutler to Edgar Kaiser, 10 March 1958, EK 145:35, KI, BL. The Itamaraty is the Brazilian Foreign Ministry. It is perhaps the single most respected and elite institution in the government.

32. R. J. Jespersen to Paul J. Stiel, 1 December 1958, EK 145:36, KI, BL.

33. *Revista de Automóveis*, February 1955; S. D. Hackley to E. E. Trefethen Jr., 30 March 1959, EK 289:5d, KI, BL; Oswaldo G. Aranha to Edgar Kaiser, EK 145:35, KI, BL; "WOB Fiscal 1960 Results," 20 September 1960, EK 146:5, KI, BL.

34. *Mundo Motorizado*, January 1960, 32–33; *Quatro Rodas*, September 1960, 8; and *Brazilian Bulletin*, April 1973, 2.

35. The term "Fusca" is widely used in Brazil, but there is no clear sense of its origins. The most probable basis of the word is the Portuguese pronunciation of the German name Volkswagen as "Folquisvaguem" and then shortened to "Folquis" and then finally to "Fusca."

36. *Mundo Motorizado*, November 1961, 24; *Quatro Rodas*, September 1960, 6–11; and Wilkins and Hill, *American Business Abroad*, 416–417.

37. *Revista de Automóveis*, December 1955, 52; *Cruzeiro*, May 1959, 87; *Quatro Rodas*, September 1960, 6–11; November 1962, 88–99. Wilkins and Hill, *American Business Abroad*, 416–417. After the JK, DKW planned to market

an upgraded version as the Jango, named for Kubitschek's vice-president, João "Jango" Goulart.

38. *Ford Eco,* May 1950; Ford do Brasil, *Esta é a Ford Brasileira* (São Paulo: Ford Divisão da Relações Públicas, n.d.); *Notícias Ford do Brasil,* November-December 1953, 4–5; February 1954, 6; June 1959, 5; *Cruzeiro,* 18 April 1953; *Mundo Motorizado,* November 1958, 25–32. The quote is from Wilkins and Hill, *American Business Abroad,* 414.

39. General Motors do Brasil, *70 Years of History* (São Paulo: Prãemio Ed., 1995), 54, 76.

40. The major expansions in São Bernardo do Campo, São Caetano do Sul, and Diadema south of the city, along with neighboring Santo André, became known as the ABCD. Santo André had a long history of Communist party presence in municipal politics, but the other cities had had little industry and few work conflicts in the years preceding the establishment of the auto industry in the mid to late 1950s. Indeed, the foreign companies expanded to these largely rural municipalities because they had inexpensive land and no history of industrial conflict. For a contrary view of industrial relations in the ABC prior to the 1950s, see John D. French, *The Brazilian Workers' ABC: Class Conflict and Alliances in Modern São Paulo* (Chapel Hill: University of North Carolina Press, 1992).

41. "Inquerito entre Indústria de Automóveis para Colher Dados de Consumo e Verificar Opinião sobre a Montagem de uma Fábrica de Peças de Automóvel," IBOPE, PE, 1956, AEL, UNICAMP; *Noticias Ford do Brasil*, November 1958; June 1959; WOB Report of Board of Directors, 30 June 1960, EK 289:5e, KI, BL; "Estudo de Mercado sobre Cristal para Automotores," May 1959, IBOPE, AEL, UNICAMP. Many of the industrialists who had backed Vargas's and later Kubitschek's policies came from the auto parts sector and sought the presence of the foreign companies as a means to push forward their industry. See Addis, *Taking the Wheel.*

42. *Mundo Motorizado*, October 1959, 30–31; November 1959, 28–39; and March 1959, 16–19; *O Cruzeiro,* 21 November 1959. WOB was sensitive to how its presence might stoke nationalistic challenges. Antônio Sylvio Cunha Bueno, a former Willys executive serving as a federal congressman from São Paulo, warned Edgar Kaiser that government support to foreign auto companies might cause a negative public backlash. His advice was for WOB to emphasize the role its vehicles could play in penetrating the interior of the nation and aiding Brazilian progress. See Cunha Bueno to Edgar Kaiser, 10 July 1959, EK 146:37, KI, BL.

43. *Mundo Motorizado*, September 1959, 27–33; January 1960, 26.

44. *Mundo Motorizado,* January 1960, 26–31; February 1959, 33; October 1961, 26–27; *Folha de São Paulo,* 19 November 1960.

45. On government support for exports, see "Exports from Brazil," Joseph Rucinski to Edgar Kaiser, 27 December 1962, EK 146:8, KI, BL. Willys

played up the ways exports would transform Brazil through advertising asserting that nationally produced autos were "strengthening the economy and boosting progress." See, for example, *Visão*, 12 October 1956.

46. "Willys," EK 250:2, KI, BL; *Noticiário Willys*, November–December 1963, 8–9.

47. *Globe Trotter*, May–June 1954; *Mundo Motorizado*, August 1960, 23; Willys-Overland do Brasil, S.A., *Anuário do Progresso, 1956/57*, 26; "Proposal of Kaiser Motor Corporation for Establishing an Automotive Manufacturing Company in Brazil," Book 2, Section 8, SD4-SD5, KI, BL; "Bandeirante de Hoje," EK 85/61c, KI, BL.

48. Pearce to Girard, 17 July 1962, EK 156:8, KI, BL. As is detailed later, such geographic expansion of the auto industry was encouraged through state financing made available through SUDENE.

49. *Diário da Noite*, 6 July 1959; *O Dia*, 5 July 1959; *Diário de Notícias* (Porto Alegre), 8 July 1959; *A Gazeta*, 13 July 1959; *Jornal de Commércio*, 12 July 1959.

50. *Cruzeiro*, 21 November 1959; *Quatro Rodas*, October 1960, 2, 46–47; June 1961, 1–2; "Estudo sobre Crédito," IBOPE, PE 1957. This marketing followed, in some important ways, the original propaganda around the initial Volkswagen campaign in Nazi Germany, even though no cars were sold by VW until after the war. On Volkswagen, Hitler, and the role of automobiles in spreading nationalism, see Adam Tooze, *The Wages of Destruction: The Making and Breaking of the Nazi Economy* (London: Allen Lane, 2006), 149–151.

51. Studying the ways multinational corporations adjust their products and how they sell them according to local political conditions and consumer tastes reveals the complex nature of globalization and challenges facile assertions about the homogenizing tendency of such production and sales. For a fascinating case study of the ways the McDonald's Corporation has adapted to its many locations throughout the world, see Thomas Misa's analysis of the "multilocal" enterprise in his *Leonardo to the Internet: Technology and Culture from the Renaissance to the Present* (Baltimore: Johns Hopkins U. Press, 2004).

52. H. W. Cloke to Henry Kaiser, 26 November 1956, EK 85:61c, KI, BL; Louis F. Oberdorter to Paul J. Steil, 30 June 1958, EK 146:36, KI, BL; Antônio Sylvio Cunha to Board of Directors, WOB, n.d., EK, 146:4, KI, BL; Hickman Price Jr. to Edgar Kaiser, 15 August 1958, EK 292:56, KI, BL; Oswaldo G. Aranha to Edgar Kaiser, 16 December 1955, EK 289:2h, KI, BL; Willys-Overland do Brasil, *Anuário do Progresso, 1956–1957*, 3–6, 22; *O Que É Hoje A Willys-Overland do Brasil* (n.p.: 1961).

53. *Correio Paulistano*, 7 July 1959; *Diário de São Paulo*, 7 July 1959; Gerald R. Hough (Deltec) to Henry Kaiser, 14 October 1954, HK 83/42c, 139:1, KI, BL; Girard to Kaiser, 12 November 1957, EK 85/61c, KI, BL; Hickman Price

Jr. to Edgar Kaiser, 15 August 1958, EK 292:56, KI, BL; Euclydes Aranha Netto to Edgar Kaiser, 28 July 1959, EK 146:1, KI, BL; Antônio Sylvio Cunha Bueno to Edgar Kaiser, 10 July 1959, EK 146:37, KI, BL; and "Kaiser Interests and Activities—Latin America," n.d., EK 289:5f, KI, BL. The quote is from Cox, Langford, Stoddard, and Cutler, "Willys-WOB—Production of Chrysler Products," 13 November 1957, EK 85/61, KI, BL.

54. "Inquerito entre Indústrias de Automóvel para Colher Dados... Peças de Automóvel," IBOPE, PE 1956.

55. On initial skepticism, see "Inquérito entre Proprietários de Automóveis," Rio de Janeiro and São Paulo, June 1952, IBOPE, PE, AEL, UNICAMP; *Estado de São Paulo*, 14 October 1954. On Ford and WOB management, see Mira Wilkins interview with Don Irwin, Ford International, 23 April 1960, Mira Wilkins Ford, Florida International University; Edgar Kaiser to E. E. Trefthen Jr., 29 August 1956, EK 289:2d, KI, BL; Draft Agreement 16 August 1956, EK 289:2d, KI, BL; Edward G. Miller for Sullivan and Cromwell to Time Bedford, Kaiser Industries, 6 December 1954, EK 289:2d, KI, BL.

56. *Quatro Rodas*, November 1960, 46–47; February 1961, 49; General Motors do Brasil, *70 Years of History*, 64–67; Ramos, *História de Propaganda*, 60–61.

57. *Revista de Automóveis*, July 1954, 8–9; *Mundo Motorizado*, November 1958, 25–32; April 1960, 14–15; *Cruzeiro*, 6 June 1969.

58. Thomas H. Holloway, *Immigrants on the Land: Coffee and Society in São Paulo, 1886–1934* (Chapel Hill: University of North Carolina Press, 1980); Nancy Leys Stepan, *The Hour of Eugenics: Race, Gender and Nation in Latin America* (Ithaca, N.Y.: Cornell University Press, 1991); Thomas E. Skidmore, *Black into White: Race and Nationality in Brazilian Thought* (New York: Oxford University Press, 1974); and Barbara Weinstein, *For Social Peace in Brazil: Industrialists and the Remaking of the Working Class in São Paulo, 1920–1964* (Chapel Hill: University of North Carolina Press, 1996).

59. Joel Wolfe, *Working Women, Working Men: São Paulo and the Rise of Brazil's Industrial Working Class, 1900–1955* (Durham, N.C.: Duke University Press, 1993), 160–188.

60. *Revista de Automóveis*, July 1954, 10–11; September 1954, 40–41; October 1954, 44; December 1954 42–43; General Motors do Brasil,, *70 Years of History*, 80–81; Weinstein, *For Social Peace in Brazil*, 257–258. Weinstein's account, based mostly on internal SENAI records, overemphasizes that agency's role in autoworker training. *Mundo Motorizado* (February 1959, 22–23; August 1960, 14–15; July 1960, 41) points out that SENAI worked mostly with nationally owned auto parts firms and smaller foreign manufacturers (e.g., Mercedes-Benz) to fashion industrial training programs.

61. George Washburn, Interamericana (subsidiary of the Chase National Bank) to Henry Kaiser, 16 August 1954, HK 139:1, KI, BL; Henry J. Kaiser to Robert C. Elliott, Edgar J. Kaiser, and E. E. Trefethen, 16 August 1954, EK,

85/61c, KI, BL; *Noticias Ford do Brasil*, March 1954; December 1955; June 1956; *Revista de Automóveis*, April 1955.

62. *Mundo Motorizado*, June 1959, 30; *Willys* (1962); *Noticiário Willys*, September 1961; "Investment in Willys-Overland do Brasil, S.A.," International Financial Corporation, Press Release 16, 11 July 1958, EK 145:36, KI, BL; Willys-Overland do Brasil, S.A., *Anuário do Progresso 1957/58*. The auto magazine *Quatro Rodas* (September 1961, 30–33) reported that women held the same jobs as men in the auto plants, but this was in fact quite rare.

63. *Quatro Rodas,* July 1961, 20–27; General Motors do Brasil, *70 Years of History,* p. 75.

64. Ford do Brasil, *Manuel da Integração* (São Bernardo do Campo: Ford Seção de Treinamento, n.d.). See also Orberg (SP) to Roberge (Dearborn), 21 June 1946; Roberge (Dearborn) to Orberg (SP), 4 March 1946, FMC 713:8; *Noticias Ford*, June 1953; July 1953; August 1953; October 1953.

65. *Visão*, July 1960; *Cruzeiro*, 20 June 1959.

66. *Mundo Motorizado*, February 1959, 10; March 1959, 19.

67. *Mundo Motorizado*, April 1959, 10; July 1959, 18–21; July 1960, 41; *Revista Automóvel Club*, March 1960. According to Schultz-Wenk, 1,200 Brazilian-made VWs were to be exported to the U.S. market.

68. WOB, "Report of the Board of Directors," 30 June 1960, EK 146:5, KI, BL.

69. *Cruzeiro*, 27 June 1959. See also *Revista de Automóvel Club*, May–June 1959, 20; *Mundo Motorizado*, May 1960, 17.

70. *Quatro Rodas*, July 1961, 20–29.

71. Public opinion polling shows that the majority of Brazilians asked considered the auto industry to be a significant agent for positive change. It was seen not only as transforming the economy but also as making Brazilian workers equal to their counterparts in the United States and Europe. See "Pesquisa sobre a Indústria Automobilistica Realizada nas Cidades do Rio e São Paulo," August–September 1959, IBOPE, PE. AEL, UNICAMP.

72. Harry Braverman's *Labor and Monopoly Capital* (New York: Monthly Review, 1975) remains the classic account of the transformation from the static production of vehicles involving a handful of craftsman to the moving assembly line manned by workers who are responsible for only the simplest tasks. Much of the social content of Fordism was put in place as a response to worker unhappiness with the monotony of the assembly line, which was expressed through high turnover rates in the factories. Although such labor represents a key example of so-called deskilling, work on the line often requires both training and the acquisition of factory-specific skills. An informative and entertaining account of the importance of local knowledge about how to perform certain tasks in specific settings in the U.S. auto industry is Ben Hamper's *Rivethead: Tales from the Assembly Line* (New York: Warner, 1992).

73. According to a U.S. government analysis, only 16% of Brazil's workforce was seen as skilled; 80% was unskilled, and 4% made up the professional class. See U.S. Bureau of Labor Statistics, *Labor in Brazil* (BLS #191, 1962), 12.

74. *Quatro Rodas*, August 1960, 26–28; *Cruzeiro*, 27 February 1960, 75; *O Que É Hoje a Willys-Overland do Brasil* (São Bernardo do Campo: 1961); *Noticiário Willys*, October 1961; July 1962.

75. See the photos throughout Willys-Overland do Basil, S.A., "Prospectus for Shareholders, 1956," EK 137:27, KI, BL.

76. S. D. Hackely to S. A. Grand, 11 June 1962. EK 146:8, KI, BL.

77. "O Ministro Lúcio Meira e a Indústria Automobilística," *Revista Automóvel Club*, May–June 1959; "Quanto Custarem as Metas do Governo JK," *Mundo Motorizado*, May 1960; WOB, Annual Report for Year Ending, 30 June 1963, 7–8.

78. *Folha de São Paulo*, 28 August 1960, *Correio do Povo,* 3 September 1960; *Quatro Rodas*, "Os Homens que Constroem Automóveis," July 1961, 20–27; "São Bernardo é a Detroit Brasileira," May 1962, 76–84; *Noticiário Willys*, November–December 1963.

79. *Cruzeiro*, 25 July 1959, 66–67; *Mundo Motorizado*, December 1962, 25; Ford do Brasil, *Manuel da Integração.*

80. *Quatro Rodas*, June 1964, 106–108; *O Que É Hoje a Willys-Overland* (1961); draft WOB Annual Report Year ending 30 June 1962, EK 146:7, KI, BL; Willys-Overland do Brasil, *Anuário do Progresso 1956/57*, 23; *Noticiário Willys*, July 1962, 12; December 1962, 3; March 1963, 3; August 1963; November–December 1963, 12.

81. *Quatro Rodas*, November 1960, 50–51; June 1964, 106–108; *O Bom Senso*, 1:3 (September 1963), 101–102. Reports of such social mobility even made the U.S. press. See *Time*, 20 January 1961.

82. Quoted in Margaret E. Keck, *The Workers' Party and Democratization in Brazil* (New Haven, Conn.: Yale University Press, 1992), 73.

83. The more rank-and-file oriented workers movement that moved from hidden factory commissions to take over several key unions in the 1950s was available for autoworkers, given its success in the São Paulo's Metalworkers' Union, but most autoworkers received such high wages and benefits at this time that they had little interest in joining this group of democratically oriented militants. They had even less cause to join Communist or populist unions. On the struggle for control of the unions in São Paulo in the early to mid-1950s, see Wolfe, *Working Women, Working Men*, 160–188.

84. Wage disputes that made their way into the government structure were settled by tripartite labor courts made up of one representative of labor, industry, and the Ministry of Labor. The labor representative usually voted for the workers, and industry usually opposed, leaving the Ministry of Labor with the deciding vote. On the Willys pay raises, see "WOB Fiscal 1960 Results," EK 146:5, KI, BL. For a description of the state-centered Brazilian

industrial relations as fostering "Mussolini-type labor syndicates that are now controlled by Communists," see William Rex Pearce to Edgar Kaiser, 30 January 1963, EK 147:34, KI, BL.

85. "Pesquisa sobre a Indústria Automobilística Realizada nas Cidades do Rio e São Paulo," August–September 1959, IBOPE, PE, AEL, UNICAMP. IBOPE polled 4,334 people for this study.

86. *Cruzeiro*, 18 April 1953, 98; 9 January 1960, 54–57.

87. This is a classic example of Misa's "multilocal" type of corporation. See *Leonardo to the Internet*.

88. "A Mudança do Capital," IBOPE, *Boletim das Classes Dirigentes*, 7–13 October 1951, 41–50; James Holston, *The Modernist City: An Anthropological Critique of Brasília* (Chicago: University of Chicago Press, 1989), 16–17; and Bojunga, *JK o Artista do Impossível*, 285–289. On Pombal and Tiradentes, see Kenneth Maxwell, *Conflicts and Conspiracies: Brazil and Portugal, 1750–1808* (Cambridge: Cambridge University Press, 1973). Emília Viotti da Costa provides an analytically rich portrait of José Bonifácio in *The Brazilian Empire: Myths and Histories*, rev. ed. (Chapel Hill: University of North Carolina Press, 2000), 24–52. José Carlos Reis places Varnhagen's life and work in historical perspective in *As Identidades do Brasil: De Varnhagen a FHC* (Rio: Fundação Getúlio Vargas, 1999).

89. IBOPE, *Boletim das Classes Dirigentes*, nos. 86–98 1952, 3–9 August 1952, "Opinião Pública Brasileira e a Marcha para o Oeste"; 39.5% of Cariocas and 30% of Paulistanos supported developing the interior.

90. IBOPE, *Boletim das Classes Dirigentes*, nos. 41–50 1951, 7–13 October 1951, "A Mudança da Capital"; 22–28 June 1952, "A Mudança da Capital"; 9–15 March 1955, "A Mudança da Capital"; no. 288, December 1956, "O Paulista 'Torce' pela Mudança da Capital." This final survey is from residents throughout the state of São Paulo who might have been even more open to the idea of developing Goiás than just those individuals in the city of São Paulo.

91. IBOPE, PE, "Pesquisa de Opinião sobre a Mudança da Capital para Brasília," March 1960; "Pesquisa de Opinião Pública," Rio de Janeiro, 24–31 January 1961. The approve/disapprove of moving the capital for Cariocas was December 1957, 54/27%; December 1958, 62/29%; March 1960, 73/24%.

92. Holston's *Modernist City* provides an outstanding analysis of the ideas underlying this modernist experiment. Holston forcefully argues that the city that resulted has failed to achieve its utopian aims and in many ways achieved the opposite of its stated goals. Holston's mentor, James Scott, takes up this theme and expands on it in his wide-ranging critique of high modernist statism. See Scott, *Seeing Like a State: How Certain Schemes to Improve the Human Condition Have Failed* (New Haven, Conn.: Yale University Press, 1998). Architect Farès el-Dahdah argues that Holston, Scott, and other critics have misread not only Lúcio Costa's modernist ideals but also how the city has come to function. He specifically refutes the notion that there is

little that is lively or spontaneous within the city by focusing on leisure. See, for example, el Dahdah, "Introduction: Superquadra and the Importance of Leisure," in Farès el-Dahdah, ed., *CASE Brasília's Superquadra* (Cambridge, Mass.: Harvard Design School, 2005).

93. Quoted in Holston, *The Modernist City*, 20–21.

94. Holston shows that wages for construction work in the city were higher than those elsewhere in Brazil and that work in Brasília after it opened tended to pay better than in other cities. See *The Modernist City*, 225–248.

95. Both quotes from Sikkink, *Ideas and Institutions*, 34–35.

96. Kubitschek, *Meu Caminho para Brasília*, 150–155. Interview with Juscelino Kubitschek by Robert Alexander, 28 November 1966, R. J. Alexander Collection 1957, box 2, Rutgers University. See also, Sikkink, *Ideas and Institutions*, 38–39.

97. Amartya Sen (in *Development as Freedom* [New York: Knopf, 1999]) flips this argument on its head and asserts that capitalism cannot flourish without democracy in place. Kubitschek's views on development and democracy closely followed many of the ideas coming out of the United Nations Economic Commission for Latin America in Santiago, Chile. Arturo Escobar, Michael Latham, and others have shown how such developmentalism closely followed U.S. foreign policy initiatives in the post-1945 period and then gained even more importance after the 1959 Cuban revolution. For this perspective, see Arturo Escobar, *Encountering Development: The Making and Unmaking of the Third World* (Princeton, N.J.: Princeton University Press, 1995), and Michael E. Latham, *Modernization as Ideology: American Social Science and "Nation Building" in the Kennedy Era* (Chapel Hill: University of North Carolina Press, 2000). These studies neglect the long history of such developmentalist thinking in Brazil.

98. "Pode o Brasil Progredir 50 Anos em 5?" IBOPE *Boletim das Classes Dirigentes*, No. 285, October 1956. Not surprisingly, Paulistas–who prided themselves on their forward-looking attitudes—were more optimistic than other Brazilians on this issue but were not necessarily convinced construction could be completed during JK's term in office. See "Os 50 Anos em 5 do Presidente e a Interpretação do Paulista," IBOPE, *Boletim das Classes Dirigentes*, No. 287, November 1956; and "Brasília Sim, Más a Longo Prazo," *Boletim das Classes Dirigentes*, No. 288, December 1956.

99. Howard E. McCurdy makes a similar argument about how Lyndon Johnson viewed the U.S. space program. If the government could put a man on the moon within a decade, it would be seen as competent enough to succeed in Johnson's "War on Poverty." See McCurdy, *Space and the American Imagination* (Washington, D.C.: Smithsonian Institution Press, 1997).

100. Quoted in Sikkink, *Ideas and Institutions*, 34.

101. The following day, 22 April, is considered the day Portuguese explorer Pedro Álvares Cabral first came to the mainland of what became Brazil. Italians

celebrate Rome's mythical founding on 21 April, and the Italian government sent a column with Romulus and Remus to be erected in the new
Brazilian capital. See Holston, *The Modernist City*, 326, fn. 6.

102. Quoted in Holston, *The Modernist City*, 72. For the original, see *Diário de Brasília* (Rio: Serviço de Documentação da Presidência da República, 1957–1960), 21 April 1960.

103. This account is drawn from a detailed report on the Caravan in *Cruzeiro*, 27 February 1960.

104. *Cruzeiro*, 7 May 1960.

105. *Cruzeiro*, 7 May 1960; *Quatro Rodas*, May 1961, 28–34; *Mundo Motorizado*, June 1960, 8; IBOPE, "Pesquisa de Opinião Pública sobre a Mudança da Capital para Brasília," Rio de Janeiro, March 1960; IBOPE, "Pesquisa de Opinião Pública," Rio de Janeiro, 24–31 January 1961, AEL, UNICAMP.

106. *Cruzeiro*, May 1959, 66–69; 30 June 1960, 44–47; *Revista Esso*, no. 1, 1962, 4–5; *Mundo Motorizado*, August 1960, 12; *Revista de Automóvel*, March 1960, 18–19.

107. "Planos Nacionais de Viação Rodovias," IBOPE, *Boletim das Classes Dirigentes*, no. 251, November 1955. Venezuela had 4,141 km, Chile 3,413 km, Peru 3,278, and Colombia 2,263.

108. IBOPE, *Boletim das Classes Dirigentes*, 24–30 November 1954; 5–11 January 1955; 9–15 February 1955.

109. Plano de Metas, #8, Rodovias—Pavimentação, CD 74, AN.

110. *Mundo Motorizado*, January 1960; *Cruzeiro*, 27 February 1960, 97–99, 112–113.

111. Karl M. Mayer, Dir. Marketing & Planning, Lockheed-Georgia to S. D. Hackely, VP Kaiser Industries, 7 September 1962; S. D. Hackley to Edgar Kaiser, 5 September 1962, EK 289:5, KI, BL.

112. *Quatro Rodas*, October 1985, 231–242; June 1963, 36–43; "Entre Omibus e Avião," IBOPE, *Boletim das Classes Dirigentes*, 3–9 August 1952, 86–98; "Qual É a Condução que o Sr. Prefere para Ir à São Paulo?" IBOPE, *Boletim das Classes Dirigentes*, 5–11 January 1955.

113. *Cruzeiro*, 29 August 1959; *Mundo Motorizado*, February 1960, 6, 44; October 1960, 33. See also *Revista de Automóveis*, July 1954, 10–11; November 1954, 36–39.

114. *Mundo Motorizado*, December 1960, 13. See Marcio Souza's fictional account of the railroad's construction, *Mad Maria* (Thomas Colchie, trans.; New York: Avon, 1985), for an entertaining and informative account of the complexities of transportation in the Amazon.

115. *Cruzeiro*, 2 May 1959; 17 October 1959; *Globe Trotter*, May–June 1954; Conselho de Desenvolvimento, Grupo Executivo de Automóveis, Processo 53, AN. The report in *Globe Trotter* preceded the manufacture of jeeps in Brazil and so focused on the Ohio plant as the home of this vehicle.

116. Bertha K. Becker and Claudio A. G. Egler, *Brazil: A New Regional Power in the World-Economy* (Cambridge: Cambridge University Press, 1992), 74–78.

117. *Mundo Motorizado*, March 1958, 17; April 1960, 12; December 1960, 11; January 1962, 21. See also *Revista de Automóveis*, September 1954, 40–41. As late as 1960, the Brazilian government attempted to use surplus coffee to trade for machine tools from the German Democratic Republic and Czechoslovakia, deepening the ties between export agriculture and the development of industry. See Adolfo Becker, Insituto Brasileiro de Café to Lúcio Meira, 5 December 1960. GEIA, Conselho de Desenvolvimento, CD 45, AN. Tractors were of little use in coffee cultivation but were key tools on soybean farms.

118. Furtado's autobiography details his work for SUDENE; see Celso Furtado, *A Fantasia Desfeita* (São Paulo: Paze e Terra, 1989). Indeed, SUDENE's initial program closely followed the recommendations of the so-called Furtado Report on the northeast that had been prepared the previous year.

119. Joseph Page, *The Revolution That Never Was: Northeast Brazil, 1955–1964* (New York: Grossman, 1972), 64–74.

120. Albert O. Hirschman, "Brazil's Northeast," in *Journeys toward Progress: Studies of Economic Policy-Making in Latin America* (New York: Norton, 1973).

121. It is worth noting that drought and mass migrations were key preconditions for the establishment of the Canudos millenarian community and the federal government's war against it in the 1890s.

122. Conselho de Desenvolvimento to Juscelino Kubitschek, 21 November 1960, "Plano de Metas," no. 19 Siderurgia and no. 22 Cimento, CD 74, AN.

123. All this information is contained in the 18 November 1960 report, "Meta 27, Indústria Autombilistica," Conselho de Desenvolviment to Juscelino Kubitschek, AN. Tractors were required to have only 70% domestic content by weight by 1960. The much higher estimates of auto sector employment (of 500,000 to 700,000) cited in some press accounts include all workers tied to the industry through backward and forward linkages.

124. Conselho de Desenvolvimento to Juscelino Kubitschek, 18 November 1960, "Meta 27, Indústria Autombilistíca"; *Folha de São Paulo*, 18 November 1960 and 24–27 November 1960; Willys Divisão de Relações Públicas, no. 2, 20 December 1960, KI, BL.

125. *Mundo Motorizado*, January 1960, 12; April 1960, 24–25; March 1961, 22; August 1961, 30; and July 1962, 26.

126. IBOPE, "Pesquisa sobe a Indústria Automobilística Realizado nas Cidades do Rio e São Paulo, August–September 1959," IBOPE, PE, AEL, UNICAMP.

Chapter 6

1. Kubitschek was 53 years old when he took office in 1956. Although Quadros was only nine and a half years younger than JK, he had burst on the political scene at only 35, when he was elected mayor of São Paulo, and then 37, when elected governor of the state.

2. Goulart had been Kubitschek's vice president and one of Vargas's ministers of labor before that. Quadros, although at one point a member of the PTB, ran for president as a candidate of the UDN (União Democrática Nacional). His fluid relationship to Brazil's major political parties is a reflection of both Quadros's independence and charisma and the weakness of parties in this era. See Thomas Skidmore, *Politics in Brazil, 1930–1964: An Experiment in Democracy* (New York: Oxford University Press, 1967), 187–200.

3. William Max Pearce, WOB to Edgar Kaiser and others at Kaiser Industries, Confidential Memo, 22 March 1961, Edgar Kaiser 289:5f, Kaiser Industries (KI), Bancroft Library (BL).

4. The distinctions Paulista industrialists made among different types of labor leaders are detailed throughout Joel Wolfe, *Working Women, Working Men: São Paulo and the Rise of Brazil's Industrial Working Class, 1900–1955* (Durham, N.C.: Duke University Press, 1993). See especially chapters 5 and 6.

5. Skidmore, *Politics in Brazil*, 187–204.

6. Skidmore, *Politics in Brazil*, 205–252.

7. Skidmore, *Politics in Brazil*, 253–302.

8. For the impact on Brazil's Left, see Daniel Aarão Reis Filho et al., *História do Marxismo no Brasil* (Rio: Paz e Terra, 1991). A good overview of how the Cuban revolution altered U.S. foreign policy in the early 1960s is Stephen G. Rabe, *The Most Dangerous Area in the World: John F. Kennedy Confronts Communist Revolution in Latin America* (Chapel Hill: University of North Carolina Press, 1999).

9. A classic view of the evolving state of rural politics from 1970s is Shepard Forman's *The Brazilian Peasantry* (New York: Columbia University Press, 1975). On the increasing incidence of rural protest in this era and its impact on politics, see Cezar Benevides, *Camponeses em Marcha* (Rio: Paz e Terra, 1985); and Fernando Antônio Azevedo, *As Ligas Camponesas* (Rio: Paz e Terra, 1982). The ongoing process of rural organizing and protest are detailed in Biorn Maybury-Lewis, *The Politics of the Possible: The Brazilian Rural Workers' Trade Union Movement, 1964–1985* (Philadelphia: Temple University Press, 1994).

10. The best work on the tenuous state of civilian politics in the post-1945 period remains Skidmore, *Politics in Brazil*. On the military's views of civilian politicians and the military's duty to "fix" Brazil, see Frank D. McCann, *A Nação Armada: Ensaios sobre a História do Exército Brasileiro* (Recife: Guararapes, 1982), and Alfred C. Stepan, *The Military in Politics: Changing Patterns in Brazil* (Princeton, N.J.: Princeton University Press, 1974).

11. In addition to fuel and assorted machine lubricants, the United States also made small arms available to the Brazilian military. Telegram, U.S. Department of State to Amb. Gordon, U.S. Embassy, Rio de Janeiro, 31 March 1964; and Memorandum, Meeting at the White House 1 April 1964, President Johnson, Secretary of State Rusk, Secretary of Defense McNamara,

et al. Both at the Lyndon B. Johnson Presidential Library, Austin, Texas. See also Phyllis R. Parker, *Brazil and the Quiet Intervention, 1964* (Austin: University of Texas Press, 1979).

12. Over the course of the twentieth century, the Brazilian military was large and diverse. Throughout the century, an important segment of its leadership conflated economic development and national security. Indeed, this tendency was so prevalent that developmentalism had adherents among both conservative and progressive segments of the officer corps. The *tenentes* and other military men supporting Getúlio Vargas's economic policies in the 1930s shared these political views.

13. U.S. Bureau of Labor Statistics, Report # 309, *Labor and Law and Practice in Brazil* (Washington, D.C., 1967), 25–26; *Notícias Ford do Brasil*, April 1955; *Cruzeiro*, 7 May 1960.

14. Ford Brasil, *A Ford no Brasil* (São Paulo, n.d.), 9–10. *Quatro Rodas*, December 1962, 41–54.

15. Orlando Valverde and Catarina Dias, *A Estrada Belém-Brasília* (Rio: IBGE, 1966), 342–343; *Quatro Rodas*, January 1966, 153; Governo do Estado de São Paulo, *Trends in the Automotive Industry* (São Paulo, n.d.), 3–6. On the economic impact of BR-14, see W. H. Allderdice, "The Belém-Brasília Road and the Advance of Agriculture in Northern Goiás, Brazil" (PhD diss., Columbia University, 1972).

16. *American Machinist*, 12 September 1966; *Manchete*, 16 July 1966, 53. See also *New York Times*, 10 July 1969.

17. *American Machinist*, 12 September 1966; *Quatro Rodas*, January 1966, 142–170.

18. IBOPE, PE, "Atitudes do Eleitorado em Relação aos Programas da Região Amazonica," Belém, June–July 1968; "Atitudes do Eleitorado em Relação aos Programas da Região Amazonica," Rio Branco, July 1968, AEL, UNICAMP.

19. Thomas E. Skidmore, *The Politics of Military Rule in Brazil, 1964–85* (New York: Oxford University Press, 1988), 144–145.

20. The single best source on the development of the military's worldview is Frank D. McCann's *Soldiers of the Pátria: A History of the Brazilian Army, 1889–1937* (Stanford, Calif.: Stanford University Press, 2004). For a broad overview of the military in power, including analysis of the ESG and its developmentalism, see Maria Helena Moreira Alves, *State and Opposition in Military Brazil* (Austin: University of Texas Press, 1985); and Alfred Stepan, "The New Professionalism of Internal Warfare and Military Role Expansion," in Stepan, ed. *Authoritarian Brazil: Origins, Policies and Future* (New Haven, Conn.: Yale University Press, 1973), 47–65.

21. Bertha K. Becker and Claudio A. G. Egler, *Brazil: A New Regional Power in the World Economy* (Cambridge: Cambridge University Press, 1992), 82–116.

22. William James Ketteringham, "The Road to Belém" (PhD diss., UCLA, 1972); and Ketteringham "Amazonian Road and the Brazilian Economic

Miracle," manuscript, Land Tenure Center, University of Wisconsin–Madison, Br. 95, k28.

23. Not coincidentally, the military government created another state agency, SUDAM (*Superintendência do Desenvolvimento da Amazônia*) that had similar aims as SUDENE. See Richard Pace, *The Struggle for Amazon Town: Gurupá Revisited* (Boulder, Colo.: Lynne Reinner, 1998), 94–97; and Sylvia Ann Hewlett, *The Cruel Dilemmas of Development: Twentieth-Century Brazil* (New York: Basic Books, 1980), 171–174.

24. Quoted in Skidmore, *The Politics of Military Rule*, 145. See also Emílio Garrastazú Médici, *A Verdadeira Paz* (n.p.: Imprensa Nacional, 1970); and H. Jon Rosenbaum and William G. Tyler, "Policy-Making for the Brazilian Amazon," *Journal of Inter-American Studies and World Affairs* 13:3/4 (July–October 1971): 416–433.

25. President Emilio Médici, *National Integration Program* (Rio, 1970). Skidmore, *The Politics of Military Rule*, 145; World Bank, *An Interim Assessment of Rural Development Programs for the Northeast* (Washington, D.C.: World Bank, 1983). For details of the so-called miracle period, see Werner Baer, *The Brazilian Economy: Growth and Development*, 2nd ed. (New York: Praeger, 1983), 98–113.

26. *Brazilian Bulletin*, November 1972; *Brazil Today*, 27 July 1973.

27. At its most basic level, the state was attempting to transform "space" into "place" by opening the interior to migration and economic development. There is a well-developed literature on how societies imagine space and what policies states follow to remake it. Among the most provocative are Henri Lefebvre, *The Production of Space*, Donald Nicholson-Smith, trans. (Oxford: Blackwell, 1991); Edward W. Soja, *Postmodern Geographies: The Reassertion of Space in Critical Social Theory* (London: Verso, 1989); and Derek Gregory, *Geographical Imaginations* (Oxford: Blackwell, 1994). David Harvey's analysis of the "spatial fix" or "spatial displacement" usually involves a form of imperialism in which more economically advanced nations solve the problem of excess capital accumulation by investing abroad in areas such as Latin America and Asia. As we have seen, the broad concept of the spatial fix certainly applies to internal Brazilian economic policy throughout the twentieth century. On the spatial fix, see David Harvey, *The Limits to Capital* (Oxford: Blackwell, 1982). On spatial displacement, see Harvey, *The Condition of Postmodernity: An Enquiry into the Origins of Social Change* (Oxford: Blackwell, 1990).

28. Charles H. Wood and Marianne Schmink, "The Military and the Environment in the Brazilian Amazon," *Journal of Political and Military Sociology* 21:1 (Summer 1993): 81–105; Susana Hecht and Alexander Cockburn, *The Fate of the Forest: Developers, Destroyers, and Defenders of the Amazon* (London: Verso, 1989), 101–12; Douglas Ian Stewart, *After the Trees: Living on the Transamazon Highway* (Austin: University of Texas Press, 1994), 1–25.

29. John O. Browder and Brian J. Godrey, *Rainforest Cities: Urbanization, Development and Globalization of the Brazilian Amazon* (New York: Columbia University Press, 1997), 73–82; Anna Luiza Ozorio de Almeida, *The Colonization of the Amazon* (Austin: University of Texas Press, 1992), 65–117; Stewart, *After the Trees*, 10–15. By 1976, there were 2 *agrôvilas* on one segment of the highway and 22 on another. The *agrôpolis* Brasil Novo opened on the eastern end of the road, and Presidente Médici was the lone *rurôpolis* in operation. It is located at the intersection of the Transamazonian Highway and the Cuiabá-Santarém Highway.

30. Browder and Godfrey, *Rainforest Cities*, 76–78; Ozorio de Almeida, *The Colonization of the Amazon*, 44–51, 70–84. Although Scott (via Holston) may exaggerate the extent to which Brasília is a "failure" of high modernism, his critique of state-directed, scientific agricultural projects in the developing world is supported by the experience of INCRA in the Amazon. See James Scott, *Seeing Like a State: How Certain Schemes to Improve the Human Condition Have Failed* (New Haven, Conn.: Yale University Press, 1998), 223–306. In the aftermath of INCRA's failure, large-scale commercial agricultural interests, with national and multinational capital backing them, turned to cattle grazing and other enterprises that severely degraded the already fragile ecosystems along the Transamazonian Highway. See Browder and Godfrey, *Rainforest Cities*, 78–82, 202–210; Stewart, *After the Trees*, 86–90, among others.

31. On the Dutra, see *Quatro Rodas*, June 1963, 36–43; October 1985, 231–242. On Embraer, see Roberto Bernardo, *EMBRAER: Elos entre Estado e Mercado* (São Paulo: Hucitec, 2000). São José dos Campos is also home to the Instituto Tecnológico de Aeronáutica, one of Brazil's leading engineering schools.

32. Edgar Kaiser, 146:7, Draft Annual Report WOB, year ending 30 June 1962; Edgar Kaiser 249:3, press releases 8 February 1965 and 19 July 1966, KI, BL. *Diário de Notícias*, 22 March 1964; *O Globo*, 29 May 1964; *O Cruzeiro*, 6 March 1965; *Noticiario Willys*, March 1966 and July 1966; *Oakland Tribune*, 4 August 1966; *Pittsburgh Press*, 26 October 1966. Such industrial development in the northeast was a key component of the original SUDENE plan.

33. *Noticiário Willys*, July 1966; *Manchete*, 16 July 1966 and 4 August 1967; *Quatro Rodas*, January 1966; *American Machinist*, 12 September 1966.

34. *Revista Esso*, 1966, 14–23. The town was founded in 1947 and became an official municipality in 1952. It had approximately 300,000 residents in 2000, with an additional 200,000 in its metropolitan area.

35. Jorge Calmon, *As Estradas Corriam para o Sul: Migração Nordestina para São Paulo* (Salvador: EGBA, 1998), and Aidil Sampaio and Risalva Vasconcelos Rocha, *Tendências das Migrações no Nordeste, 1940–1980* (Recife : Ministério do Interior, Superintendência do Desenvolvimento do Nordeste, Diretoria de Planejamento Global, Departamento de Planejamento Sócio-Econômico, 1989). For an overview of migration and population in Brazil, see Thomas

William Merrick and Douglas H. Graham, *Population and Economic Development in Brazil, 1800 to the Present* (Baltimore: Johns Hopkins University Press, 1979), 118–145.

36. Milton da Mata et al., *Migrações Internas no Brasil* (Rio: IPEA/INPES, 1972); *Brazil: Human Resources Special Report* (Washington, D.C.: World Bank, 1979); and *Population Growth and Problems in Mega-Cities: São Paulo* (New York: United Nations, 1993), 5–6. Internal migration accounted for 73% of São Paulo's population growth in the 1940s, 60% in the 1950s and 1960s, and 51% in the 1970s.

37. For a careful study of Afro-Brazilian migration to Rio from the 1920s through the 1950s, see Luiz de Aguiar Costa Pinto, *O Negro no Rio de Janeiro: Relações Raciais numa Sociedade em Mudança*, 2nd ed. (Rio: Ed. U. Federal do Rio de Janeiro, 1998). On the changing nature of celebrations of the anniversary of abolition in São Paulo during these years, see George Reid Andrews, *Black and Whites in São Paulo, Brazil: 1888–1988* (Madison: University of Wisconsin Press, 1991), 211–233.

38. Anthony Leeds and Elizabeth Leeds, *A Sociologia do Brasil Urbano* (Rio: Zahar, 1978), 235–238; Marcelo Baumann Burgos, "Dos Parques Proletários as Favela-Bairro: As Políticas Públicas nas Favelas do Rio de Janeiro," in Alba Zaluar and Marcos Alvito, eds., *Um Seculo de Favela* (Rio: Fundação Getúlio Vargas, 1998); Janice Perlman, *The Myth of Marginality: Urban Poverty and Politics in Rio de Janeiro* (Berkeley: University of California Press, 1976), 205–207, 258–260; and Enrique Desmond Arias, *Drugs and Democracy in Rio de Janeiro: Trafficking, Social Networks, and Public Security* (Chapel Hill: University of North Carolina Press, 2006), 22–30. For a similar process in an earlier epoch, see Teresa Meade, *Civilizing Rio: Reform and Resistance in a Brazilian City, 1889–1930* (University Park: Pennsylvania State UniversityPress, 1998).

39. Teresa P. R. Caldeira, *City of Walls: Crime, Segregation, and Citizenship in São Paulo* (Berkeley: University of California Press, 2000), 219–222.

40. Wolfe, *Working Women, Working Men*, 106–108, 125–126.

41. Metropolitan São Paulo had 1,568,045 people in it in 1950, while the city proper (the *município*) had 1,326,261; in 1960, those numbers were 4,739,406/3,781,446;1970:8,139,730/5,924,615;1980:12,588,725/8,493,226; 1991: 15,444,941/9,646,185/; and 2000: 17,878,703/10,434,252; IBGE, *Censos Demográficos*. Caldeira, *City of Walls*, 221–228. For a similar developments on a smaller scale, see the analysis of the city of Florianópolis and race at this time in Márcia Fantin, *Cidade Divida: Dilemas e Disputas Simbólicas em Florianópolis* (Florianópolis: Cidade Futura, 2000).

42. As the São Paulo state governor, Mário Covas (1995–2001) began work on a beltway around the city; SP-21, also known as the Rodoanel Metropolitano Mário Covas, that could take more than 20 years to construct. A section of the western portion opened in 2002.

43. Caldeira, *City of Walls*, 221–228; Heraldo da Gama Torres, "Segregação residencial e políticas públicas: São Paulo na década de 1990," *Revista Brasileira de Ciências Sociais*, 19:54 (February 2004), 41–55; São Paulo Secretaria Municipal de Planejamento (Sempla), *Dossiê São Paulo* (São Paulo: Sempla, 1995); Carlos R. Azzoni, "São Paulo Metropolitan Area: Size, Competitiveness and the Future," *TD Nereus*, 10–2005.

44. Caldeira, *City of Walls*, 235–252; *Quatro Rodas*, February 1961, 79–81. Marshall Berman has commented on the ways differing moments in modernity have moved public life away from the streets. His analysis of the role of automobility in the decline of the Bronx in the post-1945 era also points to the ways sprawl and automobility have affected urban life in the twentieth century. See Berman, *All That Is Solid Melts into Air: The Experience of Modernity* (New York: Viking, 1988), 287–348. São Paulo's experience from the 1960s through the end of the twentieth century may be more similar to the development of the U.S. sunbelt than to Europe or New York City. Its development pattern is perhaps best put in context by Robert Venturi et al., *Learning from Las Vegas: The Forgotten Symbolism of Architectural Form* (Cambridge, Mass.: MIT Press, 1977).

45. Although a combination of Greek ("alpha") and French ("ville") words that make "First City," the name is also that of the metropolis in Jean-Luc Godard's New Wave film, *Alphaville, une étrange aventure de Lemmy Caution* (1965). The movie centers around the mindless and sexual lives of the residents of a futuristic city who have given over their free will to a computer, "Alpha 60." Indeed, an alternative working title for the movie was *Tarzan vs. IBM*. See Jean-Luc Godard, *Godard on Godard: Critical Writings by Jean-Luc Godard* (Cambridge, Mass.: Da Capo, 1986). Godard's film and its dystopian view of life in a futuristic city are often invoked by critics of this massive suburban development.

46. Caldeira, *City of Walls*, 272, 277–278.

47. Other small-scale developments are located in Fortaleza in Ceará, Goiânia in Goiás, Belo Horizonte in Minas Gerais, Natal in Rio Grande do Norte, Manaus in Amazonas, Salvador in Bahia, and Gramado in Rio Grande do Sul.

48. On the SFU in Brazil, see Fernando Diniz Moreira, "Shaping Cities, Building a Nation: Alfred Agache and the Dream of Modern Urbanism in Brazil, 1920–1950," (PhD diss., University of Pennsylvania, 2004). See also Hugh Schwartz, *Urban Renewal, Municipal Revitalization: The Case of Curitiba, Brazil* (Alexandria, Va.: n.p., 2004), 27–33.

49. Lerner became a three-term mayor of Curitiba (1971–1975, 1979–1984, 1989–1992) and was twice elected governor of Paraná, in 1994 and 1998.

50. The city's master plans have tackled more than transportation problems, although these have been prominent components of subsequent reforms. The Curitiba Master Plan restricted development in some areas to prevent traffic

congestion from migrating and ensuring population density in certain areas. It also condemned parcels of land prone to flooding and opened city parks in their place (which also serve as holding ponds during periods of heavy rains).

51. Curitiba's success has garnered broad international acclaim. A detailed article in the *New York Times Magazine* noted the eco-friendly nature of the city's reforms. See Arthur Lubow, "Recycle City: The Road to Curitiba," *New York Times Magazine,* 20 May 2007.

52. The context of Geisel's reaction to the oil price shock is well detailed in Skidmore, *The Politics of Military Rule*, 178–180. On oil and alcohol, see Michael Barzelay, *The Politicized Market Economy: Alcohol in Brazil's Energy Strategy* (Berkeley: University of California Press, 1986); and Laura Randall, *The Political Economy of Brazilian Oil* (Westport, Conn.: Praeger, 1993), 96–98.

53. In the short term, Geisel maintained a high growth rate for the economy by dramatically increasing the foreign debt. See Skidmore, *The Politics of Military Rule*, 179–180.

54. José R. Moreira and José Goldemberg, "The Alcohol Program," *Energy Policy* 27 (1999): 229–245. See also *Quatro Rodas*, August 1980, 218. The magazine article claims the program was created in October 1975, but the law was signed in November.

55. *Quatro Rodas*, April 1980, 56–60, 91–94; June 1980, 36–42; July 1980, 44–52; August 1980, 44; February 1981, 84–89; and September 1984, 139; *Veja*, 23 January 1980, 75; 9 July 1980, 96–97; and 20 August 1980, 42–43; *Indústria e Desenvolvimento*, January 1980, 2–7; Ciro Dias Reis, *Salão de Automóvel: Trinta Anos de História* (São Paulo: 1990). There was some initial disagreement about whether *álcool* produced less overall pollution (*Veja*, March 1981, 34–35), but later studies seemed to prove that vehicle fleets powered by ethanol are less destructive to urban air quality than those fueled by gasoline. See Moreira and Goldemberg, "The Alcohol Program," 235–237.

56. The promilitary ARENA party, which later became the PDS (Partido Democrático Social), was most powerful in the northeast and far west. This division of the PDS controlling the northeast and the opposition PMDB (Partido Movimento Democrático Brasileiro) stronger in the center-south, was clearly seen in the 1982 elections for Congress and governorships. See Skidmore, *The Politics of Military Rule*, 233–236.

57. Gathered Brazilwood exports preceded the development of the sugar economy, but sugar was the first agricultural commodity specifically planted and harvested for export.

58. *Mundo Motorizado*, April 1962, 21; *Quatro Rodas*, May 1962, 80–93; June 1962, 10; April 1963, 111; August 1963, 19; and April 1966, 6; *O Bom Senso*, December 1963, 124; *Manchete*, 16 July 1966, 56–57; Edgar Kaiser,

147:34, memo 31 January 1963, Pearce to Girard, KI, BL; *Noticiário Willys*, October 1965, 3; January 1966, 12; August–September 1966, 3; Governo do Estado de São Paulo, *Trends in the Automotive Industry* (São Paulo, 1973), 3.13–3.20.

59. Baer, *The Brazilian Economy*, 100. Transportation equipment grew at an annual rate of 32.6% from 1967 to 1970. The rates though 1977 are 1971, 19%; 1972, 22.5%; 1973, 27.6%; 1974, 18.9%; 1975, 0.5%; 1976, 7.2%; and 1977, -2.6%. The drop-off in the mid-1970s was ameliorated by the introduction of the Proálcool program and the development of ethanol-powered cars in the late 1970s and early 1980s.

60. Baer, *The Brazilian Economy*, 161–164.

61. In 1968, Ford purchased Willys Overland do Brasil, although this was presented as a merger. Former Willys factories in São Paulo produced Ford-Willys products until 1984, when the Willys name disappeared from the market. Ford closed the Recife plant soon after the merger. For information on the purchase, see *Notícias Ford*, no. 97, November–December 1967. On the growing market for trucks and buses for the interior, see *Manchete*, 16 July 1966, 66, 79, 130; *Quatro Rodas*, December 1963, 146. The Fábrica Nacional de Motores declined precipitously in the mid-1960s in terms of quality and profitability. See *Quatro Rodas*, August 1963, 32–33; September 1963, 47. In 1968, it was sold to Alfa Romeo. After Alfa Romeo was privatized, it became part of Fiat, which closed the FNM in 1986.

62. Ford Brasil, *A Ford no Brasil*, 9 May 1969, 11; General Motors do Brasil, *70 Years of History* (São Paulo: Prãemio Ed., 1995), 88–89, 95.

63. Fiat Automóveis, S.A., "Fiat Automóveis Completa 28 Anos de Brasil"; "Growing Strong: South America Is Cornerstone of Fiat's Global Push, *Wards Auto World*, May 1997. In its first 25 years in Brazil, Fiat produced 404,803 vehicles and exported almost 25% of that total.

64. According to General Motors (*70 Years of History*, 100–103), the world car "was an industrial concept involving a basic design and the worldwide supply of components, thus permitting its assembly in different countries, with common or interchangeable parts." For more on the concept, see Stuart W. Sinclair, *The World Car: The Future of the Automobile Industry* (New York: Facts on File, 1983). By the early twenty-first century, many manufacturers had turned to cars designed for segmented regional markets over the standardization inherent in the world car. See "Unlocking Ford's Secret Plan: The World Car Is Dead. Long Live Global Architecture," *Motor Trend*, July 2007.

65. The so-called New Beetle was introduced as the VW Concept 1 at the 1994 North American International Auto Show in Detroit. It came to market in 1998 and was produced exclusively in Puebla, Mexico. Beyond completely new styling, the New Beetle featured a water-cooled engine (in the front, not the rear, which now has storage), as opposed to VW's traditional air-cooled Beetle engine. On Brazilian Fuscas becoming American Beetles, see

Automotive News, 14 October 1985. On the Escort, see *Quatro Rodas*, October 1980, 36.

66. *Quatro Rodas*, May 1981, 34; June 1982, 9–10; and February 1981, 34–38. On Brazilian trucks and buses being exported at this time, see *Indústria e Desenvolvimento*, May 1980, 43; October 1980, 28.

67. *Quatro Rodas*, October 1985, 139–142; *Automotive News*, 29 July 1985;*Veja*, 26 November 1986, 122–123, and 22 July 1987.

68. *Veja*, 26 February 1986, 70–74, 92; 29 October 1986, 115; 6 May 1987, 116.

69. *Automotive News*, 16 November 1998, 6; 29 March 1999, 3; 11 October 1999, 32.

70. It was precisely during these years that the term *globalization* made its way into the lexicon, albeit from the marketers at American Express and not from economists or other academic commentators. See David Harvey, *Spaces of Hope* (Berkeley: University of California Press, 2000), 13. Standardization precedes and enables the transition of technologically advanced products to commodities. For this process in the production of personal computers, see David P. Angel and James Engstrom, "Manufacturing Systems and Technological Change: The U.S. Personal Computer Industry," *Economic Geography* 71:1 (January 1995): 79–102. Standardization in computer software transcended commodification with the development of the open source movement. See Eric S. Raymond, *The Cathedral and the Bazaar: Musings on Linux and Open Source by an Accidental Revolutionary*, rev. ed. (Cambridge, Mass.: O'Reilly, 2001).

71. Baer, *The Brazilian Economy*, 105, 141. The skewing expanded in the 1960s and then continued at a slower pace in the 1970s. The statistics probably underestimate the impact of the military's wage policies because the dictatorship did not begin until April 1964, and the process of political opening, which is analyzed later, brought some wage relief for workers. Skidmore (*The Politics of Military Rule*, 70–71) argues that the military sought to improve working-class purchasing power in the early 1970s, but with ineffective and ultimately unsuccessful policies.

72. In 1965, Brazil had one car for every 44.7 people; Uruguay, 12.9; Argentina, 16.8; and Venezuela, 18.4. Still, owing to its large population, Brazil had the ninth highest number of vehicles worldwide. See *Noticiario Willys*, March–April 1965, 4; May–June 1965, 4. *Manchete* reported (16 July 1966, 55) that by 1966, the number had reached one car per every 37.8 Brazilians and that 10 years earlier, the figure had been one for every 78 inhabitants. On the percentages, see *Quatro Rodas*, August 1980, 10–17. Brazil had a population of about 71,695,000 people in 1960; it was 122,958,000 in 1980. In 1960, about 408,661 people owned cars; in 1980, that number was 6,147,900.

73. IBOPE, "Conceito de Marcas de Automóveis, Guanabara e Baixada Fluminense, December 1969–January 1970," AEL, UNICAMP; IBOPE,

"Transporte-Guanabara, April 1967." By October 1972, polling found that Cariocas listed the styling and prestige of a car model over its cost. IBOPE, "Concentuação e Razões de Escoha de Marce e Modelos de Automóvies, 14–18 October 1973," IBOPE PE, AEL, UNICAMP.

74. Governo do Estado de São Paulo, *Trends in the Automotive Industry*, 3.24. The south had 21% of the cars; the northeast, 10%; the center-west, 4%; and the north, 2%.

75. IBOPE, "Concentuação e Razões de Escoha de Marce e Modelos de Automóvies, 14–18 October 1973," IBOPE PE, AEL, UNICAMP; *Quatro Rodas*, August 1980, 84–88; April 1981, 91–94. *Quatro Rodas* reported that women were considered better drivers than men but still faced discrimination in hiring for jobs as drivers. The metropolitan transit authority in São Paulo had only 10 female drivers, and while the number of women taxi and truck drivers was increasing, the total remained small. See *Quatro Rodas*, September 1984, 100–105.

76. *Quatro Rodas*, August 1980, 90. This article notes that Brazilians had not traditionally used cars for such activity. Sexual freedom and danger had been an integral part of American automobility since at least the 1920s. See, for example, Virginia Scharff, *Taking the Wheel: Women and the Coming of the Motor Age* (New York: Free Press, 1991), and Robert S. Lynd and Helen Merrell Lynd, *Middletown: A Study in Modern American Culture* (New York: Harcourt, Brace, & World, 1929), 257–260. On feminism in the 1970s and 1980s, see Sonia E. Alvarez, *Engendering Democracy in Brazil: Women's Movements and Transition Politics* (Princeton, N.J.: Princeton University Press, 1990).

77. A 1966 IBOPE poll seems to indicate a low interest in auto racing, reporting that under 3% of the 600 respondents in Rio and São Paulo had an interest in this sport, while 74% had an interest in *futebol*. The poll seems to conflate being a spectator and a participant and so is of little value. For example, swimming is the second most popular sport (32% of respondents had an interest in it), followed by basketball at 13%. See IBOPE, "Esportes—Rio e São Paulo, December 1966." On the popularity of auto shows, see IBOPE, "Opinião a Respiteo da Exposição Aerospecial, Anhembí, São Paulo, September 1973, AEL IBOPE."

78. *Manchete*, 16 July 1966, 76–77, 116–117; *Quatro Rodas*, March 1964, 3–6; *O Bom Senso*, March 1964, 103–108.

79. *Quatro Rodas*, April 1964, 106–107; May 1964, 110–113; December 1964, 220–221; August 1980, 186–188; and Luiz Fernando Andreatta and Paulo Roberto Renner, *Automobilismo no Tempo das Carreteras: Em Especial no Rio Grande do Sul* (Porto Alegre: Metrópole, 1992), 159. According to Andreatta and Renner (p. 69), the famed Gaúcho *futebol* club Grêmio had sought to build its own racetrack as early as 1953 and maintained a Department of Auto Sport.

80. Formula One or F1 racing is the direct descendant of the old grand prix events; F1 races are often still referred to as grand prix. CART was created in the United States and is governed by a different group. CART cars are often heavier than those in F1. CART vehicles also have turbocharged engines, which are forbidden by F1. Although CART and F1 govern different races, many drivers participate in both, and they are more similar to each other than to NASCAR cars and races.

81. Although Fittipaldi first gained international recognition in Europe, Emerson won his first F1 race in the United States at the Watkins Glen (New York) Grand Prix in October 1970. *Quatro Rodas*, August 1980, 24–29, 186–205, reviews the growth of Brazilian motor sports from the mid-1960s through the 1970s.

82. Apart from broad national pride in the accomplishments of these young drivers, Brazilians also no doubt enjoyed their prominence after years of watching the great Argentine driver, Juan Manuel Fangio (1911–1995), dominate the sport. Fangio was so dominant and famous in the 1950s that at one point Fidel Castro's rebel army kidnapped him for the publicity. After his release, Fangio praised Castro's 26th of July Movement. See Rosalie Schwartz, *Pleasure Island: Tourism and Temptation in Cuba* (Lincoln: University of Nebraska Press, 1999), 171, 187–189.

83. Senna's early years in São Paulo through his professional career are documented in a film he collaborated on, *Ayrton Senna: Racing Is in My Blood* (1990).

84. Senna left his car to help Erik Comas during time trials for the 1992 Spa-Francorchamps in Belgium, and again in Belgium in 1993, he left his car to help Alex Zanardi.

85. Christopher Hilton, *Memories of Ayrton Senna* (Somerset, England: Haynes, 2004), 154.

86. On Xuxa, see Amelia Simpson, *Xuxa: The Mega-Marketing of Gender, Race, and Modernity* (Philadelphia: Temple University Press, 1993). No small part of Xuxa's iconic status for Brazilians is due to the fact that in addition to her own success, she dated Pelé for six years and then was linked with Senna. For the Audi incident, see *Caras*, 28 July 1995.

87. Sergio Margulis, "Causes of Deforestation of the Brazilian Amazon," World Bank Working Paper No. 22, 2004.

88. On pollution in urban Brazil, see Claudio Ferraz and Renaldo Seroa da Motta, "Automobile Pollution Control in Brazil," no. 670, *IPEA*, 1999. On traffic from the 1960s through the 1990s, see E. A. Vasconcellos, "Urban Development and Traffic Accidents in Brazil," *Accident Analysis and Prevention*, 31:4 (July 1999): 319–328.

89. Data for the overall cost of living in Brazil from 1964 to 1980, for example, show a total rate of inflation of about 23,489%. More exact wage and price data for São Paulo mirror these nationwide figures. See, among others,

Instituto Brasileiro de Geografía e Estatística (IBGE), *Estatísticas Históricas do Brasil* (Rio de Janeiro: IBGE, 1990); and Seiti Kaneko Endo and Heron Carlos Esvael do Carmo, "Breve Histórico do Índice de Preços ao Consumador no Município de São Paulo," *FIPE*, 1985.

90. According to the most definitive study of torture during the dictatorship, executives from a number of multinational corporations, including Ford and GM, financially supported the semiofficial vigilante Operation Bandeirante (*Operação Bandeirante*). See *Torture in Brazil: A Report by the Archdiocese of São Paulo*, Jaime Wright, trans., Joan Dassin, ed. (New York: Vintage, 1986), 64–65. In Argentina, automobiles themselves came to be associated with arrests and torture. Many of the disappeared were taken away by military men who drove Ford Falcons. This was so prevalent that that sedan became a symbol of dictatorship and torture. See Karen Robert, "The Falcon Remembered," *NACLA Report on the Americas*, 39:3 (November–December 2005).

91. Skidmore, *The Politics of Military Rule*, 204–205; John Humphrey, *Capitalist Control and Workers' Struggle in the Brazilian Auto Industry* (Princeton, N.J.: Princeton University Press, 1982), 153–154.

92. Reported in *Veja*, 24 May 1978, 91–95.

93. *Veja*, 24 May 1978, 91–95. After the 1964 coup, the military strengthened the government's hand in the labor system.

94. *Jornal do Brasil*, 17 May 1978; *Veja*, 24 May 1978, 91–95.

95. *Veja*, 31 May 1978, 75.

96. *Veja*, 31 May 1978, 19.

97. "Em paz, mas em greve," *Veja*, 31 May 1978, 68–72. The strikers' status as neither populists nor communists interested a number of military leaders.

98. See, for example, *Veja*, 7 June, 14 June, 26 July, 20 September, and 11 October 1978.

99. *Tendências do Trabalho*, July 1986, 10–11.

100. *Veja*, 31 May 1978, 72; 30 January 1980, 88; and *AJB Informe Sindical*, March 1990.

101. Brazilian industrialists had a complex relationship with the factory commissions. Although they tended to view them more favorably than they did the established labor leaders tied to the government (*pelegos*), many employers were uncomfortable with the strikers once the Ministry of Labor declared their activities to be illegal. See Leigh A. Payne, *Brazilian Industrialists and Democratic Change* (Baltimore: Johns Hopkins University Press, 1994), 68–83.

102. *Veja*, 17 September 1980, 116–118; 1 October 1980, 118; *Tendências do Trabalho*, July 1986, 4–6; August 1986, 16–17.

103. For Figueiredo's comments that Lula belonged in jail for breaking the labor laws, along with predictions that the new union movement was doomed to fail, see *Veja*, 23 April 1980, 20–23.

104. *Tendências do Trabalho*, September 1987, 25–27; and *AJB Informe Sindical*, December 1989.

105. *Veja*, 30 April 1980, 3–4, 16; 22 October 1980, 3–6. The PCB's position had been consistent over the years. It supported working with the Ministry of Labor even when the vast majority of workers rejected the corporatist system. The party famously called upon São Paulo's workers to "Tighten Your Belts" and return to work during the great strike wave of 1945. See Wolfe, *Working Women, Working Men*, 121.

106. This breakdown is detailed in an often-reproduced two-page chart titled "Sindicalismo Brasileiro: Quadro Resumido das Influências Partidiarias," first published in *Tendências do Trabalho*, August 1986, 16–17.

107. Francisco José Marcondes Evangelista, "Relações Trabalhista," *Tendências do Trabalho*, February 1992, 11–12.

108. This picture of automobile workers is in direct contrast to that provided by John Humphrey in *Capitalist Control and Workers' Struggle in the Brazilian Auto Industry* (Princeton, N.J.: Princeton University Press, 1982).

109. It is hard to locate groups of workers or unions that actively sought out such alliances in the past. John D. French has argued that that was the case, but his evidence is the Communist party's disastrous record of making ties to political parties in response to Moscow's dictates. For an optimistic view of the Communists' history of making such deals in Brazil, see French, *The Brazilian Workers' ABC: Class Conflict and Alliances in Modern São Paulo* (Chapel Hill: University of North Carolina Press, 1992).

110. Margaret E. Keck's *The Workers' Party and Democratization in Brazil* (New Haven, Conn.: Yale University Press, 1992) remains the best work on the subject.

111. Keck, *The Workers' Party*, 79; and Skidmore, *The Politics of Military Rule in Brazil*, 220–221, 230.

112. See, for example, *Veja*, 10 December 1986, 14–15.

113. These demographic data are from Leôncio Martins Rodrigues, "Pesquisa: O Empregado de Ford," *Tendências do Trabalho*, April 1986, 7–9.

114. The following data are from Rodrigues, "Pesquisa; O Empregado de Ford," 7–9. Among his studies on working-class attitudes, *Conflito Industrial e Sindicalismo no Brasil* (São Paulo: Difusão, 1966) is no doubt Rodrigues's most significant. See also *Industrialização e Atitudes Operárias: Estudo de um Grupos de Trabalhadores* (São Paulo: Brasiliense, 1970).

115. Of workers in São Bernardo do Campo, 71.5% supported their union. Given the history of *peleguismo* in the São Paulo city metalworkers union, which covered Ford employees in the Ipiranga plant, only 44.6% supported the union; 55.4% claimed the São Paulo union was run by *pelegos*.

116. Given differences in the makeup and experiences of the workers at the two locations, there is a slight difference in responses by factory. The data are

nonetheless fairly straightforward: Company gains, workers lose. Agree: São Bernardo do Campo 34.9%, Ipiranga 30.8%. Company gains, workers gain. Agree: São Bernardo do Campo 65.1, Ipiranga 69.2%.

Epilogue

1. Presidência da República, Casa Civil, *Constituição da República Federativa do Brasil de 1988.*

2. For a concise and thoughtful analysis of the intellectual origins and operation of these policies, see David Harvey, *A Brief History of Neoliberalism* (New York: Oxford University Press, 2007).

3. Werner Baer, *The Brazilian Economy*, 4th ed. (Westport, Conn.: Praeger, 1995), 392–393.

4. Fernando Henrique Cardoso, *The Accidental President: A Memoir* (New York: Public Affairs, 2006), 179–275.

5. Thomas E. Skidmore, *Brazil: Five Centuries of Change* (New York: Oxford University Press, 1999), 226–228.

6. Marco Aurélio Bedê, "A Política Automotiva nos Anos 90," in Glauco Arbix and Mauro Zilbovicius, eds. *De JK a FHC: A Reinvenção dos Carros* (São Paulo: Scritta, 1997), 357–387.

7. Maureen O'Dougherty, *Consumption Intensified: The Politics of Middle-Class Daily Life in Brazil* (Durham, N.C.: Duke University Press, 2002), 38–47, 117.

8. Skidmore, *Brazil: Five Centuries of Change*, 201–202.

9. Joseph E. Stiglitz, *Globalization and Its Discontents* (New York: W. W. Norton, 2002), 89–98.

10. An informative chronicle of Lula's first campaign for the presidency is in Emir Sader, *Without Fear of Being Happy: Lula, the Workers Party, and Brazil* (London: Verso, 1996).

11. Alarm over the prospect of Lula's election was reflected in the financial press. See, for example, "The Disorders of Progress: A Survey of Brazil," *Economist*, 27 March 1999; "Situation Critical" and "Attempt to Calm Fears over Brazil's Growing Crisis," both in *Financial Times*, 24 June 2002; "Region Faces Popular Pressures for Change," *Financial Times*, 8 March 2002; and early on in his administration, the cover story in *New York Times Magazine*, "Latin America's Last Leftist Hero? The Hard Times and Letdowns of Lula," 27 June 2004. To protest Lula's leftist politics, the U.S. government refused to send a high-level delegation to his inaugural. Instead, the Bush administration sent only the U.S. trade representative to the swearing in of the democratically elected president of Latin America's largest and most populous republic. See *New York Times*, 2 January 2003.

12. Private industry accelerated its investment in literacy and other education programs for workers in the 1990s. See "The A B C's of Business in Brazil," *New York Times*, 16 July 1998.

13. See Ipsos/O Observador, *O Observador: Lar, Doce Lar* (São Paulo: IPSOS, 2008), and Ipsos/O Observador, *Barômetro* (São Paulo: IPSOS, 2008). Data were collected in 70 cities and nine metropolitan areas in December 2007.

14. For detailed coverage of this, see *Wall Street Journal*, 27 October 2006. Lula, of course, is a resident of São Paulo and represented a district in the state in the national legislature.

15. For details on the strike and the central role of truck transport in the Brazilian economy, see *Época*, 2 August 1999. See also *Folha de São Paulo*, 29 July 1999.

16. Godfrey Devlin and Mark Bleackley, "Strategic Alliances—Guidelines for Success," *Long Range Planning* 21:5 (October 1988): 18–23; and Ana Maria Catalano and Marta S. Novick, "The Argentine Automotive Industry: Redefining Production Strategies, Markets, and Labor Relations," in John P. Tuman and John T. Morris, eds. *Transforming the Latin American Automobile Industry: Unions, Workers, and the Politics of Restructuring* (Armonk, N.Y.: M. E. Sharpe, 1998), 26–76.

17. For a detailed analysis of the Resende plant, see Alice R. de P. Abreu et al., " 'The Dream Factory': VW's Modular Production System in Resende, Brazil," *Work, Employment and Society* 14:2 (2000): 265–282; and Glauco Arbix and Mauro Zilbovicius, "Consórcio Modular da VW: Um Novo Modelo de Produção?" in Arbix and Zilbovicius, eds. *De JK a FHC*, 449–469.

18. A detailed description of the plant can be found in "Ford's Test Bed: Brazil's Camaçari Plant Is a Model for the Future," *Detroit News*, 22 August 2007. Ford also boasted about the factory's environmental record, which is based on extensive recycling and replanting parts of the Atlantic forest. One fascinating aspect of this extreme form of just-in-time manufacturing is that it is a near-complete repudiation of Henry Ford's attempts to vertically integrate every aspect of car manufacture, from mining iron ore in the Upper Peninsula of Michigan to producing rubber in the Amazon.

19. Honda opened a plant in Sumaré, São Paulo, in 1997 to build Civics; Chrysler opened in Campo Lago, São Paulo, in 1998 for Dakotas; Toyota in Indaiatuba, São Paulo, in 1998 for Corollas; Renault in São José dos Pinhais, Paraíba, in 1998 to manufacture the Scenic; Mercedes-Benz in Juiz de Fora, Minas Gerais, in 1999 for the Classe A; VW in São José dos Pinhais in 1999 for the Golf; General Motors in Gravataí, Rio Grande do Sul, in 2000 for the Blue Macaw; and Peugeot in Porto Real, Rio de Janeiro, in 2000 for the 206.

20. See, for example, *Newsweek*, 8 December 1997.

21. The most extreme example of an advanced technology becoming a commodity was the rise of the "Wintel box," or personal computer powered by an Intel chip that ran some version of the Microsoft Windows operating system. Commodity computing eventually involved the clustering of such machines to emulate the power of supercomputers, which had not

become commoditized. Such clusters, though, often relied on Java and other non-Microsoft programming languages. See Geoffrey C. Fox and Wojtek Furmanski, "High-Performance Commodity Computing," in Ian Foster and Carl Kesselman, eds. *The Grid: Blueprint for a New Computing Infrastructure* (San Francisco: Morgan Kauffman, 1999), 237–255.

22. In November 2001, the investment bank Goldman Sachs created a new cluster of nations whose economic performance was seen as key for understanding the direction of the global economy. Brazil, Russia, India, and China comprised the so-called BRIC. See "Building Better Global Economic BRICs," *Goldman Sachs Global Economic Paper*, 30 November 2001.

23. Eduardo Galeano focuses on this and other negative aspects of Latin American automobility without any reference to its accomplishments in "*Auto*cracy: An Invisible Dictatorship," *NACLA: Report on the Americas* 28:4 (January–February 1995): 26–27.

INDEX

CPSIA information can be obtained
at www.ICGtesting.com
Printed in the USA
BVOW06s0306060817
491226BV00002B/8/P